S0-EGN-175

WITHDRAWN
UTSA Libraries

Environmental Political Philosophy

THE LEARNED SOCIETY OF PRAXIOLOGY

PRAXIOLOGY:
The International Annual of Practical Philosophy and
Methodology Vol. 19

EDITOR-IN-CHIEF
Wojciech W. Gasparski
Kozminski University
57-59, Jagiellonska St., 03-301 Warsaw, Poland wgaspars@alk.edu.pl

INTERNATIONAL ADVISORY BOARD:

Timo Airaksinen, Finland
Victor Alexandre, France
Josiah Lee Auspitz, U.S.A.
Mario Bunge, Canada
Arne Collen, U.S.A.
Friedrich Rapp, Germany
Leo V. Ryan, U.S.A.
Ladislav Tondl, Czech Republic

Environmental Political Philosophy

Praxiology: The International Annual of
Practical Philosophy and Methodology

Volume 19

Edited by

Olli Loukola and
Wojciech W. Gasparski

Transaction Publishers
New Brunswick (U.S.A.) and London (U.K.)

Copyright © 2012 by Transaction Publishers, New Brunswick, New Jersey.

All rights reserved under International and Pan-American Copyright Conventions. No part of this book may be reproduced or transmitted in any form or by any means, electronic or mechanical, including photocopy, recording, or any information storage and retrieval system, without prior permission in writing from the publisher. All inquiries should be addressed to Transaction Publishers, Rutgers—The State University of New Jersey, 35 Berrue Circle, Piscataway, New Jersey 08854-8042. www.transactionpub.com

This book is printed on acid-free paper that meets the American National Standard for Permanence of Paper for Printed Library Materials.

Library of Congress Catalog Number: 2011020482
ISBN: 978-1-4128-4297-6
Printed in the United States of America

Library of Congress Cataloging-in-Publication Data

Environmental political philosophy / Olli Loukola and Wojciech W. Gasparski, editors.
      p. cm. — (Praxiology : the international annual of practical philosophy and methodology ; v. 19)
   Includes bibliographical references.
   ISBN 978-1-4128-4297-6
   1. Environmental policy.   2. Environmental protection--Philosophy.
   I. Loukola, Olli.   II. Gasparski, Wojciech.
   GE170.E57697 2011
   363.701—dc23

                              Library   2011020482
                     University of Texas
                       at San Antonio

Contents

Editorial

Wojciech W. Gasparski
Editor-in-Chief

Readers who carefully follow praxiological considerations related to different areas of human activity are familiar with the praxiological dimensions of *effectiveness* and *efficiency*, and of an ethical one *ethicality*. They are collectively identified as the "triple Es." There are also other Es added to the triad depending on the particular area of a discourse. Sometimes it is the E of education. This time yet another "E" is going to the fore—the E of *ecology* is ready to join the collection of profound Es. Ecology is the dimension which represents the context of human action, that is its environment, whether natural or social.

The area of problems presented in this volume has its predecessor in the action theory section of the Mario Bunge's *Treatise on Basic Philosophy*, Vol. 8 *Ethics* (1989). The book was about axiology, moral theory, and praxiology. Special chapter of the treatise, closely related to the action theory, was devoted to social philosophy within which the quoted author had pointed out the idea of social reform based on "global or systemic view" (p. 356). The view was described in the following way:

"We reject pure environmentalism because the economy must be kept going lest we all starve; pure biologism because we cannot keep in good health without a clean environment and an adequate income; pure economicism because economic prosperity is worthless unless we enjoy good health and can make use of our income; pure politicism because freedom and participation are pointless if we are sick, destitute, or ignorant; and pure culturalism because the production and consumption of cultural goods take health, economic means, and a modicum of freedom and leisure.

> To put it in positive terms: Progressive social reform, that is social development, is at the same time environmental, biological, economic, political, and cultural." (Bunge 1989, p. 256)

The reform appealed by Bunge was named as *ecosociodevelopment* (p. 358) and characterized not only as a protection against harm, but also actions for a reform needed:

> "Designing and implementing ecosociodevelopment involves much more than such purely environmental protection measures as rational waste management, reforestation, and desert reclamation. To be effective and lasting, the reform must cover nearly every aspect of social life everywhere and it must win the support of all but those who are sick with economic or political greed." (Bunge 1989, p. 358)

Bunge suggested that the reform should include long list of different types of actions: disarmament, international cooperation, environment security, nuclear security, alternative energy sources, pure technology and agriculture, careful consumption, upgrading education, improving quality of life, etc. He knew it would not be possible to fulfill the reform overnight. Therefore, the suggestion was a direction rather than a construct, however, although:

> [. . .] we must protect our planet, but not at the cost of social development. The alternative is neither environmental protection nor social development, but either a continuation of the present course toward ultimate environmental catastrophe, or the improvement in the quality of life for everyone in and through ecosociodevelopment. The order is tall but the stakes are high. (Bunge 1989, p. 362)

It is striking how actual it still is, even more now than two decades ago. This is why it is proper to refer to the idea presenting the contemporary version of the issue as perceived by eminent scholars who raise environmental policy-making as perceived from praxiological point of view.

The idea is convergent with what is called now as sustainable development, or simply sustainability (Gomis et al. 2010), i.e., continuous and harmonious process of a chain of careful use of resources, of wise production, and of recycling whatever is possible to be used again. Sustainability is one of the main issues of the Fifth World Congress of the International Society of Business, Economics, and Ethics organized in Warsaw, Poland, in 2012 at the premises of Kozminski University. This is why this book is dedicated to the Congress[1] with the hope that it will give additional important impulse to the efforts of protecting the planet.[2] Once the Congress is organized in Europe, the contributors to this volume are mainly scholars of European affiliation.

Notes

1. Two of the earlier volumes of the Praxiology series were dedicated to the previous ISBEE congresses: Vol. 5—Wojciech W. Gasparski & Leo V. Ryan, eds., *Human Action in Business: Praxiological and Ethical Dimensions* was dedicated to the 1st ISBEE Congress held in Tokyo, Japan in 1996; Vol. 8—Leo V. Ryan, Wojciech W. Gasparski, Georges Enderle, eds. *Business Students Focus on Ethics* was dedicated to the 2nd ISBEE world Congress held in Sao Paulo, Brazil in 2000.
2. It was the ISBE promoter Professor Richard T. De George who pointed out the dubious effect of environmental issues: "In many instances of environmental harm, the harm done is not wanton and produces some good. From a utilitarian point of view we must ask whether more good is done than harm, looking at all those affected, not only immediately but in the long run as well. From a deontological perspective we need to ask whether the activities violate people's rights. From either perspective we must remember that though harming the environment is bad, at least to the extend that it directly or indirectly harms people, the actions that cause the harm frequently have positive effects as well, as in the case of pesticides, which can be of great help in keeping people alive because of higher crop yields than would otherwise be possible. In dealing with environmental harm, therefore, the task is to minimize the harm done while maximizing the benefits made available by increased scientific knowledge and technological advances, and while respecting the rights of all those affected." (De George 1995, p. 208)

References

Bunge, M., 1989, Treatise on Basic Philosophy, *Ethics: The Good and the Right*, Vol. 8, D. Reidel Publishing Co., Dordrecht.

De George, R.T., 1995, *Business Ethics*, 4th Ed., Prentice-Hall, Englewood Cliffs, NJ.

Gomis, A.J.B., Parra, M.G., Hoffman, W.M. & McNulty, R.E., 2010, *Rethinking the Concept of Sustainability*, Paper presented at the EBEN Annual Conference, Trento.

Acknowledgments

The Learned Society of Praxiology expresses gratitude to the Ministry of Science and Higher Education for supporting the preparation of this volume.

Introduction

Olli Loukola
Social and Moral Philosophy
Department of Political and Economic Studies
Faculty of Social Sciences
University of Helsinki,
Finland

> *Environmental concerns are political concerns and*
> *the best way to understand environmentalism is as a*
> *complex set of political ideas.*
> *Environmentalism and the Future of Progressive*
> *Politics,*
> Robert C. Paehlke, 1989

1.

The need for remedies for the environmental problems of our world is today more urgent than ever before in the history of humankind. Environmental issues have been high on the social agenda since the 1970s, but compared to the current situation, the previous worries concerned mainly particular instances of use of natural resources, regional pollution, or animal rights. These concerns appeared in public discussion only occasionally raised by some radical activists or academic dissenters. The philosophical quest of environmentalism, which emerged, focused more on creating an understanding of the apparent neglect of nature in the human mind and history. The practical measures and policies needed to resolve existing environmental problems were more or less left to the activists to deal with. Today, the immense expansion of environmental research and knowledge along with heightened popular interest in environmental issues has penetrated the social agenda thoroughly, and has directed attention much more noticeably to their social, political, and practical implications. Environmental catastrophes appear more concrete and tangible to us; they are also seen as results of human action, and not as mere contingencies and accidents of the capricious and unpredictable forces of nature. People today are much more conscientiously aware of issues such as climate change, species extinction, resource depletion, and land degradation, and recognize the requirements they impose on us through calls for sustainability, environmental protection, ecological diversity, environmental justice, and the rights of animals and of future generations, to name a few.

The politicized and social nature of environmental issues is by no means a novel suggestion, as is apparent in the opening quotation from 1989 by Robert Paehlke. Yet the mainstream orientation in environmental philosophy at the end of the twentieth century was that of environmental ethics, concentrating on individuals' ethical relationships with nature. At the same time, a parallel orientation was developing, focusing on outlining the relationship between nature and society. The classics in this field were Andrew Dobson's *Green Political Thought* (1990) and Robert Goodin's *Green Political Theory* (1992). The emphasis of these works—which soon become central tenets of environmental political philosophy—was to reflect on environmental issues, especially environmental protection, in a critical tone through notions and principles derived from social and political theories and ideologies, such as liberalism, socialism, and ecosocial theories (cf. Murray Boochin: *The Ecology of Freedom*, 1982). Notably, also a number of writers who had previously been oriented towards environmental ethics, such as Robin Attfield (*Environmental Ethics*, 2003) and Bryan Norton (*Sustainability*, 2005), have over the past years focused more conscientiously on environmental political principles.

2.

In environmental political philosophy the questions raised are: What are justified common environmental values, goals, and policies in society? How can we legitimize the primacy of environmental protection over certain other central human goals? Can we justify infringements on rights, and on what basis? The essential undercurrent here is that environmental issues are not questions of mere efficiency or technology, solvable through increased knowledge of processes and mechanics of nature, or by boosting or targeting research, or by more conscientious allocation of resources and the development of technology. Neither are they issues resolvable solely by increased civic edification and environmental campaigns, or endless appeals to eco-friendly actions. What is typical of environmental issues is their character as problems of collective action, ensuing counterproductive or even tragic results for the whole of humankind. For such reasons, environmental political philosophy directs its attention towards human action from a social and political point of view: it focuses on social morality, theories of justice, judicial regulation, and democratic decision making through the notions of social rights, duties, and responsibilities. What is sought after is a broad framework of social and political norms, a system of principles, laws, and sanctions targeted specifically to understanding and governing human action in radically changed environmental conditions. Such a framework is necessary to effectively solve environmental problems.

An inherent element of this wider socio-political orientation is then to look at environmental issues from a more dynamic perspective. The underlying idea is put forth well by Robin Attfield in his contention that "the very changed context of ethics requires us to rethink not only our responsibilities and related ethical questions, but also how we should collaborate to discharge responsibilities in a technological and interconnected world" (Attfield 2009, p. 233). "Environment" is conceptualized not as a stagnant, unfaltering, and fixed entity or state of affairs, but as a dynamic and developing phenomenon with various instantiations, among others as a resource-pool necessary for human existence, a locale for our everyday activities, or a source of unique aesthetic pleasure, in addition to the traditional notion of "Mother Nature" filling us with awe and wonder. This is "environment" with a plurality of guises which manifest themselves in active interaction with human beings and form the inherent locus of our common life and survival in the contemporary world. The mere fact that there is no one "environment" but a plurality of "environments" is a source of a multitude of confusions and conflicts in values. It also raises serious questions about the relationships and interconnections of these disparate "environments" which we live in.

As these considerations show, the emphasis on practicality that is under discussion here surely does not mean merely opting for a swift solution, but refers much more importantly to the need for a deeper understanding of the complicated connection between theory and practice. Such an orientation is the central element in environmental pragmatism, which commits itself to an "open-ended inquiry into the specific real-life problems of humanity's relationship with the environment, ... fueled by recognition that theoretical debates are problematic for the development of environmental policy" (Katz and Light 1996, p. 2). It is easy to agree here with the well-known philosophical article of faith that practice is patently blind without theory, just as theory is empty without its practical instances.

One of the purposes of this book is to show that the focuses and methods of environmental philosophy, surveyed above, may be enriched though praxiological considerations. In general, praxiology refers to the study of human conduct, examination of the general concepts of individual as well as collective action. Thus a further crucial element of environmental political philosophy is brought out through such studies: that is, the question of what constitutes efficient action or effective decision making, including their planning and implementation. The tools of praxiology are the "triple E" criteria, that is, effectiveness, efficiency, and ethics as the central determinants of merits of actions from the point of view of how well they reach their objectives.[1] This opens up a whole new palette for evaluating conflicting environmental objectives, their relative importance, the degrees of efficiency, and risks and expectations, among other things. With this focus, praxiology is clearly a study which starts from an empirical orientation, and that in the evaluation of actions and policies, ethical considerations are seen in conjunction with effectiveness and efficiency. This emphasis is bound to create debates and conflicts, and certainly a search for rules of priority.

At the same time, this starting point reflects truthfully the central tensions of the current conceptualization of environmental problems: how to use resources sustainably and how to control and direct policies efficiently and outcomes effectively, while respecting the principal ethical guidelines and practices. Contemporary environmental problems are often seen—as are most economic and political issues of our society— as the push and pull of ethics and efficiency, of means and purposes, of instruments and goals. This is a starting point which clearly needs to be criticized for its narrowness and constricted nature, as a number of philosophers in this collection have done, yet the criticism needs to be reformulated to be accessible within other environmental disciplines, primarily environmental politics, economics, and law.

3.

Environmental political philosophy operates in the dynamic and exacting intersection of severe contemporary problems of a local and global nature. Most of the ethically challenging environmental issues and hard cases arise in novel and outlandish situations and circumstances for which we have no ethical precedents, established codes of conduct, or approved or legitimate practices. These are the kinds of situations, which challenge many of the traditional dogmas of political philosophy, especially the principles of political democracy, canons of rights, notions of justice and fairness, and convictions about human duties and responsibilities. Understanding the underlying ideas and meanings of these concepts helps us to understand what they can offer us when applied to environmental issues. This helps us further when we analyze and trace the origins of the contemporary debates and solutions that are offered in these situations.

However, in order to construct normative guidelines telling us what we *should* do, we need to know first what we *can* do. And this lack of knowledge is one of the characteristic features of contemporary environmental problems: we are uncertain of the chains of cause and effect, and what exactly are the effects of our actions. Because of our contemporary technology, we now have the power to affect large swathes of the biosphere and mould the circumstances of the future generations for centuries to come. Yet technology as such is blind; it can be used for good as well as for bad. The moral issue here is discretion in the use of that power, for instance, estimating those substantial and fatal impacts of our actions and omissions that matter most. We need to appraise carefully whether we may do what we have the power to do, and what the results of our actions are. This is the kind of conceptual consideration which drives environmental political philosophy to focus more attentively on human liabilities and responsibilities than theories of traditional political philosophy are accustomed to. Time and history are patently present here: we can see now where we have come from and what we have done; at the same time, we are well aware that something has gone terribly wrong, and we are capable of causing an enormous amount of damage and suffering, and not only to humans, but also to the whole world.

The justification for redefining the notions and principles of political philosophy is exactly this need to properly, accurately, and fairly address new and challenging environmental predicaments. Thus the central idea of this volume is that ethical and practical studies should be commenced side by side, each reflecting, analyzing, and profiting from the work of the other. It is, as Mario Bunge so aptly put it, that "[o]nly the union of the two fields can tackle the problems surrounding the full legitimacy— both praxiological and moral—of action" (Bunge 1999, p. 2).

Ultimately, environmental political philosophy is revealed to be a highly critical enterprise. It involves exploring environmental pasturelands armed with customary philosophical skepticism and distrust: criticizing the concepts, theories, and results of the environmental sciences; suspecting the resolutions, policies, and goals of public and private institutions; and mistrusting the moral opinions, motives, and capacities of individual actors. In this enterprise our goal is to utilize the traditional notions of political philosophy, while at the same time carefully evaluating the habitual substance of these notions in the face of new environmental challenges. Thus we need to ask such critical questions as "What sort of societal principles would promote effective and just solutions to the environmental problems we face today?"; "Are rights as we conceive of them today sufficient for the protection of nature and the environment?"; or "How should decision making and governance be organized in order to promote environmentally benign practices among individual citizens and other societal actors?" These and similar questions you will find in this collection of essays.

4.

The essays collected here bring together a group of young writers with selected senior scholars, and the result is a colorful and lively selection of perspectives from disparate fields and from different generations of academia. With such a variety of viewpoints, it is naturally difficult to find any one decisive and tenacious trend of thought which would systematize the field of environmental political philosophy into a coherent discipline. Yet there is one persistent thread built into the collection, one which connects the diversity of topics, and that is the clearly urgent need for change and to determine the practical measures these changes require. As many of the writers of this collection emphasize, these changes are to be radical and overarching, penetrating all our worlds and the worlds around us, requiring thorough modifications to human thinking, human behavior, and human societies. Answering this challenge requires that we relate theoretical knowledge to practical action, or as it is phrased below, "Theorizing the World" along with "Acting in the World."

Following this train of thought, the essays are divided into three parts, all congregating around the concept of change and its requirements. The first chapter, "Changing Concepts," gathers together articles that focus on the need to change and rephrase our conceptual frameworks, to re-evaluate and reinterpret those central traditional concepts of our moral, social, and political discourses, such as rights, justice, and democracy.

What exactly they amount to under these new circumstances are discussed in the first five articles. The second call for change is dealt with in the chapter "Changing Society," which examines how we should restructure society to better meet these new environmental needs and challenges. The third chapter, "Changing Human Beings", focuses on the need to change our attitudes, values, and thinking to give proper attention to other than merely human interests.

Yet the changes called for and dealt with in this collection are by no means located on a one-dimensional continuum. The main inter-relationship in the analysis of the environmental challenges, that is, the interaction between theory and action, is sketched in the graphics as the second dimension. The essays with more theoretical or conceptual orien-tation are located towards the top, while the ones with more practical or empirical orientation are closer to the bottom. On the other dimension, essays dealing with issues traditionally belonging to political philosophy, political theory, or the political sciences can be found on the left, while the right-hand side encompasses more individually oriented essays, with a moral or humanistic disposition. In between these dimensions, certain key terms and distinctive properties are named and specified in order to help the reader identify relevant topics.

5.

Part I—"Changing Concepts"—gathers together articles that focus on the need to examine and reevaluate our conceptual frameworks of political and social philosophy under these new circumstances. The topics concentrate on analyses of central concepts such as "justice", "rights" and "democracy", and of their foundations, especially in the contemporary mainstream theory of political philosophy, that is, liberalism.

The first essay, Olli Loukola's "Environmental Justice: From Theory to Practice and Back to Theory," concentrates on environmental justice, which is a typical example of the new concepts of the field, though it has its roots deep in history and philosophy. Over the past decades "environ-mental justice" has referred almost exclusively to the social movement of the same name, while the mainstream theorists of justice have more or less avoided the whole subject. Yet the general contemporary field of justice—from conceptual considerations to concrete requirements—is shaped anew today because of the new dialogue between theory and practice, a process in which environmental issues importantly figure.

The close connection between activism and theorizing has always been an important part of environmental thinking. This becomes apparent

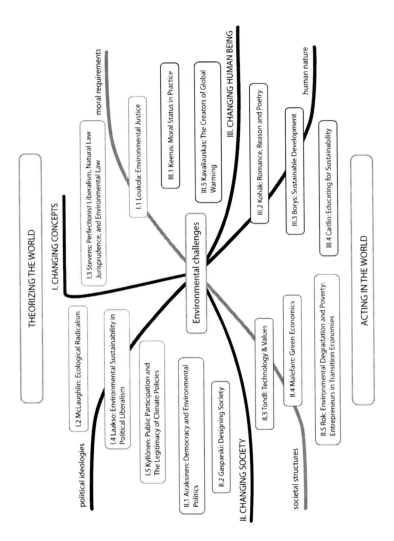

also with Paul McLaughlin's examination of the roots of radical political philosophy in "Remarks on Ecological Radicalism." As a species of
this type, he defines ecological radicalism as an argumentation about
the interaction between socio-political norms, practices, and institutions
and other elements of the natural world. As such it represents a kind of
"natural turn" in political philosophy: an extension of concern beyond
traditionally understood socio-political matters, motivated by a profound
sense of ecological crisis.

In "Perfectionist Liberalism, Natural Law Jurisprudence, and the
Philosophical Foundations of Environmental Law," Christopher Stevens
continues the task of argumentation and redefining, this time with the
concept of environmental human rights. He argues that the current interpretations in human rights-based legislation threatens the environment
and ecological integrity, and offers alternative grounds for its reform. In
this essay rich in philosophical topics, Stevens discusses the concept of
intrinsic value, natural law, and moral and political perfectionism. Most
of this discussion is undertaken within the framework of liberal political
and moral theory, which is also the background of the essays of Laakso
and Kyllönen. The starting point here is that liberal theory is in difficulty
when trying to demonstrate its applicability in environmental contexts.

In "Environmental Sustainability in Political Liberalism: Meeting the
Alleged Inadequacy Posed by the Neutrality Thesis," Marjukka Laakso
discusses the compatibility of environmental sustainability and liberal
democracy, in the Rawlsian framework. She argues that environmental
sustainability requires public coordination and public decision-making
procedures. The reason for this is that individual volition does not suffice
to guarantee a place of priority for environmental concerns in societal
decision-making. Nor is individual responsibility alone effective enough
for managing environmental issues, a discussion that will continue in
Part III.

In liberal theory, these considerations are linked with questions concerning the justificatory legitimacy of environmental policies. Those
policies often need to make radical requirements of citizens' private
behavior, in the area where coercion is customarily regarded as illegitimate. For this reason, many are highly skeptical of the efficacy of
democratic decision-making in environmental issues. To remedy this,
public participation and deliberation has been introduced as a way to
legitimize environmental policies and the infringements they make on
individual liberty. Simo Kyllönen examines this claim in his "Public
Participation and the Legitimacy of Climate Policies: Efficacy versus

Democracy?" and finds the arguments inadequate in a number of ways. His main argument is that if and when a justification can be given that makes drastic climate policies legitimate, it is based only partially on public deliberation among citizens. More important here is the publicity of the political decisions and their justifications: citizens should be able to see that the process has been fair and inclusive so that no relevant perspective has been left out and the outcome is not biased.

Part II—"Changing Society"—continues this theme but shifts the focus towards a wider look at the changes required in the name of environmental concerns. We need not only to reevaluate our central political concepts, but also our existing political structures and principles.

Timo Airaksinen frames the theme of the efficacy and legitimacy of democratic decision-making in environmental issues with the question whether politics is capable of not only protecting our natural environment but also destroying it. In "Between Democracy and Antagonistic Environmental Politics," he reaches a conclusion through an enticing argumentation—and with a little help from the Tasmanian tiger—which reflects well the convictions of the articles of the previous chapter. That is, that politics conceived as an open and democratic debate of the realization of common good—as in the liberal theory—is in fact impotent and incapable of controlling the forces which damage and destroy our natural environments.

Wojciech W. Gasparski continues the discussion by examining the requirements for designing of society in "A Designing Human Society: A Chance or a Utopia?" In the essay, he pinpoints the three central problems of decision-making, that is, the rejection of the axiom of unlimited resources, setting the survival of mankind as the supreme goal, and the vital role of practical problem-solving. What is especially interesting here is to notice the continuing importance of the questions raised in this article, which was originally published almost thirty years ago.

In "On the Role of Values in the World of Technology," Ladislav Tondl discusses the role and possibilities of technology as a means for solving societal problems. According to Tondl, since construction of technical works and technical artifacts are goal-directed activities, they contain an inherent attitude of value. This is especially vital in the application of new and previously unknown technologies, which open up new visions, spheres, and challenges to human thought. The human capability of moving in and between different "possible worlds" is vital here as a method of charting the emerging new requirements and responsibilities.

The last two essays concentrate on the capability of the economic structures of society to cope with environmental concerns. One popular attempt to institutionalize the various value-aspects of nature in the markets and society has been to translate them into monetary measures, that is, by giving them a price as natural resources. These are today conceptualized as "ecosystem services," whose prices can be estimated through economic methods of valuation. Gabriel Malenfant analyses these methods in "On Green Economics: The Limits of Our Instrumental Valuations of Nature," and even though the notion as such sounds appealing, and the methods are highly technical and sophisticated, they fall desperately short for providing morally sound guidelines for decision-makers. The reason for this is the simple fact that individually expressed preferences and desires, which these methods are capable of measuring, do not amount to genuine values.

In "Tackling Environmental Degradation and Poverty: A New Agenda for Entrepreneurs in Transition Economies," Boleslaw Rok focuses on the close and interdependent relationship between poverty and environmental sustainability, issues which are particularly burning in the so-called transition economies, the countries of Eastern Europe (EE) and the Commonwealth of Independent States (CIS). Rok argues that the reduction of poverty and environmental degradation requires active participation from the various market actors and concentrates on analyzing how to best engage or motivate these actors into creating "an economic playing field based on the principles of fairness and justice." The motivation of such actors takes place from their own starting point, by showing that they can at the same time create financial value but also improve people's lives and environmental conditions.

Part III—Changing Human Beings"—returns the discussion to the more traditional themes of environmental philosophy, those of individual action, behavior, and motivations. The emphasis here is on societal considerations, that is, asking questions such as what do such considerations require of us as individuals, as members of society, or as citizens of the local and global community? One central theme of the chapter is the possibility of extending moral consideration towards the various kinds of entities inhabiting the natural world with us—animals, plants, organisms, microhabitats, ecosystems, or even non-living things.

The chapter starts with Külli Keerus's attentive analysis of "Moral Status in Practice." A central feature of our Western moral discourse has been its inherent individualism, meaning here the unfortunate inclusion of solely human individuals within the realm of moral consideration.

Other worldly entities have only been granted a secondary moral status, as subsidiaries in the service of man. The notion of "moral status" or "moral standing" has been frequently raised as capable of extending moral consideration to these other entities. It would also serve as a justification of equitable treatment, thus motivating us to action. In her essay, Keerus demonstrates, however, that in spite of its initial appeal, the notion of moral status does not possess the required binding force that would oblige us to treat other entities with the same respect as our fellow human beings.

This theme is continued at more general level in "Romance, Reason, and Poetry in Ecological Philosophy," where Erazim Kohák paints a wonderfully vivid picture of the sensibilities of the earlier romantic environmental movement from the end of the last millennium. He discusses the way environmental issues have been conceptualized in philosophy as well as art, as ways to capture human existence and meaning. Most importantly, he tries to draw imperatives for action from this rich cultural background, and combines it with certain characteristics of human nature when asking the very relevant question whether "we humans are capable of so great a behavior modification," as survival within the Earth's limitations would require.

In "Sustainable Development as an Axiological and a Civilizational Challenge," Tadeusz Borys takes a broader view of these topics by discussing a new development paradigm. Borys emphasizes the need for a clear articulation and construction of our existing values—the task which was driven to the margin in the twentieth century—because ". . . without disclosing our systems of values, we are not able to clearly answer the question as to which social, economic, ecological, spatial, political, and institutional orders we want to accomplish." For this purpose, "an axiological diagnosis of a human" is needed, and it is to be conducted by asking the fundamental question of the true nature of human beings. According to Borys' enquiry, this diagnosis leads us to endorse more moderate anthropocentrism which is based on a "holistic vision of humaneness."

Another angle is presented by Caitlin Wilson in "Educating for Sustainability." She describes her experiences when facilitating a group of students from North America studying in Iceland on a summer program on renewable energy and sustainable development (SIT Study Abroad, 2009). A number of experimental pedagogies were used during the program, and Wilson draws from these experiences, aided by an analysis of the literature, two interesting conclusions. The first is that education for sustainable development is a particularly suitable field for using manifold pedagogical and didactic methods, with "multidisciplinarity, active student participation, immersion in nature, experiential learning elements such as field study, a critical approach, holistic presentation, firm grounding in reality, as well as consideration of ethical issues on the personal, subjective, and sociocultural levels." The other interesting result is that this mixing of skills, talents, knowledge, and personal commitment created a strong positive outlook for the future among the students. Instead of being overwhelmed by the intensified flow of information of environmental problems and dangers, the students felt that a sustainable future was possible and feasible.

The last essay of this collection is Tomas Kavaliauskas' "The Creators of Global Warming" which deviates from the other contributors by raising a serious skeptical doubt. He asks whether we humans are excessively priding ourselves on our capabilities to change the world, by "treating ourselves as the exceptional life form that has extraordinary say in the planet's well-being, quality of functioning, cycles of seasons, and its evolutionary rhythm." Kavaliauskas asks whether such an "anthropogenic approach" is truly able to overcome the dualism between nature and humankind, or whether we are merely exhausting ourselves with the burdens of social and environmental responsibilities.

6.

As can be seen, this collection of essays is crowded with common themes, with threads linking contributions from various areas, from one discipline to another, and with very little apparent systematic connection apart from the general anxiety about the whole situation. But rather than being an indication of missing logic or internal coherence among the disciplinary contributions, it is rather a symptom of the various and so far undetermined challenges posed by environmental concerns.

All this may well indicate failures of the traditional disciplines to properly address these problems, but more importantly, it indicates the need and opportunity for new and interdisciplinary work, and novel and innovative linking of theoretical analysis to practical conclusions. This is what I hope to be the most important lesson to be learned from this colorful collection of essays.

Note

1.   The first two concepts also have established applied environmental equivalents, namely "eco- effectiveness," and "eco-efficiency." And environmental ethics has naturally been around since the very beginning.

References

Attfield, R., 2009, Mediated Responsibilities, Global Warming, and the Scope of Ethics, *Journal of Social Philosophy*, 40 (2): 225–36.

Katz, E. & Light, A. (ed.), 1996, Environmental Pragmatism (Environmental Philosophies), Routledge, London.

Bunge, M., 1999, Ethics and Praxiology as Technologies, *Journal of the Society for Philosophy and Technology* 4: 4.

Part 1
Changing Concepts

Environmental Justice: From Theory to Practice and Back to Theory[1]

Olli Loukola
Social and Moral Philosophy
Department of Political and Economic Studies
Faculty of Social Sciences
University of Helsinki
Finland

> *Over hundreds of years, writers on justice in different parts of the world have attempted to provide the intellectual basis for moving from a general sense of injustice to particular reasoned diagnoses of injustice, and from there to the analyses of ways of advancing justice.*
>
> The Idea of Justice (Sen 2009, p. 5)

1. Introduction

In this essay, I will present certain observations about the background conditions involved in the analysis of the concerns for justice within the environmental field. These conditions are entangled, affecting both of the contemporary justice discourses in the field, that is, environmental justice theories and the environmental justice movement. They also explain some of the specific emphasis that marks both discourses.

As I see it, the conditions that are entangled here are the following: Firstly, there is the continuous search for a description of the current state of the environment which is attached to certain normative rules and goals which are expressed as various kinds of concerns for justice. Secondly, this search is undertaken with the purpose of outlining practical actions to be institutionalized as guidelines, principles, practices, customs, policies, or the like. Thirdly, it is understood that in order for individuals, companies, offices, institutions, or countries to be motivated to act accordingly, these actions and policies need to be supported by the best possible arguments, that is, they need to be justified, legitimized, validated, sanctioned, or authorized in some manner.

Although these three conditions are surely present in most similar instances of societal or political changes and turning points, there are certain elements in the environmental sphere, which I think makes them a special case, critically challenging our contemporary scientific and philosophical thinking and practice. We can indeed learn much from them. The first element is the three-centuries-old, but still topical, question of the place of normative elements, often expressed as the separation between facts and values, which continues to puzzle philosophers and scientists in their enquiries. The second is the special nature of environmental problems. Such problems are extremely complex in structure, involve complicated chains of causality, and are often wide-ranging or global not only in space but also in time (i.e., future generations). Most importantly, they seem dramatic and impactful to the verge of being untreatable.

In this essay, I will analyze these aspects mainly from the viewpoint of environmental justice. Some of these considerations surely apply to environmental action, some to environmental philosophy, and some only to environmental justice, though I will not analyze these issues here. Instead, the main focus of this paper is to evaluate the two-way relationship between environmental justice theories and environmental justice movement. This involves the idea that environmental justice theories can be used to analyze, distinguish, and assess the moral concerns of the environmental justice movement. At the same time, these analyses can be used to broaden the perspectives of the theories by pinpointing new, potentially relevant aspects of justice. Even though this idea seems appealing and commonsensical, a number of difficulties are still involved.

2. The Environmental Justice Movement and Environmental Justice Theories

For an astonishingly long time, it has been doubtful whether "environmental justice" actually exists in its own right as part of the field of political philosophy, and as such is involved in the theoretical enquiry of questions of justice within the spheres of the environment and nature. For the past twenty years or so, the concept has referred almost exclusively to various environmental political movements. A prime example of such usage—and of the tensions involved with the scholarly analysis and activist elements of justice—can be found in Carl Talbot's 1997 article "Environmental Justice." Here, the writer describes the characteristics of the environmental justice movement, but at the same time has a strong critical attitude toward what the notion should imply. Problems that are mentioned in the article, such as dumping waste and hazardous products in the Third World countries, siting of polluting industry in poor neighborhoods, and people of color becoming concentrated in occupations with high health risks are surely cases of infringements of justice. Indeed, Talbot is right in claiming that such issues are too rarely discussed in mainstream philosophical literature. There is specifically one suggestion in his article which deals with the potential basic orientation of a "new" movement of environmental justice, and which at the same time illustrates something important about the nature of the environmental justice movement:

> For this new movement for environmental justice, matters of the environment are not confined to how to best manage or preserve some extra-urban "wilderness"; rather, the environment is part of a broader framework of economic, racial, and social justice. This perspective represents a significant challenge to the way mainstream environmental groups have commonly presented the environmental agenda as primarily occupied with the conservation of pristine wilderness and wildlife. The exclusion of any discussion of urban or industrial concerns in mainstream environmentalism is reflected in the histories of environmentalism, which concern themselves with the romantic champions of wild "Nature", such as the 19th century national parks advocate John Muir and Aldo Leopold, whose "land ethic" has become so revered by much of modern environmentalism, but say nothing of struggles to improve the urban and industrial environments.[2]

The message that could be read from this passage is that the environmental justice movement was no longer addressing the proper concerns of justice, and reason for this was that the movement was changing, had changed, and was in need of a change. As such it is a social movement, and this is an indicative feature of the environmental justice movement as such: instead of practical harmonization in the attainment of a common goal, it is plagued by competing movements, conflicting policy recommendations, and antagonistic doctrines.

The second message of Talbot's text and another indicative feature for the whole field is described in the popular media: "Environmental Justice is a movement . . . [which] seeks an end to environmental racism and [seeks to] prevent low-income and minority communities from an unbalanced exposure to highways, garbage dumps, and factories. The Environmental Justice movement seeks to link 'social' and 'ecological' environmental concerns, while at the same time preventing de facto racism, and classism."[3] Thus there exists today, and has in fact existed throughout the movement's history, a pronounced goal to "link" together social and ecological environmental concerns.[4] The environmental justice movement is a typical social and political movement in the sense that it to tries to couple existing empirical problems with goals judged worthwhile, valuable, or necessary. The debates which surround these goals are naturally intense.

The third indicative feature is that there is a strong inclination to justify these goals, as all social movements try to do. Justification is sought for a number of things, and an analysis of their nature and importance is sorely needed. Some have got to do with the empirical feasibility and efficaciousness of the proposed measures and instruments, with their inherent uncertainty and doubtfulness. Others deal with the applicability and practicality of the goals and ideals at a more general level, especially when legitimizing resulting policies, strategies, and goals. In short, environmental movements are trying to do the right things for the right reasons; in the terms used in academic enquiry, they are trying to link correct descriptions and working instruments with right goals, such as savings the world. Facts, motivations, and normative goals all play central role in this package.

These three features are typical characteristics of those social and political groups that make up the environmental justice movements, and are also the reasons, why they are not mere scholarly theories. Environmental movements have always been searching for plausible ways of legitimizing the policies, strategies, and goals they suggest and advocate. This need has amplified exceedingly over the past years for various reasons: to start with, in contemporary democratic societies all societal decisions need to be legitimized. A further reason is that the natural ally of all environmental decisions and policies over the past decades, the natural sciences, have turned out to be far less capable of supplying scientific bases for these decisions. They have not been able to provide descriptions and predictions of the state and development of nature and the environment as hoped for. Especially, the various uncertainties in scientific research have produced spin-off effects often directly undermining the goals and demands of the environmental movements. Scientific uncertainties have laid a shadow on the overall reliability of scientific knowledge, and more concretely, they have made environmental decision-making increasingly difficult. Measures and methods for determining policy options and possible actions have proved to be highly unreliable, and the various kinds of ethical, economic, and societal uncertainties accruing further complicate the picture.

All this has led the environmental movement to search for common grounds with not only the natural sciences, but increasingly often with the social sciences and philosophy. To put this simply, the environmental movement's search for broader and more convincing perspectives to solve the various serious environmental crises of our world is not a question of merely finding straightforward technical answers. Much more is at stake in these crises.

With these developments, the role of philosophers has expanded over the past decades. The demand for expertize in dealing with normative questions enabled the outbreak of applied and practical ethics from the 1980s onwards. This was made possible by the major shift at the end of the 1970s in moral philosophy, sometimes called "the Great Expansion of Ethics,"[5] which suggested that moral and political philosophers would be able to articulate normative and substantial assessments on contemporary practical issues and problems. Certain socially pressing moral questions such as abortion, animal rights, or euthanasia served as a marketing window of these capabilities of philosophical enquiry.

Despite these attempts by different discourses to approach each other, they are still far apart. Even though many of the problems of the environmental justice movement follow from the fact that their theoretical input is limited, not always scientific, and sometimes plainly false, there is a clear tendency to downscales the impact of theory for various reasons.[6] Very often their analyses is merely varying and strong beliefs of a speculative nature. The movements deal with empirical cases, and their assumptions, concepts, and explanations as well as justifications are strongly dependent upon each other, and the result is that they are too often curious and/or misconceived mixtures of normative goals and descriptions of social and natural sciences. Even though this is often the case with various social movements, it seems to be particularly prevalent within the environmental movement.

Or what should one say of a claim like "elite-driven environmental programs act as a disciplining mechanism against the poor," also to be found in Talbot's text? With such an extremely strong claim, one would clearly need more explanations and theoretical input on a number of questions, starting with the potential truth of the whole claim: Is it really the case that environmental problems are elite-driven programs targeted against the poor? What constitutes a "disciplinary action"? Who are the elite doing that? How does such a mechanism emerge? How does it work? And how do you prove such claims? I am not saying here that these explanations are necessarily false, but that they need to be verified, and that is the task for (usually social) scientific inquiry. Thus more theoretical input is needed, and at various levels.

Moreover, it is also claimed we are dealing with issues of justice: but what kind of a breach of justice exactly is it, and on what basis? Which exactly are the injustices here and why do they take place? How and where are we to look for the roots and solutions to this contravention? What are the moral statuses of the people involved? Who are the exploiters and exploited here? What are the canons of justice in operation here? If we do not have a plausible theory of justice at our disposal, we cannot analyze these questions very far; even if we see this situation amounting to an infringement of justice at face value, we may well disagree of its nature, and what it requires of us. Indeed, the movement has not been particularly active in searching for support for their convictions from existing theories of justice.

There is therefore a need to clarify the roles of two kinds of scholarly theories here—scientific theories describing and explaining the situation, and justice theories defining, classifying, and analyzing the moral problems involved.

The scientific input in the concerns raised by the environmental justice movement usually comes from the results of "Environmental Science." The discipline is, however, far from being a settled, accepted, and established academic enterprise, with a variety of disciplines crossing each other's disciplinary borders. But if the scientific study of nature and the environment is in a state of confusion and change, the philosophical study of the environment is pretty much in a similar state. Environmental philosophy, the area where philosophical questions concerning nature and the environment are generally dealt with, is also an intensely debated and contested field. Although being the mainstream emphasis of environmental philosophy over the past two decades, environmental ethics never managed to produce the kinds of conclusions that would have addressed the kinds of practical concerns the environmental movement raised. This is in part due to the fact that environmental philosophy has never really been able to set its agenda independently of the practical concerns raised by the environmental movement as some other traditional fields of philosophy have been able to do in their respective fields.

But this is not just a drawback for the enterprise, since it is here, in environmental problems, that theoretical questions and practical concerns collide in a most profound manner, and this is bound to be instructive and edifying in a number of ways. This makes environmental philosophy an especially interesting field of contemporary philosophy: it is a wonderful example of the difficulties and problems incurred when philosophy is used as an applied discipline, and especially in conjunction with other sciences. It is also here that philosophy runs not only into a crash course with other sciences, but also with everyday moral feelings and intuitions. We are indeed here, as Sze and London phrase it, at a crossroads of social movements, public policy, and academic research.[7]

My focus here is, where exactly do the normative considerations of justice fit into this framework? Moreover the starting problem with environmental justice theories is quite simply that we do not really have such theories, or certainly we did not have them at the time of Talcot's article. Our general theories of justice over the past few decades have been rather limited topically. In fact they have dealt with a restricted set of questions, and environmental issues have never really been on this agenda. Yet this problem of the missing theories of environmental justice is not an isolated problem from the rest of social and political philosophy; so let us take a brief look at the historical origins of this problem.

3. Theories of Justice

In order to evaluate the ways of theorizing environmental justice, it is necessary to reflect what the theories of justice in general are and have been. Do environmental justice concerns differ from the general concerns of justice? Do they have some sort of special character?

These are indeed two separate questions, and the first—what is the nature of justice?—is discussed intensely within the contemporary mainstream of political philosophy, while the second —what is the nature of environmental justice?—has not been a mainstream topic in a similar way. So far there exists no comprehensive and systematic analysis of the justice concepts used and appealed to in the various environmental justice contexts,[8] be they academic or activist by nature. One goal of this chapter is to outline some of the preliminaries for such an analysis.

The central figures of political philosophy in the early 1980s were such philosophers as John Rawls, Ronald Dworkin, and Robert Nozick, and later David Gauthier. These theorists wrote extensively about justice in their works, and presented precise, constrained, and focused analyses from their perspective of what justice means and what it consists of. This amounted to the idea expressed in the first sentences of Rawls's *Theory of Justice* from 1971: "[j]ustice is the first virtue of social institutions, as truth is of systems of thought."[9] With this straightforward definition this central concept of political philosophy is given a precise interpretation. At the same time it is cleared from all the previous transcendental and metaphysical notions, such as of justice as discovery of harmony, justice as divine command, or natural law, in addition to the various religious conceptions of justice. Rawls located justice firmly and concretely in the basic structures of society, as a safeguard for individuals against unjust political arrangements: "A theory however elegant and economical must be rejected or revised if it is untrue. Likewise, laws and institutions, no matter how efficient and well-arranged, must be reformed or abolished if they are unjust. Each person possesses an inviolability founded on justice that even the welfare of society as a whole cannot override."[10] This sort of definition limited potential questions and topics concerning justice to more manageable chunks, thus allowing for more precise and coherent analysis of these topics. Nozick, for his part, fixed the central notions of political philosophy tightly into his individualism, conceptualizing justice as a question of distribution of property.

Along with these ideas, justice came to mean the distribution of the benefits and burdens of the liberal society, carefully safeguarded by individual rights. Accordingly, the study was conceived as the search for the principles of distributive justice. Influenced by certain simple theorems of economic theory, these were conceptualized as a set of normative principles designed to allocate goods of limited supply relative to demand. The principles suggested have been categorized in a number of ways,[11] for instance: (1) Which are the benefits and burdens we are to distribute? Are we talking of money, wealth, opportunities, or the like? (2) Who are the subjects of this distribution? Are they natural persons, groups, reference classes, professions, or the like? and (3) On what basis should the benefits and burdens be distributed? Is equal division vital, or should we pay attention to individual characteristics, such as merit, or should we resort to free market transactions? The dominant principles supported on the basis of these distinctions enumerated in the textbooks are usually versions of egalitarianism, utilitarianism, libertarianism, or variations on liberal theories.

During the past twenty years of increased interest in environmental issues, this discourse of justice never really touched the discourse of the environmental justice movement. The academic discussions of political philosophy along the principles of justice set by John Rawls were highly theoretical, concentrating on distributional patterns and principles, while the discussions within the environmental justice movement have been conspicuously practical, concentrating on empirical breaches of justice. The latter discourse has focused on analyzing and outlining the processes that construct maldistributions of societal bads and goods; or to give a representative example from Talbot again, ". . . to analyze patterns of disproportionate exposure to environmental hazards experienced by minority and low-income communities, to understand how such patterns have developed, and to develop programs by which disproportionate exposures can be remedied and prevented."[12]

In its analyses of concrete maldistributions, the environmental justice movement has utilized a plurality of different more or less articulated conceptions and notions of justice, adopted from various sources such as traditional notions of justice, strong intuitions, societal values, or political and religious doctrines. As if an answer to the call of Talbot presented in the beginning of this essay, definitions have increasingly often been drawn from theoretical discussions of political theory and philosophy. This discussion has, however, been found restricting and limited in a number of ways. As a result, there is an intense development under the way in both discourses—environmental justice movement, and political theory and philosophy. Along with the development of justice theories, and the various needs posed by applied ethics and applied philosophy, academic theorists have started to search for new ways of analyzing and conceptualizing the notion of justice. In a similar manner, environmental activists have realized the increasing need for theoretical analysis in order to fruitfully and efficiently analyze contested practical situations. Thus there is a reciprocal pull within both discourses—justice theory and the justice movement—toward each other. But what exactly are these centripetal forces, what are these needs that these two discourses are looking for in each other?

One way to look at this relationship is through the recent analysis of Amartya Sen in *The Idea of Justice* (2009). As descendants of the eighteenth and nineteenth century Enlightenment thought, the theories of justice as distribution have an emphasis on reforming political institutions and the protection of individuals and their rights.[13] According to Sen, there were in fact two lines of reasoning about justice emerging "with the radical thought of that period." The first, which he calls "transcendental institutionalism," originated from Thomas Hobbes and was followed by Jean-Jacques Rousseau, and concentrated on identifying just institutional arrangements for society, what "perfect justice" is comprised of in the sense of "identify[ing those] social characteristics that cannot be transcended in terms of justice." The goal was to "get the institutions right," to find perfectly or ideally just institutions, and the methodological tool for these purposes was the social contract theory. This is indeed the very same mainstream of justice theories that I have been talking about here. Sen also names Ronald Dworkin, David Gauthier, and Robert Nozick as representatives of such theorists, since they "share the common aim of identifying just rules and institutions, even though their identifications of these arrangements come in very different forms."[14]

Sen outlines the second "line of thought" by contrasting it to transcendental institutionalism and what it was lacking. It did not concentrate on relative comparisons of justice and injustice, and it did not analyze "moral or political imperatives regarding socially appropriate behavior." The idea here is that the society based on a favored set of principles and institutions of transcendental institutionalists would still crucially "depend also on noninstitutional features, such as actual behaviors of people and their social interactions." And it is these behavioral assumptions, "norms of behavior," that have been neglected within this line of reasoning. These kinds of "comparative approaches" were taken seriously by Enlightenment theorists such as Adam Smith, the Marquis de Condorcet, Jeremy Bentham, Mary Wollstonecraft, Karl Marx, and John Stuart Mill. In contrast to transcendental institutionalists, they were "concerned with social realizations (resulting from actual institutions, actual behavior and other influences)."[15]

Sen invokes another distinction that is apparently the basis for the distinction between the two types of justice thought, but is nevertheless a more general categorization. This is the distinction between the "arrangement-focused view of justice" as practiced by the mainstream theorists of (distributive) justice and "realization-focused understanding of justice" as practiced by the latter theorists, Mill, Marx, etc. The first refers to "organizational propriety and behavioral correctness, while the latter stands for "a comprehensive concept of realized justice": "In that line of vision, the roles of institutions, rules and organization, important as they are, have to be assessed in the broader and more inclusive perspective . . ., which is inescapably linked with the world that actually emerges, not just the institutions or rules we happen to have."[16] Where the mainstream of justice then goes wrong here, according to Sen, is that "we have to seek institutions that promote justice, rather than treating the institutions as themselves manifestations of justice, which would reflect a kind of institutionally fundamentalist view."[17]

Sen sums up his idea in the following way:

> The former line of thought proposes that justice should be conceptualized in terms of certain organizational arrangements—some institutions, some regulations, some behavioural rules—the active presence of which would indicate that justice is being done. The question to ask in this context is whether the analysis of justice must be so confined to getting the basic institutions and general rules right? Should we not also have to examine what emerges in the society, including the kind of lives that people can actually lead, given the institutions and rules, but also other influences, including actual behaviour, that would inescapably affect human lives?[18]

When we shift our focus from these reflections back to environmental justice concerns, I believe it is evident now that we could categorize the environmental justice movement to present just this latter kind of comparative approach. Its analysis of the actual infringements on justice, such as "maldistributions" and "disproportionate exposure to environmental hazards," is intended for example "to prevent environmental racism and classism," and all its attempts to influence the behavior of individuals, companies, officials, and states, surely satisfies Sen's characteristics of the "realization-focused understanding of justice."

When talking of general theories of justice, Sen directs his attention to what he sees as the imbalance in the current situation, namely that transcendental institutionalism is dominating the theory of justice. But the thing is that in environmental contexts the reverse is true in the sense that the dominating thinking of the field is the "realization-focused understanding of justice," and not the "arrangement-focused view" concentrating on principles and institutions. Thus it is the other side of the equation that is lacking, at least for the time being; theories of environmental justice are still under development.

The first thing to note, of course, is that we are not operating completely in a vacuum here. We do have well-developed theories of environmental ethics, which have an effect on the concerns of environmental justice too, in a similar manner as ethical theories in general provide background conditions, postulations, and other preconditions for political philosophy. Secondly, and most importantly, we are constantly testing and applying the general theories of justice to see how well they fit these circumstances. This is, after all, the work that needs to be done here, to determine what are those rules, principles, or canons of justice that are best for the purposes of environmental justice.

But this latter point leads us to the next question, which is two-fold. Firstly, how are we to conceive the relationship between the environmental justice movement and environmental justice theories today? Put in Sen's terms, what would the relationship be between environmental arrangement-focused and environmental realization-focused understandings of justice? The second question is, whether there is a theory of environmental justice, with its own subject area, or is it just an application of the more general theories of justice? In other words, is there something special in environmental justice concerns?

I will continue with a discussion of the relationship between arrangement-focused and realization-focused understandings of justice in general, although I will not here concentrate on what Sen himself has to say about the issue at a general level. Instead it is necessary here to clear up the background in moral philosophy during the last century, which set the stage for the development of contemporary theories of justice. Sen does admit that despite this focus, transcendental institutionalists, such as Kant and Rawls, were nevertheless able to develop realization-focused understandings of justice, and in fact did present "deeply illuminating analyses of moral or political imperatives regarding socially appropriate behaviour."[19] And the central tool for Rawls and his contemporaries was the "reflective equilibrium," which consists of critical dialectical scrutiny of socially approved values and priorities in contrast to relevant theories.

4. Reflective Equilibrium

In the analytic philosophy of the last century, and especially in meta-ethics with the dominance of noncognitivism, inquiry into existing moral opinions and socially approved values was classified as belonging under "descriptive ethics," or "moral sociology," that is, to the scientific domain of sociologist, anthropologists, or historians.[20] This was seen as an empirical enquiry that does not yield normative conclusions for philosophical ethics. One concrete reason is the manifest infallibility of existing values, the fact that human moral beliefs—individual or collective—and the homologous social and cultural traditions are often short-sighted, stagnated, or prejudiced. As such they cannot be used as measure sticks for moral truths. The task of philosophical ethical enquiry was something different than mere observation of moral phenomena.

This is, as said earlier, very much the character of the concerns expressed by the environmental justice movement as well. One difference, though, is that these moral convictions are rarely traditional and stagnated and supported by traditional customs; quite the contrary, they are more often revolutionary and reformist. But this difference does not amount to raising their status to make them any more genuine moral norms.

How seriously should we then take these moral concerns, and here especially with regards to justice? Are moral intuitions subtle or perceptive enough to detect and clarify relevant differences between the existing relations of social entities? Does common sense, conceived either as a collective mind, or an aggregate of individual opinions, amount to a clear and justified judgment on important social issues? In other words, can we draw normative conclusions from the facts of moral sociology? All through the twentieth century, the analytic moral philosophers' answer to this question was negative.

Further questions are, what is the role of those moral emotions, intuitions, and convictions that environmental movement utilizes in advocating the concerns for justice? How seriously are we to take them? And what is the role of scientifically produced knowledge of a supposedly impartial and objective nature when it is coupled with these concerns for justice? In other words, what is the distinction between facts and values? In summary, how do we deal with concerns for justice as raised by the environmental justice movement? How does one argue within these circumstances?

These are all issues that keep posing compelling challenges to the contemporary practice of moral philosophy, especially in its theoretical trends. Different and interesting answers have been provided by theorists supporting diverse metaethical views of morality, concerning the factual and nonfactual nature of moral statements, their truth-conditions, motivating force, or action-guidingness. I have no intention of trying to deal with these questions here—their scope is simply too wide for the purposes of this short essay. But what I do try to show by raising them here is how these questions have influenced our conceptions of what environmental justice consists of. A short survey of the history of moral philosophy is again needed.

An insightful account of the origins of the questions relevant here is the article "Toward Fin de siecle Ethics: Some trends," by Darwall et al. (1992). They talk about the period of the great boom of applied ethics as "the Great Expansion" which was initiated once again by John Rawls's *Theory of Justice*:

In the Great Expansion a sense of liberation came to ethics. Moral philosophers shed the obsessions of analytic metaethics, and saw—or thought they saw—ways of exploring normative morality as a cognitive domain, without a bad philosophical conscience. The result was an unprecedented pouring of philosophical effort and personnel into ethics, which in turn spread out into the most diverse issues and applications.[21]

The central tool for the Great Expansion was the method of "reflective equilibrium," which is basically a way of checking the consistency or coherence of our moral judgments with our theoretical engagements, and utilizing the results as a means of justification. The method can be used for evaluating the moral nature of specific questions, such as, "what is the moral thing to do under circumstances X" or in a more general way like asking, what would be the correct theory of justice in environmental contexts. One of the central results of the reflective equilibrium arguments was that moral intuitions, such as those put forth by the environmental justice movement, could be taken seriously as a potential source of moral knowledge. As Darwall et al. put it, "[t]he method of reflective equilibrium accorded a cognitive and evidential status to moral intuitions or 'considered moral judgments,' particular and general alike."[22] Utilizing this idea, the applied theories of the late twentieth century tested traditional normative theories dialectically against moral intuitions and socially approved values concerning various empirical and philosophical questions. And the field expanded further as the variety of considerations involved with morality was expanded, and new methods and theories were adopted:

> New forms of naturalism and non-naturalism [became] competitive with noncognitivism, which itself has been significantly refocused, for example, to encompass rationality as well as ethics. And postwar work in game theory and rational choice theory has opened the way to rethinking and sharpening questions of practical justification, bringing them into a prominence they had not enjoyed under analytic metaethics. Finally, as we approach the fin de siecle, self-consciousness leaves little untouched; philosophy, including metaethics, has become reflective both about the limitations of the notion of meaning and about the point or prospects of philosophical inquiry itself.[23]

This development engendered an expansion of applied and practical ethics, and the result was "[. . .] an unprecedented pouring of philosophical effort and personnel into ethics, which in turn spread out into the most diverse issues and applications."[24] This expansion of the fields of academic ethics was indeed a major movement in the moral philosophy of the late twentieth century, although its genuine importance to the whole enterprise still remains to be assessed.

A number of versions of reflective equilibrium have been developed since, and there is abundant discussion about the various features of the concept, and their usefulness and plausibility. One of the central theorists is Norman Daniels, who describes what is often called the "wide reflective equilibrium" in the *Stanford Encyclopedia of Philosophy*:

The method of reflective equilibrium consists in working back and forth among our considered judgments (some say our "intuitions") about particular instances or cases, the principles or rules that we believe govern them, and the theoretical considerations that we believe bear on accepting these considered judgments, principles, or rules, revising any of these elements wherever necessary in order to achieve an acceptable coherence among them. The method succeeds and we achieve reflective equilibrium when we arrive at an acceptable coherence among these beliefs. An acceptable coherence requires that our beliefs not only be consistent with each other (a weak requirement), but that some of these beliefs provide support or provide a best explanation for others. Moreover, in the process we may not only modify prior beliefs but add new beliefs as well. There need be no assurance the reflective equilibrium is stable—we may modify it as new elements arise in our thinking.

. . . The method of reflective equilibrium has been advocated as a coherence account of justification (as contrasted with an account of truth) in several areas of inquiry, including inductive and deductive logic as well as ethics and political philosophy. The key idea underlying this view of justification is that we "test" various parts of our system of beliefs against the other beliefs we hold, looking for ways in which some of these beliefs support others, seeking coherence among the widest set of beliefs, and revising and refining them at all levels when challenges to some arise from others.[25]

The actual significance of the method is a debated issue.[26] As a coherence method of justification, the central question boils down to whether it amounts to nothing more than a sophisticated way of clarifying, categorizing, and systematizing our existing moral beliefs. Darwall et al. criticized the concept in the following manner:

For what does broad reflective equilibrium demand if not that we bring morality into some congruence with whatever else we hold in our going view of the world? . . . But what is our going view of the world? Perhaps most contemporary philosophers would agree that our going view treats empirical science as the paradigm of synthetic knowledge, and that an acceptable account of ethics must "place" it with respect to this paradigm, either by effecting some sort of methodological (and perhaps also substantive) assimilation (which might include a correction of some stereotypes of empirical science), or by establishing a convincing contrast.[27]

The nature of the background theories is still vague, as is the quality of the support they supposedly give to moral principles. It is questionable whether it is able to transcend our moral intuitions; they are always susceptible, short-sighted, stagnated, or prejudiced, even if they were genuinely believed to be carefully and impartially considered judgments. We have plenty of historical evidence of that. This poses a problem, because these judgments are part of the justification process. Further, how is one to choose the background theories, and moreover, if two persons choose different theories they will probably end up with completely different points of equilibrium. A further question is the span or scope of the intuitions and background theories to be included in the deliberations. Should the intuitions and theories used as a reference points be those of professional philosophers or the community at large?

Let me translate this idea now to the questions of the present context. It suggests that we can justify environmental justice theories through a process of deliberation in which we evaluate the considered judgments, that is, those concerns for environmental justice as expressed in society, especially by the environmental movement (or of anyone else with a relevant opinion in the issue, for that matter), together with the principles of environmental justice and with the theoretical background consider-ations that are relevant here. In the process we may then improve and refine our theories, endorse or debunk them, and treat moral intuitions similarly[28] while clarifying their roles and connections with other (theo-retical) considerations relevant here.

The concept of reflective equilibrium has in fact been explicitly sug-gested by Avner de-Shalit as particularly useful for dealing with environ-mental questions. In his *The Environment: Between Theory and Practice* (2000) he endorses what he calls "the public reflective equilibrium." His emphasis, however, is more on the question whose intuitions should be taken into consideration. This is in fact the reason why he calls his own model the "public" reflective equilibrium, contrasting it to the more limited models with Rawls's as the extreme case, where "the philosopher just sits in an armchair and reflects":[29]

> It seems simply arbitrary to divide the discourse between professional philoso-phers (e.g., those paid by the university) and amateur ones. The division should be between well and badly constructed arguments. Moreover, not only are there many interesting intuitions and many good arguments made by the general public and the milieu of environmental activists, but also it is extremely important that professional philosophers bend their ears to the voices of those who are active; the latter know the real philosophical problems emerging from the political and social debate.[30]

Reflective equilibrium forms an important element in Avner de-Shalit's and Andrew Light's *Moral and Political Reasoning in Environmental Practice* (2003), where they discuss the role of political philosophy in environmental reasoning, the relationship between cases and theories and between activism and philosophizing. In their enterprise of making environmental philosophy more practical and pragmatic, they consider that the ". . . role of the philosopher, according to this model of reflective equilibrium, is to engage in the public discourse, refine the arguments coming out of this discourse, and help to foment public debate about important issues." However, their goal is much more comprehensive than my concerns here; their aim is to turn environmental philosophy into a practical venture, a genuine public philosophy.[31] This is discernible in that they seem to me to be harnessing reflective equilibrium as a means for the development of public dialogue, and to justify it through as wide a public participation as possible.

But when it comes to using reflective equilibrium in the contexts of the notion of environmental justice I am discussing here, the goals are different in the sense that it is not a project to promote democracy. Which theories of justice should we reflect our intuitions on? This seems to me to be the area where the equation described by the reflective equilibrium is unbalanced in the following sense. The goal is different: we are not evaluating which of our theories of environmental justice is the best or accords to our intuitions—we are simply not that far in our enquiry yet. Instead we are still trying to estimate, what these theories are in the first place. And we are doing this by checking out what the general theories of justice are, and trying to determine to what extent they are applicable to environmental justice concerns.

I will rephrase the point I am trying to make here in Sen's terms. In order to construct a wholesale picture of environmental justice, we need both arrangement-focused and realization-focused understandings of it. But at the moment we have only mostly realization-focused understandings of environmental justice (the convictions of the environmental justice movement), while arrangement-focused theories are more or less missing. The former do not even amount to proper theories, but shift between being mere considered judgments or "theoretical considerations that we believe bear on accepting these considered judgments."[32] And the latter are not particularly convincing, as I tried to demonstrate in the beginning of this essay. On the other hand, the general arrangement-focused theories of justice of the mainstream do not address environmental concerns in a satisfactory manner, if at all. They usually do not even have in their vocabulary words such as nature, animals, or ecosystems. Therefore, reflective equilibrium is not particularly useful here: we lack candidates to become the theories of environmental justice needed in the process of reflection. Nor can intuitions produce these theories. For this purpose, theoretical inquiry of the structures, rules, and other arrangements of the society regarding environmental issues is needed. Here the process, as it is described by de-Shalit and Light, is surely useful: "It is only when the philosopher realizes that she is 'professional' not by having 'better' intuitions, but rather by having the skills and the means (including time), to devote herself to a profound reflection—i.e., the formation of a proper theory—about the intuition."[33]

To summarize the chapter, the task of environmental justice theorists is to develop general theories to suit environmental contexts with the help of environmental concerns as they are expressed in the considered judgments of the environmental justice movement, especially taking into consideration the contextualizing background conditions.

5. Developing Theories of Environmental Justice

Developing the account I have outlined above, environmental justice then requires us to target our theories of justice to address the various environmental concerns more carefully. This is done by modifying and adjusting our existing theories of justice and reflecting them on the various background considerations that are believed to bear on the intuitions ("considered judgments") concerning particular instances or cases (usually the perceived maldistributions) of environmental justice. As I see it, a central part of such an analysis is the examination of the background considerations, and these are the ones that the mainstream theories of justice have neglected.

Here the background considerations would serve two roles. Firstly, they are those considerations which tie these questions specifically to the field of environment, that is, make them explicitly questions of environmental justice, in contrast to general questions of justice. Their second role is to present a bridge between theoretical considerations and practical concerns. In both roles they serve in an important role as *contextualizing conditions*.

The work which seems to me to start from these kinds of presuppositions is David Schlosberg's *Defining Environmental Justice: Theories, Movements, and Nature,* which is also to date the most comprehensive work in the field of environmental justice.[34] Even though he never mentions reflective equilibrium, his work proceeds along the lines I presented in the previous chapter. He states as one of his goals the following:

> So the distance—and relationship—between justice theory and environmental justice movements is the first gap I hope to span in this book. I use the first to explore the latter, and use the latter to expand upon the first. My hope is to bring empirical evidence and activist definitions to the attention of theorists of justice for their serious consideration, and to offer activists and movements a theoretical overview of the positions and demands they express.[35]

With this starting point, Schlosberg's work gives a number of answers to the questions raised in this essay. He itemizes the four basic notions of justice that the environmental justice movement uses when expressing their concerns: (1) the equitable distribution of environmental risks and benefits; (2) the possibility for fair and meaningful participation in environmental decision-making; (3) the recognition of community ways of life, local knowledge, and cultural difference; and (4) enhancing the capabilities of communities and individuals to function and flourish. I would classify these notions as belonging in theoretical background commitments—those principles I have called intermediate principles.

Schlosberg notes the insufficiency of mainstream theories of justice and has built his own pluralistic account of environmental justice theories on the ideas expressed in general theories of justice. He deals explicitly with theories by justice of Iris Young, Nancy Fraser, and Axel Honneth— with their focus on individual and social recognition—and Amartya Sen and Martha Nussbaum—with their focus on the capacities necessary for individuals to fully function in their lives. A further element of these new theories is the emphasis on procedural or participatory justice: "For Fraser, participation is the third leg of a triad that also includes distribution and recognition; for both Sen and Nussbaum, participation is a key political capability, necessary for individuals to ensure functioning."[36] These accounts enlarge the scope of general justice theories beyond the mainstream conception.

As a result, a wholesale account of justice consists of concerns for fair distribution, recognition, capabilities, and functioning. These are the theories of justice Schlosberg uses in a reflective manner to analyze the perceived or felt injustices as expressed by the environmental justice movements, and outlined along the lines of the four basic notions of justice.

This is thus my account of the present situation of concerns for environmental justice. There are deficiencies of two kinds here: firstly, the mainstream accounts of justice—the institutional theories—are well developed and sophisticated, but are constricted (to questions of distribution) and too abstract (concentrating on transcendental rules and institutions of the society) to apply to environmental contexts. The other deficiency is that even though there are—mainly within the environmental movement—plenty of concerns for justice in existence, and a lot of practical analysis has been carried out, and evidence of infringements, and the will and motivation to rectify these injustices can be found, the terms of their realizations is not adequately conceptualized and theorized.

Here I therefore agree with Sen, who says, though targeting this criticism against mainstream theories of justice, that "[t]he question to ask in this context is whether the analysis of justice must be so confined to getting the basic institutions and general rules right. Should we not also have to examine what emerges in the society, including the kind of lives that people can actually lead, given the institutions and rules, but also other influences, including actual behavior, that would inescapably affect human lives?"[37] Of all the potential areas of human lives influenced by concerns for justice, environmental concerns are surely the most urgent ones.

6. Conclusion

To conclude, it is necessary to reflect on the nature of justice in general terms. The concerns of environmental justice, coming from the movement as well as from theorists, are apparently of a special kind. In *Moral and Political Reasoning in Environmental Practice* (2003), Andrew Light and Avner de-Shalit make a short but interesting note in their assessment of the relationship of environmental philosophy to the traditional modes of philosophical enquiry: "[i]f environmental philosophy is to marry more practical political theory, environmental justice is likely to be critical to the success of their union."[38] They may just be referring to that fact that environmental justice was firstly and foremostly a social movement, and this is the reason for their critical attitude toward theory—the textual context would seem to indicate this—but I believe that there are better reasons for such an assertion.

As I see it, justice is the fundamental normative question of the way people should treat each other. As such, it concerns the prerequisites of good life for the political animal living in the midst of similar beings. In this sense all other moral requirements are subordinate to it. This is something that is deeply immersed in Plato's idea that justice consists of creating harmony between the different elements of society. This harmony, on the other hand, is created by common rules, which are institutionalized (as institutions or as customs) and publicly known, and this requirement is well acknowledged by the contemporary mainstream theories of justice. But a further requirement is that everybody should subject themselves to these rules, to see their point and purpose, and be motivated to uphold them. Thus the concerns for justice contain, in addition to rules and institutions, the "moral or political imperatives regarding socially appropriate behavior," as Sen puts it.[39]

The normative concerns for justice are therefore our fundamental concerns. But they are also very extensive concerns in the sense that they imply the inclusion of all members of ones community or society. Even though number of theorists emphasize that the task of justice is to protect the individual, justice also includes an important element of reciprocity, i.e., the requirement that all relevantly similar creatures should be treated similarly. Environmental issues are extensive precisely in this sense, and this in turn poses problems of the most serious kind for social animals: they seem to endanger the future of not only their own kind but of the whole world. And here "the whole world" is meant to be understood literally, as all entities existing on Earth. We are no longer making a separation between us and them, Greeks and barbarians, the latter of which fall outside the concerns of justice. Everybody and everything is today included in the concerns for justice, and not only now, but also in the future. All this is straining our moral imagination today to its extremes.

This situation has also created considerable pressure for philosophers,[40] forcing them to try to make good their claims. To start with there has been an increasing pressure for more concreteness, more details, more praxis, more particularity, and more down-to-earth approaches and topics. It is required of philosophers and philosophical theories that applications and concrete results are supplied. Philosophers are invited to perform all sorts of cross-activities that are claimed to be the proper engagements for them: analyzing interdisciplinary research and its methods, combining theory and practice, conjoining facts and values, evaluating normative aspects in various academic projects, etc. Philosophers are obligated to answer these calls, since a number of them are raised by philosophers themselves in their proclamations of the inadequacies of the scientific enterprise. Moreover, the promises of applied philosophy and practical ethics have reassured others of their competence to undertake the job. All this has resulted in miscellaneous assessments of the role and nature of the whole philosophical enterprise, which of course is always a welcomed thing.

But let me return to the concerns of justice for the last time. An important fact here is that injustices are usually felt very strongly. They raise robust and intense emotions in us, to the extent that we may want to completely desist from theorizing these issues. As Sen puts it, "[w]hen we find, for example, a raging famine, it seems natural to protest rather than reason elaborately about justice and injustice."[41] This is very much the case with the environmental problems of our world, and the drastic and dramatic character of these problems immensely enhances such attitudes. We are constantly reminded of their life-threatening nature with doomsday visions and ghastly illustrations of the ensuing damages. These catalogues and picture books belong to the commonplace syllabuses of environmental education. In such a situation, "assessment [with] an observable calamity"[42] is often indeed felt to approach these problems in a wrong way, undermining their full and devastating meaning. When it is further realized, as is the case with environmental justice theories, that their moral theoretical input is not even focusing on what is felt to be the right concerns—or that they are far too abstract and theoretical to even touch these cases—it is understandable that many are tempted to demote theorizing to a subordinate role.

But since one of the purposes of environmental movements is advocating goals and motivating action, undermining theoretical considerations may prove counterproductive. We may well end up reducing serious concentration on burning social issues to becoming items of merely passing interests, with the result that they fade from public knowledge just as quickly as they were raised. The subsequent policy resolutions probably also reflect this situation and turn out to be temporary, short-term, and short-sighted, when in environmental issues quite the opposite would be needed. And this, as we know from history, is also a dangerous road. In order to avoid being driven to extremes, to moralizing and to parochial solutions, which often emerge when we rely blindly on intuitions and emotions, we need to enhance the role of reasoning here. As Sen states in the epigraph of this essay, "[t]he requirements of a theory of justice include bringing reason into play in the diagnosis of justice and injustice. Over hundreds of years, writers on justice in different parts of the world have attempted to provide the intellectual basis for moving from a general sense of injustice to particular reasoned diagnoses of injustice, and from there to the analyses of ways of advancing justice." Indeed, what else is this reasoning here but analyzing, conceptualizing, and theorizing? Nor does it mean turning a blind eye to actual infringements of environmental justice. Instead, at best, such an approach attaches infringements to their wider contexts and clarifies their effective causes as a necessary basis for any resolutions that purport to be sustainable.

Notes

1.   The research for this essay was funded by HENVI, the Helsinki University Centre for the Environment. My thanks are due to Dr. Mark Schacleton from University of Helsinki for checking my English.

2. Talbot 1997, p. 94.
3. http://en.wikipedia.org/wiki/Environmental_movement, retrieved 18.1.2010.
4. In fact the environmental justice movement, in the United States in particular, is a combination of two earlier movements, that is, the environmentalist movement and the civil rights movement.
5. The nature of this expansion will be dealt with in more detail in Chapter 3.
6. de-Shalit and Light describe some of them (2003, p.):

   "Excluding from environmental philosophy arguments and theories that are raised in real-life cases will only fortify the sense of alienation that activists sometimes have toward environmental philosophers . . .

   In too many cases . . . the discussion between philosophers and activists ended up in despair, with the latter claiming that environmental philosophy was a far cry from what was needed in practice. "All this is very beautiful, but how can I make the layperson see it?" they asked. Environmental activists have often pointed to a need for an environmental philosophy constructed in language and arguments accessible to wider audiences. Moreover, they maintain, arguments are needed that are relevant to the debates in which they are engaged.

   Even more important, if we analyze the gap between environmental philosophers and environmental activists, we see that the two groups sometimes disagree about the causes of environmental problems as well."
7. Sze and London 2008, p. 1331.
8. The closest analysis of this kind is surely Schlosberg 2007.
9. Rawls 1971, p. 3.
10. Ibid.
11. One of the first general analyses of this kind was Nicholas Rescher's *Distributive Justice* 1966, where he defines the seven "canons" to be "the Canon of Equality, . . . of Need, . . . of Ability and/or Achievement, . . . of Effort, . . . of Productivity, . . . of Social Utility, and . . . of Supply and Demand".
12. Talbot 1997, p. 93.
13. Sen 2009, pp. 5–6. Interestingly, Sen states as a reason for this "especially strong boost" to the justice discipline of the time "the political climate of change and also by the social and economic transformation taking place then in Europe and America." This has a lot in common with the urgency of the environmental problems of our time.
14. Ibid., pp. 6–8.
15. Ibid., pp. 7–9.
16. Ibid., p. 20.
17. Ibid., p. 82.
18. Ibid., p. 11.
19. Ibid., p. 11.
20. See R.M. Hare's entry "Ethics", in J. Ree & O.J. Urmson (eds.), 1990, *The Concise Encyclopedia of Western Philosophy and Philosophers*, Routledge.
21. Darwall et al. 1992 p. 123.
22. Ibid. One purpose of the usage of the term "considered moral judgments" is to exclude from consideration at least the most outrageous, unacceptable, or unfair convictions, such as those of extreme racists.
23. Ibid.
24. Ibid., p. 122.
25. Daniels, N., 2003, Reflective Equilibrium. Retrieved 21.1.2011, from http://plato.stanford.edu/entries/reflective-equilibrium/.
26. A compact exposition of the central points of criticism can be found in Juha Räikkä's entry "Reflective equilibrium" in IVR Encyclopaedia of Jurisprudence, Legal Theory

and Philosophy of Law, http://ivr-enc.info/index.php?title=Reflective_Equilibrium, retrieved 20.1.2011.
27. Darwall et al. 1992, p. 126.
28. Depending of course whether we can think of intuitions as improvable; considered judgments can of course be refined and improved.
29. de-Shalit 2000, p. 24.
30. Ibid., p. 30.
31. "Using this method of reasoning, environmental philosophy could become truly public and practical. This is so for two reasons. First, it derives from, and speaks to, people previously denied access to the shaping of the morality of our institutions. Second, environmental philosophy that uses public reflective equilibrium will derive from issues and questions previously marginalized by what has been considered the "real" or important issues on the moral agenda. Notice that this critique is pointed at two groups simultaneously. The first group consists of the developers and politicians who maintain that growth, economic considerations, and so on are the only important issues on the environmental agenda. The second group is made up of those environmental philosophers who seem to have ignored what activists have defined as urgent and important—for example, the effectiveness of arguments that try to persuade developers to act more responsibly (rather than simply the truth of those arguments), or moral dilemmas deriving from activism. Instead, many environmental ethicists have decided that the philosophically important and interesting issues are intrinsic value, nonanthropocentrism, and other philosophical concepts. An environmental philosophy based on public reflective equilibrium would not fall into this trap because it would start from questions and arguments that are raised in real-life, public debates." (Ibid., p. 15).
32. Daniels, Ibid.
33. Ibid., p. 15.
34. The summary below refers to various places in Schlosberg 2007. Other interesting works along these lines include his *Environmental Justice and the New Pluralism: The Challenge of Difference for Environmentalism*. Oxford; New York: Oxford University Press (1999), and "Reconceiving Environmental Justice: Global Movements and Political Theories", in *Environmental Politics*, Vol. 13, No. 3, Autumn 2004, pp. 517–40.
35. Schlosberg 2007, p. 5.
36. Ibid., p. 4.
37. Sen 2009, p. 11.
38. de-Shalit and Light 2003, pp. 19–20.
39. Sen 2009, p. 6.
40. de-Shalit for instance talks of "public reflective equilibrium" in a chapter entitled "The Social Role of the Philosopher"; see de-Shalit 2000.
41. Sen 2009.
42. Ibid.

References

Darwall, S.A., Gibbard, A. & Railton, P., 1992, Toward Fin de siecle Ethics: Some Trends, *The Philosophical Review*, 101 (1): 115–89.
de-Shalit, A., 2000, *The Environment: Between Theory and Practice*, Oxford University Press, USA.
de-Shalit, A. & Light, A. (eds.), 2003, *Moral and Political Reasoning in Environmental Practice*, The MIT Press, Cambridge, MA.

Rawls, J., 1971, *A Theory of Justice*, Belknap Press of Harvard University Press, Oxford.

Rescher, N., 1966, *Distributive Justice*, Bobbs Merrill, Indianapolis, IN.

Schlosberg, D., 2007, *Defining Environmental Justice: Theories, Movements, and Nature*, Oxford University Press, USA.

Sen, A., 2009, *The Idea of Justice*, Belknap Press of Harvard University Press, Cambridge, MA.

Sze, J. & London, J.K., 2008, Environmental Justice at the Crossroads, *Sociology Compass* 2/4: 1331–54.

Talbot, C., 1997, Environmental Justice, in R.F. Chadwick, (ed.), *Encyclopedia of Applied Ethics*, vol. 2. Academic Press, London, pp. 92–103.

Remarks on Ecological Radicalism

Paul McLaughlin
Department of Philosophy
University of Tartu,
Estonia

1. Introduction

"Radicalism" is a term that is frequently ascribed (or self-ascribed) in ecological circles. Quite often, it is regarded as some kind of badge of honor by ecological thinkers and activists, who proudly declare themselves "more radical" than their rivals. But what are the positive associations of this term? What exactly does radicalism in general, and ecological radicalism (here taken to be synonymous with radical ecology) in particular, actually mean? And what is the relationship between ecological radicalism and the radical tradition more generally?

It is these questions that I attempt to answer in this chapter. I will therefore begin in the first section by noting some connotations of the term "radicalism"; as will be seen, ecological discourse is somewhat unusual in this respect (in so far as the connotations of this term are broadly positive). In the second section, I will analyze the concept of "radicalism" and specify some of the primary forms of radicalism so understood. Then, in the third section, I will turn to ecological radicalism more particularly and comment on its distinctive concerns as well as some of the disputes that have marked its development. Finally, in the fourth section, I will attempt to pinpoint the place of ecological radicalism in the broader tradition of (modern, Western) radicalism, noting some relevant continuities and discontinuities.

Before I move on, I should emphasize that my purpose here is not to defend ecological radicalism in general or in any particular form. Thus, I will not engage in the "external" debate between, for example, radical ecology and environmentalism, or in the "internal" debate between, for example, deep ecology and social ecology. While I go some way toward explaining the basis of these disputes, my main interests in this chapter are in conceptual clarification (of what it means to be an ecological radical) and historico-philosophical reflection (on the place of ecological radicalism in the history of radical ideas).

2. Connotations of Radicalism

In everyday social and political discourse, the words "radical" and "radicalism" conjure up a number of images—attractive to some, repulsive to others—images of heroism and villainry, of hope and fear. Such associations depend, perhaps, on political outlook and cultural context. Thus, to many socialists in a time of economic crisis, radicalism is considered a good thing. To many ordinary citizens in a time of political violence, on the other hand, radicalism is considered a bad thing. But why so? What accounts for the positive and negative connotations of "radicalism"?

Starting with the negative or pejorative connotation, which is arguably dominant today, we may note the common association of radicalism with extremism. In certain contexts, these terms are taken to be practically synonymous. These seemingly synonymous terms are exonymic; that is to say, radicalism and extremism are ascribed to others—those from whom we would wish to dissociate ourselves culturally or politically, whether we are willing to understand their views or not (as is usually the case). Thus, in journalistic writing, we often encounter the following kind of discourse: "With few prospects, these young men [in North Sinai, Egypt] are particularly susceptible to the extremist ideas of radicals, like Al Qaeda's Osama bin Laden, calling for global jihad or holy war against non-Muslims."[1] On the theoretical side, it would seem that radicalism-extremism takes fundamentalist form; that is to say, radicalism is bound up, theoretically, with simplistic, dogmatic, and reactionary world views (religious or ideological). On the practical side, it would seem that radicalism-extremism takes violent form; that is to say, radicalism is bound up, practically, with discriminate and especially indiscriminate violence (including "terrorism"). Clearly, radicalism as extremism-fundamentalism-terrorism is a repulsive phenomenon to most ordinary citizens going about their daily lives. However, it is not clear that such an association is justified. The analysis of radicalism we offer below will enable us to determine whether it is.

The positive connotation of "radicalism" is perhaps less prominent. It is also somewhat more difficult to explain. But one possible explanation might focus on the association of radicalism with progressivism: that is, with the endeavor to achieve "change for the better" in society and other domains—practically, for example, with respect to the development of freedom, and theoretically, for example, with respect to the development of reason. In this positive sense, the term "radicalism" is endonymic; that is to say, it is ascribed by "progressives," for example, to themselves as well as to those with whom they identify in some way (the "like-minded"). Examples of such usage are common enough, but here is a rather curious example from David Cameron, leader of the British Conservative Party, during his successful general election campaign: "the Conservatives are today the radicals . . . we are now the party of progress."[2]

Whether the association of radicalism with progressivism is justified remains to be seen, but we should be cautious with such an account of the positive connotations of "radicalism" since there are those who embrace radicalism but denounce progressivism. Thus, some other account must be offered, and we will offer such an account below. For the present, we simply observe that some ecologists fall into this category, or that some ecologists denounce progressivism while they ascribe radicalism to themselves (and the "like-minded") in a positive sense. At the very least, certain radical ecologists denounce a particular understanding of progressivism, as the following statement by two leading deep ecologists indicates:

The ultimate value judgment upon which technological society rests—progress conceived as the further development and expansion of the artificial environment necessarily at the expense of the natural world—must be looked upon from the ecological perspective as unequivocal *regress*.[3]

3. The Meaning of Radicalism

The words "radical" and "radicalism" are often used—and carry the kind of associations discussed above—but they are rarely clarified; and when they are, the clarification typically begins *and ends* with etymology. Accordingly, the word "radical" is typically traced back to the Latin word *"radix,"* meaning root (as in the root of a plant). Thus, in the etymological sense, that which is radical pertains to the root of something. Such an etymological clarification would not be very helpful in itself were it not for the fact that radicals themselves embrace this sense of the term. For example, Karl Marx famously wrote in 1844 that "To be radical is to grasp things by the root."[4] Few thinkers have tried to flesh out this sense of the term, and etymological use of the term "radical" has therefore tended to remain rather more suggestive than descriptive. But one thinker—the Polish sociologist, Zygmunt Bauman—has recently developed this kind of etymological analysis somewhat. Bauman writes:

> Acts, undertakings, means, and measures may be called "radical" when they reach down to the roots: of a problem, a challenge, a task. Note, however, that the Latin noun "radix," to which the metaphorical uses of "radical" trace their pedigree, refers not only to *roots*, but also to *foundations* and to *origins*.[5]

Bauman goes on to ask the obvious question: "What do these three notions—root, foundation, and origin—have in common?" His answer singles out two features. First, there is a common element of *concealment* involved: "the material referents of all three are hidden from view and impossible to examine, let alone touch directly." And, second, there is a need for notional deconstruction or material dismantling—that is, for some kind of *destruction*—in order to reach (to comprehend or influence) the concealed roots. Thus, on Bauman's account, to be radical is *to seek to "dis-cover"—theoretically or practically—the roots, foundations, or origins of a problem or a project.* Bauman concedes that this account "leaves the criteria of recognizing the claim to radicalism sorely under-defined." For my own part, I think that Bauman's analysis—moving from mere etymology toward substantive analysis—provides a reasonable point of departure.

On the basis of Bauman's analysis, then, we might define radicalism very generally as *the orientation toward roots, foundations, or origins in a particular domain.* But an immediate objection can be raised here—against Bauman as well as our definition—about the inclusion of foundations in such a definition, or the identification of foundations with roots. Returning to mere etymology, and inspired by contemporary "anti-foundationalism," Jeremy Gilbert and Jo Littler note that the word "foundation" derives from the Latin *"fundamen,"* and that it is therefore etymologically distinct from the word "root." Why should this matter? Is this not just a point of etymological pedantry? Not according to Gilbert and Littler, who claim that foundations and roots differ in an important respect: foundations are singular (seemingly inorganic) determinants of what is "built" upon them, whereas roots are organically interdependent on other elements that "grow" out of them. So, from a contemporary (anti-foundationalist) radical perspective, what is of interest is not foundations but roots: not any "one element, institution, or group," for example, which is "determinant or constitutive of all others," but "the *interrelatedness* of different elements of the social."[6] That is to say, in basic terms, contemporary (anti-foundationalist) radicals "seek to dis-cover" (or at least explore) complex roots rather than simple foundations (as articulated by the radical "metanarratives" of the past). However, assuming that Gilbert and Littler are not getting carried away with etymology, they certainly seem to be getting carried away with their imagery of the organic and inorganic. Our general definition of radicalism implies nothing about singular foundations or interrelated roots; that is to say, we make no presumption in favor of foundationalist, anti-foundationalist, or any other kind of explanation.

Our next task is to specify the *forms* of the orientation toward roots, foundations, or origins *in a particular domain*. Indeed, it is the particular domain in which this orientation is apparent that determines the form of radicalism. Thus far, we have been emphasizing the *political* form of radicalism: that is, *the orientation toward roots, foundations, or origins in the sociopolitical domain*. However, radicalism is not limited to the political form: there are numerous *nonpolitical* forms of radicalism (which may be more or less politically relevant). Thus, we come across references to aesthetic radicalism, for example, as when Theodor Adorno writes: "Now that American hotels are decorated with abstract paintings . . . and aesthetic radicalism has shown itself to be socially affordable, radicalism itself must pay the price that it is no longer radical."[7] We also come across frequent references to religious radicalism, which might in fact be regarded as the most closely related form of radicalism to political radicalism, both historically and contemporaneously. Historically, the Reformation of the sixteenth century represented an attempt to "discover" the foundations of Church authority. This project was pushed further still by Radical Reformers, who challenged the authority of all churches and the nobility too. That is to say, these Reformers "moved from rejecting clerical privilege to the rejection of noble privilege as well; their republicanism led them to break with a concept of authority based on social estate."[8] Contemporaneously, religious radicalism is generally associated with (Islamic, Christian, etc.) fundamentalism, or versions of religions which (arguably) seek to rediscover the roots or fundamentals of these faiths—and then to put them into political practice.

Our focus in this chapter is not on aesthetic, religious, or any other form of nonpolitical radicalism, but on political radicalism itself. Political radicalism is recognizable both as *a mode of action* and as *a mode of thought*. Political radicalism as a mode of action can be defined as *the attempt to exercise social power with respect to fundamental sociopolitical relations and institutions*. This definition raises two questions: first, how is social power exercised *radically*?; and, second, what are *fundamental* sociopolitical relations and institutions? These are questions of radical means and ends. The ends of radical action are the fundamental relations and institutions that are to be subjected to social power or transformed in some way. These relations and institutions define a particular society "politically"—were they absent, for example, the society would be fundamentally different in a "political" sense—and they include class, gender, and racial relations as well as political, legal, and economic institutions. The means of radical action, by contrast, are those forms of social power which can be availed of to fundamentally transform a society (or to alter its fundamental or defining relations and institutions).

Radical means are often regarded as "extreme" such that radicalism—at least as a mode of action—is identified with extremism. The extremist connotation of radicalism was touched on in the first section, but we should look at it a little more closely in this context. How might we understand extremism? What does it mean to call someone's politics "extreme"? Two factors are arguably most significant: first, we can say that "a person is more extreme, the further away her views are from the mainstream or centre view"; and, second, we can add that a person is more extreme "the more willing she is to use violent methods in support of those views."[9] In this sense, the extremist is characterized, theoretically, by outlandish views (including those of a "fundamentalist" nature) and, practically, by violent tendencies. Assuming for a moment that outlandish views are not particularly troublesome in themselves (at least, practically speaking), we might wonder whether political radicalism as a mode of action gives rise, more worryingly, to violence. Here we need to consider the forms of political radicalism as a mode of action: if there are nonviolent forms, then there is clearly no necessary connection between radicalism and extremism. The first distinction that can be drawn here is between the *revolutionary* and *nonrevolutionary* forms of radicalism. For the purposes of the present discussion, we can say that this distinction hinges on a distinction between *immediate* and *gradual* transformation of the fundamental relations and institutions of a society. Thus, transformation can take place over an extended period of time, contrary to certain caricatures of radical action. But taking just the revolutionary form of radicalism, we can distinguish further between violent and nonviolent revolution. That is to say, there is no necessity for immediate social transformation to occur by violent means (and history attests to this fact, such that refer to "velvet" and "singing" revolutions of the relatively recent past). Thus, political radicalism as a mode of action can take nonrevolutionary and *nonviolent* form; and neither of these points suggests a necessary relationship with extremism. That said, political radicalism as a mode of action *can* take revolutionary and violent shape; it *can* involve acts of terrorism, for example, and *can* amount to a form of extremism. In evaluative terms, therefore, while it is difficult (though not impossible) to speak against radicalism in general, certain cases of radicalism are certainly morally suspect, to put it mildly. Thus, we would not wish to suggest that radicalism as a mode of action is a good thing in and of itself.

At this point, given a relatively benign account of radical means, one might be inclined to ask about the opposite of radicalism, or to ask: what are the forms of political nonradicalism as a mode of action? Put simply, they are forms of political action that involve no attempt to transform fundamental relations and institutions. There are two principal forms of "nonradicalism" in this sense: *conservation and reform.* Conservation is the attempt to maintain existing relations and institutions in their present shape. Reform, by contrast, is the attempt to make adjustments to existing relations and institutions; not to replace them, not simply to maintain them as they are, but to modify them to a lesser or greater degree (presumably "for the better" or in a "progressive" direction). Of course, the dividing line between nonradical reformism and nonrevolutionary radicalism is not always clear, and is often aggressively contested in real-world cases. But the distinction should be fairly clear at a certain level of abstraction: certain parties wish to change the world "in a deep sense" over time; other parties simply wish to make improvements to the world as it stands. In evaluative terms, once again, no judgment should be made against nonradicalism in general. There are cases where the best course of action is to maintain a given state of affairs (in certain life-or-death situations, for example); there are also cases where the best course of action is to adjust the given state of affairs (in nonrevolutionary conditions, for example). However, it should be remembered (by conservatives and reformists) that these states of affairs are very often the outcome of radical action at some prior point—or that radicalism at least sometimes brings about desirable consequences. So, once again, it appears difficult to speak against radicalism as a mode of action in general.

Moving on to political radicalism as a mode of thought, it can be defined as *inquiry into fundamental sociopolitical norms, relations, and institutions*. (Inquiry is loosely identified with theoretical "dis-covery" here.) There are many forms of radicalism as a mode of thought or particular modes of thought which exemplify the general radical mode. The main distinction I will make here is between *philosophical* radicalism and *nonphilosophical* radicalism. As examples of the latter, we might think of radical approaches in the social sciences: radical sociology, radical economics, and so on. So, what constitutes the former and how does it differ from the latter? What, in other words, is radical political philosophy? In order to answer this question, we need to characterize philosophy itself. But, in doing so, we should exercise extreme caution. Our aim here is not to *defend* a particular account of philosophy or to *convince* others of its merits, but simply to *present* one account and to explore its implications for the analysis of radicalism. (A defense of this account is beyond the scope of this chapter, in any case.) Moreover, the account we present is an intentional simplification in certain respects, notably with respect to the distinction drawn between different modes of thought, modes which are often very difficult to distinguish in practice—which overlap, which are apparent simultaneously, which may be criticized by alleged practitioners of the respective disciplines, etc.

Philosophy is often defined etymologically as the "love of wisdom" or, in rather looser terms, as a "wondering" activity. However, such a definition is misleading in two respects. Firstly, owing to certain connotations of the word "wisdom," it suggests that philosophy is a somewhat mystical enterprise, perhaps undertaken by elderly eccentrics who consider themselves "above and beyond" real or earthly concerns. This is certainly not the case with the form of philosophy under consideration here, though certain philosophical disciplines and traditions might be characterized or caricatured in this manner. Secondly, the etymological definition implies that most forms of intellectual activity can be called philosophy, including fortune-telling and scientific research, in so far as these are also directed toward "wisdom" of some kind. (Similar problems arise, incidentally, with etymological definitions of science.) However, philosophy is "essentially" different to other intellectual activities: it differs with respect to its primary mode of thought. Thus, we can say that while science is distinguished by its experimental mode of thought, and art is distinguished by its expressive mode of thought, philosophy is in fact distinguished by its argumentative mode of thought. What is more, we can—in principle—think experimentally, expressively, or argumentatively *about anything*. Thus, philosophy has no distinct subject matter, which is not to deny, of course, that certain subjects (such as the nature of argumentation itself) are of special interest to philosophers. These distinctions are, we reiterate, simplifications; they serve a more illustrative than definitive purpose. But the crucial point here is that it is a *method* (however, it is to be understood more adequately) that distinguishes philosophy, not a *goal* (say, "wisdom") or *subject matter* (say, "Being").[10]

Our distinction in terms of methods or modes of thought should not be taken to mean that scientists, for example, cannot offer arguments, or that philosophers cannot conduct experiments: scientists often do offer arguments (over the outcome of research, for example) while philosophers sometimes do conduct experiments (to test their arguments, for example); but neither activity characterizes its respective discipline; neither represents its distinguishing mode of thought. Accordingly, we might have serious misgivings about a scientist who thinks that offering good arguments is his main line of business, or a philosopher who thinks that conducting interesting experiments (or at least collecting empirical data) is his. Some philosophers, such as experimental philosophers, might question these misgivings, however. But even experimental philosophy, qua philosophy, is an argumentative discipline—one which holds that the armchair intuitions of traditional philosophers are untrustworthy or at least inadequate and that they should be tested, supplemented, or replaced by empirical findings. Thus, experimental philosophy straddles the gap between disciplinary modes of thought, but it does not dismiss philosophy or argumentation as such.

On our account, then, philosophy is (i) an *argumentative process* and, as we noted, (ii) a *comprehensive discipline*. That is to say philosophy is an argumentative process concerning anything and, indeed, everything. But this argumentative process requires something quite basic if it is to go anywhere (or to make any progress); that is, (iii) philosophy requires *conceptual clarification*. In simple terms, as philosophers, before we enter into substantive argumentation, or argue about anything, it is necessary that we know what it is that we are arguing about. This is, of course, easier said than done: concepts are difficult to pin down for a number of reasons [historical (they change over time), sociological (they may be bound up with issues of culture and power), and so on]. But, at least in one line of the philosophical tradition, clarity is held to be intellectually desirable (if not necessary) and possible (to some extent at least). To summarize, then, we can say that philosophy is, on our account, *a comprehensive argumentative process premised upon conceptual clarification.*

What we are concerned with in this chapter is only one aspect of the comprehensive argumentative process that is philosophy, namely, the sociopolitical aspect. Moreover, having defined radical political thought in general as inquiry into fundamental sociopolitical norms, practices, and institutions, we are now in a position to define radical political philosophy as *the argumentative process concerning fundamental sociopolitical norms, practices, and institutions* (premised upon conceptual clarification); that is, radical political philosophy is inquiry of the relevant kind (fundamental and sociopolitical) *conducted primarily by argumentative means.* Now, as a definition, this may seem to lack a crucial component. Some might argue for a motivational component of radical political philosophy (or all radical political thought); they might even argue that this is a necessary condition for the application of such terms. In other words, some might think that radical thought is necessarily motivated by a sense of sociopolitical disorder or injustice: by the sense that there is something fundamentally unsound or wrong with our sociopolitical arrangements. I suspect that such a sense usually does motivate radical inquiry (by argumentative or other means), but I see no reason why it should necessarily do so. A thinker might very well inquire into our fundamental sociopolitical norms, relations, and institutions out of simple intellectual curiosity, without any sense that anything is amiss. This might be a risky enterprise for those who favor or wish to conserve the status quo, since it might lead them unwillingly (as it were) to critical conclusions. And presumably this is why philosophical conservatives are as opposed to critical inquiry as they are supportive of the status quo.[11] But, once again, there is no necessary reason for the radical to be motivated in the manner indicated.

Radical political philosophy involves fundamental sociopolitical inquiry and is conducted primarily by argumentative means. But what constitutes fundamental inquiry? What constitutes a fundamental philosophical problem or question in the sociopolitical domain? These are matters of some controversy. What is more, reflection on these matters may lead us to conclude that there are no such fundamentals or that they are arbitrarily designated by supposed radicals; that is, that there is no such thing as radical political philosophy or that it is conceptually redundant. However, we do not speak here of fundamental problems in an *absolute*, timeless, (theoretically or practically) context-independent sense. There are *perennial* problems of philosophy, basic problems that have preoccupied Western political philosophers throughout the history of their discipline, such that the writings of the Ancient Greeks on justice and government still speak to us (to a debatable degree) today. For the most part, though, we speak of fundamental questions in a *relative* sense. In other words, we recognize certain questions as fundamental relative to the existing state of philosophy or the existing state of affairs. Thus, what appeared to be theoretically radical a few centuries ago (liberalism, for example) seems less so in the twenty-first century; and movements that appeared to be practically radical in the recent past (Catholic nationalism in Poland in the 1980s, for example) seem highly conservative today. Terrell Carver (who cites the latter example) makes this point, commenting that "It would seem that political backdrop is perhaps the greatest determinant in producing a politics that qualifies as 'radical.'" And, for this reason, he denies that radicalism should be identified, ahistorically, with "Left" or "Right." Indeed, it would be "unhelpful" to do so in any case, since "Left" and "Right" are also "moving targets" or categories that are subject to historical change and conceptually slippery.[12]

Another problem with the concept of radical political philosophy, assuming that fundamental problems can be specified in some (perennial or relative) sense, is that such problems may appear to be the subject matter of *all* philosophy. Arguably, all philosophy—qua philosophy—involves fundamental inquiry. Arguably, philosophy is a fundamental discipline, in which case "radical philosophy" is, once again, conceptually redundant. But this view is demonstrably mistaken. There are a number of forms of nonradical political philosophy, for instance. First, to return to an example introduced above, conservative political philosophy is *explicitly* nonradical: that is to say, conservatives renounce the project of fundamental inquiry, considering it theoretically misguided and practically dangerous. This distinction is so striking that conservatism is sometimes represented as the very antithesis of radicalism. A second example of nonradical philosophy is applied philosophy. The aim of applied philosophy, to put it crudely, is to apply existing philosophical theory to real-world situations (in business, medicine, etc.), not to engage with or advance philosophical theory (at a fundamental or rather less fundamental level). A third and more problematic case of nonradical political philosophy might be called "postradical" political philosophy. On the face of it, much postradical thought shares traditional radical concerns. However, postradicals reject certain core beliefs which they associate (justifiably or otherwise) with the radical tradition. The concerns they share and the beliefs they reject are disputed, but they seem to share a concern for distributive issues of social power, for example, while rejecting certain essentialist beliefs (metaphysical and moral) that they identify with traditional radical thought. A fourth category of non-radical political philosophy involves nonradical inquiry in the broadest sense: not the reticent inquiry of conservatives, application of existing philosophical theory, or postradical critique, but higher-order inquiry— by argumentative means—in the sociopolitical domain.

Admittedly, it is difficult to generalize about the distinction between radical political philosophy and nonradical political philosophy in the fourth sense. The best we can do in this context is to provide some examples of the respective forms of inquiry in specific areas of sociopolitical concern. Consider as very general examples, then, "levels of inquiry"— fundamental and nonfundamental—into five key socioeconomic questions: the first two more "economic"; the next two more "political"; and the last more "social." (Note, of course, that we have yet to introduce more "ecological" questions.) One might inquire fundamentally into the question of *political power*, evaluating the very *legitimacy* of such power. Or, without inquiring at that level, one might proceed nonfundamentally, evaluating the proper *limits* of a power that is taken to be legitimate. One might also inquire fundamentally into the question of *political violence*, evaluating its *justifiability* in principle (irrespective of the agency in question, be it the supposedly privileged state or otherwise). Or, proceeding in nonfundamental fashion, one might evaluate the principles of *just war* (assuming that some such principles must apply to states). In more "economic" terms, on the other hand, one might approach the problem of *distributive justice* by seeking to determine a *fair distribution* of social goods among individuals. More fundamentally, however, one might raise the *property* question, asking whether any party (notably private parties) has a legitimate claim in this respect. One might also investigate the problem of *labor* nonfundamentally, by seeking to determine the *fair wage*; or, more fundamentally, by examining the problem of *exploitation*, "fair" or otherwise. Finally, in more "social" terms, one might inquire into the problem of *cultural difference* either nonfundamentally, by raising the issue of *toleration* (of that which, in principle, we find disagreeable), or fundamentally, by raising the issue of *dignity* (of all those who, in principle, are deserving of respect).

Such distinctions are by no means clear-cut, and much work would be required to substantiate them. Moreover, the list of distinctions we have just drawn up is far from exhaustive. But the most important point that I wish to emphasize here is that these distinctions are, in themselves, descriptive or nonevaluative; that is, my general claim is not that one form of philosophy (radical philosophy) is better than another (nonradical philosophy). Nonradical philosophy (in the fourth sense, at least) poses vitally important questions: questions of toleration, for example, are of real importance to those whose dignity goes unrecognized (rightly or wrongly); and principles of just war really do matter to citizens of threatened states (legitimate or illegitimate). Nevertheless, these questions are not the sole subject matter of philosophy: philosophers, given the opportunity which many often overlook, can also assert the significance of, and pursue inquiry into, more fundamental matters—both as members of a philosophical community in which a social division of labor is fruitful (notwithstanding problems of over-specialization) and as individual thinkers who might at other times proceed (nonradically) *as if* the foundations were in place. In other words, one could claim that radical and nonradical inquiry both matter and that they are not mutually exclusive.

4. Ecological Radicalism

We arrive now, after a prolonged discussion of radical political philosophy in general, at a particular area of inquiry within this overall field. An initial point to be made, however, is that not all ecological radicalism is theoretical (a mode of thought), philosophical (conducted by argumentative means), or political (directly concerned with sociopolitical norms, practices, or institutions). Thus, one can point to ecological radicalism that is practical or religious in nature, or to radical ecological philosophy that is wholly metaphysical. But our sole concern in this paper is radical ecological political philosophy which, for convenience, we will subsequently refer to (with these words of warning in mind) as ecological radicalism. We have already claimed that radical political philosophy is an argumentative process concerning fundamental sociopolitical norms, practices, and institutions (premised upon conceptual clarification). Now the question is: what sets ecological radicalism apart? What is ecological radicalism's specific domain of inquiry? An obvious answer is that its domain of inquiry is the "ecological," rather than the "political," "economic," or "social" as such. But what should this be taken to mean? And in what sense does it bear on "sociopolitical" inquiry?

While "ecology" involves inquiry into the interactions between different elements (including populations, communities, and ecosystems) of the natural world, "ecological political philosophy" involves argumentation about the interaction between sociopolitical norms, practices, and institutions and other elements of the natural world; or, for short, between society and nature. The development of such a form of political philosophy represents a kind of "natural turn" in political philosophy: an extension of concern beyond narrowly sociopolitical matters, as they were traditionally understood (as matters of human significance only), toward more inclusive matters which arise when we consider the interaction between human beings and other elements of the natural world—nonhuman animals, ecosystems, the planet itself. This development was motivated by a profound sense of ecological crisis associated with the recognition of the threat posed, minimally, to human well-being or even survival— and, beyond that, to the well-being or survival of other elements of the natural world—by human practices and the beliefs which underpin them or at least justify them. (The precise nature of these practices and beliefs is not the topic of this chapter.)

One might, for philosophical rather than historical purposes, reconstruct this development, or this "natural turn," in four stages. In the first (anthropocentric) stage, we question the effect of existing human practices on human well-being in the natural world. Then, in the second (ecocentric) stage, we begin questioning the effect of existing human practices on the well-being of nonhuman elements of the natural world. In the third (critical) stage, we start to question our beliefs about our relationship to the natural world. And in the fourth (constructive) stage, we entertain questions about the desirability and possibility of alternative beliefs and practices. It is during this final stage that the idea of the "ecological society" enters into political philosophy as a vision of the "good society." But the most important point for us to make here is that conflict emergences within this process between those (nonradicals) who remain at the first stage—trying to figure out how we might modify existing human practices for the sake of continued human well-being—and those (radicals) who insist that we go further—challenging our existing beliefs and practices in a more fundamental way. Thus, within the relatively new field of ecological political philosophy, we witness a familiar distinction between radical and nonradical approaches; but the language in which this distinction is expressed may be somewhat unfamiliar. I will point to two examples.

In a lecture of November 1971, Murray Bookchin made a sharp distinction between (nonradical) environmentalism and (radical) ecology.[13] As he saw it, environmentalism was to be identified with an "instrumentalist" attitude to "the serviceability of the human habitat, a passive habitat that people use, in short, an assemblage of things called 'natural resources' and 'urban resources.'" Thus, for Bookchin, environmentalists think of nature as something to be used by humans, at best in a more "sustainable" or better-managed fashion; they do not demand that we rethink our relationship to the natural world or transform society in any fundamental way. Ecology, by contrast, is for Bookchin "an outlook that interprets all interdependencies," or interactions in the natural world, "nonhierarchically" and regards human beings as "only one part of the whole" of nature. That is to say, ecologists deny that nature exists simply for human use or that mankind has a privileged place in the natural world. More positively, according to Bookchin, ecologists affirm "that diversity and spontaneous development are ends in themselves, to be respected in their own right." Whatever the merits of ecology, so understood, Bookchin's conception certainly diverges in quite fundamental respects from (what he sees, at least, as) long-held beliefs about human mastery of nature (which supposedly justifies the domination of some social groups by others) and environmentalist beliefs about the need to manage the environment for our own good.

In September 1972, a matter of months after Bookchin had distinguished between ecology and environmentalism, Arne Naess made a similar distinction between (radical) "deep ecology" and (nonradical) "shallow ecology."[14] Shallow ecology, for Naess, is concerned primarily with the problems of "pollution and resource depletion" and seeks to promote "the health and affluence of people in the developed countries." Deep ecology, on the other hand, has "deeper concerns which touch upon principles of diversity, complexity, autonomy, decentralization, symbiosis, egalitarianism, and classlessness." (Naess elaborates somewhat upon these principles in his paper.) In general, Naess's criticism of shallow ecology is that it is "one-sided" in its emphasis on particular environmental problems; deep ecology, by contrast, expresses a "forcefully normative" position that is founded upon a fundamental "ecophilosophical" worldview or "philosophy of ecological harmony or equilibrium."

Whether we think it better to distinguish between ecology and environmentalism or deep ecology and shallow ecology (or perhaps prefer some alternative distinction), within the field of ecological political philosophy a firm distinction has been made between ecological radicalism and nonradicalism, or between those approaches which raise fundamental questions about the interaction between society and nature and those which do not, focusing instead on modifications to existing practices in the here-and-now.[15] It seems that from Bookchin's rather sectarian point of view, those approaches which do not raise fundamental questions are to be rejected, whereas from Naess's more ecumenical point of view, they are simply to be regarded as (of value but) inadequate. Given what has been said about the relative merits of radical and nonradical philosophy in the previous section, I am inclined to side with Naess on this issue (which is somewhat surprising, even to me). In other words, while questions of pollution and resource depletion certainly do not exhaust the field of ecological political philosophy, and need to be rethought quite fundamentally within the philosophical community as a whole, these questions can still be said to matter to those faced with environmental disaster or dwindling water reserves, for example, and are worth pursuing at least to that extent.

Of course, while I claim here that Bookchin's ecology—which he labels "social ecology"—and Naess's deep ecology are similarly radical, in so far as they focus on fundamentals, we should note that there is significant disagreement about these two radicalisms over the extent to which they are radical enough, or that they go far enough in "discovering" the roots of our ecological crisis. The basic grounds for this disagreement are as follows: social ecologists hold that deep ecology is prone to mysticism and misanthropy (basically, that it is irrational and can be dangerous). Deep ecologists, on the other hand, hold that social ecology is prone to rationalism and anthropocentrism (basically, that it is old-fashioned and un-ecological). However, there is nothing especially shocking about disagreement between radical theorists in particular fields (other than the all-too-frequent ferocity of dispute, perhaps). And our interest here is rather more in the shared form of radical philosophy rather than the disputed content of particular radical philosophies. That said, in the next section I will outline some of the more familiar subject matter of the radical tradition in order to locate the place of ecological radicalism within this tradition.

5. The Radical Tradition

In discussing "the radical tradition," an immediate question arises: is there such a tradition? Many would argue that "the radical tradition" is historically redundant: that there is no such tradition and that nothing is gained (historically, at any rate) by speaking as if there were such a thing. Some ecologists might add that even if there were such a tradition, ecologism wouldn't be part of it. For our purposes, a tradition can be understood as an *organic phenomenon or an intellectual construction*. In the former sense, members of an intellectual tradition identify with one another (to a lesser or greater degree) in some real, historical sense and (more or less) self-consciously draw on one another's work. To the extent that, for example, Saint-Simon, Fourier, Proudhon, Marx, and others so identify and influence one another, they can be said to be part of the socialist tradition in an organic sense. But doubt may be cast on whether, for instance, La Boétie in the sixteenth century and Pateman in the twentieth century belong to such a tradition, whatever similarities one might find between their ideas. Nevertheless, one might, for good reason, *construct* a tradition and situate these figures within it. Why would one wish to do so? What could justify such historical "fabrication"? Very simply, one would do this for systematic, rather than historical, philosophical reasons: in order to advance philosophical inquiry in a given (fundamental sociopolitical) area by making use of the resources of the history of ideas. By means of such "impure" history of ideas, one hopes to gain methodological, conceptual, and argumentative insight into (fundamental sociopolitical) philosophical problems. In proposing such construction, I do not mean to dismiss the role of history, or history for its own sake; nor do I deny the indirect role that good history can play in systematic philosophy. But my own interest, within the broader community of scholars, is in systematic rather than historical work per se.[16]

In this context, two claims can be made: it doesn't really matter for our purposes whether the radical tradition can be said to exist as an organic phenomenon (we can fruitfully proceed, from a systematic point of view, as if it did); and, likewise, it doesn't really matter whether ecologism belongs to such a tradition, assuming, for the present, that it does exist as an organic phenomenon (we can, once again, fruitfully proceed, from a systematic point of view, as if it did). For what it is worth, my own view is that there are organic elements in the tradition under discussion, but I have no real interest (from my systematic point of view) in justifying such a historical claim.

So, to be more precise, what are the resources that we hope to make systematic use of in the history of radical ideas? Given the analysis of radical political philosophy above, this should be relatively clear. In the first place, we can single out a number of *fundamental questions* with which radicals have dealt. We can also determine a number of *methodologies* that radical philosophers have employed in dealing with these questions. Thirdly, we can draw on the basic *conceptual work* that radicals have offered in order to pursue these questions. And, finally, we can make use of the *argumentation* they have provided in the substantive philosophical attempt to answer these questions. Obviously, we are not in a position to do all of this—to engage in comprehensive systematic treatment of the history of radical ideas—in this chapter. Nor would we wish to offer such a treatment of the entire history of radical ideas. My own interest is in modern, Western radical political philosophy, since my main political interests lie in the problems of European modernity. Nevertheless, there are certainly premodern radicalisms (if not postmodern radicalisms) that could be systematically and fruitfully explored; the same is undoubtedly true of non-Western radicalisms. But to merely hint at what might be revealed by such work on modern, Western radicalism, we can at least enumerate a number of its central (fundamental) questions (without dealing here with methodology, conceptual work, or argumentation). I submit that many of these questions are still live, to a lesser or greater extent, and that much can be learned (systematically) from earlier treatments of them (which is not to deny the significance of historical context altogether); that is to say, one can make systematic use of the works in question while recognizing the limits of time and place. The goal is to learn (systematically) from the past without succumbing to the (historical) illusion that we are still living there.

In the early modern period, during the French Reformation, we find Étienne de La Boétie in his *Discourse of Voluntary Servitude* (c. 1552) raising the problem of *civil obedience* (to tyrants in particular, and arguably government in general). Moving into the Enlightenment period, Jean-Jacques Rousseau attempted to locate the ethico-historical origins of *social inequality* in his Second Discourse (1755). In the context of the French Revolution, William Godwin's *Enquiry Concerning Political Justice* (1793) focused on the moral foundations of *government*. Charles Fourier, writing in the aftermath of that revolution, examined the problem of poverty associated with commercial capitalism in his *Theory of the Four Movements* (1808). A few decades later, Pierre-Joseph Proudhon questioned the moral right to private property in his *What is Property?* (1840). Proudhon's most famous associate from this period, Karl Marx, originally took up the problem of *alienation* (or specifically alienated labor) in his Paris Manuscripts (1844) before focusing his theoretical attention on *exploitation* under capitalism in his subsequent masterpiece, *Capital*, Volume I (1867). Mikhail Bakunin, Marx's subsequent political rival, focused on the question of *authority* (theoretical and practical, religious and political) in works such as *God and the State* (1871). At the start of the next century, Rosa Luxemburg examined the growing belief in the *adaptability and reformability* of capitalism in *Reform or Revolution* (1908). In the interwar period, Antonio Gramsci studied the problem of *ideological and political power* in capitalist society in his

Prison Notebooks (1929–36). Max Horkheimer and Theodor Adorno, writing during World War II, questioned the very foundations of *modernity* in the *Dialectic of Enlightenment* (1944). Written in the context of African decolonization, Frantz Fanon's *The Wretched of the Earth* (1963) investigates the issues of *colonialism and race*. In contemporary political philosophy, Ernesto Laclau and Chantal Mouffe have questioned the viability of a *postmodern radicalism* in *Hegemony and Socialist Strategy* (1985), Carole Pateman has questioned Western and liberal forms of *patriarchy* in *The Sexual Contract* (1988), and so on.[17]

Of course, this list of figures, texts, and problems is rather arbitrary, and it probably under-represents radicals "of the right"; but it should give us some idea of the scope of traditional radical concerns. If we were to generalize, then, it seems that radical political philosophers are traditionally preoccupied with fundamental problems related to the *distribution of social power* (in dominative, exploitative, and other forms), from the perspective of those who wield such power (governments, for example) and especially those who are subject to it (colonized peoples, for example). (To say, of course, that they are traditionally so preoccupied does not mean that radical political philosophers are necessarily so preoccupied: other kinds of fundamental sociopolitical problems are arguably evident or conceivable.)

So, how does ecological radicalism fit into this tradition? Does ecological radicalism exhibit the traditional form of argumentation concerning fundamental problems related to the distribution of social power? On the one hand, the answer might appear to be negative. After all, we stated that ecological radicalism represents an extension of concern beyond the strictly sociopolitical, taking into account the perspective (so to speak) of nonhuman elements, as well as human elements, of the natural world—a perspective lacking in our characterization of the radical tradition above. On the other hand, we stated that ecological radicalism was motivated by a sense of human responsibility for ecological crisis—by a sense that we, as wielders of social power, have threatened the well-being of not just ourselves, but of other aspects of the natural world (animals, ecosystems, the planet itself). As such, ecological radicalism does raise a fundamental problem related to the distribution of social power, at least from the perspective of those who wield it (namely, human beings in general or as particular individuals, groups, institutions, etc.)—that is, the problem of *environmental destruction*. In the course of dealing with this problem (which is formally consistent with the radical tradition), however, ecologists encounter another problem (which is formally inconsistent with the radical tradition); that is, the problem of *nonhuman considerability*, viewed from the *ecological perspective*; or, in cruder terms, the sociopolitical problem of nature. The discovery of the ecological perspective marks a revolution in radical thought—though the necessary preservation of the human perspective (the perspective of the wielder of social power) reminds us that this is a revolution within traditional radical thought. Thus, ecological radicalism can be said to be part—but a very different part—of the radical tradition.

6. Conclusion

In this paper, I have tried to demonstrate that, notwithstanding the diverse connotations which surround the term "radicalism," one form of radicalism—radical political philosophy—can be understood fairly neutrally as an argumentative process concerning fundamental sociopolitical norms, practices, and institutions (premised upon conceptual clarification). I have also attempted to establish that one kind of radical political philosophy—ecological radicalism—can be understood as an argumentative process concerning the relationship between society (or its fundamental norms, practices, and institutions) and nature (or other, nonhuman aspects of the natural world). Finally, I sought to identify the place of ecological radicalism within the radical tradition, noting that its emphasis on the human perspective is consistent with that tradition, while its discovery of the ecological perspective represents a revolution within it. Though I have therefore said very little about specific ecological radicalisms, I hope that I have at least succeeded in the rather modest task of clarifying the meaning and historical significance of ecological radicalism.

Notes

1. Extremism among Egypt's poor Bedouin, *Christian Science Monitor*, May 24, 2006.
2. Labor are now the reactionaries, we the radicals, *The Guardian*, April 9, 2010.
3. Bill Devall & George Sessions, *Deep Ecology: Living as if Nature Mattered*, Salt Lake City: Gibbs M. Smith, 1985, p. 48.
4. Toward the Critique of Hegel's Philosophy of Law: Introduction, Loyd David Easton & Kurt H. Guddat (eds.), *Writings of the Young Marx on Philosophy and Society*, Hackett, Indianapolis, 1997, p. 257.
5. Getting to the Roots of Radical Politics Today, Jonathan Pugh (ed.), *What is Radical Politics Today?*, Palgrave Macmillan, Basingstoke, 2009, p. 25, note 1. All subsequent quotations from Bauman are from this note.
6. Beyond Gesture, Beyond Pragmatism, *What is Radical Politics Today?*, pp. 127–28.

7. *Aesthetic Theory* (ed.), Robert Hullot-Kentor Continuum, London, 2005, pp. 37–38.

8. Introduction, Michael G. Baylor (ed.), *The Radical Reformation*, Cambridge University Press, Cambridge, 1991, pp. xx–xxi. Baylor notes that the radicals in question were not democrats or economic egalitarians.

9. Albert Breton et al., *Political Extremism and Rationality*, Cambridge University Press, Cambridge, 2002, p. xiii.

10. Among other difficulties here, the distinction between philosophy and rhetoric may seem to break down. These disciplines arguably share an argumentative mode of thought and differ in some other way: their goals, perhaps (knowledge as opposed to persuasion); or their disciplinary dynamics (progressive as opposed to cyclical). But this issue can be set aside for the purposes of this chapter.

11. This suggests that conservatives can do radical political philosophy, but that traditional philosophical conservatives have recognized the dangers of doing so. To put it in Enlightenment terms, then, philosophical conservatives are opposed not only to (practical) progress but also to (theoretical) reason; and this two-sided nature of the conservative position should not be overlooked.

12. Moving Targets and Political Judgments, *What is Radical Politics Today?*, p. 52.

13. See 'On Spontaneity and Organization' in Murray Bookchin, *Toward An Ecological Society*, Black Rose Books, Montreal, 1980, especially pp. 270–71.

14. See *The Shallow and the Deep, Long-Range Ecology Movement: A Summary* in Alan Drengson & Yuichi Inoue (eds.), *The Deep Ecology Movement: An Introductory Anthology*, North Atlantic Books, Berkeley, 1995, pp. 3–9.

15. Since we are not concerned with the concept of "ideology" here, I will not attempt to answer the question of whether this philosophical distinction gives rise to ideologies that are different in kind (or only different in degree). For a more ideologically-oriented approach to these matters, see Andrew Dobson, *Green Political Thought: An Introduction* (2nd ed.), Routledge, London, 2000.

16. For a more historical approach, see Jason Edwards, *The Radical Attitude and Modern Political Theory*, Palgrave Macmillan, Basingstoke, 2007. Unsurprisingly, Edwards is, from his historical rather than systematic perspective, much more skeptical about talk of a "radical tradition" than I am.

17. One may reasonably doubt whether the theorists in question regarded their problems as philosophical problems (to be dealt with primarily by argumentative means). (Marx's work on exploitation, for example, was more scientific than philosophical.) But, at the very least, these theorists inspired the philosophical investigation of such problems. (Marx's work on exploitation still plays a central role in philosophical discussion of the problem, for example.)

Perfectionist Liberalism, Natural Law Jurisprudence, and the Philosophical Foundations of Environmental Law

Christopher Stevens
Department of Philosophy
University of Maryland at College Park
USA

1. Introduction

The philosophical foundations of environmental law as they are typically conceived, or as they would appear by inference from the forms the law typically takes, support and in that sense have also partly motivated the formulation of a body of human rights-based legislation that is, I believe, unsuited to serving the function for which some and probably many policymakers intend it. This is because those foundations—the *will theory* of the function of rights, the *status theory* of the justification of rights, and the *pluralist* liberal democratic theory from which they partly spring—support a type of legal right which, though serving an ostensible good, serves also to delimit a realm of putatively morally-permissible free choice so broad as to allow serious environmental infelicities to go unnoticed or undealt with.

The environmental infelicities I speak of are those due to the choices we make, as consumers and citizens, that collectively threaten the environment by shrinkage and threaten the ecological integrity of its surviving bits.[1] The ostensible good I speak of is one served by these legal rights securing environmental means for some basic human needs' satisfaction, and this satisfaction is in turn required for the exercise of the capacities definitive of it, viz., the rational and volitional capacities definitive of the good that is autonomous agency. Though seemingly a good outright, in the context of the growing environmental crisis autonomous agency is, paradoxically, a merely ostensible one, in that the particular conception of it which such rights help realize is itself what delimits that overly broad, environmentally-threatening realm of putatively morally-permissible free choice. But there exist alternative foundations for rights, and these foundations have as much a recognized lineage as do those which support environmental human rights as most now conceive of them.

Debates about details of some features of the rights theories I discuss are complex and ongoing.[2] Rather than attempt to fairly deal with those details by, say, citing extensively from the voluminous relevant literature, I instead present those features in a more translucent manner, unhampered by exegesis of numerous others' views, so as to present a relatively accessible introduction to one instance of a more general and, so far as I am aware, unexamined option for the formulation of environmental human rights.[3] The option offers, I believe, a more satisfactory basis for environmental law.

In Section 2, I discuss what type of right an environmental human right (EHR) is according to the well-recognized Hohfeldian analytical scheme for rights analysis; present an unrecognized distinction between EHRs and most other rights falling under their Hohfeldian type; and show both that the distinction matters for evaluating EHRs and that, in the light of the distinction, EHRs as typically conceived are deficient with respect to their efficacy for realization of the widely-held environmental aims they are intended to help meet. In Section 3, I begin working to overcome that deficiency. This involves discussion of the two main theories of rights' function and their concomitant theories of rights justification, the place of one of the pairs in the mainstream conception of an environmental human right, and the unacknowledged potential of the other, less popular pair for serving to found a very different, novel environmental human rights conception.

I argue for the superiority of that less popular pair—the interest theory of rights' function and the instrumental theory of rights justification—in Sections 4 and 5, where I present and assess the most daunting common objection the instrumental theory and its rival—the status theory—each face, present a new objection against the status theory, and discuss at length Thomas Nagel's version of what is probably the *prima facie* most promising response the status theorist has to offer to that daunting common objection his theory faces. The discussion in Section 5 turns on the concept of intrinsic value, a key component in Nagel's response, and on an account of the metaphysics of value which obviates that concept. I argue in favor of that account as part of an argument against Nagel's defense of the status theory in an effort to show the instrumental theory superior. I offer, in effect, a novel conception of the instrumental theory of rights justification, one that looks to both natural law, ethical theory, and a sophisticated attitudinal hedonism for making sense of what rights do for us and, in turn, for making sense of how best to conceive of their justification. These sections, Sections 4 and 5, are the argumentative heart of the essay.

In the concluding section, Section 6, I discuss one possible cause, arising from within rights theory, of this novel instrumentalist conception of rights justification being so far unformulated despite what it has to offer rights theory. Because that cause has also partly to do with the widespread misunderstanding of perfectionist liberalism as a hopelessly inconsistent theory of politics, I discuss the misunderstanding so as to go some way toward remedying it in an effort to gain the novel conception a fair hearing. That effort involves, in turn, a brief discussion of natural law theory in ethics, as part of the cause of the misunderstanding of perfectionist liberalism is the mistaken notion that appeal to natural law, and appeal to the moral and political perfectionism natural law moral theory can involve, is antithetical to any form of political dispensation reasonably referred to by the term "liberal."

The short response to those who hold the mistaken notion is that not all forms of liberalism include (i) "an irreducible pluralism about the good," despite the inclusion, within all forms of liberalism, of (ii) "a desideratum about freedom along the lines of J.S. Mill's Liberty Principle," which limits legitimate coercive force, applied by authorities or mere members of the society and against the individual citizen, to cases in which doing so is necessary to avoid that citizen's doing harm to another.[4] Embracement of (ii) does not require for the avoidance of a practical inconsistency the embracement of (i).[5] The relevance of that fact to both environmentalism and the movement for the widespread state adoption of environmental human rights is this: conceptions of the good more substantive than pluralist liberalism allows, and which include environmentally-had human goods more complex than those among common lists of basic human needs, can constitute part of a liberal democratic theory while also securing environmental preservationist ends of the strong sort which interest the many policymakers for whom the basic needs EHR approach is recognized as a stopgap measure on the way toward stronger means to environmental preservation. Those means would limit environmental harms, incurred via preferences running against environmental preservation, whose satisfaction is permissible in the broad realm of morally-permissible free choice promoted by the pluralist liberalism from which the standard, basic needs view of EHRs partly springs.

I conclude with a brief sketch of one complex environmentally-had human good of the sort mentioned above so as to offer a glimpse of one way forward in filling out the conceptual space won in earlier sections against the standard view. I emphasize that the instance is just that, an instance. There are no doubt others.

2. What Type of Right Is an Environmental Human Right?

EHRs are typically conceived as entitlements to the provision of basic needs such as clean air and water.[6] On that conception, EHRs are what in the widely-accepted Hohfeldian analytical scheme are referred to as "passive and positive claim-rights."[7] They are claim-rights in that they involve a duty owed to the right-holder, such that there could be made a claim, by him, calling for the duty-bearer's fulfillment of whatever obligation is specified by the duty's description. They are positive rights, rather than negative ones, in that they involve an entitlement not to noninterference but to provision. They are passive rights, rather than active ones, in that they pertain not to the right-holder's actions but to the actions of others.

Behind the normalcy of that result of the application of the Hohfeldian scheme to EHRs, though, hides an interesting fact about them, a fact that I have not found discussed elsewhere with the care it deserves: unlike with most passive positive claim-rights, fulfillment of the duties of provision that standard EHRs involve principally requires the protection of an extant good rather than the creation of a good. That is, the duty-bearer's meeting the obligation of the EHR principally requires his protecting a healthy environment from harms that would taint its capacity for provision of the basic goods to which EHRs pertain. In this way, EHRs are different from, say, the purported positive social and economic rights that some argue exist, for some claimants, for such goods as sustenance, housing, healthcare, or employment. Those goods cannot typically be secured, for the claimant, by merely the duty-bearer's prevention of harm coming to an extant resource. Rather, prior to provision those resources must be created, even if they are created by some third party and then secured by the duty-bearer via purchase or the further provision of regulation safeguarding a right-holder's privileged access to them.

We have, then, a distinction between *created provisions* and *merely-protected provisions*. There are significant further differences between the two. Owing to the long-term cost-lowering benefits a high-quality good offers its provider, a created provision's overall quality is likely to be given significant consideration, and because even its consideration alone leads to a higher probability of that quality being imparted, there is a higher probability of its being so. With regard to a merely-protected provision, authorities are less likely to be concerned with considerations for the overall quality of the source of the good. Why? Because given the relatively *ad hoc* nature of the claims generating the call for the duty's being fulfilled, duties of this sort are more easily thought sufficiently dealt with—even with regard to considerations of long-term cost benefit, if these indeed arise at all—by equally *ad hoc* solutions. And *ad hoc* solutions, by their very nature, do not give rise to extraneous considerations. Claims made, for example, by persons suffering harms due to groundwater-tainting toxic effluents from a local plant are likely to be dealt with, and thought sufficiently so, via a combination of financial reparations, application of state or federal legal code specifying allowable levels of the offending chemical constituents of the plant's effluents, and scientific survey ensuring compliance with code. Notice that unlike instances of nonenvironmental provision, such environmental ones do not involve to the same degree, if they involve them at all, concerns for doing what may be necessary to ensure long-term integrity of the good's source. They instead involve but minor repair of what may, overall, be in decline.

One way to put the main point here is to say that fulfillment of such duties, whether or not it occurs as per the example above via recognition of violation of existing code, does not typically result in concerns for the baseline measure of integrity of the source of the provision. There are at least three reasons for this. First, and obviously, for instances in which those duties are fulfilled as a matter of course, attention to the long-term integrity of the resource does not come into play, since they can be fulfilled by simply the avoidance of doing the resource harm of the egregious sort, nearly the only sort with the potential for triggering response from the diffuse monitoring efforts resulting from economic realities. Second, in legal cases reparations may quell such claims, robbing them of the force they might otherwise have for helping foster environmental concerns of a longer-range and so ultimately more significant sort. Third, and more importantly, legal rulings in favor of claimants in such cases require a mere return of the good's quality to the baseline measure, so that subtle and long-term, slow-changing decreases in source quality go unaffected. They go unaffected by claims of this sort because the way to reduce costs of fulfilling the duty is to do merely what the law requires and no more. Another and more pithy way to put the main idea here is this: the created provision's source is the creator, while the merely-protected provision's source is not.

The problem is that this "basic needs" approach to EHRs allows long-term, serious damage to environmental integrity via gradual, incremental human-induced degradation of measures too small to register the sorts of concern that trigger EHR claims. This problem matters not only because an ecosystem service quality baseline level might very well imperceptibly shift for the worse and so degrade human welfare over generations, but even more so because this degradation is inconsistent with what many who support the EHR approach to resolving the problem of achieving long-term sustainable growth understand as a necessary part of the ultimate though perhaps grand aim of the sustainability movement, viz., environmental preservation, whereby "environmental preservation" is meant "preservation of (and restoration leading to) an ecologically sound natural environment of reasonable size proportionate to the size of the human population," or something roughly semantically equivalent. To avoid confusion and misunderstanding about the claim I have just made linking EHRs and environmental preservation, comments are in order.

First, though most environmental ethicists will balk at the claim that an EHR approach could ever reasonably be thought a hopeful part of an ultimately successful preservationist strategy, the sincerity of the preservationist hopes of EHR advocates should not be doubted on the sort of grounds environmental ethicists invoke. Understanding this requires some background information. Because environmental ethicists typically believe that treating nature as an instrumental rather than a final end is, in one or more of its various manifestations, the main cause of the environmental crisis, they also then believe dubious and misguided those preservationist strategies which offer a solution to the crisis in terms of some novel, supposedly preservation-securing formulation of the instrumental treatment of nature. An EHR approach to preservation falls into that category. Instead, environmental ethicists invoke reasons for preservation which are variations of the view that living nature is owed respect or special treatment in virtue of value or a moral status they claim nature has due to some of its intrinsic features alone.[8] The sincerity of the preservationist hopes of EHR advocates should not be doubted on the sort of grounds environmental ethicists invoke, because environmental ethicists' reasons are no more effective or satisfactory politically than are basic needs EHR advocates' reasons effective or satisfactory from a less practical, more straightforwardly moral-theoretical point of view. That is, while in principle not strong enough to yield preservation of the degree wanted from the outset by environmental ethicists, the reasons for environmental protection invoked by basic needs EHR advocates do, unlike environmental ethicists' reasons, have a pedigree which earns them serious consideration in policy debates. Because practical considerations have a weight environmental ethicists typically fail to acknowledge, one can indeed reasonably be for EHRs as an important part of a preservationist strategy despite environmental ethicists' balking.

Second, consider the following approach for bringing that central environmental ethical idea—i.e., the idea of owing nature treatment as a final end in virtue of its purported intrinsic value or moral status—into line with requirements for policymakers taking notice: claim that living nature itself ought to be thought to have negative rights of noninterference owing to that value or moral status.[9] The promise of this approach, if indeed it has promise, depends upon the likelihood of successfully making the case for the reasonableness of categorizing nature as an instance of the sort of thing capable of being legitimately given legal standing. The approach has been with us now for some time, but has yielded little fruit.[10] This is no doubt due to the mockery which, giving legal standing to things devoid of the capacity for consciousness, would be seen by most as making of rights talk in general, not to speak of the contortions in reasoning that would need to be made, and somehow made from without the borders of philosophy proper, in order to show nature as having features construable as necessary and sufficient for legal standing. The approach, beyond its interestingness for die-hard environmentalists concerned with rights issues in the philosophy of law, is notable, despite its failure, for being an attempt to bring concerns central for environmental ethics into line with real-world policymaking strictures. The lesson to be learned from the failure is that in the search for practical and so legal means to preservationist ends one had best look elsewhere.

Third, recall that a basic needs EHR approach to environmental preservation is deficient for the following reason: the environmental protections it provides are in principle too weak to prevent harms that some human activities do to natural environments and that work against long-term preservationist goals, but which do not immediately affect its capacity to satisfy basic needs referred to in descriptions of the duties required for meeting claims made by holders of basic needs EHRs. But, in fact, the bad effects of the deficiency's cause—the deficiency being, again, EHRs' limited preservationist force—are much worse than merely the lack of preservationist force in which the deficiency itself consists. The deficiency's cause is a limitation, on the type of positive right typically thought justifiable in a liberal democracy, that restricts the realm of rights to those required for agents functioning autonomously, as rational choosers and pursuers of the good as they themselves understand it. The bad effects of that cause are all it allows for, and what it may even insidiously promote, in the way of the pursuit of agent-chosen ends that run against not only preservationist goals but which, I believe, run also against the realization of nature-related components of a defensible conception of the common good which requires that those goals be met.[11]

Contrary to communitarian environmental thought, however, it is not the atomistic agent individualism at the heart of pluralist liberalism that, due, for instance, to the lack of fellow-feeling and so lack of coordinated behavior it allows, so problematically threatens the environment. This is because the individuals whose views form the consensus in a community can, too, choose to pursue ends they believe to be of value but which are needlessly inconsistent with sustainability aims. I say "needlessly" in the sense that there may be other ends which are of equal or greater value than those of that majority but which run against neither sustainability aims nor a reasonable, defensible conception of the common good, which could, then, include the nature-related components I alluded to above.

The problem, rather, is that the subjectivity or incommensurability about the value of ends which is at the heart of pluralist liberal theory and is a principal motivation for limiting positive rights to those required for agent autonomy—autonomy, that is, as conceived in accord with that theory—is inconsistent with a preservationist agenda. It is inconsistent with that agenda because the claim that "nature ought to be preserved, for more than merely its provision of some of the basic needs" is in effect to assert that whatever reasons justify that *ought* trump the reasons agents give themselves for some or all of the ends which run against preservation but which in accord with pluralist liberal theory are typically thought sacrosanct.[12]

The lesson those three considerations teach is troubling: the EHR approach to preservation as it is now practiced—i.e., as founded in basic needs—is fundamentally flawed and yet, at the same time, a rights approach, because of the prevalence and power the language of rights has come to have in the policy world, is probably the only viable mechanism for making significant environmental policy change, despite the fact that appeals for giving nature itself rights were probably best thought hopeless from the start. The good news is that there is less need to despair of this situation than one might at first believe there to be, since there exists a theory of rights arguably more suitable to the environmental cause than the one working behind the scenes of much of what I have so far discussed. Rather than unquestioningly accepting the *will* theory of rights, which undergirds the basic needs approach, we may do better to embrace the *interest* theory.

3. Theories of Rights' Function and the Foundation of EHRs

The Will Theory. According to the *will theory* of rights' function, the function they serve or, in other words, what rights do for the right-holder, is bestow upon him a power over another's duty. For example, if another has a duty of noninterference with respect to certain of my actions (as is typically taken to be the case, so long as those actions do not infringe upon the liberties of others to perform analogously noninfringing actions), then according to this theory my right to noninterference is best understood as my having a power to waive or otherwise alter the other's duty. I might waive it conditionally, were I, for example, to deem her intervention in some way helpful given what I so far know of her intentions, or I might annul it, were I more confident of the predictive reliability of that knowledge. Key to the theory is the idea that rights allow the right-holder's determination of privileges afforded others with respect to treatment of him. And in that sense, advocates of the will theory are concerned foremost with negative rights, i.e., rights conceived of as protections against a range of kinds of harm to person.

The Interest Theory. According to the *interest theory* of rights' function, they serve, rather, to further the right-holder's interests. For example, a right to personal property is not thought on this theory to be principally a power over another's duty of noninterference with right-holder acquisitions, but is instead thought principally a legal mechanism for ensuring something his welfare requires. Considering the distinction as I have just made it, one might come to think there may be little substantive difference between the two theories. And that thought would in one sense be correct. The will and interest theories are outcome equivalent with respect to the capacity each has to account for what rights in one particular domain do for us, viz., the domain of potential harms due to action, rather than to inaction or failure to provide something, by another. For example, we can say, in line with the interest theory, that the following is in my interest: to have control over what others *may* do or not do to me, since it is in my interest that harms to me be prevented. The domain might be called the "domain of permissions," since it centrally involves the right-holder giving permission to another with respect to the other's treatment of him. The domain of permissions is in this sense a domain of negative rights, as these are rights of noninterference.

But with respect to positive rights—i.e., rights to provision of something—the theories are partially but not entirely outcome equivalent. This is because the domain of permissions is only partially overlapping with what might be termed the "domain of reasonably-required provisions."

To understand this, note first that, by way of example, one need not think complete the analysis of basic needs EHRs' type as I presented it in Section 2. One might, instead, categorize them as negative protection rights rather than positive rights to provision, in that they protect agents from harms caused by interference with a good's quality, the access to the unadulterated form of which might best be thought had by default. In terms of this recategorization or reconceptualization of a positive right as, instead, a negative one, the domain of permissions can be helpfully thought of as including at least some rights more typically thought of as positive ones. This is helpful, because it allows a tidy reckoning of the status theorist's concern as one with a single domain of rights—the domain of permissions.

I have written "need not think complete" rather than "need not think correct" with regard to the original analysis because the alternate categorization includes, though in an opaque way, the notion of provision, as these are negative rights against noninterference with access to something. So even if one prefers the alternative categorization, one's preferring it should not lead one to decry the original analysis. Likewise, the notion of harm plays a part, though an even less conspicuous one, in the original categorization of basic needs EHRs I offered earlier, and it does so for much the same reason, viz., that lack of provision causes harm. The significance of the difference between the two categorizations does not amount, however, to a mere matter of emphasis. The difference is significant to what might be termed the "scope of rights," as will become clear.

Second, note that the will theorist construes the rights had by a right-holder as had by him irrespective of their furthering his interests, even though they might help to do so. A being's metaphysical status as a moral agent, i.e., a being with the capacity to form a unique life plan and make choices which further his realization of that plan, is sufficient, on the will theorist's view, for the *justification* of protections safeguarding his ability to exercise that capacity, should he so choose, and to do so to whatever extent he wishes, provided compatibility with the like exercise of others. This notion of rights justification is known as the *status theory*, since the justification is made via reference to the moral status of the agent.

Another way to make this same point is to say that rights are justified with respect to the value of their function. If the function of rights is to give the right-holder control over another's duty with respect to the other's obligation of noninterference with right-holder action, then the justification of rights conceived of that way will include reference to the value of the agent sovereignty which such rights serve to protect. The sphere of unhampered action secured via rights construed in that way is, in a manner of speaking, the will's sphere, and rights construed that way are typically justified via reference to the value of the autonomous, freely acting agent, i.e., the agent understood as defined in part by his volitional capacity. The idea is that the moral status of agents is due to their having the rational and volitional capacity to act autonomously. Hence, the will theory of the function of rights and the status theory of the justification of rights go hand in hand, and it is no coincidence we find that will theorists are also status theorists.

These differences in strategy for the justification of rights yield a practical difference of import. The interest theorist's construal of rights as being had by the right-holder with a normative force proportional to the extent which the fulfillment of the corresponding duties furthers his interests yields access to a conceptual apparatus not readily available to the will theorist: if we conceive of "furthering the agent's interests" in an objective rather than subjective sense, so that the realization of some agent-perceived interests or the satisfaction of some agent preferences might not further his interest, with "interest" conceived as "what is in his best interest objectively speaking," then unlike with the will theory, we can conceive of a range of rights, from strongly nonoverridable to merely weakly nonoverridable, with the strength of nonoverridability depending upon the extent to which observance of the corresponding duty fulfills that function (of furthering what is, from an objective point of view, in his best interest). Another way to express this conception is to say that rights are justified via reference to the degree of value of the outcome which their observance yields. This kind of theory of rights justification, i.e., one having to do with outcomes, is known as the *instrumental theory*.

Third, last, and most importantly, note the following: because will/status theorists justify rights via reference to the moral status of the autonomous agent, the scope of provision-rights is, on their theory, limited to goods required for avoiding harms to agent autonomy.[13] These goods are, in part, the basic needs goods, some of which are environmental. Hence, for the will/status theorist, EHRs are the basic needs EHRs. The upshot here is this: the philosophical foundation of the basic needs EHR view is the will/status theory of rights.

In case this upshot need be made clearer, note that environmental provision beyond the basic needs reduces agent autonomy, as the will/status theorist conceives of it, in that such provision reduces possibilities for the agent to exercise his will in actions that use nature in ways not reducing its capacity for yielding the environmentally-had basic needs. With that upshot of the third point behind us, we are now prepared for another and related upshot which brings those three points together in terms of the claim which brought their discussion about, viz., that though the will and interest theories are outcome equivalent with respect to the capacity each has to account for what rights do for us in the domain of permissions, they are only partially outcome equivalent with respect to what I termed the "domain of reasonably-required provisions." This is easiest to understand via three further but thankfully much less involved steps.

First, recall the third point from above: because will/status theorists justify rights via reference to the moral status of the autonomous agent, the scope of provision-rights is, on their theory, limited to goods required for avoiding harms to agent autonomy. It is in this sense, i.e., in terms of this limitation that, second, the domain of permissions is only partially overlapping with the domain of reasonably-required provisions. This is because there might be defensible arguments in favor of eschewing the limitation, as would be the case if it were reasonable to believe that, for meeting threshold levels of some very significant component of human well-being, there were required provision of goods other than merely those the will/status theorist allows for. Given one of any number of instances of an objective theory of well-being of the sort I mentioned earlier in connection with my presentation of the instrumental theory, that case might not be difficult to make, and I will in fact sketch one way of attempting to make it in Section 6. Third, and also in terms of that limitation, because the domain of permissions is in this way only partially overlapping with the domain of reasonably-required provisions, and because the domain of permissions exhausts the will/status theory but not the interest theory, the two theories of rights' function are not outcome equivalent with respect to the capacity each has to account for what rights might do for us in every domain. Another way to put this point is to say that there may be a larger domain of rights than merely the domain of permissions.

To conclude Section 3, it is worth mentioning that I suggested in passing that the importance of the point about the philosophical foundation of the basic needs EHR view being the will/status theory is related to the two theories of rights' function not being outcome equivalent with respect to the domain of provisions. If that relation is not yet obvious given what has come before, it can be made so by bringing to the fore the background against which the discussion of them has so far taken place: because the basic needs view of EHRs provides insufficiently strong protectionist reasons for environmental preservation and because the rights mechanism is the only policy-practical one for the reaching of preservationist aims (those constitute the background), then because the basic needs view of EHRs is founded on the will/status theory and the interest theory offers an expanded domain of rights, we had best look to the interest theory in search of a rights-based mechanism for environmental preservation.

4. A Better Foundation for Environmental Human Rights

Any convincing reason for favoring the interest/instrumental theory of rights as a foundation for EHRs must not compromise the reasons one might give in favor of the theory's being superior as a theory of rights.[14] In the strongest case, reasons of the latter sort would, in addition, function as reasons also of the former kind. I believe that case can be made. Common objections against the status and instrumental theories of rights justification are that the former is too strong and the latter too weak. Thinking through these and some related objections can offer, I think, good reason for believing the instrumental theory superior not only as a theory of rights in general but superior also as a foundation upon which to build a theory of environmental human rights.

The status theory can be thought too strong in that if status alone justifies rights, then since status, unlike instrumentalist outcomes, is not amenable to gradation, then for any status right—say, for example, a very broadly defined right to life—that is claimable by two or more agents in a situation for which action arguably requires, per a very strong moral intuition, the recognition of the rights of some but not all, the theory gives us no practical reasons for action. This is an unwelcome ramification of the status theory because real-world situations sometimes call for such action. For example, status theorists will typically agree that, despite their theoretical commitment to rights' nonoverridability, in some such situations and at some sufficiently high ratio of agent-right-recognized to agent-right-overridden, the status-grounded right of the fewer should be overridden in favor of the recognition of the rights of the many. And the making of a decision on that basis is not merely a failure to recognize the rights of some. It is also an acknowledgment of the place of instrumental reasons in the realm of rights. We can characterize in the following way the force of this way of construing the objection that rights as conceived by the status theorist are too strong: general acknowledgement of the place of instrumental reasons in the realm of rights, by those who conceive of rights as justified noninstrumentally, is good evidence that their conception is either to some extent misguided or, at least in the guise in which I have so far presented it, somehow incomplete.

Theoretical cases have to do, for example, with the torture and possible death of one for the increased probability of saving many threatened lives (as in terrorist bomber cases), or the letting die of one to save at least some (as in deserted island dearth of water or lack of food/ cannibal cases). It is true that the distinction between "letting die" and "killing" arises with good reason in discussion of these kinds of case, as it enables the status theorist to avoid the objection by providing him a means for offering a reason for action, rather than none: if letting die is not a failure to recognize right to life then those many lives can be left unsaved in the first case, or the many can be saved in the second, without one's having to conceive of oneself as having done, per the status theory, a moral wrong.[15] With respect to the first case, embracement of the distinction allows the status theorist to remain consistent, and so uphold the result of the application of the status view, by rejecting the instrumentalist intuition that letting the many die is morally wrong. With respect to the second, the distinction's embracement allows the status theorist to again remain consistent, this time by aligning the status theory's result with the instrumentalist's intuition rather than by rejecting it.

Admittedly, I have in the above taken the point of view of the interest/instrumental theorist when referring to some "rights," in that what might be referred to as the "right" of the many in the terrorist bomber case and of the sick/injured in the deserted island case is not a negative right having to do with noninterference but is, instead, a right, if it is a right, to the provision of something—to the provision of aid potentially sufficient for saving lives in the former case, and to the provision of aid sufficient for sustaining life in the latter one. The distinction between killing and letting die falls out of the predilection of status theorists for limiting rights to the realm of permissions in its more restricted sense (i.e., not in the expanded sense I discussed in Section 2), and since these "rights" lie outside that realm, they need not be thought by the status theorist as being rights at all.

Nevertheless, for the sake of a consistency that will help limit confusion, I will continue throughout to refer to the moral basis of claims to such provisions in cases like these using the term *rights*, no matter whether the reference occurs in the context of a discussion of the instrumental or the status theory. And, anyway, it is unclear whether those who limit legitimate rights to negative ones will be able to do so with consistency. The reason for this is interesting and worthy of a brief aside, especially since, as far as I am aware, it has not been discussed elsewhere.

Despite the negative rights emphasis, and the distinction that falls out of it, providing means for the status theorist's avoiding the difficulty of being unable to offer reasons for action in such cases rather than none, it should be noted that a tension exists between that emphasis on the one hand and, on the other, the allowance of a place for positive rights within the rights sphere that is implicit in the widespread concern for the institutionalization of rights. That is, there would seem to be many who conceive of the place of third parties, in helping to establish institutionalized human rights in states where serious rights abuses are rife, as itself based in such a strong humanitarian obligation that this obligation might best be understood as a duty corresponding to a claim-right. That claim-right, if it is one, is a positive right to aid in the establishment of a set of rights most of which are, however, negative rights of noninterference. Those rights being negative should not blind us to the positive nature of that second-order right, that right to aid in the establishment of rights. This is a problem for those who limit rights to negative ones, in that the more strongly they conceive of the nature of the injustices done in the failure of the recognition of those negative rights, the stronger would appear the positive right to aid in their establishment.

Be that as it may, another way of expressing the connection between the status theorist's limitation of rights to negative ones and the killing/letting die distinction is to say that the right to life, though a bona fide right on the status view, is typically conceived of as one that is so only with express respect to the duty each of us, individually, owes to other individuals, such that we are each individually obligated to not kill another. The notion undergirding this conception is that moral reasons are agent-relative: the agent whose life is in a particular circumstance threatened has a claim-right to life not against members of society in general, in which case moral reasons would be in that sense agent-neutral, but against the one who would in that circumstance kill him.[16] The duty to fulfill the claim falls on the agent who would perform the offending act, and the moral reason grounding that duty is in that sense agent-relative. On this view, I am not obligated, for example, to do what might be required for preventing some other individual from killing, even if I am in a position enabling me to significantly and positively alter the outcome.

That strikes me as a strange view to take, though as far as I am aware the strangeness I recognize is of a different sort than that noted by others of an instrumentalist mindset. Typically noted is the difficulty, for the advocate of agent-relative reasons, of his somehow justifying the over-riding of agents' rights—rights grounded in agent-relative reasons—for cases in which the advocate himself concedes that those rights should be overridden. That is the sense in which rights as per the status theory are typically thought too strong. That is, the killing/letting die distinction may be criticized not only in terms of its unsuitability for making sense of what seem to some to be good and binding reasons for giving aid, but also in terms of its being something the status theorist must in all cases embrace due to his inability to offer such justification. I will criticize the distinction in passing but will not question the status theorist's ability to formulate that justification.

Instead, I will question the capacity of the status theory for offering resources to make sense of the moral phenomenology the justified over-riding of rights involves. My assessment will be negative, and it is the view's inability to offer such resources that I find odd; we want a theory of rights to be able to account for the moral badness that even the justi-fied overriding of rights involves, so as to enable our making sense of the feeling of having done some wrong in having overridden them.

But that inability is not the only or even the most interesting oddity I will discuss. Another is the direct contradiction I have found by chance to exist between the claim describing the result of that assessment—the sta-tus theory being incapable of accounting for that moral phenomenology—and the upshot of a well-known response to a second but seemingly unrelated common objection to the status theory having to do with the distinction between agent-relative and agent-neutral reasons. This second objection is that the status justification of rights is really no more than mere stipulation, and one upshot of the well-known response is that, instead, the status theory is indeed capable of accounting for the moral phenomenology the justified overriding of rights involves. The oddness lies in two such seemingly unrelated matters being so related.

As to what the deep cause of their being related is, I admit I remain unsure. But the relation itself is what matters here, for it has spurred my investigation into whether the reasoning backing the response to that second objection is sound, and my assessment crowns the discussion forming this portion of the essay. The discussion proceeds in two parts in the remainder of this section, and spills over into Section 5.

Part One. Rule consequentialists, who might conceive of rights as rules justified instrumentally in terms of their observance producing good outcomes, can, unlike the status theorist who embraces the killing/letting die distinction, admit that such rights as the right to life are indeed such a strong expression of inviolability that, in a sense, all of us, including those who in a particular situation would not kill but would merely let die, have an obligation to do what we can to uphold them. I have written "in a sense," because not all of us bear the same measure of the burden of obligation, i.e., this is not the unreasonably strong obligation it might be thought to be, since the obligation can be conceived of as one whose strength varies proportionally to the ease with which one can help uphold the right. The key idea here is that, on this rule consequentialist view, instrumental reasons for overriding a right leave the right recognized though overridden. And that is because the consequentialist decision procedure has the capacity to include, via its accounting of good and bad outcomes, reference not only to the good produced by overriding a right but also to the badness the overriding of that right yields. The badness is part of the calculation, even if deliberation tells ultimately for a decision in favor of some good whose production requires the production of that badness. On this view, we do wrong when overriding a right, but we do less wrong by overriding it than not, because of the numbers of persons whose right we thereby recognize. That assessment of the making of such a decision for such cases as those mentioned above aligns well with their moral phenomenology. Letting die feels wrong.

The first oddity I recognize in the status view, to the extent which the status theorist is wedded to the killing/letting die distinction, is that the distinction robs its advocates of resources to account for that moral phenomenology. The status theorist may, though, simply deny the aptness of that phenomenology by holding fast to the distinction; if letting die is not strictly speaking a failure to recognize a right, then perhaps we ought not give into a feeling which, conceived of as based on such a failure, is in that way misconceived. But as mentioned earlier, status theorists will typically concede that at some sufficiently high ratio of agent-right-recognized to agent-right-overridden, the status-grounded right of the fewer should be overridden, and it is in that sense justifiably overridden, in favor of the recognition of the rights of the many. So the status theorist does not in all cases hold to the distinction. What of his ability to account for the moral phenomenology of these cases?

He is here, as I understand matters, in just as grave a spot—he cannot claim that the feeling of having done wrong to the fewer is due to a right having been overridden. This is because a right is, on his view, a kind of inviolability or nonoverridable protection, so that for cases in which an agent's inviolability has been justifiably transgressed, or more pointedly there has been what might be called a "justified infraction" of that inviolability, then because the inviolability, as so breached, thereby justifiably no longer exists as a property of the agent, then the right can no longer be legitimately said to exist as something that protects him in a strictly nonoverridable way, in which case we have not a right remaining in force yet overridden but, for that agent, the nonexistence of, or inapplicability of, a right. A right conceived of as nonoverridable might be unjustifiably overridden, or violated, in which case the right's force remains in play despite the violation, but to justifiably override a right, if rights are construed as nonoverridable protections, is to effectively annul it. Another way to put the gist of this point is to say that (z) "the status theorist is unable to account for the badness of the overriding of the rights of those whose rights are overridden in cases for which he concedes that instrumental reasons for overriding those rights should be acknowledged."

Since rights are, as per the status view, not rules that can in some circumstances be overridden, but are instead conceived of as nonoverridable, and also partly because of the status theorist's penchant for limiting rights to those of noninterference and the related widespread embracement among status theorists of the doing/allowing or killing/letting die distinction, the status theorist is left with few resources to make sense of the moral phenomenology of the sorts of situation discussed above, which can be characterized as follows: a moral failure to act in accord with the reasons for upholding the right(s) of some, due to the existence of stronger reasons for some action upholding others' rights that is inconsistent with action having the potential for preventing the failure. Yet another way to put the point is to say that the status theory, being without and being even antithetical to the incorporation of more sophisticated instrumentalist resources for making sense of the workings of their own concession to instrumental reasons, is incapable of providing resources necessary for its advocates' making sense of the moral phenomenology such situations involve.

Part Two. The second oddity is that some status theorists deal with another, different, and standard objection in a way that yields the negation of (z), i.e., the negation of my earlier objection that "status theorists are unable to account for the badness of the overriding of the rights of those whose rights are overridden in cases for which they concede that instrumental reasons for overriding those rights should be acknowledged." That might be thought a good thing for the status theorist. But insofar as the status view would, as I have discussed, seem in principle to preclude the status theorist's dealing successfully with that first objection, soundness of the reasoning leading to the response to the second is open to doubt and so the response is worth investigating.

The second objection is that, unlike with the instrumental theory—on which rights are justified via reference to things whose fittingness for being highly valued is relatively uncontroversial, like human happiness— the justification of rights via reference to agent moral status can appear little more than mere stipulation, and stipulation provides little if any leeway for argument in favor of the stipulated.[17] Thomas Nagel describes the problem exposed by this objection in terms of the status theorist's needing to find an explanation for what he refers to as "the "paradox" of rights."[18] This is the logical difficulty of noninstrumentally-justified rights, being of course not amenable to being made sense of in terms of good outcomes, being also incapable of being made sense of even in terms of the value of what they protect, for if they were made sense of in that way, it would then appear consistent with the status view, for all or nearly all cases, to override the rights of some in the service of recognition of the rights of others, if more of the protected good were to result from doing so. The paradox is this: to the extent that rights are understood as an expression of unconditional inviolability— i.e., understood as the status theorist suggests—they can to that same extent not be understood in terms of the value of the inviolable thing they protect, and to that same extent they are or appear to be ungrounded or merely stipulative. The attempt to ground rights on the unconditional inviolability of the agent would appear to yield a grounding of the weakest possible sort.

One of the *prima facie* most promising responses to this second objection is the following: inviolability is valuable in an understandable but noninstrumental way—it is intrinsically valuable. I say this is *prima facie* promising because it would seem to be the only way to avoid the paradox, since it is the only way to account for something's purported value without referring to instrumental or relational value. But what matters for the success of the strategy is of course the unpacking of the notion of intrinsic value in the particular guise in which it appears in this context. Consider the following, from Nagel: "To be inviolable does not mean that one *will not be violated*. It is a moral *status*. It means that one *may not* be violated . . .."[19] The point here is that what is being claimed to be intrinsically valuable is not the property of being inviolable—since given the status theorist's concession to the place of instrumental reason in moral deliberation, agents are not, on his view, inviolable—but is, rather, the *status* of being inviolable.

To clarify this distinction between what I will term "agent-inviolability" and "agent-status-inviolability," Nagel claims that "[i]f he has it [agent-status-inviolability], he does not lose it when his rights are violated [i.e., when there is an infraction of agent-inviolability]—rather, such treatment counts as a violation of his rights precisely because he has it."[20] Note that if this distinction is viable then, contrary to my earlier claim that status theorists cannot make sense of the notion of a right justifiably overridden and so cannot make sense of the moral phenomenology of cases involving what would seem to be justifiably overridden rights, the status theorist will indeed be able to make sense of it, in that he can, via the distinction, accommodate within his theory the notion of a right the force of which is retained despite the right's having been overridden. On the view that rights are an expression of agent-status-inviolability, the overriding of a right, no matter whether justified or unjustified, leaves the right in an important sense unaltered, because what is infringed is not agent-status-inviolability but merely agent-inviolability.

In the above presentation of the distinction, it has been made understandable in terms of its use for overcoming the objection, but clearly more will have to be said about it to render it more than merely an *ad hoc* one. In what does this status of being inviolable consist—or, what function does it serve—if not in its being an effective preventative to having one's rights violated? That is, in precisely what does the distinction between agent-status-inviolability and agent-inviolability consist? This is the pertinent question to ask in the context of a discussion of the benefits and drawbacks of the status and instrumental theories because, without an answer to it, claims of the following sort, which turn on the distinction and which Nagel offers in defense of the status theory, can appear empty:

> So even if we suppose, for the sake of argument, that in a moral world in which such rights exist [agent-status-inviolability] and are moreover recognized and respected by most people, the chances of being killed would be higher than in a world in which there are no such rights . . . still, this would not be the only difference between the two worlds. In the world with no rights and fewer killings, *no one* would be inviolable in a way in which, in the world with more rights and more killings, *everyone* would be . . .[21]

It sounds a bad thing for agents to not be inviolable, but none of the badness we find in it should be residual badness bleeding over from associations having to do with the more standard usage of the term "inviolable," by which is typically meant agent-inviolability. If the badness seems to one obvious and yet one is without a clear understanding of the distinction, then it is safe to say that one has allowed such bleed over. If the perceived force of the claim relies on such bleed over, then it can also safely be said that, unless the distinction matters, this claim that agents are not inviolable may be hyperbole.

Or consider the following claim, which includes implicit reference to agent-status-inviolability or intrinsically valuable moral status while also being an instance of the standard criticism of instrumental rights as being too weak:

> . . . [E]ven if there is a general right not to be tortured or murdered, perhaps there are evils great enough so that one would be justified in murdering or torturing an innocent person to prevent them. But this would not change the basic character of the right [agent-status-inviolability], since the threshold will be high enough so that the impermissibility of torture or murder to prevent evils below it cannot be explained in terms of the agent-neutral badness of torture or murder alone. Even if it is permissible to torture one person to save a thousand others from being tortured, this leaves unexplained why one may not torture one to save two.[22]

That is an argument, in favor of the status theory, via the recognition of a purported drawback of the instrumental theory: advocates of the instrumental theory, unlike advocates of the status theory—who have at their disposal the notion of a agent-status-inviolability—are purportedly unable to explain the widely-accepted intuition that, as Nagel puts it, "one may not torture one to save two." That, however, is an underestimation of the instrumentalist's resources; contrary to Nagel's claim, the intuition can indeed be explained, as follows, in terms of only agent-neutral badness, i.e., in terms of only the badness that results for everyone and not merely in terms of the moral wrongness instantiated by the agent who kills and the moral badness of the deaths of those killed. The measure of agent-neutral badness is inversely proportional to the measure of the ratio of *number saved*, S, to *number killed in order to save S*, K. As S/K rises, the agent-neutral badness decreases, since with the rise, there is a fall of the measure of concern amongst individual agents that they might be so murdered. Saving two by killing one produces so much anxiety-badness or badness in terms of the well-being of all, that the measure of anxiety badness is greater than the measure of good that results from having saved two by killing one.

That is an instance of a standard consequentialist response to objections like Nagel's, but it is a response worth having made in this context. This is especially so, since Nagel pushes his point about the instrumentalist's purported inability to give such an explanation, as he does again when claiming that ". . . in the absence of such a right [agent-status-inviolability], no one is inviolable: Anyone may be killed if that would serve to minimize the number of killings."[23] Notice that, contrary to Nagel's claim, and in the light of the standard response, it is false that minimization of killings alone is sufficient on the instrumentalist's view for any single agent's being killed. One cause of his mistake of failing to mention the standard response and to instead persist in pushing his point may be the status theorist's predilection for unwittingly conceiving of agent-neutral badness along the lines of agent-relative badness. For the status theorist, who is concerned mainly with agent-relative badness, the badness or goodness of killing can too easily be thought as having to do with only agents being alive or dead, since deaths suffered, killings done, and lives saved are the direct or agent-relative results of killing or not killing in such cases. But for the instrumentalist, who embraces agent-neutral badness and goodness, goodness can more naturally be thought to have to do not only with lives saved but with the quality of lives lived. The notion of something like anxiety badness may simply not have come to Nagel's mind.

With respect to the considerations above, we have, then, what may be an overstatement of the favorability of the status theory and an underestimation of the favorability of the instrumental theory. If Nagel's claim about the intrinsic value of inviolability is credible, then the two theories are on a par with regard to these standard objections. If it is not credible, then we have good reason to believe that the instrumental theory is, at least with respect to those objections, superior. I have written "at least with respect to those objections," but those objections are arguably the most daunting the two theories face. So an investigation into the credibility of the claim will, I think, be telling, no matter what the result. What, then, of the claim of the intrinsic value of the status of inviolability?

Here are the beginnings of Nagel's argument for that intrinsic value:

> . . . this explanation of rights in terms of the value of the status they confer might be thought instrumental . . . .. For what is the value of this status, if not the value for the people who have it of being *recognized* as not subject to certain kinds of treatment, which gives them a sense of their own worth? It seems difficult to distinguish this argument from an instrumental argument for the institutional establishment of rights as a means to improving people's well-being. The answer to this objection is that we cannot understand the well-being in question apart from the value of inviolability itself.[24]

By "the value of inviolability itself," Nagel intends to mean what most might refer to as "the intrinsic value of inviolability." The idea behind his invocation of intrinsic value in the passage above and in those appearing below is this: without his having to renounce the instrumental value of that inviolability and so without having to disagree with the instrumentalist's intuition that inviolability status is instrumentally valuable, Nagel retains the status theorist's view that rights are best conceived of as, in a strong sense, nonoverridable, by founding the instrumental value of inviolability status on inviolability status' intrinsic value. Here is another key passage, this one making even more explicit the connection between inviolability's instrumental and purported intrinsic value: "What is good about the public recognition of such a status is that it gives people the sense that their inviolability is appropriately recognized. Naturally they are gratified by this, but the gratification is due to recognition of the value of the status, rather than the opposite—i.e., the status does not get its value from the gratification it produces."[25] Or most emphatically: "It may be that we get the full value of inviolability only if we are aware of it and it is recognized by others, but the awareness and the recognition must be of something real."[26]

In that last and most emphatic passage, as it appears in the context of the other quoted passages, Nagel has equated the metaphysical realness of value with its being intrinsic. And his doing so is important with respect to his response to what I have referred to as the "second objection" because, as he claims, "[t]he answer to this objection is that we cannot understand the well-being in question apart from the value of inviolability itself [i.e., from the intrinsic value of inviolability]."[27] There are, as I understand matters, two flaws in Nagel's line of reasoning, and they are related. One is his having equated the metaphysical realness of value with its being intrinsic. On the contrary, if there is any sort of putative value that is a likely candidate for being unreal, it is, I believe, the sort referred to as "intrinsic value." The other is that, contrary to Nagel's response to that objection, and in virtue of what I believe to be an account of value more worthy of accepting than any that countenances the notion of "intrinsic value," we can indeed understand the well-being in question apart from the value of inviolability itself.

5. Inviolability and Doubts about the Concept of Intrinsic Value

5.1.

So I am a doubter about the concept of intrinsic value. But I have, I think, good reason to be, and so should others think themselves to have. This is not only because the concept of intrinsic value is a concept of a mysterious property—the value a thing has in virtue of only its intrinsic properties—but also because it is sometimes invoked at just the point in responses to objections where there seem to be few resources remaining for successfully dealing with them.[28] The invocation of the concept of intrinsic value is in such instances too convenient to be thought an innocent one. I do not have access to Nagel's view about the metaphysics of value, if only because, to my knowledge, he, as so many others who invoke the concept, has never offered one.[29] So I am unable to argue against his view, whatever it may be. But what I can do is offer a description of a concept of value rendering the metaphysics of value and talk about value in general less mysterious. If we accept the concept, and if it can be reasonably thought to offer an elucidating interpretation of Nagel's description of agents' well-being-related responses to the public recognition of what he conceives of as agent-status-inviolability, then we can, without a loss in our ability to explain a very real phenomenon, jettison the notion of intrinsic value from Nagel's claims while retaining the explanatory power they seem at first to offer.

Here is the concept of value I suggest be adopted: value is the second-order property of a thing's having first-order nonevaluative properties which, if and only if referred to by the agent in reasons, justify the taking, toward the object, of a particular pro-attitude.[30] Value is on this view a relational property, since its existence requires one's awareness of, or one's being able to provide, reasons which justify the taking of a particular pro-attitude toward the thing. On this view, neither is the truth of value claims subjective nor is value something mysterious. The truth of value claims is not subjective, despite some of the valuer's mental states being involved in constituting the value to which those claims refer, because only some and not all of the thing's properties can serve as justifiers for, if indeed they do justify, the taking of some particular attitude toward it. And value is not on this view something mysterious, floating apart from valuers, as though it were somehow something like a physical property. Instead, the existence of value requires the existence of valuers.

One such pro or positive attitude is, for example, pleasure, if pleasure is understood, as I believe it ought to be, as a propositional attitude, i.e., an attitude complete with propositional content.[31] It should be understood like this partly because to capture some of the more significant of the many ways we typically use the term "pleasure," the concept underpinning its meaning is best understood as an intentional one: our pleasures have objects. The objects of our pleasures are what we might refer to generally as "states of affairs."[32] One might, for example, be pleased that he is off from work, or be pleased that his daughter has been accepted to a good college. Pleasure is often in this way straightforwardly taken in something's being the case, and is in that sense an attitude fundamentally grounded in propositional content, rather than, as some conceive of it, primarily a sense-induced bodily "feel," each instance of which involves merely whatever mental states were causally necessary for its production. Propositional content's being part of one's taking of such pleasures is significant because it allows instances of the taking of pleasure to be subject to assessment. If, for example, pleasure is taken in something's being so-and-so, but the thing is not so-and-so, then the pleasure is inappropriately taken. It is an unjustified pleasure. This, in turn, is significant because instances of pleasure-taking include the presumption, on the part of the pleasure taker, that the state of affairs which is the object of his pleasure does indeed obtain.

With the discussion of the concept of pleasure behind us, we can return to the discussion of the credibility of conceiving of inviolability as intrinsically valuable. Here is the way in which the statement "the status is valuable" and Nagel's two claims—"[w]hat is good about the public recognition of such a status is that it gives people the sense that their inviolability is appropriately recognized" and "[n]aturally they are gratified by this"—can be captured or analyzed in terms of the concept of value introduced above: "the status is valuable" means "the status has the first-order nonevaluative property of 'providing agents, via a public recognition of that status, with a felt sense that they are recognized as inviolable', such that, when referred to in reasons, the property justifies the agent's taking toward that status the pro-attitude of pleasure".

One reason for my having discussed attitudinal pleasure is that the right side of this definition of "the status is valuable" includes reference to the concept of attitudinal pleasure, along with reference to properties of the object of pleasure that might justify instances of taking pleasure in it. If the appearance of "pleasure" seems out of place here, note that it functions as Nagel's "gratification." There may be other pro-attitudes one might take toward that status, but this is the one Nagel has mentioned, and, anyway, his mentioning it in this context does nothing in particular to endanger the integrity of his claims explaining the value of the status, even when interpreted in accord with my favored concept of value. I say, in virtue of the following line of reasoning, that it does no such harm. The key question provoked by the analysis is this: "Is the attitude of pleasure a fitting one to take toward something which has that property?" That is, does that property, if referred to in reasons intended to justify the taking of the pro-attitude, indeed justify one's taking it?[33] The answer to that question is, *prima facie*, a resounding "yes," for whom amongst us would not be pleased to be recognized as inviolable? In being so pleased, one is or ought then to be naturally pleased, too, in one's having the inviolability status the recognition requires.

But it of course does not follow from one's being pleased with something that one ought to be pleased with it. If there are reasons for being pleased to be recognized as inviolable, then insofar as those are good reasons, the property of being so recognized does justify one's taking the pro-attitude of pleasure in having inviolability status. And there are indeed good reasons—reasons which also explain the unanimity with which agents are pleased at their being thought inviolable.

One reason for this unanimity of pro-attitude toward being thought inviolable is that an agent's awareness of his being thought so yields for him an awareness, too, of there being in place at least a *pro tanto* assurance against a multitude of infringements of a lesser kind, infringements the disvalue of which can be conceived of as their power to preclude his taking of other pleasures. Infringements of his inviolability are greater ones in the sense that, if they are not assaults on his very person, they are then assaults on liberties whose exercise is fundamental to his sense of well-being in that his being denied any one of them amounts to a debilitating denial of access to a whole sphere of activity, while an infringement against freedoms to pursue any particular type of activity within any of these spheres is by the very nature of its lesser reach a lesser infringement, though it is nevertheless a significant one in that it may preclude his pursuit of some activity which he is interested in pursuing and so believes worthy of pursuit and so believes valuable, in which case it is, on one version of this account of what it is for something to be valuable, a candidate for his fittingly taking pleasure in.[34] Recognition of inviolability protects the possibility of such pleasures being taken in that it protects the possibility of the pursuit of such activities, and it does the latter insofar as it renders difficult the institutionalization of lesser infringements, since those lesser infringements are, at least *prima facie*, inconsistent with the protection against greater infringements that is embodied in the notion of inviolability.

A second good reason for that unanimity of pro-attitude is that one's being thought of as inviolable is, presumably, at the expense of no one else, and so produces no displeasure in others, and so has no capacity for producing a particular displeasure for the one thought inviolable— the particular displeasure that is a constituent in the conception of that expense as a disvalue, i.e., a disvalue in terms of one's fittingly taking toward the state of affairs instantiating the expense the propositional attitude of displeasure. In other words, the pleasure one takes in being so recognized need not be lessened or entirely offset by displeasure one takes in others' being displeased in their having as a result been unrecognized as inviolable. One need not do so because, as per the presumption, one's recognition need not be the cause of others going unrecognized.

5.2.

In criticism of the line of thinking the second reason just mentioned involves, one might point to the existence of those who would take plea-sure in others' displeasure. Consideration of their existence suggests the thought of there being two possible worlds, both of which have the same amount of pleasure generated either directly or indirectly by the recogni-tion of inviolability, but with *world one* having all agents recognized as inviolable, and *world two* with merely some being so recognized. This could be the case if the recognition of those in *world two* were for some reason at the expense of others being so recognized, with the difference in measure of pleasure between the two worlds which that generates being made up for in *world two* via the pleasure those recognized might take in the failure of the recognition of the inviolability of others. This is the beginnings of an argument to the effect that pleasure is a feeble ground for value.

It might be thought, in revolt against this analysis of the value of something so fundamental to the strongest of rights as is inviolability, that pleasure is not only a feeble ground for value in general, but that it is in particular not the sort of thing capable of grounding rights' value. The thought is mistaken on three counts. A first response is that, if the truth of the proposition the thought expresses is taken by its proponent as obvious, then he should note that his taking it to be so, if not backed by argument against the analysis or by the suggestion of an alternative grounding, amounts to his merely begging the question. Nagel suggests and argues for what is, in effect, an alternative grounding, and it is Nagel's argument I am here in the midst of offering a refutation of.

A second response is that pleasure alone is not the ground; nonevaluative properties of the status also ground the value. That is a simple point, but it is also one whose significance for making sense of value naturalistically, i.e., for making sense of the way value claims connect with facts in the world, can too easily and unwittingly be overlooked or underestimated precisely because of that simplicity. The point's simplicity belies its significance.

A third response is an answer to a question that for someone willing to concede to the initial plausibility of the analysis might nevertheless trouble him and lead him in the direction of its rejection: why is *this* pleasure—i.e., the pleasure one takes in being provided a felt sense that one is recognized as inviolable—a pleasure of such measure that it marks the value it partly grounds as one towering above others, as would befit the value we figure that inviolability, something so fundamental to our conception of the strongest of rights, must have? The answer can be stated in two different but related ways: recognition of inviolability is a fitting object of a higher pleasure; or, pleasure taken in being recognized as inviolable is a pleasure that compared to most other pleasures involves a far greater degree of exercise of the human affective, rational, and volitional capacities.

These two ways of answering are related in that the second cashes out part of the notion of a higher pleasure, a notion appearing explicitly in the first: higher pleasures are those pleasures which more fully than most other pleasures exercise the human affective, rational, and volitional capacities. Note, though, that if pleasure is conceived of as a propositional attitude, then because higher pleasures involve a sufficiently high measure of the exercise of those human capacities, then a pleasure's being a higher pleasure depends upon the capacity of the pleasure's object for effecting such exercise. And indeed the first way of answering—i.e., that recognition of inviolability is a fitting object of a higher pleasure—for that reason emphasizes properties of the object. Only those objects having the capacity to effect such exercise are ones fitting for a higher pleasure being taken in them.

The second way of answering—i.e., that pleasure taken in one's being recognized as inviolable more fully than most other pleasures exercises those human capacities—emphasizes properties not of the object but of the subject or pleasure-taker. The point here is that just as some objects of pleasure are more apt than others for taking pleasure in—viz., those objects befitting the higher pleasures—likewise some pleasures are more apt for taking than others—viz., the higher pleasures. That point can be difficult to grasp despite its simplicity.

Here it is in the remainder of 5.2, stated with greater precision. One can take pleasure in having taken particular kinds of pleasure. The former is a second-order pleasure and the latter are first-order pleasures. One might take pleasure, as far as is practicable given the different sorts of activity that make for a life, in having taken on the whole a preponderance of higher rather than lower first-order pleasures. Properties of the subject are emphasized here, then, in that the object of the second-order pleasure is an event of pleasure-taking—and so this object, in comparison with the object of a first-order pleasure, includes the subject as a constituent—and it is not only a pleasure but is a higher pleasure, so that not only is the subject a conspicuous constituent, but so also are the subject's relevant human capacities, in that their exercise is definitive of the higher pleasures.

Particular kinds of thing are more apt than others in exercising our cognitive, affective, and conative capacities. Reading a novel, for example, has the capacity for exercising them more so than does cleaning the manure from a stable, despite one's perhaps choosing, if given a choice between but the two following alternatives, to clean the stable rather than read a vapid novel. Though one may while shoveling think hard about the nature of the digestive tract, suffer from nausea due to the stench, and have a strong urge to physically escape the task, the reading of a novel in comparison can, conditional on its quality, involve or stimulate complex thought processes about the ideas its story is expressive of, can evoke or give rise to rumination about complex emotions, and might even plant the seeds for one's willing a change in one's own general outlook, life plans, or ways of interacting with others.

Just as particular kinds of thing are in that way more apt than others in exercising those capacities, so too some instances of a kind of thing are more apt than others in exercising the capacities in ways characteristic of all instances of the kind. These are the instances that are the more excellent ones of their kind.

It may typically not be useful to conceive of pleasures in orders higher than second, as these can turn out to be artificial in that they may lack robust descriptive content and so can be reduced to lower-order pleasures without loss of explanatory power. But there is at least one third-order pleasure not like that. Just as one might look back on his life thus far and take a second-order pleasure in having taken on the whole a preponderance of higher rather than lower first-order pleasures, so too might he consider his life not in comparison with only what it might given the circumstances otherwise have been, but in comparison with a life's ideal. He might take pleasure in having with diligence pursued and to some threshold level of success lived the sort of life that is the best kind of life for a human being to live, i.e., a life that warrants his taking that second-order pleasure in having taken on the whole a preponderance of higher rather than lower first-order pleasures. If he does this, he is taking pleasure in having lived a life of excellence. And he is also taking a third-order pleasure: since a life of excellence is one that warrants the taking of that second-order pleasure, then taking pleasure in having lived a life of excellence is taking pleasure in having been able to justifiably take that second-order pleasure, in which case it is a third-order pleasure.

Consideration of that third-order pleasure helps make sense of one reason that recognition of inviolability is a fitting object of a higher pleasure, a pleasure of such measure that, as I suggested above, it marks the value it partly grounds as one befitting the value we figure that inviolability, something so fundamental to our conception of the strongest of rights, must have. There are two steps in making sense of the reason. The first is a description of the way in which that pleasure-taking can involve the rational, affective, and volitional capacities. Prior to consideration of the second step, these may appear too pedestrian to be a mark of a higher pleasure.

Step One. To take pleasure in recognition of inviolability—to take pleasure in it actively—is to take pleasure in doing activities in those spheres of activity the status protects. As mentioned near the close of Section 3, liberties to pursue activity in these spheres are liberties whose exercise is fundamental to one's sense of well-being, since the liberties include, e.g., self-expression and association. Such pleasures surely often involve an affective component, as do others. Likewise they involve a rational component, as per the conception of pleasure as a propositional attitude. Another way to express the idea underlying this line of thought as described so far is to say that pleasure is an affect-laden judgment or evaluation having the power to motivate the pleasure-taker to action. It is with further consideration of the rational or cognitive component of pleasure taken in recognition of inviolability, though, that its fittingness for higher pleasure becomes apparent.

Step Two. Note the way J. S. Mill conceives of the justification of basic rights: for Mill, rights are justified instrumentally in terms of their protecting spheres of activity necessary for the existence of a kind of culture that most effectively promotes the production and appreciation of objects of the higher pleasures. In that sense, rights are instrumental for the realization of the greatest or highest kind of good for the greatest number. The culture is one in which individuality and entrepreneurship thrive, and the open and frank discussion of contrary views is not only tolerated but promoted. Those three features are necessary for a culture's promoting the originality in thought and deed, experimentation, and maintenance of love for and healthy informed criticism of tradition so important not only for the coming into being of those rare objects, events, and ways of life worthy of the higher pleasures, but also of the conservation of such things, since only be extending the tradition via informed innovation do those things come to take their acknowledged place in the story we tell ourselves, as members of such a culture, about the history of our greatest accomplishments, a history that helps us understand not only who we are but who we have aspired to be. Maintenance of an awareness of this history is maintenance of an awareness of collective excellence.

Next, recall the third-order pleasure that is taking pleasure in having lived a life of excellence. Recall also the active, affect-laden pleasure-taking in inviolability recognition discussed in step one. If an agent does that active pleasure-taking with an eye toward living a life of excellence, a life which also then may contribute if even in some small way to that history of collective excellence, then the cognitive component of his taking that pleasure in being recognized as inviolable is, in a sense, as fully exercised in terms of significance of content as it could possibly be. This is because he takes those pleasures against the background of an awareness of the philosophical underpinnings of a conception of what it is to be an excellent human being. He takes those pleasures, that is, against the background of an awareness of what for beings with such capacities constitutes their proper final end. Recognition of inviolability is a fitting object of a higher pleasure, then, because it exercises the human affective, volitional, and cognitive capacities in this very significant way.

5.3.

As I mentioned near the close of sub-section 5.1, Nagel's invocation of pleasure in his discussion of the value of inviolability status does nothing in particular to endanger the integrity of some of his claims explaining this value, even when interpreted in accord with my favored value conception. It does not do so because, as discussed in sub-sections 5.1 and 5.2, the property of "providing the agent, via a public recognition of his inviolability status, with a felt sense that he is recognized as inviolable" does indeed justify the agent's taking toward his having that status the pro-attitude of pleasure. And this is because public recognition of inviolability status, which presupposes his having been given that status, is itself a fitting object of a higher pleasure.

But Nagel's invocation of pleasure does, in a more general sense, do his view harm. Because understanding why this is so requires recollection of some of the ground we have already covered, and because the discussion has covered much ground, it is best at this point that I mention where we left off with the comparative evaluations of the status and instrumental theories of rights justification begun in Section 3, including the assessment of Nagel's claims against the instrumental theory and in favor of the status theory of rights discussed there, and where we left off with the discussion of his response to what is probably the most serious objection against the status theory, viz., the objection that the status theory's purported grounding is merely stipulative or, what amounts to much the same thing, that the status theory falls afoul of the paradox of rights.

With respect to Nagel's initial claim in favor of the status theory, the result of the assessment was that Nagel overstates its favorability in that his claim in its favor, relying as it does upon the integrity of the notion of agent-status-inviolability, relies also then implicitly upon the notion of the intrinsic value of inviolability status, a notion the credibility of which remained at that point very much open to question. I suggested that the force of his claim should be understood, that is, to be weaker than it might appear, since the claim's appeal relies upon an unfounded and controversial notion. With respect to Nagel's claim against the instrumental theory, the result of the assessment was that, in contrast to the overstatement of the favorability of his own theory, he underestimates the resources of its competitor for dealing with what is one of the most serious objections the instrumental theory faces. With respect to the paradox of rights and the standard objection that the status theory's grounding is merely stipulative, Nagel's response turns, as we have seen, on that very same notion of the intrinsic value of inviolability status, as does a possible response to the oddity I noted about the status theorist's difficulty in accounting for the moral phenomenology the justifiable overriding of rights involves, a difficulty not shared by the instrumental theory.

The upshot of the comparative evaluation, then, was this: if Nagel's argument for believing inviolability status intrinsically valuable is a convincing one, then the two theories are on a par with regard the standard objections, in that both are met, and both are then on a par, too, with regard that issue of moral phenomenology. If it is not convincing, then we have good reason to believe that the instrumental theory is, at least with respect to those objections and the oddity, superior. But, again, those objections are reasonably thought the most daunting the two theories face; Nagel's response to the one against the status theory may be representative of the best type of response available; and an ability to account for that moral phenomenology is, as I hope I have made clear, an important feature for any theory of rights.

With that retrospective behind us, it is now possible to more easily understand the way Nagel's invocation of pleasure does, in a more general sense, do his view harm. It does harm because it allows, via the pleasure-based account I have offered of the meaning of "inviolability status is valuable," for a negative assessment of Nagel's three key claims intended to show inviolability status intrinsically valuable. The first of these key claims, once more, is that with regard to the instrumental value of inviolability status or, in other words, with regard to the well-being the status promotes, ". . . we cannot understand the well-being in question apart from the value of inviolability itself," whereby "the value of inviolability itself," Nagel means "the intrinsic value of inviolability."[35] On the contrary, I have in sub-sections 5.1 and 5.2 shown that we can indeed understand this well-being while decrying the concept of intrinsic value. And I have not invoked the concept anywhere in my account of the value of inviolability status.

Nagel's second key claim is a variation of his first. On the account I have offered of the meaning of "inviolability status is valuable," this second key claim in favor of the status theory, his claim that ". . . the gratification is due to recognition of the value of the status, rather than the opposite— i.e., the status does not get its value from the gratification it produces[,]" is false.[36] Why? Because on the account I have offered, the gratification is *partly constitutive* of the value of the status. That is, the value is not intrinsic, and so contrary to Nagel's claim, the instrumental value of the status need not be thought parasitic upon its purported intrinsic value.

Nagel's third key claim in the context of his discussion of this purported intrinsic value, though of lesser importance to an assessment of the successfulness of his argument for the intrinsic value of inviolability status than the first two, is nevertheless telling because it is suggestive of an intuition that may serve as a deep motivation for Nagel's insistence that the value of inviolability status is intrinsic. Nagel's claiming, in the context of his argument for this intrinsic value, that "[i]t may be that we get the full value of inviolability only if we are aware of it and it is recognized by others, but the awareness and the recognition must be of something real" suggests that he may intuitively, and in general, take the metaphysical realness of value to require its being intrinsic.[37] I say this because he has here equated the value of inviolability, as something metaphysically real, with the intrinsic value of inviolability.

As I hope is abundantly clear from my discussion of value in earlier sections, there is no need to hang on to the intuition, if indeed one has the intuition, that to make sense of objective value claims requires the invocation of the concept of intrinsic value. On my account of the value of the status of inviolability, inviolability status is not intrinsically valuable, for on the account nothing is. Nevertheless, something that is wanted by those making the claim "inviolability status is intrinsically valuable," and wanted by them in their making of that claim, can be had via the account of value I have offered. Something they want is something that can be inferred from claims to the effect that a thing is intrinsically valuable, viz., second-order claims to the effect that a first-order statement describing the thing as valuable is not subjectively true. Such a statement would not be subjectively true, were it true, because intrinsic value is conceived of as the value a thing has in virtue of its intrinsic properties alone, and that conception rules out a dependence, for such statements' truth value, upon extrinsic or relational properties.

As I have taken pains to show, my favored account of value, the one I have used in defending the instrumental theory of rights, secures the objectivity of the truth value of value claims via the assessability of the truth value of the propositional content of the affect-laden propositional attitudes partly constitutive of the value any such claim refers to. The propositional content is, on this view, to be understood as a means for justifying the taking of whatever pro-attitude is partly constitutive of the value the claim refers to. Assessability is significant not only because it offers this objectivity. It is significant also because the objectivity it allows for, in combination with the account's reduction of value claims to ones that are straightforwardly naturalistic, in turn allows the account to render value real in the sense of its being constituted by natural properties while retaining the objectivity of value claims wanted by many who invoke the concept of intrinsic value, a concept not obviously rendering value real in any straightforward sense.

The point here is that since Nagel considers the construal of value as something real a plus for any theory of rights justification, and if he is correct in doing so, as he undoubtedly is, then it is not the status theory that comes out ahead. The instrumental theory, at least as I have interpreted it, is on this count the winner. And as I have shown, it is the winner not only on this count, but it is so with regard to the overall evaluation of the two theories that I have offered in this and the preceding section, Section 4. Recall that near the close of that section, at the midway point of the evaluation just prior to introducing Nagel's argument for the intrinsic value of inviolability status, I stated the following: if Nagel's argument for believing inviolability status intrinsically valuable is a convincing one, then the two theories are on a par with regard the standard objections, in that both are met, and both are then on a par, too, with regard the significant issue of accounting for the moral phenomenology of rights justifiably overridden, but if it is not convincing, then we have good reason to believe that the instrumental theory is, with respect to those objections and that issue, superior. Nagel's argument has turned out to be unconvincing. So the instrumental theory is superior.

Three matters remain to be discussed. One is the lack of appearance in the literature of any such defense of the instrumental theory as I have offered here. If it is, as I believe it to be, such a hopeful defense of the instrumental theory, then what has kept it from being formulated and offered? As it turns out, there is indeed a likely explanation for this. Another matter is perfectionist liberalism and a reminder of its place in the overall account of rights I have offered. The third remaining matter to be discussed is some example of an environmental human right, founded on the interest/instrumental theory of rights and their justification, that offers greater potential than does the will/status theory's basic needs approach for meeting the stronger environmental preservationist ends which concern many who understand the rights-based approach to preservation as offering one of the only real world, policy-based means to reaching those ends. In the final and concluding section, I briefly discuss all three.

6. Conclusion

One likely reason that no such defense of the interest/instrumental theory as I have offered appears in the literature on rights is that the defense is built on commonly misunderstood or underappreciated theories of ethics and politics. The ethical theory is a nonstandard form of hedonistic utilitarianism. It is nonstandard in that it includes a perfectionist component. And the theory of politics that would support an environmental human right of the sort that might be built on the version of the instrumental theory I have offered is a nonstandard form not only of liberalism—viz., perfectionist liberalism—but this perfectionist liberalism is itself of a nonstandard sort.[38] The latter is nonstandard in that it includes among its list of perfectionist ends, and includes it, furthermore, as an overarching perfectionist end, pleasure.

Hedonistic consequentialism is, roughly, the view that what ought to be done is whatever will bring about the best consequences, with the notion of the best consequences understood in terms of some conception of pleasure. J.S. Mill is the most well-known exponent of this view. His hedonism, however, has been much maligned. And the significance of its place in his ethical and political views has been nearly universally misunderstood.[39] Hedonistic consequentialism is misunderstood, I think, mainly because pleasure is unreflectively thought necessarily a subjective concept in the sense that one's experience of taking pleasure in something is thought conceptually tied to the satisfaction of desire, and desires are themselves thought subjective in the sense that they are thought not susceptible to critique. But Mill, as I understand him, conceives of pleasure in a perfectionist vein: a pleasure is objectively better for someone as a being with the particular capacities pleasure-taking involves, proportional to the degree that the pleasure is the satisfaction of an informed preference. By "informed preference" I mean, roughly, a preference grounded in knowledge of the pleasure-relevant properties of the object the pleasure is taken in; grounded in judgments, about the pleasure-worthiness of objects, rendered reliable via development of the sensitivity required for the discernment of those properties, including the affective sensibilities or capacities for affective response; and grounded not only in that knowledge, those judgments, and that sensitivity, but also in the development of a capacity for emotive response to the object's perceptual properties had against background knowledge marking out the object of pleasure as a better or worse member of its kind.

That is admittedly a complex and under-described notion of informed preference as it relates to the taking of pleasure, but this essay is not the place to elaborate upon it. All of this should be familiar enough, anyway, from my discussion of value and pleasure appearing in the sections above dealing with the defense of the instrumental theory. I have, in effect, simply channeled Mill, or at least my version of Mill. The crux here is that the reason Mill has in this way been nearly universally misunderstood, if I am pushed to conjecture, is that most have the intuition that hedonism and ethical perfectionism are antithetical, and so the perfectionist part of Mill's hedonistic utilitarianism—those parts dealing with a conception of pleasure rendering it an objective one via reference to the perfection of human capacities—is simply dropped, by most who read Mill, as incoherent.[40]

Recognition of the coherence, though, of Mill's view as I have laid it out in my own way in earlier sections may make one wonder why anyone could have the intuition that hedonism and perfectionism are inescapably inconsistent.[41] The only explanation of this widespread intuition I have so far come up with, and it is not much of an explanation I admit, since I do not share the intuition, is that pleasure, when conceived of against consideration of one's own experience of it, is quite naturally conceived of as dependent upon present preference; one cannot derive pleasure from the satisfaction of preferences one does not presently have. While that is of course true, it does not render false the claim that "were one to have some preferences other and inconsistent with those he now has, and were they satisfied, he would be better off in that the pleasure-taking related to them would be of a more worthy kind." It is the line of thinking behind this sort of claim that is central to a perfectionist account of pleasure and to the sort of welfarist normative ethic having such an account of pleasure at its core.

And there is to be had further evidence of the prevalence of the intuition that hedonism and perfectionism are inescapably inconsistent.

Aristotle's ethics is standardly understood as perfectionist. Excellences of various kinds are central to his account of the character of virtuous persons. What is not a central part of the standard understanding of his virtue ethics, however, is recognition of the very significant place he gives to pleasure in his overall conception of both the virtuous person and the good life.[42] And the claim of the prevalence of that oversight is corroborated by pleasure having been quite simply dropped from most modern variants of his view, despite Aristotle's lengthy and repeated positive discussions of it.[43] Part of the reason for this is no doubt the decision on the part of most modern-day virtue ethicists to demote to a lesser place the notion of prudential reasons and the virtue of prudence, a master virtue on Aristotle's account, in favor of virtues and values of a kind more obviously connected to the concern for other-regardingness that characterizes modern moral philosophy.[44] But the intuition that pleasure and perfectionism are antithetical is surely also a significant factor both in pleasure having been dropped in the standard account of his virtue ethics and in its failure to make much if any an appearance in modern-day variants.

The view of Aristotle's that is most clearly connected with my discussion of value and pleasure is the view that the good life can be characterized as one justifying pleasure being taken in it, in that it is a kind of life that is an excellent one with respect to the development and exercise of the central human capacities.[45] Aristotle's ethics is typically understood as an ethical natural law theory, in the sense that a correct understanding of the good centrally involves an understanding of human nature—i.e., an understanding of the central human capacities definitive of beings like us—and in the sense that the good, once correctly understood, is what structures practical reason, giving us our proper final ends, the ends suited to us, as the sort of being we are. It may seem strange or a staggering oversight, though, that pleasure appears on so few of the lists of final ends or basic goods offered by modern-day natural law theorists of ethics, because a life without pleasure would so obviously be one hardly characterizable as one that is good from the point of view of the person whose life it is, and also because pleasure of the characteristically complex sort of which humans are capable would seem to be such a central distinguishing human feature.[46]

The bearing which this very brief discussion of Mill's hedonistic consequentialism and Aristotle's ethical natural law theory has on the question of likely reasons for the failure of any such defense of the instrumental theory as the one I have offered appearing in the literature is this: the conception of the instrumental theory I have offered, by combining features of a natural law view with those of hedonistic consequentialism, yields an instrumental theory that in effect, and with the potential for causing undue confusion, borrows something from the theory to which the instrumental theory is opposed, viz., the status theory. What it borrows is a concern for the central human capacities (though not merely of the rational and volitional capacities definitive of the autonomous agent as conceived per the status theory), and that alone would render it an extremely unlikely product of the thought of a rights theorist.

What theory of politics would support a right built on such an interest/instrumental conception? The most likely candidate for this would be, as I mentioned in the essay's introduction, perfectionist liberalism. The classic account is, again, Mill's, though given the standard interpretation of the way Mill's moral and political views inform each other, one might not think that the case.[47] The key to understanding the view as it relates to a hedonist consequentialism of the form I have discussed in earlier sections is this: a strategy for the justification of liberties yielded via a sociopolitical dispensation ensuring the citizen the greatest measure of freedom consistent with the like freedom of others need not be a strategy involving principal reference to the value of that liberty conceived as a final end. Rather, those liberties, and so that dispensation, may be justified with principal reference to something further they bring about, and that is so with the justification the perfectionist liberal will offer. But it should be understood that this line of thought does not involve a denial of the value of agent autonomy. Rather, autonomy is conceived here as valuable in terms of the role it plays in one's choosing, for oneself, and pursuing with due independence, objects and activities worthy of the choice and pursuit.[48]

As I discussed at greater length in sub-section 5.2, the instrumental theorist of perfectionist and hedonist persuasion may justify rights in terms of their protecting spheres of activity necessary for the existence of a kind of culture that effectively promotes the production, conservation, and appreciation of objects and activities of the higher pleasures, with "higher" conceived of along the lines of ethical natural law theory in the sense of there being involved a central reference to fundamental human capacities. It is important to note in the context of a discussion of such elitist sounding notions as the "higher pleasures," though, that hedonist perfectionist liberalism is not a theory supportive of cultures that would aim to provide or conserve objects of the higher pleasures for the benefit of a chosen few. To see this, just recall the utilitarian slogan "the greatest (i.e., highest) good for the greatest number."

There is one final matter left to discuss. This is the nature of one such higher pleasure that might reasonably be thought the basis upon which to build an environmental human right in line with the perfectionist, hedonist conception of the interest/instrumental theory for which I have argued. Here, first, is the way in which a concern for the environment and the concern with rights reunite after so much discussion of rights alone. For the following reason, I believe, nature ought to be preserved: it is the sole means to such a significant constituent of human well-being that provision of and ready access to indigenous and ecologically sound nature are worthy of being secured by legal right. The constituent is a complex cognitively-grounded and perceptually-induced emotive experience.[49] The experience is best characterized as an aesthetic one, though in the current policy and social climate this characterization will to most policymakers and concerned citizens hardly convey its significance for either well-being or the preservationist cause. This is, however, to be expected, if a large part of the cause of our environmental problems is, as I suspect it may be, the widespread absence of the experience and so also of the moral motivation for preservation it yields, and of both the knowledge and perceptual sensitivity required for having it. This essay is not the proper place for a detailed explanation of the experience, which would take us far afield into the aesthetics literature, though after discussing some more general features of the connection between the experience and environmental preservation below, I will have a bit more to say about the experience to begin to satisfy the curious.

This view of the justification of environmental preservation is different from those common in the environmental ethics literature and in environmental policy. It includes neither an appeal to nature's purported intrinsic value, which I decry on metaphysical grounds and count a philosopher's expedient for some of the same reasons I have done so with regard to Nagel's defense of the status theory, nor an appeal to provisioning, regulating, or supporting ecosystem services such as clean air and water, climate control, and biomass production, though these are secured secondarily if indigenous and ecologically sound nature is primarily secured as a means to the experience. Another consideration of natural law theory is helpful at this point. There is a slot that most natural law theorists allot to particular kinds of aesthetic experience as necessary for a flourishing life, which for the purposes of my discussion and the concerns I have shown for hedonism can be conceived of as a life as full as is practicable with higher pleasures, including the second-order and third-order pleasures of the kind discussed earlier. The philosophy of law, and the notion of natural rights discussed in that literature, enter here much as they do for natural law theorists of ethics whose jurisprudence is based in moral theory. These philosophers understand positive law as legitimated, to the extent that it is so, via moral reasoning, so that law's proper function is conceived partly as the protection of the social and real capital that are, according to the natural law view in ethics, the means to human flourishing, with flourishing understood objectively as per human capacities, much as I have understood a proper account of pleasure.[50]

That explains the connection between rights and the good life. What, though, of that part of the good life having necessarily to do with a higher pleasure related in some way with the environment? That is, just what is the aesthetic experience of natural environments I mentioned above in connection with the formulation of an environmental human right requiring nature's preservation? To understand the answer to that question, first recall that according to the account of value presented in sub-section 5.1, value is explained as follows: value is the second-order property of a thing's having first-order nonevaluative properties such that, when referred to in reasons, these properties justify claims to the effect that the thing is the fitting object of a particular pro-attitude. This has been referred to in the literature as the 'buck-passing account of value', because the buck is passed, with respect the ontology of value, from the object and its purported first order nonrelational evaluative properties, to this second-order, relational, extrinsic property of their existing a merited relation between response and an object's nonevaluative features.

Here is one way of thinking about how the view works that is a bit different from its application earlier in assessing Nagel's argument and defending the instrumental theory: a thing might be thought valuable in virtue of its meriting the pro-attitude of awe, and if that thought is taken to be correct, then there must be good reason to believe the thing has natural, nonevaluative properties which are the mark of the awe-inspiring. Much could be said about the many ways we might isolate such a property, and they will differ with the particular pro-attitude in question, but here is one of many examples of such a way: biological facts learned from evolutionary theory provide us with the means to refer to phenotypic properties which, when considered against the background of further knowledge about natural selection, justify the response of awe, and wonder, at the vast array of phenotypes which have evolved through variation and natural selection to fit the multitude of niches living organisms have come to occupy. If those factors yielding the response are combined with attention paid to perceptual properties of one or more of these creatures and its habitat, then the response of awe becomes visceral, and the experience, being of perceptual properties and grounded in propositional content referring to relevant properties of the object, is an aesthetic experience whose object merits the cognitively-grounded, emotive aesthetic response.

Naturalists, environmentalists, and environmental aestheticians have repeatedly suggested, and in some cases pleaded, for the uninitiated to come to appreciate, understand, and perceive natural environments in this way.[51] One reason for this has to do with the very great instrumental value provided by the aesthetic experience of wonder at our natural world: the experience, being visceral, provides strongly motivating reasons for preservationist action directed at safeguarding the object of the experience, and, more importantly, the experience offers insight into what is perhaps the most significant reason for preservation there is. This is the reason provided by the sense of emotively-felt meaningfulness the experience offers those who undergo it. There may be no greater constituent of well-being, no higher pleasure, no pleasure more fitting for the kind of being we are, than the pleasure had via cognitively-grounded and volition-activating aesthetic experience of the natural world, a world from which our species has sprung, and to which each of us will return upon death, mere dust, but dust that is one with the mountains, deserts, and floors of the deepest parts of the seas across which future individuals of our species may travel, contemplating, as did we, the beauty of this planet and the life upon it.[52]

Notes

1. For two of the many available discussions of the environmental dangers consumerism poses, see Herman E. Daly, "Consumption: Value Added, Physical Transformation, and Welfare," in David A. Crocker and Toby Linden (eds.), *Ethics of Consumption* (Lanham, MD: Rowman and Littlefield, 1998); and Mark Sagoff, "Consumption," in Dale Jamieson (ed.), *A Companion to Environmental Philosophy* (Malden, MA: Blackwell, 2001), pp. 473–85.
2. See, e.g., Matthew H. Kramer, N. E. Simmonds, and Hillel Steiner, *A Debate Over Rights* (New York: Oxford University Press, 1998).
3. Options on offer include those appearing in the following: Tim Hayward, *Constitutional Environmental Rights* (New York: Oxford University Press, 2005); Richard P. Hiskes, *The Human Right to a Green Future* (New York: Cambridge, 2009); Alan Boyle and Michael Anderson (eds.), *Human Rights Approaches to Environmental Protection* (New York: Oxford University Press, 1996).
4. For Mill's presentation of the principle, see any of the numerous reprintings of his *On Liberty*.

5. For one of the most well-informed and accessible discussions of this point as it applies in particular to Mill's political views, see John Skorupski, *Why Read Mill Today?* (New York: Routledge, 2006).

6. See, e.g., James W. Nickel and Eduardo Viola, "Integrating Environmentalism and Human Rights," in Andrew Light and Holmes Rolston III (eds.), *Environmental Ethics* (New York: Blackwell, 2003), pp. 472–77; James W. Nickel, "The Human Right to a Safe Environment: Philosophical Perspectives on Its Scope and Justification," *Yale Journal of International Law* Vol. 18 (1993), pp. 281–95; Richard P. Hiskes, *The Human Right.*

7. He presents the scheme in Wesley Hohfeld, *Fundamental Legal Conceptions* (New Haven, CT: Yale University Press, 1923). 'Passive' and 'positive', and 'active' and 'negative' are not, strictly speaking, part of the Hohfeldian analytical framework, but are just as widely accepted a part of the formal apparatus, and more often than not accompany uses of it.

8. Classic accounts of this view include Paul W. Taylor, *Respect for Nature: A Theory of Environmental Ethics* (Princeton: Princeton University Press, 1986); Holmes Rolston III, *Environmental Ethics: Duties to and Values in the Natural World* (Philadelphia: Temple University Press, 1988). For what is probably the most careful, thorough, and convincing criticism of such views, see John Nolt, "The Move from *Good* to *Ought* in Environmental Ethics," *Environmental Ethics*, Vol. 28 (2006), pp. 355–74.

9. See Christopher W. Stone, "Should Trees Have Standing?" *University of Southern California Law Review*, Vol. 45 (1972), pp. 450–501.

10. See Sam Kalen, "Standing on its Last Legs: *Bennett V. Spear* and the Past and Future of Standing in Environmental Cases," *Journal of Land Use and Environmental Law*, Vol. 13 (1997), pp. 1–68. Kalen canvases numerous relevant cases, nearly all of which involve the question of standing with respect not to the environment directly but to those who claim harms to themselves due to the occurrence of environmental damage. And Stone himself (see footnote 8), after receiving compelling criticism, in effect much weakened his view that nature is best thought a legitimate bearer of rights; see his "Should Trees Have Standing? Revisited: How Far Will Law and Morals Reach? A Pluralist Perspective," *Southern California Law Review*, Vol. 59 (1985), pp. 1–154.

11. More of which I discuss briefly in Section 6, after paving the way for doing so by the further discussion of rights here and in Sections 4 and 5.

12. These ends are thought sacrosanct in the sense that their pursuit is conceived of as part of a more general pursuit of something much more significant—one or another way of life, self-chosen, infringing on no one else's claim to do likewise, and deemed available, to citizens of a pluralistic liberal democratic state, as something that freedom demands.

13. The formulation "avoiding harms to agent autonomy," though awkward in the sense that harms are typically said to be done to persons rather than to something else, is in another sense less awkward and so more fitting in this context, since it is more in accord with the negative rights tenor of the will theory than would the following, more typical formulation: because will/status theorists justify rights via reference to the moral status of the autonomous agent, the scope of provision-rights is, on their theory, limited to goods required for enabling autonomy. There is, though, no substantive difference.

14. One such unconvincing reason is this: favoring the interest/instrumental theory as a foundation for EHRs for the reason that granting legal standing to the environment, in virtue of living nature's purportedly moral status *as living*, is in the human interest because doing so helps to overcome environmental coordination problems

that may be the undoing of future generations. That reason undercuts the interest theory because it requires a status theory, which is invoked for reasons analogous to those for which a status theorist would invoke a status theory on behalf of human agents.

15. See, e.g., Alastair Norcross, "Killing and Letting Die," in R. G. Frey and Christopher Heath Wellman (eds.), *A Companion to Applied Ethics* (Malden, MA: Blackwell, 2007), pp. 451–63. The distinction can be understood as an instance of the more general one between doing and allowing, though Norcross is keen to discuss cases which contravene the universal applicability of that understanding.

16. The distinction between agent-relative and agent-neutral reasons has been much discussed. One of the earliest discussions, with the terms going by other names, appears in Thomas Nagel, *The Possibility of Altruism* (Princeton: Princeton University Press, 1970). A particularly well-known discussion appears in Derek Parfit, *Reasons and Persons* (Oxford: Clarendon Press, 1984).

17. An objection in the same spirit as this one was most famously put by Jeremy Bentham in *Anarchical Fallacies*, which is available in numerous reprintings. To describe natural rights he uses the epithet "nonsense upon stilts." More helpful is this, in which Bentham, writing of the notion of natural rights, claims that it ". . . is from beginning to end so much flat assertion . . . it lays down as a fundamental and inviolable principle whatever is in dispute . . . ." See Jeremy Waldron, *Nonsense upon Stilts: Bentham, Burke and Marx on the Rights of Man* (London: Methuen, 1987), pp. 53, 74.

18. Thomas Nagel, "Personal Rights and Public Space," *Philosophy and Public Affairs* Vol. 24 (1995), p. 90.

19. Ibid., p. 89 (italics in original).

20. Ibid., p. 90.

21. Ibid.

22. Ibid., pp. 88–89.

23. Ibid., p. 90.

24. Ibid., pp. 92–93 (italics in original).

25. Ibid., p. 93.

26. Ibid.

27. Ibid.

28. For skepticism about the integrity of the concept of intrinsic value, see "Doubts About the Concept of Intrinsic Value," Part II of Toni Rønnow-Rasmussen and Michael J. Zimmerman (eds.), *Recent Work on Intrinsic Value* (Dordrecht: Springer, 2005), pp. 61–168.

29. Nagel does mention the concept repeatedly in "The Fragmentation of Value," chapter nine of his *Mortal Questions* (Cambridge: Cambridge University Press, 2000, originally published 1979), though without the explanation for which one concerned with the metaphysics of value would hope.

30. This sort of account of value is now typically referred to in the literature as the "fitting attitudes account." It is also referred to as the "buck passing account" owing to Thomas Scanlon, one of the first to present it. See Scanlon's *What We Owe to Each Other* (Cambridge: Harvard University Press, 1998), pp. 95–100. A useful presentation of the history of buck passing views appears in Jonathan Dancy, "Should We Pass the Buck?" in Rønnow-Rasmussen and Zimmerman, *Recent Work*.

31. Pleasure's being properly conceived as an intentional state is defended in Fred Feldman, *Pleasure and the Good Life: Concerning the Nature, Varieties, and Plausibility of Hedonism* (New York: Oxford University Press, 2004).

32. The taking of pleasure in such things as the taste of a food or the feel of the sun on one's face, though seemingly involving little cognitive content, can be understood on this model via appeal to dispositional belief.
33. The relevant instantiated form of that general question is this: Does the property of "providing the agent, via a public recognition of his inviolability status, with a felt sense that he is recognized as inviolable" justify the agent's taking toward his having that status the pro-attitude of pleasure?
34. Consider, for example, the freedoms of speech and assembly guaranteed in the First Amendment to the US Constitution. The "one version of this account" I refer to here is the version according to which all pro-attitudes are reducible to the pro-attitude of pleasure. That version is therefore a form of hedonism, though a sophisticated one.
35. Nagel, "Personal Rights and Public Space," p. 93.
36. Ibid., p. 93.
37. Ibid., p. 93. One might think upon reading Nagel's statement, as I have presented it here in isolation from its original context, that he is claiming not that the object of recognition which must be real is the *value of the status*, but that the object of recognition which must be real is merely the status alone. The context, however, makes Nagel's intending meaning clear: in the sentence immediately preceding the one quoted, he speaks of the "recognition of the *value of the status*" (italics are mine).
38. Perfectionist liberalism is, however, beginning to be taken more seriously, due to a small number of recent book-length treatments of it. See George Sher, *Beyond Neutrality: Perfectionism and Politics* (Cambridge: Cambridge University Press, 1997); and Steven Wall, *Liberalism, Perfectionism and Restraint* (New York: Cambridge University Press, 1998).
39. For an antidote to some of the misunderstanding, see John Skorupski, "Quality of Well-Being: Quality of Being," in his *Ethical Explorations* (New York: Oxford University Press, 1999), pp. 107–30; and "Liberal Elitism," ibid., pp. 193–212.
40. A famous example of an interpretation of Mill in which this occurs is Isaiah Berlin's; see his "John Stuart Mill and the Ends of Life," in John Gray and G. W. Smith (eds.), *J.S. Mill On Liberty in Focus* (New York: Routledge, 1991), pp. 131–61. For a discussion of some of the ways in which Berlin goes wrong, see Richard Wollheim, "John Stuart Mill and Isaiah Berlin: The Ends of Life and the Preliminaries of Morality," ibid., pp. 260–77.
41. Something that has not helped the matter is some having stipulated a definition of 'perfectionism' according to which excellences are valuable regardless of whether or not they contribute to well-being. Thomas Hurka does this in his *Perfectionism* (New York: Oxford University Press, 1993).
42. For antidotes to the oversight, see the following: Johan Brännmark, "'Like the Bloom on Youths': How Pleasure Completes our Lives," in Timothy Chappell (ed.), *Values and Virtues: Aristotelianism in Contemporary Ethics* (New York: Oxford University Press, 2006), pp. 226–38; Gabriel Richardson Lear, "Aristotle on Moral Virtue and the Fine," in Richard Kraut (ed.), *The Blackwell Guide to Aristotle's Nichomachean Ethics* (New York: Blackwell, 2006), pp. 116–36; Francis Sparshott, *Taking Life Seriously: A Study of the Argument of the Nicomachean Ethics* (Toronto: University of Toronto Press, 1996).
43. Despite a lengthy discussion of the benefit the virtues offer the agent, Rosalind Hursthouse mentions pleasure or pleasure-related notions so little in her *On Virtue Ethics* (Oxford: Oxford University Press, 1999) that "pleasure" does not even appear in the index. It seems to me that modern virtue ethicists have done their best to avoid using the concept of pleasure for cashing out the

notion of flourishing understood as a kind of well-being, so as to avoid charges of hedonistic ethical egoism that have so often been brought against virtue ethics understood as including claims about the agent's final end being happiness as some form of pleasure. Such a strategy can be thought strange, given the commonsense understanding of happiness as irreducibly involving positive affect, Aristotle's frequent references to pleasure, and Aristotle's sustained discussions of pleasure in books seven and ten of the Nicomachean Ethics. And attempts to flesh out the concept of flourishing without reference to pleasure can—I would add "predictably"—lead to the sort of theoretical vacuousness Copp and Sobel notice in some of Hursthouse's book: ". . . Hursthouse does not offer an explicit definition of the key concept of eudaimonia." [David Copp and David Sobel, "Morality and Virtue: An Assessment of Some Recent Work in Virtue Ethics," *Ethics*, Vol. 114 (2004), pp. 514–54, p. 526.] In fairness to Hursthouse, though, it should be noted that some virtue ethicists object from the start to the demand that the virtue ethicist give the sort of definition Copp and Sobel might be taken as asking for, viz., one that, in Julia Annas' words, ". . . is both substantive and makes no reference to the virtues . . . virtue ethics tells us that a life lived in accordance with the virtues is the best specification of what flourishing is." [Julia Annas, "Virtue Ethics," in David Copp (ed.), *The Oxford Handbook of Ethical Theory* (New York: Oxford University Press, 2006), p. 521.]

44. See Christopher Miles Coope, "Modern Virtue Ethics," in Chappell, *Values and Virtues*, pp. 20–52.
45. See Brännmark, "Like the Bloom."
46. Of four of the most prominent natural law ethicists, only one—Timothy Chappell—include pleasure among the list of basic goods. See his *Understanding Human Goods* (Edinburgh: Edinburgh University Press, 1996); John Finnis, *Natural Law and Natural Rights* (Oxford: Oxford University Press, 1980); Germain Grisez, *The Way of the Lord Jesus, Volume I: Christian Moral Principles* (Chicago: Franciscan Herald Press, 1983); Mark C. Murphy, *Natural Law and Practical Rationality* (New York: Cambridge University Press, 2001).
47. For an account that takes seriously their informing each other, see John Skorupski, "Liberal Elitism," *Ethical Explorations*. See also "The Ethical Content of Liberal Law," and "Liberty's Hollow Triumph," in his *Ethical Explorations* (New York: Oxford University Press, 1999), pp. 213–33, 234–54.
48. Joseph Raz is a prominent defender of this sort of conception of the value of autonomy. See his *The Morality of Freedom* (New York: Oxford University Press, 1986); and his "Liberty and Trust," in Robert P. George (ed.), *Natural Law, Liberalism, and Morality* (New York: Oxford University Press, 2002), pp. 113–29.
49. See, e.g., Allen Carlson, "Nature, Aesthetic Judgment, and Objectivity," and "Nature and Positive Aesthetics," in his *Aesthetics and the Environment* (New York: Routledge, 2002), pp. 54–71, 72–101; Ronald W. Hepburn, "Landscape and the Metaphysical Imagination," *Environmental Values*, Vol. 5 (1996), pp. 191–204; and Kenneth Simonsen, "The Value of Wildness," *Environmental Ethics*, Vol. 3 (1981), pp. 259–63.
50. See, e.g., John Finnis, *Natural Law and Natural Rights*.
51. Among the more prominent naturalists are Rachel Carson, Aldo Leopold, and John Muir. Among aestheticians are Allen Carlson, Glenn Parsons, and Marcia Muelder Eaton. All are environmentalists.
52. Thanks go to the Fulbright Foundation for supporting a year-long visit as fellow at the University of Oslo's Centre for Development and the Environment, during which ideas for this essay developed.

References

Annas, J., 2006, Virtue Ethics, in Copp D. (ed.), *The Oxford Handbook of Ethical Theory*, Oxford University Press, New York.

Berlin, I., 1991, John Stuart Mill and the Ends of Life, in *Gray and Smith*, pp. 131–61.

Boyle, A., and M. Anderson (eds.), 1996, *Human Rights Approaches to Environmental Protection*, Oxford University Press, New York.

Brännmark, J., 2006, 'Like the Bloom on Youths': How Pleasure Completes our Lives, in T. Chappell (ed.), *Values and Virtues: Aristotelianism in Contemporary Ethics*, Oxford University Press, New York, pp. 226–38.

Carlson, A., 2002a, Nature, Aesthetic Judgment, and Objectivity, in *Aesthetics and the Environment*, Routledge, New York, pp. 54–71.

———, 2002b, Nature and Positive Aesthetics, in *Aesthetics and the Environment*, Routledge, New York, pp. 72–101.

Chappell, T., 1996, *Understanding Human Goods*, Edinburgh University Press, Edinburgh.

Coope, Ch.M., 2006, Modern Virtue Ethics, in T. Chappell (ed.), *Values and Virtues: Aristotelianism in Contemporary Ethics*, Oxford University Press, New York, pp. 20–52.

Copp, D. & D. Sobel, 2004, Morality and Virtue: An Assessment of Some Recent Work in Virtue Ethics, *Ethics*, Vol. 114, pp. 514–54.

Daly, H.E., 1998, Consumption: Value Added, Physical Transformation, and Welfare, in D.A. Crocker and T. Linden (eds.), *Ethics of Consumption*, Rowman and Littlefield, Lanham, MD.

Dancy, J., 2005, Should We Pass the Buck?, in Rønnow-Rasmussen and Zimmerman (eds.), pp. 33–44.

Feldman, F., 2004, *Pleasure and the Good Life: Concerning the Nature, Varieties, and Plausibility of Hedonism*, Oxford University Press, New York.

Finnis, J., 1980, *Natural Law and Natural Rights*, Oxford University Press, Oxford.

Gray, J. & G.W. Smith (eds.), 1991, *J.S. Mill On Liberty in Focus*, Routledge, New York.

Grisez, G., 1983, *The Way of the Lord Jesus, Volume I: Christian Moral Principles*, Franciscan Herald Press, Chicago.

Hayward, T., 2005, *Constitutional Environmental Rights*, Oxford University Press, New York.

Hepburn, R.W., 1996, Landscape and the Metaphysical Imagination, *Environmental Values*, vol. 5, pp.191–204.

Hiskes, R.P., 2009, *The Human Right to a Green Future*, Cambridge, New York.

Hohfeld, W., 1923, *Fundamental Legal Conceptions*, Yale University Press, New Haven, CT.

Hurka, T., 1993, *Perfectionism*, Oxford University Press, New York.

Hursthouse, R., 1999, *On Virtue Ethics*, Oxford University Press, Oxford.

Kalen, S., 1997, Standing on Its Last Legs: Bennett V. Spear and the Past and Future of Standing in Environmental Cases, *Journal of Land Use and Environmental Law*, Vol. 13, pp. 1–68.

Kramer, M.H., N.E. Simmonds & H. Steiner, 1998, *A Debate Over Rights*, Oxford University Press, New York.

Lear, G. Richardson, 2006, Aristotle on Moral Virtue and the Fine, in R. Kraut (ed.), *The Blackwell Guide to Aristotle's Nichomachean Ethics*, Blackwell, New York, pp. 116–36.

Mill, J.S., 2010, *On Liberty*, Classic Books, New York.

Murphy, M.C., 2001, *Natural Law and Practical Rationality*, Cambridge University Press, New York.

Nagel, T., 1970, *The Possibility of Altruism*, Princeton University Press, Princeton.
———, 1995, Personal Rights and Public Space, *Philosophy and Public Affairs*, Vol. 24, pp. 83–107.
———, 2000, The Fragmentation of Value, in *Mortal Questions*, Cambridge University Press, Cambridge.
Nickel, J.W., 1993, The Human Right to a Safe Environment: Philosophical Perspectives on Its Scope and Justification, *Yale Journal of International Law*, Vol. 18, pp. 281–95.
Nickel, J.W. & E. Viola., 2003, Integrating Environmentalism and Human Rights, in A. Light & H. Rolston III (eds.), *Environmental Ethics*, Blackwell, New York, pp. 472–77.
Nolt, J., 2006, The Move from *Good* to *Ought* in Environmental Ethics, *Environmental Ethics*, Vol. 28, pp. 355–74.
Norcross, A., 2007, Killing and Letting Die, in R.G. Frey and Ch. Heath Wellman (eds.), *A Companion to Applied Ethics*, Blackwell, Malden, MA, pp. 451–63.
Parfit, D., 1984, *Reasons and Persons*, Clarendon Press, Oxford.
Raz, J., 1986, *The Morality of Freedom*, Oxford University Press, New York.
———, 2002, Liberty and Trust, in R.P. George (ed.), *Natural Law, Liberalism, and Morality*, Oxford University Press, New York, pp. 113–29.
Rolston III, H., 1988, *Environmental Ethics: Duties to and Values in the Natural World*, Temple University Press, Philadelphia.
Rønnow-Rasmussen, T. & M.J. Zimmerman (eds.), 2005, *Recent Work on Intrinsic Value*, Springer, Dordrecht.
Sagoff, M., 2001, Consumption, in D. Jamieson (ed.), *A Companion to Environmental Philosophy*, Blackwell, Malden, MA, pp. 473–85.
Scanlon, T.M., 1998, *What We Owe to Each Other*, Harvard University Press, Cambridge.
Sher, G., 1997, *Beyond Neutrality: Perfectionism and Politics*, Cambridge University Press, Cambridge.
Simonsen, K., 1981, The Value of Wildness, *Environmental Ethics*, Vol. 3, pp. 259–63.
Skorupski, J., 1999a, *Ethical Explorations*, Oxford University Press, New York.
———, 1999b, Quality of Well-Being: Quality of Being, in *Skorupski*, pp. 107–30.
———, 1999c, Liberal Elitism, in *Skorupski*, pp. 193–212.
———, 1999d, The Ethical Content of Liberal Law, in *Skorupski*, pp. 213–33.
———, 1999e, Liberty's Hollow Triumph, in *Skorupski*, pp. 234–54.
———, 2006, *Why Read Mill Today?*, Routledge, New York.
Sparshott, F., 1996, *Taking Life Seriously: A Study of the Argument of the Nicomachean Ethics*, University of Toronto Press, Toronto.
Stone, Ch.W., 1972, Should Trees Have Standing?, *University of Southern California Law Review*, Vol. 45, pp. 450–501.
———, 1985, Should Trees Have Standing Revisited: How Far Will Law and Morals Reach? A Pluralist Perspective, *Southern California Law Review*, Vol. 59, pp. 1–154.
Taylor, P.W., 1986, *Respect for Nature: A Theory of Environmental Ethics*, Princeton University Press, Princeton.
Waldron, J., 1987, *Nonsense upon Stilts: Bentham, Burke and Marx on the Rights of Man*, Methuen, London.
Wall, S., 1998, *Liberalism, Perfectionism and Restraint*, Cambridge University Press, New York.
Wollheim, R., J.S. Mill & I. Berlin, 1991, The Ends of Life and the Preliminaries of Morality, in *Gray and Smith*, pp. 260–77.

Environmental Sustainability in Political Liberalism: Meeting the Alleged Inadequacy Posed by the Neutrality Thesis[1]

Marjukka Laakso
Social and Moral Philosophy
Department of Political and Economic Studies
University of Helsinki Finland

1. Introduction

In this article, the limits and possibilities of a green, public, and liberal political sphere are explored. The article argues for public and political decision-making in environmental regimes, also in liberal theory when principles and norms are chosen. Due to the need for a good environment for decent human life, it is necessary to justify these normative claims of the environmental regime at the public and political level of liberal society. Consequently, justifications for public environmental policies and institutions are explored and presented. I will define the environmental elements relevant to the public sphere as those of environmental sustainability. The core question, whether environmental sustainability and liberal democracy are compatible, will result in an exploration of how the neutrality thesis as the guarantee of individual autonomy and the ensuing restrictions on state intervention can be combined with environmental concerns.

In liberal political theory, justifiability of objectives and principles are usually understood against two fundamental commitments. The first concerns individuals' rights and liberties, for instance, their right to choose their conceptions of good. This leads to the second commitment, to neutrality, according to which it is considered undemocratic and illegitimate for the government to align itself to any of the existing conceptions or ideals of the good (e.g., De Marneffe 1990, Rawls 1996). Several authors have claimed that liberalism in general is incapable of dealing with broad environmental problems successfully or in a manner satisfying even the most basic preconditions established by environmentalists. On the one hand, the liberal emphasis on individual rights as well as the limitations to governmental interference in individual action are claimed to hinder environmental policies other than those based on individual, voluntary choices. On the other hand, environmental problems as problems of commons require collective solutions and coordination, which cannot be implemented through individual action alone.

De-Shalit (2000, pp. 64–66, 72) argues that severe difficulties arise in addressing environmental issues properly at the political level. While liberalism encourages discussion on environmental issues, it can neither implement nor justify environmental policies. This inability is mainly dependent on the requirement of majority decisions, democratic elections, election periods, and free markets. Marcel Wissenburg echoes this as follows:

> The latter caveat indicates exactly where the problem lies: although liberalism offers room to green ideas at the level of individuals, and can if necessary even appreciate a unanimous preference for green policies among them, it can apparently not accept that one particular and very substantive theory of the good be prescribed and be made the yardstick of all political institutions. By the same token, ecologism apparently excludes as a matter of principle liberalism's love for individual diversity and constitutional neutrality (Wissenburg 2006a, p. 122).

Hannis (2005) challenges liberal theorists advocating both neutrality and environmental concerns, and concludes that "we can have neutrality or ecological sustainability, but not both" (Hannis 2005, p. 578). According to him, e.g., David Miller[2] gives no good reason why environmental goods should be considered as individual preferences: Miller seems to draw the normative conclusion that environmental goods cannot be impartial and necessary conditions for human flourishing simply from the empirical fact that some people do not value these goods enough (Hannis 2005, p. 583). To strengthen Hannis's point, we could also argue that individuals are neither capable nor willing to weigh the value of environmental issues. It is actually unbearable from the point of view of individuals if decisions about such complex, uncertain, and unexpected issues as environmental procedures, consequences, and phenomena are only their responsibility. It is obvious that efficient environmental policy requires coordinated cooperation by several actors as well as a political infrastructure in society, as mentioned earlier in this paper.

2. Political Liberalism and Environmental Sustainability

From different liberal versions of a theory, Rawlsian political liberalism (Rawls 1996) offers a consistent theoretical framework for public—i.e., political—procedures, their justification and legitimacy in the society. The description of this approach can be summarized as a four-level model of the societal structures. These levels are: neutral principles, societal institutions, individual autonomy, and public goods derived from individual preferences. The first level is that of neutral principles, which regulates all societal cooperation and political action at general level. In line with the neutrality commitment, these principles are accepted by all reasonable "comprehensive doctrines" of the society, which represent the different individual conceptions of good life. At the second stage are the societal institutions built on these principles. They provide e.g., law, order, democratic decision-making mechanisms, health care, and the market. The third level consists of individual autonomy, which includes, for example, the personal values and preferences that each individual is free to have and promote. On the fourth level are the public goods of the society, which are democratically chosen as worth promoting (Cohen 2003, Rawls 1996).

Traditionally, the liberal theorists have placed environmental concerns on the fourth level, that of public goods. Yet, because of the deep disagreements and pluralistic goals that characterize modern societies, common agreement on any further substantive public goods, such as the details of fair distribution, has usually been considered impossible. As a result, liberalism is committed to emphasize the fair procedures of the fourth level as basic justification for legitimate public goods, such as the environment.

Derek Bell argues for a consistent account which would require liberals to "prioritise a conception of the environment as a provider of basic needs over a conception of the environment as property" (Bell 2005, pp. 183–84). Bell constructs an account of a liberal environmental citizen's rights and duties, where the rights would consist of substantive and procedural rights to basic needs, and their correlative duties. For political liberals, it is the state that is responsible for dividing up of duties among citizens, and in many cases, it also takes on the role of primary duty-bearer itself. But to be regarded as duties of liberal (environmental) citizens, the source of these duties must be based in some way on the correlative rights of other citizens (e.g., the right to air quality might create a correlative duty to limit car use), and their fulfillment must not mean prioritizing some particular "green" conception of the environment (Bell 2005, p. 190). Arguments defining the environment as anything beyond "the provider of our basic needs" will be understood as a comprehensive doctrine, and therefore considered under disagreement. According to Bell, reasonable debate is thus possible only on environmental political procedures, not the substance of environmental decisions (Bell 2005, p. 185).

This argumentation reflects well the central problem in the debate on environmental issues and liberalism, namely the suggestion that substantive environmental elements cannot be secured in liberalism. Bell constructs his argument from the viewpoint of an individual citizen. In the private sphere, "[c]itizens must formally—in state-sponsored deliberative spaces and in civil society—have the opportunity to try to persuade others to adopt their conceptions of the environment and our place in it (Bell 2005, p. 186)."

However, the environment is hardly correctly understood if it is defined as one entire entity from the moral viewpoint. For example, a choice for a vegetarian diet is entirely up to an individual to decide for in the liberal framework. Motives for it vary from ecological reasons (vegetarianism is more climate friendly option compared to meat-eating) to concern for nonhuman animals. Even though there are regulations and laws concerning the treatment and living conditions of farm animals, the ultimate decision whether nonhuman individual animals are to be used is a moral question and to be evaluated by each and every one individually reflecting her moral value judgment of the role of nonhuman animals— whether animals are valued intrinsically or instrumentally. Still the public regulation mirrors a common concern for living animals, but the exact content of these regulations is debated constantly, like in the case of e.g., battery farming. Climate-related reasons, like emissions of carbon dioxide, are on one hand scientifically indisputable but other arguments in favor or against can be presented: the impact of diet choice on local farming and employment, cultural reasons, etc.

Consequently, it seems that Bell bundles environmental entities all together, and argues that any value position given to this one entity will fall into the category of "a comprehensive moral doctrine." But those elements of the ecology vital to beings, like climate and ecological chains or ecosystemic structures, can and should be understood as morally different from e.g., nonhuman individuals and their living conditions. These critical elements would include not only those that are vital directly to human survival, such as air, water, food and shelter, but also those larger-scale ecological processes and systems which sustain production of breathable air, drinkable water, eatable food and satisfactory environment. However, often these systems change so slowly that their dynamic is unnoticeable to shortsighted human beings and therefore, might not be preferred by individuals and their voluntary choices. One important feature of these holistic systems is, that consequences of change are hard to predict, and there lies risk of severe harms and effects on large amount of people, not only on those who make the choices. This dilemma between individual autonomy and publicly decided societal goals is one of the core issues in environmental sustainability and sustainable development.

Environmental sustainability refers to the level below which biodiversity, environmental integrity and the ability of ecosystems to regenerate, become endangered. Thus essential requirement of the environmental sustainability is to address the impacts on these slower ecological scales. *Environmental sustainability* refers to, at a minimum, maintained human environment and vital elements of the ecology, like biodiversity and other ecological processes. Environmental sustainability includes the human viewpoint of the situation while *ecological sustainability* analyses the situation purely through ecological processes and changes therein (Wissenburg 2006b, p. 427).

Dobson defines environmental sustainability as a normative concept. He describes how in the realm of environmental policy it is often thought that "sustainability" is a question of scientifically defined thresholds between sustainable and unsustainable states of affairs. But a natural scientific analysis of the means and measurement is not enough, but it is here that a philosophical and normative analysis enters (Dobson 2003, p. 147). In other words, there needs to be procedures to allow society to define what sort of issues matter, for whom they matter and why these issues are worth consideration: why (intrinsic or instrumental value) and for whom (for ourselves or for the future generations) we are to conserve certain elements of ecology—whether we are talking about a conservation park or carbon-dioxide circulation and its impacts.

Because sustainable development as the foremost concept of environmental sustainability is a process rather than an institution, its defining characteristic is the sustainment of development and its goals, rather than the conservation of nature. For environmental sustainability, this implies, first, that not every environmental problem is related to sustainable development; an activity with negative environmental effects is not necessarily contradictory to sustainable development, rather it is the context that determines whether an activity is sustainable or not. For instance, there is nothing inherently wrong with clearing forests for farming, as long as this is done prudently and the land thus used is not taken from other, more useful purposes (e.g., essential for ground-water). If clearing the forest meets these ecological preconditions and still is necessary, for example, local livelihood, the goal of sustainable development is met. Second, an activity that is not sustainable itself can still be part of a broader process that is. Otherwise, nonrenewable materials, for instance, could not be consumed at all. Again, the needs of humanity (especially needs of poor as argued in the definition of sustainable development by the Brundtland Commission) override slower and partly invisible ecological processes (Langhelle 1999).

The elements of environmental sustainability are by nature such that their consequences affect all members of society. This, in turn, leads us to the conclusion that the basic principles of environmental sustainability should be treated differently from those which can be included in the private sphere and in the category of individual moral commitments. The main concern of this paper regarding environmental sustainability involves the elements of holistic systems, ecological processes, and the interaction of human beings with surrounding ecological systems as being relevant to public decision-making. These holistic elements require common decisions and often also publicly decided, long-term procedures and institutions. For instance, recycling waste is rather impossible without both common agreement on its necessity and public infrastructure.

3. What Sorts of Goods are Environmental Goods?

The concept of ecological citizenship with its emphasis on citizens' rights and obligations also calls for a general political framework for establishing and implementing environmental rights and duties. Also, for citizens to fulfill their voluntarily chosen green aims, like decreasing car use or choosing organic food produced nearby, an infrastructure is needed, which in turn must be adequately justified. For example, decreasing car use requires societal infrastructure, e.g., public transportation that is provided by the society.

The locus of the environment, as already implied, consists of several diverse categories of entities, which can be represented by different levels of societal decision-making. The Rawlsian description of society implying a four-level model of societal structure presented above in short, would consist of the following aspects in detail. From the bottom up, these levels are as follows: neutral principles, societal institutions, individual autonomy, and public goods derived from individual preferences.

The first level is that of *neutral principles* derived in the original position, the ones regulating all societal, cooperational, and political actions. In addition, certain limitations imposed on individual behavior concerning interaction with other persons are allowed. On this level, principles consist of rules of justice (distributional and redistributional) and law, for example. Dobson sees the importance of neutrality and explores where this will lead us in terms of environmental sustainability. He suggests that ". . . liberalism and the liberal state, should be in favor of strong sustainability—and not because of any special commitment to "nature," but because a structured bequest package amounts to a wider range of options from which to choose good lives (Dobson 2003, p. 168)." So, sustaining nature and its crucial elements is actually what liberalism calls for, because acting otherwise would limit the range of options future generations will have.

This raises the question of what neutrality actually means in a liberal theory. Peter de Marneffe argues that neutrality has developed into two different conceptions in the recent decades, both of which have very different implications for the crucial issue of individual rights (De Marneffe 1990, p. 253). *Concrete neutrality* is applied to consequences of a policy, but political liberalism relies on *neutrality of grounds* referring to a principle *regulating the justification* of principles of justice. ". . . the principles of justice that regulate basic social and political institutions must be justifiable in terms of moral and political values that *any reasonable person* would accept as the basis of the moral claims regardless of his or her particular conception of the good (De Marneffe 1990, p. 253)."

Neutral principles are based on the idea that a reasonable person can in spite of her diverse values and aims in life recognize some general values as useful or rational to follow. For example, fair cooperation or developing and exercising the capacity of practical reasoning would exemplify such neutral values—i.e., a person who would not recognize fair cooperation as valuable would be an unreasonable person. For example, liberty as an equal basic liberty is necessary in order to ensure the fair distribution of primary goods, which are derivable from neutral principles. Primary goods are also neutral, even if they would exclude some conceptions of particular goods which conflict with the principles of justice. Liberal neutrality does not mean relativity of values but aims at promoting conceptions of the public good (De Marneffe 1990, p. 254–55). Kymlicka (1989, p. 884) compares this to a market place selling ways of life. Under conditions of individual freedom, all ways of life may be advertised, but those not considered worthy of promotion will not have enough adherents in the long run to survive. In the end, valuable ways of life override those which are not supported by a majority of individuals—eventually the outcome is non-neutral but the justification for procedures is neutral. Institutions satisfying this criterion are legitimate and justified.

It is suggested here that environmental sustainability belongs to the category of neutral principles. The general idea of maintaining vital ecological elements for human well-being differentiates this principle of sustainability from the environmental concerns of individual preferences. Case-specific elements of environmental sustainability, like the exact content of principles, belong to the sphere of constant discussion and debate in society. Individuals promoting, say, animal rights or the intrinsic value of nonhuman entities may and can freely do so, as proponents of the pure instrumental value of the natural world are also free to promote their view. Both parties may submit their values to public debate and criticism.

In the second stage, *societal institutions* are built on these principles. Institutions have, of course, an effect on individuals: on their aims, preferences, and values in forming the ideas of a good life. These institutions provide law, order, social harmony, education, democratic decision-making mechanisms (e.g., voting system, parliament, political parties), health care, and the market. They also secure and distribute the social primary goods and compensate for *natural primary goods* (health, vigor, intelligence, and imagination) according to the principles of justice. The primary goods distributed and secured by society, *social primary goods*, include basic rights, liberties, and opportunities as well as income and wealth. Rawlsian social primary goods are governed, provided, and secured mainly by the basic institutions and principles of society (Van Parijs 2003, p. 211). Institutions monitoring environmental regime and environmental regulations in accordance with environmental sustainability are necessary and belong to this level of the political system. It is of vital importance that basic environmental institutions are legitimized independently of the contingencies of political life and day-to-day political decision-making. For example, Wouter Achterberg (1994) has claimed that the liberal requirement of relatively short electoral periods weakens the possibility of efficient environmental decisions since politicians work to please voters and their short-term preferences at the cost of long-term decisions, which may not always be the best assets in election campaigns.

What is to be noted here is that primary goods are not open to public debate and are not to be decided in political processes but are determined already in the original position. They are therefore essentially different from public goods. Now, the temptation to simply add "clean environment" to the list of primary goods is high, but a more careful analysis is required. Primary goods are personal assets in the sense that they are personal individual rights which can be demanded from society. Schramme (2006) has analyzed the relationship between primary goods and the environment and interprets Rawlsian reasonable individuals as preferring equal distribution of social and material goods, unless a justification for inequality is presented, with each individual getting the biggest possible share of distributed goods. Schramme takes natural resources to be primary goods, defining nature as "all-purpose means," because resources like clean water and air are controlled by societal institutions. Primary goods, to follow Rawls himself, are to be distributed equally. According to Schramme, this is detrimental to the environment, because this principle of equality does not entail means for saving or nonusage of existing resources, but rather they are seen as resources that are to be used freely (Schramme 2006, pp. 147 and 149).

The third level is of *individual autonomy* including, for instance, comprehensive views, personal values and preferences that each individual is free to have and promote. This is the private sphere, in which the state is not allowed to intervene. This is crucial and also the most problematic area in the liberal framework in general. While the above-mentioned principles and institutions regulate and limit to some extent the scope of individual autonomy, there is still a remarkable range of issues left for individuals to decide on. These issues belonging to the private sphere as comprehensive doctrines are here at this level and are to be included in moral evaluations by individuals as best seen by themselves. An example of an environmental concern on this level is whether natural entities—nonhuman animals or species—are valued instrumentally or intrinsically.

The third and fourth levels are closely connected because individuals on level three are to decide autonomously about *the public goods* on level four. The Rawlsian conception of public goods is located here. David Miller (2004) divides public goods somewhat differently into three categories based on how their provision is justified. The two first categories of public goods are, first, those whose provision is justified by appealing to the value of justice (category A including clean air and other very basic needs); the second, category B of public goods, include those which may be provided by the relevant political community but without universal appeal to justice itself. These first two categories by Miller can be interpreted as primary goods in Rawlsian terms.

The third category C is that of public goods whose justification appeals to privately held conceptions of good and which is the proper place for most environmental concerns according to Miller. Paradigmatic examples are ideal-regarding justifications in the case of the conservation of nature (Miller 2004, pp. 136–37,140). This is the fourth level of Rawlsian pure public goods in the model presented here, where provision of public goods is dependant on those conceptions Rawls would call comprehensive reasonable doctrines. This means that some elementary environmental concerns are purely individual matters, since they belong to the third category of Miller's public goods whose justified provision arises from reasonable disagreement. As Rawls makes clear, individuals decide which sorts of public goods are worth promoting. This is where problems related to the environment start: if the environment is defined as a mere public good, it is dependent on individual values and preferences about whether to conserve nature, limit material consumption, or just aim at increasing material wealth (which is not to suggest that these are all the alternatives we have). Miller's example of this is conservation of the snail darter, a small fish whose preservation is not near to everyone's heart. Miller concludes that the state can provide only the first two categories, and the third needs to be left to individual discretion (unless, over the course of time, the pro-group can pursue the con-group to promote the good in question to be moved to the B category). It seems likely Rawls would agree with Miller in situating environmental goods mainly in category C. Obviously, this is not the conclusion arrived at in this paper, but rather that environmental public goods belonging to this level are more case-specific in their nature. For instance, what the means are for conservation of the snail darter if its decisions to protect are made at the level two of institutions?

Consequently, in the face of the possible and probable consequences of environmental hazards, it is fair and valid to say that a satisfying and safe environment—which means environmental sustainability—does belong to the category of neutral values and principles creating the primary goods necessary for individual well-being. No rational citizen would want the principles regulating the basic institutions of society to ignore such risks threatening basic human well-being.

To sum up, the main argument here is that environmental sustainability should be situated on the first level of the Rawlsian social structures, among the neutral principles regulating societal, legal and political action. Significance of this conclusion lies in the resulting possibility of forming stable and legitimate long-term environmental institutions to the second level, such as novel environmental legal principles. A further upshot is that critical environmental issues would be justifiably coordinated and maintained independently of the contingencies of individual preferences or day-to-day political decisions. In this manner, the autonomy of environmental concerns would be secured throughout the whole process of political decision-making, with the subsequent adoption of long-term regulations, such as the precautionary principle. Environmental sustainability can be understood as a new liberal principle focusing on the fair distribution of environmental goods that are indispensable for all.

4. Conclusion: Environmental Sustainability as a Neutral Regulating Principle

The pluralism of liberal society often implies contradictory and competing individuals' conceptions of goods and, therefore, the only possible agreement on the basic structure and fundamental organization of society is that of an overlapping consensus. This conception of justice, as concerning the political sphere, ensures social unity to a minimal degree in a pluralistic society over a period of generations. The political sphere and environmental public policy choices should, therefore, be defined through a mutually agreed process of political consensus. This is legitimate and in accordance with liberal neutrality as the neutrality of grounds, and does not violate individual freedom. Though Rawls himself defined the environment as categorically belonging to those public goods that depend on individual preferences, it seems obvious that his interpretation of environmental status leads to difficulties in dealing with the requirements of environmental sustainability, a concept which reflects those ecological problems and phenomena as holistic elements, and therefore having possible global consequences for human well-being now and in future. Environmental sustainability as a neutral principle of society would create side constraints to human action meaning that at least serious irreversible effects should be avoided if possible. Environmental sustainability may be subordinated to other social issues, such as equality, but the significance and status of the environment still remains central.

To include environmental concerns and aspects to the decisions, it seems necessary to do so already at the first level of principles. Then it is possible to form environmental institutions which regulate the environmental scope on level two of the model presented here. Permanent environmental institutions and defined processes for monitoring the environment would guarantee that at least important environmental issues be coordinated and maintained independently of contingencies of individual preferences or political life. In this manner, environmental concerns would be secured throughout the whole procedure of political decision-making. Environmental sustainability requires public coordination and public decision-making procedures due to the nature of environmental impacts. Individual responsibility alone is not effective enough for managing environmental issues, especially global and intergenerational ones. In addition, it is unreasonable to assume that individual capabilities would be adequate to solve environmental dilemmas, because the amount of knowledge and information alone is far too broad and complex for one person to absorb and understand, and coordination of action also requires recognized legitimate authority. In liberal theories, this authority is usually the state. Hence it is argued in this article that the environment constitutes one of the core spheres of public matters, and promoting sustainable development including environmental sustainability is essentially a neutral principle of public concern.

For example, Bell (2005) argues that the environment is something that provides for our basic needs. The difference between the argument proposed in this paper and Bell's is that Bell interprets the environment as a particular good over which individuals have a right to choose how they are to regard it. An attitude toward the environment is, according to Bell, a moral claim. Instead, this paper argues that the environment as a holistic system is not a particular moral claim or a moral doctrine but that environmental sustainability is a neutral principle underlining the conception of political justice, together with other neutral principles, such as equality. Individual well-being is impossible without elementary environmental goods maintained by environmental sustainability.

Finally, two supplementary points need to be made. First, effective management of environmental impacts and consequences also requires the inclusion of the global dimension. At the moment, it seems that the liberal global political system is best applicable as a representation of national states in global and international institutions and agreements (but analyzing the global political system is beyond the scope of this paper). International cooperation is, however, necessary in parallel with national environmental policies. Secondly, the conclusions offered here concern only public policies and justification for public action. This is to say, that the public sphere still leaves quite an extensive amount of responsibility to individuals themselves. Individual morality and ethical reasoning are not excluded in this framework. The only condition is that individual morality and responsibility are used and required when they are relevant and efficient—not when it is inefficient and irrelevant with respect to the results of action requiring more than personal morality and individual judgment, as it is in the case of environmental sustainability requiring long-term decisions on complex and uncertain issues. How people should conduct their private lives, however, is to be left to persons themselves to decide, as liberal theory requires.

Notes

1. The writing of this article has been supported with funding through the research program "Environment and Law," the Academy of Finland, in the sub-project "Redefining Concepts and Practices of Environmental Law."
2. Miller's conception of environmental rights is presented later in this paper.

References

Achterberg, W., 1994, Can Liberal Democracy Survive the Environmental Crisis? Sustainability, Liberal Neutrality and Overlapping Consensus, in W. Zweers & J.J. Boersema (Eds.), *Ecology, Technology and Culture. Essays in Environmental Philosophy*, pp. 135–57, Cambridge, UK: The White Horse Press.

Bell, D.R., 2005, Liberal Environmental Citizenship. *Environmental Politics*, 14 (2), 179–94.

Cohen, J., 2003, For a Democratic Society, in S. Freeman (ed.), *The Cambridge Companion to Rawls*, pp. 86–138, New York: Cambridge University Press.

De Marneffe, P., 1990, Liberalism, Liberty, and Neutrality. *Philosophy & Public Affairs*, 19 (3), 253–74.

De-Shalit, A., 2000, *The Environment Between Theory and Practice*, Oxford: Oxford University Press.

Dobson, A., 2003, *Citizenship and the Environment*, Oxford: Oxford University Press.

Hannis, M., 2005, Public Provision of Environmental Goods: Neutrality or Sustainability? A reply to David Miller. *Environmental Politics*, 14 (5), 577–95.

Kymlicka, W., 1989, Liberal Individualism and Liberal Neutrality, *Ethics*, 99, 883–905.

Langhelle, O., 1999, Sustainable Development: Exploring the Ethics of Our Common Future, *International Political Science Review*, 20 (2), 129–49.

Miller, D., 2004, Justice, Democracy and Public Goods, in K. Dowding, R.E. Goodin & C. Pateman (eds.), *Justice and Democracy: Essays for Brian Barry*, pp. 27–149. Cambridge: Cambridge University Press.

Rawls, J., 1996, *Political Liberalism: [with a new introduction and the "Reply to Habermas"]*, New York: Columbia University Press.

Schramme, T., 2006, Is Rawlsian Justice Bad for the Environment?, *Analyse & Kritik*, 28 (2), 146–57.

Van Parijs, P., 2003, Difference Principles, in S. Freeman (ed.), *The Cambridge Companion to Rawls*, pp. 200–40, New York: Cambridge University Press.

Wissenburg, M., 2006a, Ecological Neutrality and Liberal Survivalism, *Analyse & Kritik*, 28 (2), 125–45.

———, 2006b, Global and Ecological Justice: Prioritising Conflicting Demands, *Environmental Values*, 15 (4), 425–39.

Public Participation
and the Legitimacy of Climate Policies:
Efficacy versus Democracy[1]?

Simo Kyllönen
Social and Moral Philosophy
Department of Political and Economic Studies
University of Helsinki
Finland

1. Introduction

Public participation has become one of the central notions in environmental governance. There are two main sorts of arguments for more deliberative and participatory environmental policy processes. On the one hand, participatory means are required to ensure democratically legitimate decisions. Behind this is, first, the idea of fair procedures, i.e., that broad public participation incorporates the values and interests of affected parties into decision-making more inclusively and equally. Second, public participation should serve as a deliberative process, in which these possibly incommensurable values and interests are publicly considered, justified, and reconciled.

On the other hand, public participation, particularly in climate issues, is advocated because they improve the quality of decisions and help in outcome-oriented problem solving. The complexity of climate change and the urgency to produce effective outcomes pose considerable epistemic requirements for existing decision-making procedures. This is claimed to challenge traditional ways of democratic decision-making. The core of the challenge concerns the notion of democratic legitimacy that bases the authority of decisions on procedural rather than epistemic requirements. Contrary to this, epistemic requirements seem to entail the participation of those holding the expertise and competence of effective problem solving. Thus well-informed participation and deliberation among experts in the field (e.g., scientific experts, NGOs, governmental officials) has become vital for climate decisions. However, direct participation of the lay public has also been required for effective problem solving in climate issues, either because it promotes effective implementation of climate policies, or because it incorporates situated and context-specific knowledge of the public into the decision-making.

Primarily, participation of these "epistemic communities" is claimed to assure that outcomes are the best available effective solutions to the climate problem. Such participation does not resort to "abstract" theories of democratic legitimacy (e.g., Steel 2001). However, the lack of connection between effective problem solving and democratic legitimacy is not so straightforward. In this theoretical paper, the controversy between (deliberative) "legitimacy theories" and "problem-solving approaches" is seen to result, first, from vaguely analyzed relations between alternative ways of public participation in the climate policy-making, and second, from a too narrow understanding of the concept of democratic legitimacy. Legitimacy should be understood more broadly as a generally held social recognition that decisions are accepted as rightful. While this recognition also implies a socially sanctioned obligation to comply with these decisions, legitimacy will also have a vital impact on the effectiveness of these decisions and rules (Reus-Smit 2007, Scharpf 1999).

In this paper, alternative ways of public participation at work in problem-solving approaches are analyzed in some detail. This allows for a more comprehensive understanding of the ways in which the legitimacy and authority of epistemic participation are actually dependent on more general forms of public justification highlighted by so-called legitimacy theories. Finally, the paper aims to clarify how and to what extent public participation can enhance the authority of climate policy outcomes to command assent and compliance by citizens particularly in the areas of private behavior in which coercion or material inducement are often costly or even regarded as illegitimate. I shall argue that climate policies typically concern such areas of human behavior. Effective climate policies require drastic changes in private consumption patterns, life-styles, and conventional habits. Yet governments through legal regulation, tax incentives, etc., have only a partial impact on private decisions concerning recycling, energy use at home, holiday destination, or family planning. It is particularly here where democratic legitimacy in the form of public justification meets effective problem solving.

2. The Concept of Legitimacy

The concept of legitimacy has often been characterized as having at least two distinct dimensions: descriptive and normative (Beetham 1991, Zürn 2004). From a descriptive perspective, legitimacy refers to the societal acceptance or recognition of a political actor, institution, or decision. From a normative perspective, the focus is on the justificatory validity of a political actor, institution, or decision to claim legitimacy. These two dimensions are interrelated. Zürn (2004), for instance, argues, how the removal of numerous decisions from the circuit of national democracies gives rise to problems concerning their normative legitimacy, which in turn leads to decreasing societal acceptance of global governance. Elliot (in press) stresses, how the normative underpinnings of legitimacy are intimately connected to our ideas about "the bounds of the community of 'rightful membership,'" that is, about those whose views about legitimacy should be taken seriously. These ideas constitute particular social norms that in turn constitute our views about the acceptability of factual political authorities and political communities. The normative dimension is thus of great concern to the legitimacy of environmental governance that might comprise many contested views about these ideas.

The normative dimension has many components (Eckersley 2007, Elliot in press, Scharpf 1999). The first is the moral validity of the objectives of a political actor, institution, or decision. Providing a public good, like public security, or preventing a public bad, like catastrophic climate change, are paradigmatic examples that are generally regarded as morally valid objectives of any political order. This component has also been called "content norms" of legitimacy (Beetham 1991, Parkinson 2003). The second normative component is the expertise or special competence of a political actor, institution, or decision. As far as their competence is based on the assessment of their effectiveness or performance in achieving morally valid objectives, e.g., preventing public environmental bads, these components constitute what Scharpf (1999) has called "output legitimacy": governmental institutions, policies, and decisions should represent effective solutions to problems that the governed have in common.

But though the objective of preventing catastrophic climate change has almost generally been accepted as a morally valid goal, this has not resulted in an overall acceptance of any particular climate regime or policy as a legitimate means to achieve it. This emphasizes the fact that climate objective is just one morally valid objective among others, and they may all be in tense relations to each other. Thus the procedural "source norms" or "input" component of legitimacy is often stressed by environmental political theorists (Elliot in press, Parkinson 2003, Scharpf 1999, Bodansky 1999). Because in pluralistic societies people disagree about what is the right order of alternative objectives and what serves as the right basis for performance evaluations, the source of legitimacy must be the procedural qualities of decision-making, such as its procedural fairness, its public visibility and its responsiveness to the manifest preferences of citizens.

However, many liberals, including deliberative democrats, understand the role of fair democratic processes as being more than giving procedural justification for outcomes. Democratic procedures should also provide justified reasons for citizens to accept the content of the outcome. Contrary to fair proceduralists (e.g., Waldron 1999), who consider that brute disagreement prevents any recourse to the epistemic value of the outcomes, deliberative democrats (cf. Cohen 1989, Gutmann and Thompson 1996) are more open to the possibility that deliberative procedure could also have some epistemic value as well. Since fair deliberation involves the process of reasoned arguments and judgments, it should lead to more reasonable outcomes. Epistemic democrats (Estlund 1997, 2008) go even further and claim that it is the tendency of democratic procedures to produce epistemically superior outcomes that generates their legitimacy, not their procedural qualities.

3. Values of Public Participation in Environmental Decision-making

3.1. From fair proceduralism and constitutional liberalism to deliberative democracy

It should come as no surprise that with environmental problems, such as global warming, the normative components of legitimate governance are easily taken to be contrary to each other. Following the output components of instrumental efficacy, we can claim that protection of the environment is about aiming at specific ecological goals and values, and thus governance should be assessed exclusively instrumentally in the light of these goals. The risk is, of course, that we may end up restricting or even abandoning democracy in order to achieve these goals (Heilbroner 1974, Ophuls 1977, Westra 1998; the latest appeal to an authoritarian government to prevent climate change has been made by Shearman and Wayne Smith 2007). Emphasizing the procedural components, we are easily left in the hands of democratic procedures, the outcomes of which should be taken as justified and legitimate regardless of their environmental impacts.

Literature on environmental democracy and public participation has utilized the normative components of legitimacy in various ways to reconcile this controversy. Following a fair proceduralist approach, we may argue that participatory democracy is justified in environmental protection, because it provides more equal opportunities also to those who represent the interests of nature to defend their interests and contribute to the definition of the collective will (cf. Goodin 1996, p. 845, Webler 1995, p. 38). Though we will still have deep disagreements concerning environmental issues, procedurally environmental interests are respected more fairly and thus decisions based on broad public participation should gain more legitimacy.

For many greens such a link between environmental goals and fair democratic procedures seems too weak, since as Saward (1996, p. 84) notes, even "such a democracy may not promote green outcomes if we think in majoritarian terms." Dryzek (1987, 1996, 2000) also considers that fair and "passively inclusive" liberal democracy is incapable of responding effectively to ecological problems, since its negative feedback mechanisms are usually dominated by the representation of interests that are contrary to those of environmentalists. Moreover, since actual decision-making in liberal democracy, though based in formal equality, is typically strategic bargaining or power trading between these particular interests, it prevents them from adding up to "generalizable" ecological interests or public values.

This is why many have argued for deliberative modes of democracy in order to strengthen the link between ecological interests and democratic procedures. As noted above, the deliberative approach shares the idea of fair and equal procedure as an essential element of legitimacy but connects these procedural requirements more closely to the requirements of reasoned deliberation. For deliberative democrats it is not enough that the public's diverse interests are respected in an equal and fair way by the decision-making procedures but citizens must have "the ability and opportunity to participate" in a way that they are "amenable to changing their judgments, preferences and views" and finally capable of accepting the decisions as justified (Dryzek 2000, p. 1).

The deliberative approach can work at different levels. One can use it in order to make "matters of constitutional essentials and basic justice, the basic structure and its public policies" justifiable to all citizens (Rawls 1993, p. 224). However, deliberative justification does not need to be limited to constitutional matters. In fact, most deliberative democrats see this as a too restricted way to understand the value of public deliberation (Dryzek 2004, Gutmann and Thompson 1996). This is seen to be particularly important in the context of environmental decision making, because a great deal of environmental problem solving takes place in locations that are scarcely reached by constitutional specifications—international climate regulations that are unregulated by a constitutional rules are paradigmatic example of such locations. Private decisions in which governments can through their legal specifications have only a partial impact constitute another example. Thus public deliberation should rather be understood "as an extra-constitutional ordering device," that may be protected by constitutions but operates in the public sphere outside the formal institutions of the state (Dryzek 2000).

Here, advocates of deliberative democracy usually refer to the instrumental values of public deliberation. First, public deliberation is said to be vital for enhancing certain desirable qualities in citizens. As Sagoff (1988, p. 96) has put it, political participation is "supposed to educate and elevate public opinion." Public deliberation should be understood as a "school for democracy," in which citizens and their political representatives are "actively schooled in deliberative democracy" (Eckersley 2000, p. 126). Since public deliberation favors unconstrained and uncoercive argumentation among free and equal participants, it is claimed to be more likely to lead people to "rise above their self-interest" and be willing to protect public values. Moreover, the ability of the political process to cause people to make their values more public-oriented is considered to be crucial for the legitimacy of environmental policies (cf., Goodin 1996). In other words, through public deliberation people should be able to develop or recognize shared public values that form a basis for legitimate environmental decisions and policies (Sagoff 1988).

3.2. Legitimacy and real processes of public participation

At the same time, what Arias-Maldonado (2007) has called "the democratising tendency in green political theory" has provided approaches that cast serious doubt on the likelihood that these values of deliberative democracy can ever be actualized in real processes of public participation. According to Williams (1994), the assumptions of deliberative democracy are most implausible in the context of environmental decision-making, where deep disagreements about environmental facts, values, and even the premises of reasonable justification may characterize the whole process of decision-making (cf., also Kyllönen et al. 2006). According to Williams, the very nature of an environmental problem changes as it is moved from institution to institution, which all define and characterize the issue in their own manner.

Though we might be able to agree that climate change poses a serious threat that requires drastic changes in our patterns of energy use and consumption, this shared public value does not prevent heated disputes concerning acceptable climate policies when we move "to a debate in the legislature, then to the particularities of rulemaking by administrative agencies, then to the decisions of the courts, and finally throughout the political community" (Williams 1994, p. 24). As Williams notes, each of these institutional contexts requires its own structures of justification and may involve disputes about the appropriate premises from which justification for climate policies should emerge. Alleged public value gives only very limited justification for the authority to legitimately exercise climate policies in the face of these disagreements generated by deliberation from these disputed premises.

Furthermore, it has been noted how people usually have their own private stake in seeing a given deliberative process as valuable, and thus they undertake strategic action to achieve their goals rather than providing other-regarding arguments (Parkinson 2003). Though public deliberation may make participants' arguments more other-regarding or even the content of their preferences may be shaped, because they have to justify their proposals to others in the public deliberation (Cohen 1989, Goodin 1996), it seems inevitable that the participation of the public is influenced by their private interests and strategies to achieve them.

Thus talking about the public values or "generalizable" interests that participants in public deliberation should discover during the process is too optimistic and simple a view about the legitimacy of (environmental) decisions. Only in very ideal circumstances in which all affected are included and they all have equal standing in the deliberative process, would the outcome qualify to be the public value that would suffice to justify its (even coercive) implementation. As critical notes here emphasize, these ideal circumstances hardly ever occur in actual participatory processes. Even in their most deliberative forms (e.g., citizens' juries, consensus conferences) they are easily influenced by the existing power structures within which these processes are embedded. Furthermore, while these processes have to limit the number of participants in order to enable reasoned and fair deliberation, the more they do it the more their outcomes can be challenged to represent only a partial value, not the public value of the people (Parkinson 2003).

3.3. Public participation promoting effective problem solving

These critical doubts have led many to seek more defensible grounds for public participation in the context of environmental decision-making from the practical problem-solving capacity of participatory processes (Davies 2001, Newig 2007, Steel 2001). Steel (2001), for instance, claims that it is not the "abstract models of legitimacy" that are behind the present increased use of participatory processes in environmental law and policy-making, but rather what she calls "the problem-solving approach." This approach stresses particularly that reasoned participation and "broadly-based deliberation is a superior means of reaching [the best available] practical decisions, as opposed to seeking the most legitimate or defensible form of democracy" (Ibid., p. 432).

These claims concerning the effective problem-solving capacity of participatory processes are grounded by at least three distinct arguments. The first and the second mainly concentrate on the implementation phase, while the third epistemic argument supports public participation due to its contribution to the epistemic quality of decisions.

The first view, what Bulkeley and Mol (2003, p. 148) call the "information deficit model," sees public participation as a mode of public education. But contrary to the views of deliberative democrats, this model sees the public as ill equipped to take environmental decisions and actions. Thus public participation is not so much about collective deliberation but is a way to provide the public with still more information about the issue and actions that individual citizens can undertake. The European Commission's "You Control Climate Change" campaign and analogous national climate campaigns of the member states[2] are good examples how the persuasive logic of such "information deficit" participation is designed to activate citizens to take voluntary action that hopefully will lead to more effective implementation of already decided environmental goals.

In the second type of argument, participants are given a role as input-makers into the process, but this role is seen as purely instrumental in relation to effective implementation. Here participation is taken to be an "instrument for the anticipation of resistance to planning and implementation" (Linder and Vatter 1996, p. 181). Participation is expected to reveal the preferences and values of the participants on the basis of which the measures of implementation can be shaped in order to be accepted by them (Newig 2007, p. 54).

These models see public participation serving only as a tool to secure the efficient implementation of the already made collective decisions. The previous "information deficit model" tries by informing the public to make it more willing to accept these decisions and act accordingly, whereas the latter "anticipation of resistance" model seeks to inform the authorities about public opinion, allowing authorities to shape the implementation measures accordingly.

To be sure, informing the public about, for instance, alternative lower carbon options can increase people's awareness and bring about even attitudinal change, which, in turn may also increase the acceptability and legitimacy of climate policy measures, e.g., of carbon price mechanisms (Bartle 2009). However, empirical evidence for the fact that public participation directly aids implementation is far from clear. More information about decisions has not automatically led citizens to change their environmental values and preferences, and implementation measures have not always been accepted without resistance even though they are deliberately shaped according to participants' preferences. It is, for instance, pointed out, that these instrumentalist models of public participation do not take the environmental, social, or political context in which the implementation is occurring adequately into account (Bartle 2009, Bulkeley and Mol 2003, pp. 148–49, Newig 2007). There are many other factors besides the implementation measures themselves, particularly those of context-specific environmental circumstances, social networks, and trust invested in institutions, that are more crucial in determining how willing the participants are to accept the policy measures and act accordingly. Since the above models restrict public participation only to the implementation of predetermined policy decisions and objectives, these models can hardly address the issues of these larger social and political contexts.

Finally, it can be argued that at least part of the reluctance or even resistance of the participants to accept predetermined decisions results because people expect their participation to be essential part of the production of a decision, not just a part of its implementation. They may even see these participatory models that focus on implementation phase as poor attempts of an authority to legitimize already made decisions, which may, in fact, increase their distrust of the authority instead of increasing its legitimacy

(Kyllönen et al. 2006). In many decisions, particularly concerning many of their salient interests, citizens in democratic societies do have strong expectations of seeing themselves as the source of the decisions, not just as means of their effective implementation. However, anticipating what will be argued below, this does not mean that citizens always expect them to be directly engaged in the decision-making process. More often citizens simply need to have warranted reasons for believing that their views are included in a fair and adequately inclusive way in the process before decision-making.

3.4. Epistemic argument for public participation

Arguments for effective problem solving are not limited to the implementation phase. The epistemic argument connects effectiveness more closely to the epistemic quality of the decision. Public participation prior to decision-making can serve as a way to incorporate valuable knowledge that would otherwise not be available to the authority. Participatory approaches are required, because they enable the greatest range of views and approaches to the environmental problem at hand to be represented and considered (Steel 2001). Inclusiveness of variable perspectives and situated and context-specific knowledge about the social and environmental circumstances is argued to make democracy based on broad public participation more capable of dealing with complex, variable, and uncertain environmental problems (cf., also Dryzek 1987). Particularly this is the case with "the newer generation of environmental concerns," like climate change, which involve a wide range of uncertainty concerning their future impacts. According to Steel, broad public participation, in addition to "expert" risk-assessment, is required because only a wide range of different perspectives allows us to evaluate exactly how, say, a risk of catastrophic climate change should be weighted against the current benefits of using fossil fuels.

Here the argument comes close to what John Stuart Mill has written:

> [T]he only way in which a human being can make some approach to knowing the whole of the subject, is by hearing what can be said about it by persons of every variety of opinion, and studying all modes in which it can be looked at by every character of mind. (John Stuart Mill 1956)

Following Mill's idea one can thus claim, that a society that promotes public deliberation among its citizens will often make better decisions. Decisions will likely to be more informed when a wide variety of people and groups have the opportunity to examine the facts relevant to the policy issue and test each other's views on these matters (Christiano 2008, p. 194). Such a society will also be more likely to invite "reflexivity, self-correction and continual public testing of claims" (Eckersley 2000, p. 122). Such public testing is vital because it prevents decisions from being biased toward the interests of some powerful groups like "technocratic policy professionals, politicians or corporate leaders." Thus a society promoting public deliberation is expected to be more sensitive to the interests of a broader portion of its citizens, and its decisions are likely to be more fair or just.

However, the evidence that public participation contributes to the epistemic qualities of decision-making is not straightforward. Even in small groups such effects are contingent on many variables and remain to some extent an open question requiring additional research (Larson et al. 1994, p. 459). Thus the generalization of these effects to large-scale public deliberation should be treated with caution (Christiano 2008, cf. Sunstein 2003). Furthermore, as Gaus (2003, p. 136) reminds us, people typically resort to the most vivid, psychologically salient or retrievable information, even if it is false. Hence the political judgment of people seems to be more likely to converge on stereotypical characterizations of some groups that people find attractive to themselves rather than fully-informed understandings.

Of course, the aim of participatory processes may well be just information gathering without any intention of reasoned public deliberation (Parkinson 2003). Here the reference is often made to Estlund's (1997, 2008) epistemic argument for democratic authority (cf., Parkinson 2003, Steel 2001). According to Estlund, it is the tendency of democracy to produce epistemically superior decisions that makes these decisions legitimate and authoritative. For him, democracy's epistemic virtue is not primarily based on its deliberative capacity to sort good arguments from bad, although he admits that he has "some sympathy" with appeals to "the power of free and open political discussion" in which "voters debate" (Estlund 2008, p. 256). When Estlund argues that democratic (majority) decisions are epistemically superior, he means that they are produced by a procedure that is better than random and best of among those procedures that are beyond reasonable objections of citizens. Thus democracy wins out over, for instance, a rule of experts, because even if a group of experts may sometimes produce more accurate decisions, generally their claim for authority on the basis of their expertise is not beyond reasonable objection (the same argument will be utilized in the case of environmental decision-making below).

However, Estlund's complicated argument is not easily applied when advocating direct public participation. Though it is the overall input of citizens that seems to matter for Estlund, this may lead to many different arrangements in designing democratic institutions. In some political processes, direct citizen participation may enhance total input, but even in such cases, Estlund allows some inequality of opportunities for political inputs between citizens in order to maximize the total amount of political input (Estlund 2008, pp. 195–98). But more usually the overall input depends on the unrestrictive forms of informal public communication, which may take a wide variety of forms of political participation including political confrontations as well as nonpolitical works of art.

Humphrey (2007) has also made a potent argument in favor of a wide variety of radical means for environmental activist groups who are incapable of engaging in any sort of reason-giving public deliberation that the epistemic argument for participatory approaches seems to imply. Some of these groups might be incapable of giving any justification for their particular protests in terms that their fellow citizens might accept. However, Humphrey claims that those who see political equality and the inclusive representation of all various views in the decision-making as valuable, should often support the radical means of these groups rather than condemn them. The radical means of some environmental activists can be seen as the only politically effective way to place their unpopular or unusual issue on the political agenda. The more their issue differs from established patterns of behavior, the more these groups suffer from the fact that the political agenda is dominated by established and habituated worldviews and patterns of behavior. Radical acts by climate protestors—like blocking Downing Street with tons of coal or painting the prime minister's name on the chimney of Kingsnorth coal-fired power station—could be seen as a way to lever them out of their otherwise uninfluential political position. At least they could be seen as kick-starting the process where their fellow citizens are invited to reconsider their political and ethical views and habitual patterns of behavior that in part sustain the too high levels of greenhouse gas emissions.

4. Public Deliberation, Participation and Representation

4.1. Toward procedural qualities of broad public deliberation

Public participation in decision-making can have many instrumental values that may contribute to effective environmental problem solving. However, the potential contribution appears to be conditional on many context-specific qualifications, which the most straightforward problem-solving participatory models of effective implementation easily overlook. Power asymmetries, distrust between the parties, and context-specific social relationships are more decisive for the actual effectiveness of implementation than the direct engagement of the public. The epistemic argument that values public participation prior to decision-making due to its epistemic inputs moves closer to the arguments of the deliberative approach. To the extent that public participation enhances morally and environmentally relevant qualities such as "a more long-range and risk-aversive orientation," or "more inclusive and other-regarding attitudes," there is reason to think that they will be promoted in a society that encourages public deliberation among all its citizens. However, empirical evidence for this kind of commonsensical claim still remains scanty. Climate policy decision-making is full of examples in which public deliberation also promotes poor virtues, like crude appeals to group or national interests (cf. e.g., Teräväinen (2010) on Finnish climate policy discourses).

To the extent that public participation enhances open and unrestricted forms of public communication that increases the overall input of various perspectives to the climate issue and promotes their public examination, the epistemic argument that public participation leads to more correct outcomes can also be warranted. Yet, the epistemic argument seems to be more dependent on the properties of the broad domain of public communication with a wide variety of different forms of political participation than on the quality and quantity of individual participatory processes. In individual participatory processes, the epistemic qualities of the process as well as the outcome are contingent on many context-specific variables, not least on the epistemic quality of the public sphere surrounding these processes.

The various perspectives and views that participants are expected to bring along to these processes do not arise in vacuum. Nor does their justification to be taken seriously into account in these processes. Both the content of these views and their justification are formed in close interconnection with the broader public sphere including debates between citizens and their representatives as well as opinion journalism, political demonstrations, campaigns, and so on. In highly complex policy issues like preventing global warming, where epistemic requirements are high to even understand the phenomenon itself, not to mention all its potential impacts, such interconnection is even more crucial (cf. Barber and Bartlett 2005, pp. 191–92). We, as citizens, depend upon the judgment of climate scientists and other experts in the field. Yet, the authority of these judgments is conditional on their legitimacy and acceptability in our eyes (O'Neill 2007).

Thus it is the qualities of this broad public sphere that has a vital impact on the views of participants and on the capacity of others to critically examine those views. These procedural qualities, particularly accountability and publicity, are directly connected to the questions of legitimate participation and representation that can also critically impinge on the problem-solving effectiveness of participatory processes.

4.2. Participation and legitimate representation

The idea of deliberative democracy entails the idea of universal accountability. Participants in a deliberative forum try to justify their views, opinions, and decisions to all of those that are bound by these decisions or affected by them. Some approaches to public deliberation take this idea to require the direct participation of citizens in "multiple forms of associations, networks, and organisations" (Benhabib 1996, cf. also Dryzek 1990). As a general view of public participation in environmental decision-making, this idea has been ditched, as many advocates of deliberative democracy consider representation to be a necessary element of any deliberative and ecological democracy (cf. Eckersley 2000, Goodin 2003). Bringing together all parties that are affected by climate change to deliberate among themselves would be impossible—e.g., those who are incapable of themselves participating in deliberation (future generations and nonhuman species) should be represented. Moreover, it is noted that the more serious the need for reasoned deliberation, the more stringent become the constitutive requirements for that deliberation, such as equality in deliberative competence, rules of good communication and practical limits to the number of deliberators (Estlund 2008, Gutmann and Thompson 1996).

Recognizing representation as a necessary or even as a desirable element of any meaningful environmental decision-making does not yet justify any single form of representation. One common argument often connected with participatory approaches requires that representation is possible only by those who share a common identity with those who they represent. Together with this "politics of presence" (Philips 1997) the epistemic argument above may require the direct representation of the lay public for effective problem-solving in climate issues, because it incorporates the perspectives of particularly those who are closest to the problem and its effects and are thus supposed to have greater context-specific understanding of it. Furthermore, shared identity and similar experiences can be regarded as a condition of a proper knowledge of the particular interests and context-specific circumstances of a local community. Thus it is vital that the representatives of different relevant groups, like indigenous people, women, local NGOs, are directly included in the deliberative processes. According to "politics of presence" approach, participatory process should ensure that these groups "are actually present when the decisions are made" (Sunstein 1997, p. 169).

O'Neill (2007) has cast doubt on the idea that such a link between shared identity and legitimate representation can be established:

> Individuals have a complex set of identities under different descriptions. The issues, as to which of these count, under what categories different groups are included and how legitimately particular individuals can be said to stand for or speak on behalf of others becomes increasingly problematic. [. . .] The very descriptions used in these [experiments of deliberative democracy] force a representative status on participants which may be contested, indeed by those individuals themselves. The contestation is proper. Simply being a member of a particular group does not entail that one is a representative of that group. (O'Neill 2007, p. 176)

These problems become even more acute where the formal acts of authorization (like voting) and mechanisms of accountability are absent (cf. Bäckstrand 2006). The "politics of presence" approach seems to be closer to what has been called delegate representation than so-called trustee representation. According to the delegate model, representatives are bound to follow the instructions, opinions, and interests of their principals, whereas trustees are given free rein to use their discretion and to make decisions (Parkinson 2003). For the delegation model, it is the responsiveness of the representative's decisions to the interests of the principal that is crucial. Thus the accountability of the representative's decisions becomes central to the representative's legitimacy. But to the extent that there are no (generally accepted) mechanisms of accountability, the legitimacy of this kind of "presence" representation can easily be a highly contested issue.

4.3. Epistemic representation

The complexity of the climate problem and the urgency to produce effective outcomes has intensified claims for another type of epistemic representation, namely well-informed participation and deliberation among experts of the environmental policy field (e.g., the inclusive participation of scientific climate specialists, NGOs and governmental officials). This is closer to the trustee model of representation, because it is the expertise or specific knowledge of these people that justifies their representative status in decision-making. Through their knowledge about climate change, they should have a better grasp of the objective interests of people concerning global warming and thus they should have the freedom to make decisions as they see fit within this specific policy field.

However, these arguments for the participation of "epistemic com-munities" are subject to the justificatory questions that epistemic par-ticipation generally raises in relation to democratic participation (cf. Estlund 1993): How do we justify that this (expert or local) knowledge improves the epistemic quality of decisions? How can we be certain that these actors possess this knowledge? With regard to technical knowledge, this identification is more possible. Those who are trained in a science relevant to understanding climate change should have greater say in ap-plying that science. Similarly, local actors in many cases may have the best understanding of local circumstances and should thus have more say in decisions concerning their local environment. But decisions of climate policies are not just technical questions requiring solely technical context-specific knowledge. Rather they are complex and difficult politi-cal and societal questions comprising different ethical conceptions and elements of justice. Just as we might disagree on these different ethical conceptions and elements of justice, so we might also disagree on what is the kind of moral competence required by these questions and on how we should recognize those who posses this competence. Any criteria based on education (like any criteria based on permanent inhabitation in some local neighborhood or on membership of a particular group) will hardly be beyond reasonable doubt in pluralistic societies.

Representation based solely on epistemic criteria would also make the outcomes vulnerable to the suspicion that the interests of those who are outside the group of epistemic representation are likely to be given lesser weight. So-called "Climategate" appears to support this claim. In this scandal, the Climate Research Unit of the University of East Anglia was accused of scientific misconduct and withholding information. This was followed by the scandal over the scientific accuracy of the IPCC climate report. According to polls made in several countries shortly after these scandals, the number of citizens who felt that the potential consequences of climate change had been exaggerated increased significantly.[3] This all happened at the same time as governments were negotiating ever deeper cuts in their greenhouse gas emissions (to cut them to almost zero by 2050 in industrialized countries) and planning ever stricter climate policies to achieve those cuts (e.g., the UK's Climate Change Bill allows the government to introduce a personal carbon trading scheme without any further primary legislation).

These results may be partly an outcome of a deliberate campaign by some groups of climate skeptics and might reflect only a momentary or a misinterpreted reaction of the public,[4] but they nonetheless seem to highlight that the more radical the required changes in citizens' behavioral patterns, the more vulnerable climate policies seem to be to serious doubts about their biased and inadequate justifications. Baber and Bartlett (2005, p. 192) also note that as citizens become more aware of such claims about the biased interest of science, "they feel freer to resist even the most apparently objective and factual knowledge because of its source, its implications, or the challenge it presents to their tacit knowledge."

5. Effective Climate Policies and Public Justification

5.1. From actual public participation to public justification

It was suggested in the introduction that legitimacy should be understood as a generally held social recognition that decisions are accepted as rightful. Because this recognition implies a socially sanctioned obligation to comply with these decisions, legitimacy does not only make these decisions more acceptable in the eyes of citizens, but their social recognition as legitimate finally ensures their effective implementation. In the absence of such recognition, a government which requires drastic changes in the behavior of its citizens would have to resort to ever more intensive material inducement or coercion in its policies, which would be hard to justify in liberal democratic polities.

As Scharpf (2003, p. 1) notes, if this functional definition of legitimacy is accepted, then it follows that the need for legitimation varies with the salience of the citizen's interests that are potentially interfered with by these policies. Since preventing catastrophic global warming requires policies that would most likely interfere significantly with many salient interests of the citizens, this stresses the need for strong justification of any such policies in order to be able to induce effective action by citizens. But as we have noted, none of the approaches to public participation is able to make drastic climate policies legitimate in a sense that would ensure their effective implementation. From a fair proceduralist perspective, public participation makes public decisions more justified insofar as they incorporate the interests of the society more fairly into decision-making. This "passive inclusion" of interests through formal decision-making procedures is criticized by the deliberative democrats, because of its inability to give any other justification for legitimate decisions. Yet, as questions about legitimacy of environmental or climate policies clearly exemplify, disagreements among people not only concern the substance of these policies but also the procedural qualities of decision-making. Conflicts over the legitimate political community—whose views should count in legitimate decision-making—or over legitimate representatives of this community, can become as serious as those that concern the content of the policies. Thus the demand of deliberative democrats seems to be warranted that fair procedures need to be supplemented by public deliberation that gives justification for not only the substance of decisions but also for the decision-making procedures (e.g., Gutmann and Thompson 1996).

The straightforward arguments of so-called problem-solving approaches were found to be inadequate from the same justificatory perspective. Even if the claim that public participation contributes to the epistemic quality of the decisions may in some circumstances be defensible, it does not mean that this automatically leads to more effective problem solving. Particularly in the context of climate policies, where many of the salient interests of citizens are potentially interfered with, the efficacy of climate policies becomes more dependent on citizens' recognition that the epistemic quality of those policies gives them a justified reason to comply. If people disagree about what makes the outcomes "the best available practical solutions," or if they have serious suspicions that these outcomes are biased, the epistemic qualities of these solutions can hardly induce effective action by citizens.

The deliberative approach that combines the epistemic values of the outcome with procedural qualities of reasoned and deliberative processes seems to be more capable of satisfying requirements of legitimacy from both sides. Since deliberative democracy emphasizes that a fair process of public deliberation should be a cognitive process of assessing arguments and forming judgments, it then can claim that deliberative processes should lead to more justified and reasonable outcomes, which gives citizens a good reason to accept them. But as we have seen, such idealistic qualities of deliberative processes hardly qualify as real participatory processes. Of course we can allow that "relevant constituencies are sorted out" (Knight and Johnson 1994) following the principle that participants in the deliberation should be public-oriented, and that the reasons they provide in public discourse should be articulated so that they can be accepted by other citizens. But as we have noted, there are many important environmental views that fundamentally challenge the prevailing worldviews and thus the majority of citizens does not easily accept them. Nonetheless, these views should be included in the environmental political agenda, not only because that is what political equality requires, but also because these views might be as relevant as the established worldviews for the proper understanding of an environmental question in Mill's sense mentioned above.

5.2. The value of publicity and freedom of choice

However, though we should abandon the ideal of deliberative process as a blueprint or even as a counterfactual mirror of our actual public participation, the idea of deliberative democracy entails qualities that are vital for a proper understanding of democratic legitimacy as a source of effective policy making. First, deliberative theory emphasizes the perspective of citizens themselves. It is the "reactive attitudes" of citizens that forms a basis for the requirement that public norms and policies should be justified to them (Habermas 1991, cf. also Strawson 2001). Unjustified interference with their behavior makes them feel not just angry but indignant or resentful, because no valid reasons for the interference are offered. According to Gaus (2003), analysis of such reactive attitudes like indignation or resentment reveals that our relationship with others presupposes that interpersonally valid norms—including public norms regulating our social life—have to be justified to each other. If citizens are expected to act on these norms, they have to have an adequate reason to do so.

Second, many deliberative theorists have argued that the publicity of decision-making is crucial for the legitimate democratic authority. If deliberative democracy bases the legitimacy of democratic authority on the reasons that officials and citizens give to justify their political actions, it is vital that those reasons and the information necessary to assess those reasons are public. As was discussed above in regard to the "Climategate" case, the more likely it is that required changes in citizens' behavioral patterns interfere with their salient interests, the more vulnerable climate policies seem to be to serious suspicions of their biased and inadequate justification.

The argument made by Gutmann and Thompson (1996) is that the ability of public deliberation to carefully consider relevant conflicting moral claims makes citizens more likely to accept the outcomes of these deliberations even when they disagree with them. Making justifications public should also contribute to the broadening of citizens' moral and political perspectives. Even if public deliberation does not transform citizen's self-interested claims into public-spirited ones, it does make the justifications of political decisions available to them. This should make the continuation of political cooperation possible even in the face of persistent moral disagreement.

Christiano (2008) has also listed several fundamental interests that ground the requirement of publicity.[5] According to Christiano, in a society where citizens can acknowledge fallibility and the cognitive bias of their own moral judgments and where disagreements about substantive moral issues obtain, each citizen has an interest in not only being treated as equal, but also in being able to see that he or she is treated as an equal and not in accordance with someone else's conception of equality. Furthermore, argues Christiano, the value of publicity is also grounded in the fact that citizen's diverse judgments often reflect modes of life to which they are accustomed or in which they feel at home. Thus each citizen has a fundamental interest in having a sense of being properly at home in the society in which he lives. Public knowledge can encourage this sense to the extent that everyone can see how his or her society is responsive to his or her interests. Finally, every citizen has a fundamental interest to see that he or she has an equal moral standing among his or her fellow citizens.

If Christiano is right, the publicity of political decisions and of the justifications behind them can have a significant importance on the fundamental interest of citizens. Citizens' interest in being at home and having equal moral standing may also explain why authoritative policies have only limited success in many areas of environmental regulation. It has been shown, for instance, that in certain areas of behavior, people in modern democratic countries will insist on freedom of choice. The choice of having children is one palpable area, but making holiday decisions is also seen as one critical area in which people want to have freedom of choice (Pellikaan and van der Veen 2002). Freedom of choice in these areas of behavior is seen vital, because not having this freedom would be seen as reflecting a judgment that they are not competent or do not have the same equal standing that is normally accorded other adult members of the society (cf. Scanlon 1998).

Yet climate policies that seek to prevent catastrophic global warming require drastic changes in the public's holiday decisions or even in their procreative decisions. It seems inevitable that if policies are able to have access to the decisions that citizens regard as of utmost important for their sense of being at home and having equal moral standing, they need to be based on political objectives and policy means that people can see as having public justification.

6. Conclusion

I have focused here on the analysis of various arguments offered for public participation as a vital part of legitimate and efficient climate policies. I have found each of these arguments inadequate. I have instead stressed that the values of public participation are not easily fulfilled by any single form of public engagement.

In short, the more citizens see that their salient interests are threatened by climate policies, the more likely they are to see their participation strategically as a way to defend those interests. Therefore, it is unlikely that any particular process of engaging citizens directly in decision-making will suffice to provide public justification for climate policies. If and when such justification can be given that makes drastic climate policies legitimate, it will be based on multiple sources. Some of these are based on citizens' beliefs that the policies (and the climate goals they are meant to fulfill) are actually an outcome of reasoned deliberation that discards, at least, the most unreasonable proposals. Therefore, deliberative democrats are correct in stressing the importance of actual public discussions and debates in order to justify our beliefs and norms. But while deliberative democrats believe that this reasoned debate should be able to make one policy proposal victorious against any other (i.e., a public value), the claim here is a more modest one: at the end of public deliberation there can be many policy proposals whose public justification remains "undefeated" (Gaus 2003). In deciding between these challenging proposals, resorting to fair procedures as a competent way of producing legitimate policy outcomes is often needed. Therefore citizens should be able to believe that the political process has been fair and inclusive in a way that gives reason to believe that the outcome is not biased and no relevant perspective has been left out. This belief is more warranted if citizens are able to see publicly how this process proceeds even if they do not participate themselves.

Furthermore, public justification is supported by how well citizens are able to see that their salient interests are being recognized and treated equally. In some cases, like making decisions on how to reduce energy consumption in the local neighborhood, actual participation of the inhabitants in the decision-making process may be the most viable way to achieve this publicity requirement. But as we move to more large-scale decisions and public regulation, the need for more limited participation and representation becomes a practical necessity. At the same time, contested questions about the legitimacy of participation and representation may become more and more acute.

Moreover, large-scale decision-making and public regulation usually takes place in multiple institutional contexts (scientific panels and committees, the legislature, administrative agencies, courts) that all require their own structures of justification (Williams 1994). How these justifications are opened up to public scrutiny is conditional on a set of principles, rules, and mechanisms that secure their accountability and publicity. Thus the public justification of these principles, rules, and mechanisms concerning the whole decision-making process becomes a critical source of legitimacy with large-scale policies (cf. Daniels 1999).

In conclusion: a necessary condition for effective policies to prevent global warming is that these multiple sources of public justification suffice to give reasons for citizens to change their behavioral patterns also in areas of life where their most salient interests are at stake.

Notes

1. The research was funded by HENVI, Helsinki University Centre for Environment. My warmest thanks are due to Dr. Mark Shackleton for checking my English language.
2. Cf. http://ec.europa.eu/environment/climat/campaign/index.htm.
3. Cf., Gallup 11.3.2010 (http://www.gallup.com/poll/126560/americans-global-warming-concerns-continue-drop.aspx), BBC 7.2.2010 (http://news.bbc.co.uk/2/hi/8500443.stm), Der Spiegel 4.1.2010 (http://www.spiegel.de/fotostrecke/fotostrecke-53441.html) and 10.6.2010 (http://www.spiegel.de/wissenschaft/natur/0,1518,699967,00.html).
4. In his article in the New York Times (8.6.2010), Krosnick claims that the results of the polls that purport to show that citizens are increasingly skeptical about the very existence of climate change and about climate research have been misinterpreted (http://www.nytimes.com/2010/06/09/opinion/09krosnick.html?pagewanted=2&_r=1). His own survey made by Stanford University shows that there has not been any dramatic decline in the proportion of Americans who believe in global warming. A small recent decline is likely to be a temporary reaction based on citizens' personal observations of the recent decline in world average temperatures. Particularly, according to Krosnick, the survey discredits the claim that there would have been any growing skepticism as a result of "Climategate" (http://woods.stanford.edu/docs/surveys/Global-Warming-Survey-Selected-Results-June2010.pdf).
5. It should be noted that the notion of publicity here is a weak one, because it requires only that people "in principle" can see that they are being treated justly once the basic facts about human cognitive limitations are taken into account and given a

reasonable informed effort on the part of these people (Christiano 2008, p. 48). In contrast, Rawls (1993, p. 35) requires that everyone knows that the basic institutions are just. Moreover, he requires that a society satisfies a publicly recognized conception of justice when "everyone accepts and knows that everyone else accepts the very same principles of justice."

References

Arias-Maldonado, M., 2007, An Imaginary Solution? The Green Defence of Deliberative Democracy, *Environmental Values* 16: 233–52.

Baber, W.F. & Bartlett, R.V., 2005, *Deliberative Environmental Politics. Democracy and Ecological Rationality*, The MIT Press, Cambridge, MA.

Bäckstrand, K., 2006, Multi-stakeholder Partnerships for Sustainable Development: Rethinking Legitimacy, Accountability and Effectiveness, *European Environment* 16 (5): 290–06.

Bartle, I., 2009, A Strategy for Better Climate Change Regulation: Towards a Public Interest Oriented Regulatory Regime, *Environmental Politics* 18 (5): 689–706.

Beetham, D., 1991, *The Legitimation of Power*, Macmillan, Hong Kong.

Benhabib, S., 1996, Toward a Deliberative Model of Democratic Legitimacy, in Benhabib, S. (ed.), *Democracy and Difference. Contesting the Boundaries of the Political*, Princeton University Press, Princeton, NJ.

Bulkeley, H. & Mol, A.P.J., 2003, Participation and Environmental Governance: Consensus, Ambivalence and Debate, *Environmental Values* 12 (2): 143–54.

Christiano, T., 2008, *The Constitution of Equality. Democratic Authority and its Limits*, Oxford University Press, Oxford.

Cohen, J., 1989, Deliberation and Democratic Legitimacy, in Hamlin, A. & Pettit, P. (eds.), *The Good Polity. Normative Analysis of the State*, Basil Blackwell, Oxford.

Daniels, N., 1999, Enabling Democratic Deliberation: How Managed Care Organisations Ought to Make Decisions about Coverage for New Technologies, in Macedo, S. (ed.), *Deliberative Politics. Essays on Democracy and Disagreement*, Oxford University Press, New York and Oxford.

Davies, A., 2001, What Silence Knows—Planning, Public Participation and Environmental Values, *Environmental Values* 10: 77–102.

Dryzek, J. S., 2004, Constitutionalism and its Alternatives, in van Aaken, A., List, C. & Luetge, C. (eds.), *Deliberation and Decision. Economics, Constitutional Theory and Deliberative Democracy*, Ashgate, Aldershot.

———, 2000, *Deliberative Democracy and Beyond: Liberals, Critics, Contestations*, Oxford University Press, Oxford.

———, 1996, Strategies of Ecological Democratization, in Lafferty, W.M. & Meadowcroft, J. (eds.), *Democracy and the Environment*, Edward Elgar, Cheltenham.

———, 1990, *Discursive Democracy: Politics, Policy and Political Science*, Cambridge University Press, New York.

———, 1987, *Rational Ecology: Environment and Political Economy*, Basil Blackwell, Oxford.

Eckersley, R., 2007, Ambushed: The Kyoto Protocol, The Bush Administration's Climate Policy and the Erosion of Legitimacy, *International Politics* 44: 306–24.

———, 2000, Deliberative Democracy, Ecological Representation and Risk. Towards a Democracy of Affected, in Saward, M. (ed.), *Democratic Innovation: Deliberation, Representation and Association*, Routledge, London.

Elliot, L., (in press), Legality and Legitimacy: The Environmental Challenge, in Falk, R. & Thakur, R. (eds.) *Legality and Legitimacy in the International Order*, United Nations University Press, Tokyo.

Estlund, D., 2008, *Democratic Authority: A Philosophical Framework*, Princeton University Press, Princeton and Oxford.
———, 1997, Beyond Fairness and Deliberation: The Epistemic Dimension of Democratic Authority, in Bohman, J. & Rehg, W. (eds.), *Deliberative Democracy*, The MIT Press, Cambridge MA.
———, 1993, Making Truth Safe for Democracy, in Copp, D., Hampton, J. & Roemer, John F. (eds.), *The Idea of Democracy*, Cambridge University Press, Cambridge.
Gaus, G. F., 2003, *Contemporary Theories of Liberalism*, SAGE Publications, London.
Goodin R. E., 2003, *Reflective Democracy*, Oxford University Press, Oxford.
———, 1996, Enfranchising the Earth, and Its Alternatives, *Political Studies* 44 (5): 835–49.
Gutmann, A. and Thompson, D., 1996, *Democracy and Disagreement*, The Belknap Press of Harvard University Press, Cambridge, MA.
Habermas, J., 1991, *Moral Consciousness and Communicative Action*, MIT Press, Cambridge, MA.
Heilbroner, R.L., 1974, *An Inquiry into the Human Prospect*, Calder & Boyars, London.
Humphrey, M., 2007, *Ecological Politics and Democratic Theory: The Challenge of Deliberative Ideal*, Routledge, London.
Knight, J. and J. Johnson, 1994, Aggregation and Deliberation: On the Possibility of Democratic Legitimacy, *Political Theory* 22 (2): 277–96.
Kyllönen, S., Colpaert, A., Heikkinen, H., Jokinen, M., Kumpula, J., Marttunen, M., Muje, K. & Raitio, K., 2006, Conflict Management as a Means to the Sustainable Use of Natural Resources, *Silva Fennica* 40 (4): 687–728.
Larson Jr., J.R., Foster-Fishman, P.G. & Keys, C.B., 1994, Discussion of Shared and Unshared Information in Decision-Making Groups, *Journal of Personality and Social Psychology* 67 (3): 446–61.
Linder, W. & Vatter, A., 1996, Kriterien zur Evaluation von Partizipationsverfahren, in Selle, K. (ed.), *Planung und Kommunikation*, Bauverlag, Berlin.
Mill, J.S., 1956, *On Liberty*, The Liberal Arts Press, New York.
Newig, J., 2007, Does Public Participation in Environmental Decisions Lead to Improved Environmental Quality?, *CCP* 1: 51–71.
O'Neill, J., 2007, *Markets, Deliberation and Environment*, Routledge, London and New York.
Ophuls, W., 1977, *Ecology and the Politics of Scarcity*, W.H. Freeman, San Francisco, CA.
Parkinson, J., 2003, Legitimacy Problems in Deliberative Democracy, *Political Studies* 51 (1): 180–96.
Pellikaan, H. & van der Veen R.J., 2002, *Environmental Dilemmas and Policy Design*, Cambridge University Press, Cambridge.
Philips, A., 1997, Dealing with Difference: A Politics of Ideas or a Politics Presence, in Goodin, R. & Pettit, P. (eds.), *Contemporary Political Philosophy*, Blackwell, Oxford.
Rawls, J., 1993, *Political Liberalism*, Columbia University Press, New York.
Reus-Smit, C., 2007, International Crisis of Legitimacy, *International Politics* 44: 157–74.
Sagoff, M., 1988, *The Economy of the Earth: Philosophy, Law, and the Environment*. Cambridge University Press, Cambridge.
Scanlon, T.M., 1998, *What We Owe to Each Other*, The Belknap Press of Harvard University Press, Cambridge, MA.

Scharpf, F.W., 2003, *Problem Solving Effectiveness and Democratic Accountability in the EU*, (http://centers.law.nyu.edu/jeanmonnet/hauser/FWSNYU_hauserS04.rtf).
———, 1999, *Governing Europe Effective and Democratic*, Oxford University Press, Oxford.
Shearman, D. & Wayne Smith, J., 2007, *The Climate Change Challenge and the Failure of Democracy*, Prager, Westport, London.
Steel, J., 2001, Participation and Deliberation in Environmental Law: Exploring a Problem Solving Approach, *Oxford Journal of Legal Studies* 21 (2): 415–42.
Strawson, P.F., 2001, Freedom and Resentment, in Ekstrom L. W. (ed.), *Agency and Responsibility. Essays on the Metaphysics of Freedom*, Westview Press, Boulder, CO.
Sunstein, C., 1997, Preferences and Politics, in Goodin, R. & Pettit, P. (eds.), *Contemporary Political Philosophy*, Blackwell, Oxford.
———, 2003, *Why Societies Need Dissent*, Harvard University Press, Cambridge, MA.
Teräväinen, T., 2010, Political Opportunities and Storylines in Finnish Climate Policy Negotiations, *Environmental Politics* 19 (2): 196–216.
Waldron, J., 1999, *Law and Disagreement*, Clarendon Press, Oxford.
Webler, T., 1995, 'Right' Discourse in Citizen Participation: An Evaluative Yardstick, in Renn, O., Webler, T. & Wiedemann, P. (eds.), *Fairness and Competence in Citizen Participation. Evaluating Models for Environmental Discourse*, Kluwer Academic Publishers, Dordrecht.
Westra, L., 1998, *Living in Integrity: A Global Ethic to Restore a Fragmented Earth*, Rowman & Littlefield, Lanham, MD.
Williams, D.R., 1994, Environmental Law and Democratic Legitimacy, *Duke Environmental Law and Policy Forum*, Vol. IV: 1–40.
Zürn, M., 2004, Global Governance and Legitimacy Problems, *Government and Opposition* 39 (2): 260–87.

Part 2
Changing Society

Between Democracy and Antagonistic Environmental Politics

Timo Airaksinen
Social and Moral Philosophy
Department of Political and Economic Studies
University of Helsinki,
Finland

1. The Case of the Thylacine

In Tasmania, there used to live a strange, ancient marsupial predator variously called a tiger, Tasmanian tiger, Tassy tiger, hyena, or finally and correctly a thylacine. Its color is light brown, and its lower back is striped like that of a real tiger. Its back slopes down toward its hind legs like that of an African hyena, and it has the head of a dog. The size is approximately that of an Alsatian dog. The animal is mostly nocturnal and hunts mainly wallabies. It needs one wallaby every third day, and it seems to be a skilled hunter who follows its prey's scent until it is exhausted and ready to be killed. The thylacine is not a fast runner because of the bone structure of its hind legs. The animal builds a lair for herself and her cubs under a tree or to some other suitable covered place and keeps her cubs there. The aborigines have many names for her, such as corinna, lagunta, and laoonana. The beast lives where the aborigines do and, thus, shares their natural environment and habitats. They do not seem to place any special role or meaning to the corinna in their lives, unlike the Tasmanian devil which was called the Nasty One. Devils survive to this day, although a type of mysterious mouth cancer has killed some fifty percent of their population (in the end of 2010).

The last thylacine died in captivity on the September 7, 1936, and none have been seen after that. The tiger, when it was still alive, was hated and feared almost universally and killed whenever it was met. It was kept in captivity, and local and international zoos exhibited them eagerly and also paid high prices for captured individuals. The case of the thylacine was politicized at least twice, with the first being in 1886 when the Tasmanian Parliament decided to pay a substantial bounty for each killed animal. Also, individual sheep farmers paid their own bounty, so a lucky hunter could collect twice or more. There was even a Tiger Extermination Society. The thylacine was demonized, feared, and condemned as a vermin. All kinds of fanciful stories were told by their hunters, emphasizing the combat between man and the beast and prizing the heroism of the hunter or themselves. Actually, thylacines do not seem to be especially dangerous or ferocious. They were no real man-eating tigers, and most of the killed sheep seem to have been victims of dogs. Dogs love to kill sheep, and they kill a lot when they get started. They still do. But thylacines were labelled as the culprits by big-time aristocratic sheep owners, and the parliament complied. The vote was a narrow one, but it condemned the tiger forever. The true facts were not very important for this decision. The tigers should go and that is that. No research was needed.

Natural anxiety, the hatred of the wild beast, which is so typical of the hunters and farmers, did its part, and then the parliament did its own. The country people always killed the thylacine whenever possible, but now they got paid for it. The demon beast was under the double controls of natural anxiety and financial greed and, thus, doomed to extinction. Such a natural anxiety seems to have another side too, namely, the deep conviction that there is a practically unlimited supply of game, prey, and predators. In popular imagination, then and now, the supply of natural bounty knows no reserve. The thylacines come from rainforests, fields, and hills, so when you kill one another one takes its place. In one's anxious mind the enemy always returns whatever you do, but you keep on fighting. And suddenly there is no one to kill. They are all gone forever. The people of Tasmania still do not believe this can happen. After killing them, they want them back. They are still anxious as they repent.

The second political move takes place after it is already too late. The parliament decides to protect the thylacines after they are all gone, almost on the same day in 1936. Of course, these protection measures would not have helped much because hunters would shoot a thylacine anyway. This is what they always did. And the vulnerable sheep are still out there.

Sanctuaries were suggested. The tiger would be captured and moved to a designated island where they could live and breed without being hunted and killed. But such a sanctuary came too late. And then the final irony: once the thylacine was dead, it became popular and even loved. Now it is a main Tasmanian icon and source of shared identity. People want to see it, and they see it around all the time—except that the tiger is dead. In their anxious mind, now free of fear, they imagine what could and should be the case. The beautiful, unique historical relic is still out there hunting wallabies and barking in the night. The fact that it is dead is too much to bear. Hatred and love are once again close to each other. Protection and destruction go hand in hand. The devils are getting rare, and thus, they can be loved, too. Perhaps this logic of anxiety will also apply to the poor aboriginals one day?

The thylacine is dead, but actually, they are constantly seen and reports of sightings keep coming. This is so charming. People really want to see them now. They love this mystery which seems to have a deep symbolic meaning to the Tasmanians. And when you want to see, you will see. Yet no prints or scats have been documented, and when scientists have tried automated cameras and other reliable methods they have not been successful at all. The beast is dead, but it lives in popular imaginations. The thylacine should live but it does not. It was hunted to extinction because it kills sheep; just like the Tasmanian aboriginals were hunted because they killed sheep too. This story of tiger is told convincingly by David Owen in his excellent book Thylacine: *The Tragic Story of the Tasmanian Tiger* (Owen 2003). My facts are lifted from it.

2. Political Considerations

As we saw above, the Tasmanian parliament both condemned and tried to save the tiger, first successfully and then unsuccessfully. They condemned it when their legislation could still work, and they saved it when nothing could be done anyway. But perhaps this catastrophe was just bad luck in the sense that they really tried to do their best, except that they came a little late. Anyway, they tried and this may save their reputation. Yet, there is this nagging feeling that when it is too late, the good decision is easy to make. You wash your hands and that is all.

In environmental and conservationist matters, political decision making has a major role today. Do we have a reason to be skeptical or is optimism the right attitude? In other words, are political processes able to do the right thing and make the correct laws? Or is the case of the

Tasmanian Parliament the paradigm example of politics doing first this and then that in a wrong order? How could politics destroy as well as protect our natural environment?

Not all agendas can be politicized, such as sacred and moral matters. Does this observation offer any help? No parliament would make a law which allows some utterly sacrilegious or disgustingly immoral behavior—not normally, that is. Some issues are, indeed, out of the question when we consider the lawmakers' powers. Do environmental questions belong to this class? Should they belong there? Is it good if they do? My intuition is that some questions of religion and ethics are so fundamental and intuitively clear that no political interference are needed or accepted. Environmental problems and questions are, on the contrary and in many cases, essentially contested. We need politics to deal with them, and we need legislation and the relevant laws. We also have laws that regulate our actions toward religious and moral questions, of course. Yet, certain aspects of religion and morality are outside of politics. Similarly, I do not think that it would be possible today to make a law that all hawks and eagles are to be killed, and the ideas which were prevalent, for instance, in Finland one hundred years ago are simply unimaginable now. Those times have changed. Extermination is no longer a viable policy, but everything else is debatable.

What do we mean by politics and political issues? In this paper, I speak about politics mainly in the narrow sense of the word: politics means an open and democratic debate and decision making concerning issues which are important to all citizens in such a way that common good is at least approximated. There is the loose sense of the term as well: politics means all considerations and decision which alter our common social world in an ultimately consensual manner. In the most general sense politics means nothing but an attempt to live together in an orderly fashion. There are two rules: we should do it together and we should not try to undermine the idea of open, joint decisions. We may also insist on deliberations. In other words, we cannot make a political move to end all politics. Dictators do this, and therefore, there is no political life in dictatorships or in true oligarchies in the narrow sense of the word and very little on the loose sense. Something like politics exists outside of democracies—I do not deny it—but it is not the same thing. Should important environmental questions be decided by some benevolent dictators or strong elites? In many cases this works well in religious questions, so why not elsewhere? On the other hand, no true moral élites or dictators exist, and still, we do not want to make (all) moral questions political.

One complication of politics which I want to emphasize is the question of the rationality and irrationality of the relevant debates. It is all formal, given the normal moral and religious side-constraints, and the contents may be as irrational as you want. When the death sentence of thylacines was read in the Tasmanian Parliament, the decision was rational in the sense that it was made formally in the correct order. But the contents were twofold: the big-time sheep farmers' economic interests were to be protected and general anxiety relieved. Actually, this simplifies the case too much. The express purpose of the legislation which promised to pay a bounty for the verified killings of tigers was to protect the holy sheep and investments on them. The background facilitating factor was the fear of thylacines and its associated anxiety. This is a nasty beast. The main motive is apparently, or even obviously rational, that is, legitimate economical interest. This must be protected at all times, as promised by some higher order legislation, as an interest shared by the whole population of Tasmania. It is a right.

As David Owen makes clear, there is one hidden source of irrationality here. And this source has its double nature, both cognitive and emotive. The fact is, if anything about the tiger is a fact, that dogs kill sheep and most of the destruction is due to them, not the timid thylacine. Also escaped convicts and bushrangers wanted the sheep. The tiger is condemned on the basis of false evidence which nobody wants to put straight. Of course killed dogs also brought a reward to the hunter, but the bounty was smaller and dogs were an inexhaustible resource. All the people wanted to own dogs, and they produced more of them all the time: more dogs, more feral dogs. Our lovable pets work for us and then they kill, beasts of prey as they are, true carnivores. No anxiety is visible here, unlike in the case of the tiger. Any evidence against them is good evidence, and they get killed indiscriminately.

Anxiety makes wonders. First, it motivates killings and finally it brings about love and longing. What looks rational, the political decisions are basically as irrational as anything. What we learn from the case is this. We cannot trust politics to make the right decisions which guide the citizens to do the right thing. We all know this, of course, but the strange case of the Tasmanian tiger illustrates the case well, especially when see how much the people want their tiger back. From fear and anxiety to longing and sorrow, this is how it goes. And it all is mediated by the economic interests of elites.

Politics is capricious to the extreme, and we know that. This banal observation allows us to formulate a rule, though. Political processes and decision making works well in those cases where the next decision may correct the unintended damage made by means of the first decision. One party corrects the other party's mistakes. We suffer first, but after we win the next election we change it all. We will wait patiently, and our turn will come. It follows that no one has the right to make irreversible changes to the world. This is how democracy works when problems are not irreversible. To hunt the thylacine to extinctions is irreversible, and thus, it cannot be a good political decision or no political decision at all. To reduce their number in certain areas of the country may be acceptable for many different reasons. But we must be able to fix the damage later if that happens. Also, good facts are always needed. No decisions without facts, this is a nice rule. For instance, if it as a fact that the thylacine question is highly anxiety ridden, this should be duly recognized and utilized in the decision making.

This rule of reversibility also allows us to understand some of the intuitions which are related to sacred and moral matters. They are too important, in this very sense, to be subjected to capricious political processes. They may be politicized, but the point is that this should not happen. Wrong decisions cause too much damage in the long run as their effects cannot be reversed. This is also one reason why we should not accept dictators, however benevolent they may be. They may not care about reversing their decisions. Why should they? They are dictators. In politics, decisions are reversed when new groups come to office and assume power. They are not bound by the earlier bad decisions like the original decision maker may well be. They are free to act and correct the damage. A dictator is always tied to his earlier decisions and commitments and, thus, perhaps reluctant to initiate a change and start correcting the problems caused earlier. Dictators are resilient to change (see Airaksinen 2000).

We have examples of religious dictators which illustrate the point. Their decisions last forever, as the treatment of women and gays in many churches and religious denominations prove even today. What is said is said and it must not be changed. The Lutheran church has no dictator or a dominant elite, and it at least tries to cope with such problems in a democratically political manner.

Nevertheless, it is easy to maintain that a well-informed, benevolent environmental dictator would be an ideal solution, but this must be a mistake. Would she be a highly respected scientist who is in charge of the field of her undisputed expertise? Could we ever really trust this person or elite group? I do not think so. Something else is needed. Let me make one more remark on this matter. A scientist would be a science dictator, but our natural environment is so much more than merely an object of biological learning, science, and studies. Perhaps some biologists would like to be dictators on the basis of their superior knowledge and understanding? But what about all the anxiety and elation which is also rooted in our natural environment and which may define it in an essential manner? A biologist may love and desire things which bring anxiety to many. Think of wolf protection programs in Finland, for example. Not all the people who walk in the forest want them there. On the contrary, they want them gone forever, just as they seemed to be a short while ago. Wolves do not look that good when your children play in the forest at dusk; this is how the popular argument goes. Is the anxiety here too ridiculous to be taken seriously in political deliberations? This question is not easy to answer. It creates a political problem.

As a kind of appendix to this chapter, let me add one relevant consideration concerning the role and values of scientists. When, say, a biologist studies her living creatures and their environment, she generates scientific theories and establishes some scientific facts. She knows how her objects live and function. She can answer why-questions, and she is able classify and describe them. Then she has her relevant values. Where does she get them? Certainly not from her scientific work, its theories and facts (cf. the Naturalistic Fallacy). Her values may be generated by and derived from the social community of scientists themselves. They may come from the traditional-magical view or even from the economical side of the debate. The values must come from a source which is outside of science, if science is scientific. Most naturalists love what they study and do everything to benefit them. I think this is true. But it is still a valid question where these pro-nature values are coming from and what they are exactly like. I am sure some one hundred years ago the set of values typical of naturalists were very different from what they are now, perhaps more commercial, religious, and exploitive. The modern values seem to demand goals like originality and preservation. This is a question of the hidden loyalties of scientists who work in the relevant fields. I am certain that these values are eminently respectable and correct, but what they are and where they come from is still a moot question.

3. A Model of Some Relevant Elements in Environmental Politics

Our natural environment is many things, and its political control is equally complicated. As J. C. Ramo argues in his book *The Age of the Unthinkable* (Ramo 2009), we are always trying old solutions to solve new problems. He mainly discusses global security problems, policies, and politics, but his main idea can be applied to environmental issues as well. We need new ideas when we are challenged by new and irreversible changes in our shared natural environment. The environment is as difficult to correct as the situation of the Tassy tiger used to be. Too many of the changes we cause are irreversible, even if we pretend otherwise. Corrective measures can be tried. One crucial fact was that thylacines did no breed in captivity. Could they have been saved if they did? Suppose they are saved. Then a small population exists in zoos and on a remote island outside the Tasmanian cost. Would this be the same as the thriving populations in the Tasmanian hills and forests? The answer must be in the negative, but at the same time we think that the situation would not be so bad. The worst alternative can be avoided even if some aspects of the change are irreversible. And in this less than perfect way the politics of environmental change can indeed work. What are the new ideas then? Do we have any in the field of politics which is dominated, on the one hand, by bright economic interests and, on the other hand, by the conservationist gloom? Next, let me present a simple systemic model which maps the different factors to be recognized in the reasonably rational game of politics without dictators.

Here is the schematic big picture for your consideration:

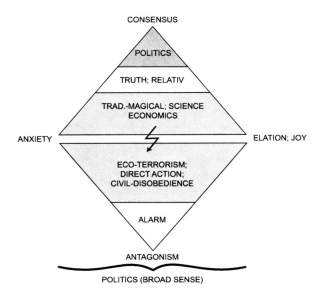

Figure 1

Figure 1 can be read as follows. Our attitudes toward nature are dominated by three different factors: traditional-magical attitude, biological science, and the economics of exploitation—which form the base segment of the upper triangle of the picture. The first is the domain of storytelling, the second of allegedly impartial and objective research, and the third, as I already put it, exploitation and utilization of some stored but unlimited resources. The first is the field of endless anxiety and some elation, the second that of cognitive interests, and the third that of our effort, labor, and success. All three fields are separate but at the same time they need each other. To make the situation worse, these needs are not really mutually and amiably recognizable or without antagonism.

Think about science now. A biologist studies nature and claims some important discoveries, theories, and facts to be his own. He rules the relevant cognitive realm here. But why does he do what he does? What is his ultimate practical goal? Or is his work purely theoretical, disinterested, and devoid of any practical utility. This is hardly the case. Our biologist can join either the traditionalist camp or sell his results to the economical field of business. We all know what happens in the second case. He tells the forest industry how to make the forests grow back after logging. He advises legislators on how many seals can be harvested every year in a given area. He thinks in terms of MSY (Maximum Sustainable Yield). His knowledge is in demand, and both sides benefit from it. All is well (see Ramo pp. 173–81).

But our biologist can join the traditionalist camp as well and, thus, turn his back to business interests and MSY. I mean by traditional-magic attitude many things which still form a continuity from the atavistic magical picture of nature as a field of spirits and gods, all the way to keeping lovable pets who can think and act like their friend-masters. In the Spanish law, some animals have human rights. In early times, a brown bear is not only an animal but also a walking ghost and a spirit who will take revenge against the killer of the bear. The bear is killed but a complicated ritual is mandated if the spirit's hatred is to be avoided. The bear is a trophy but what an anxious one it is. If it is treated wrongly, the hunter and his tribe must suffer. If the rituals are right and correct, the tribe can have their bear meat and products and enjoy their beneficial side. But it all depends.

I do not think it is too much of an exaggeration to say that this magical attitude toward nature is anxiety ridden to the core. The predators threaten our subsistence so they must be killed. They also threaten us humans. Many animals are a nuisance like the dam building beavers that must also go to extinction, or rats. Elks are given for us to eat and enjoy, and there is an unlimited supply of them—another magical attitude—so that we can hunt them forever and any time of the year. At the same time, these creatures are sacred so that their meaning to us is well beyond all practical concerns. In Finland, pike used to be a sacred fish, a fact which is now almost forgotten. In the Kalevala, the great male hero Väinämöinen makes a kind of harp out of a giant pike's jawbone. Suddenly, it appears that they are not out there for us. All this is so disturbing.

The relevant atavistic history here is truly complex, and I cannot even pretend to trace it here. Let me remark about one more thing. The beauty of the sublime nature is an essential modern aspect of this traditional-magical attitude. Many, if not most, people share this view. Nature is both sublime and beautiful, and hence, it should be protected and preserved. Science does not have much to say about this. Many people think that golf courses are wonderfully impressive natural environments. We also like the rolling fields of wheat in Champagne France, as if we were witnessing something else and not an ecological catastrophe in the biological scientific sense. All the anxiety is gone when we admire a colorful sunset on the beach, even if the color comes from the pollution in the atmosphere. When we realize that this is the case, anxiety kicks back again. We do not want to know, and we need not know when we are in the traditionalist mood. A biologist can live in this environment if he is ready to use his scientific knowledge to support, control, and enliven the traditionalist attitudes. The magical side may already be beyond his competence. He may, for instance, reinforce people's fashionable ideas of how to make our pets and other comparable animals look and feel more human-like. Such ideas are in great demand just now. Our pets should have human rights because they are just like us.

When we move one step up from the baseline of the upper triangle, we find two basic attitudes toward the natural theories, traditional-magical, scientific, and economical. These are truth and relativism. Let me explain the meaning of these words here. I mean, by truth and truthful attitude, the insistence on finding and keeping the correct theory of nature, environment, and conservation and so on. This is a kind of epistemic-fundamentalist view which does not accept compromises or conditional statements. On the contrary, it demands a fixed view which can be used as a guideline for decisions, actions, and policies.

It is certain that this can be done; that the essence of natural matters is merely hidden from us, but it is there anyway. He who reaches out will find it. Think of the thylacine again. It was known to the early Tasmanian rural population that the beast was a nasty, bloodthirsty, dangerous, and threatening sheep killing beast. From this it follows that it should be killed any time anywhere. The truth is available to us, and we must act accordingly. The problem is, of course, that the Tasmanians did not have much knowledge of the beast, only myths and hearsay. This does not matter if the context is not scientific, and in many or most real life cases it is not, for instance in politics. Combined with the traditional-magical world view and concept of nature, this is a potent mixture. The folk beliefs and theories easily assume the garb of truth, and action on that basis is then fixed in a rigid and predictable manner. This may be good or bad, it depends. Here is an example: The current urban legend and myth is, of course, that indigenous tribes and forest dwellers are naturally environment friendly and have their correct instinctive preservationist sentiments and sensibilities. Modern farmers are a much more dubious case as they tend to rely on industrial-like methods and clear their fields and forests of harmful and useless natural elements. Perhaps, the indigenous part of the story is just a sentimental myth which consoles our already urbanized and alienated citizens and easies their troubled conscience.

The next factor is relativism, the curse of critical science. Folk ideology needs and requires the truth, but science can only provide fallible knowledge and more or less hazy probabilities. Nothing else is available, so it must be enough. Science has its own peculiar place in environmental debates and decisions. On the one hand, science provides guidelines for policy making, and on the other hand, it maps the limits of what we do not know. In other words, science is supposed to know, but what it actually does is tell us the opposite, what we do not know. As an angler, my own favorite example is the life and behavior of many types of fish. On the U.S. North-East coast, good schools of bluefish emerge every July and August. For a while they are everywhere and provide good sport-fishing and lovely meals for the locals and tourists alike. When the winter comes, they disappear. Not much is known of their behavior and life. I sometimes wonder why. Our seas are vital to us, but we want to gaze at the stars. Astrophysics fascinates people and politicians more than marine life. The key words are atavistic amazement and national prestige. Why think that fishes are that interesting?

Of course, I do not want to argue that science is empty. On the contrary, we know a lot, and all of this (or almost all) is scientific knowledge. That is as it should be. And this is relativism: science maps our fields of cognitive interest pointing out what we know and what we do not know and, at the same time, providing an explanation why this is so. Good science also tells us what the likelihoods are that its theories and other results are valid, or how much weight we can put on them in practical matters. It is all open ended and temporary, yet we make progress in scientific matters. How much progress is there? It is all relative.

On top of the top triangle we have politics, understood in the narrow sense I already sketched above. I once heard Gru Harlem Brundland say in Cambridge, England, in 1991, that environmental policy making is such a simple thing. Scientists provide the right information, and we politicians then make the correct decisions. The picture was that of a boat which is steered by politicians and propelled by science and scientists. A very simple picture indeed it is. I was horrified and anxious afterward when I pondered her message and the attitudes behind it. It sure offered no hope to me. We are all doomed, I said to myself. A similar case shocked me once more. I said to Minister Eva Biaudet in Helsinki at a medical ethics conference some six years ago that decision making in medical ethics is quite difficult because of Adam Smith's invisible hand. What we achieve is seldom what we wanted to achieve, as the world is so unpredictable and capricious. I could and should have also mentioned Hegel's cunning of reason in history, but luckily I did not. Her answer was a very irritated and brief: I do not know what this invisible hand is but your point is obvious nonsense—we politicians say what should be done and then it is done. This time I loved the response. It was so utterly revealing and in a sense naked. Perhaps, politicians really think they are above the laws, rules, and problems of complexity and multi-agent planning in conflict ridden game contexts. Science and politics are supposed to do the work together, and nothing else is needed. The two power hungry and self-satisfied elites do the good work, at least in the dreams of top politicians. Somehow I cannot make myself believe that this is the whole picture.

Let us look at the top triangle once more and search vertically for some key relations between its various elements. What about politics and the traditional-magical view of nature and the natural environment? We must not forget that we are here discussing politics in its narrow sense, which is a democratic effort to live peacefully together. This means that there are political ideologies, voters, their opinions, hopes, and anxieties, opinion polls, and finally elections. Environmental politics is not yet like foreign policy which is largely beyond popular control and democratic decision making. That field tends to be beyond democracy and, therefore, also beyond politics. It has its own elites or dictators (in the special sense sketched above). But most of the social issues, including environmental questions, still belong to democratic decision making. Then the point is obvious: any politician who wants to make the relevant decisions needs the support of her electorate and, perhaps, an even wider power base. She cannot make her decision in a vacuum. Certainly she needs science, but she can also bypass scientific advice. This is because of the essential relativism of scientific knowledge. There are countless examples of this tendency. Global warming may be a fact, but politicians need not care if other considerations are more pressing. Coal mining and burning is not yet diminishing. Cars are still fast and powerful and ever more complicated machines.

It is easy to pay lip service to science. This is done because people not only want a clean environment and preservation of the original nature and wildernesses; they want a good economic life, fun, and many other mutually incompatible things. But when we think of environmental matters and democratic politics, it is clear what the direction of influence is. It mainly, if not exclusively, goes from the traditional-magical view toward politics and not the other way round. If the voters are interested in environmental issues or, perhaps, even alarmed because of the relevant problems (see below), their expectations must be met by politicians, or they are no longer in power. If people want to live in the middle of nature in their nice homes in those ever larger suburbs and commute to work in their own cars, the politicians may take steps in this direction and pretend that this is a reasonably good environmental policy, which it is not. Cars and homes are like sacred objects.

Politicians will say at this point that I am wrong. They say that they make the scientifically and environmentally correct decisions anyway, even if these decisions were unpopular at the time. The key words are education and anticipation. The politician tells and explains the case to the people who first listen and then obey because of the authority of the politicians. They are mandated to do the right thing, and they do it. Then they wait, anticipating their voters to see the good results, learning their lessons and thanking them for them. This is the essential hubris of politics. What actually happens is explained below when I introduce the lower triangle and its antagonistic elements. To make politics work in the right way we need nonpolitical measures. Or in other words, to correct politics in the narrow sense, we need politics in a much wider sense of the term. This wider sense comes close to what is called deliberative democracy, except that it contains some potentially violent elements. I do not see any possibility or even need to avoid them. Perhaps this is extended deliberative democracy where the extension means violence.

But more of that will be said later. Politics always contains an antagonistic element. It is never purely and perfectly consensual or deliberative (see Gastil and Levine 2005).

What about politics in the narrow sense and science? There is mutual interaction here. Science policy is a political process which shapes science, but science also advices politics, as I said above. My conjecture is that politics shapes science more than science shapes politics. We all hope that this would not be the case, but hopes are hopes and wishful thinking is better avoided. I will come back to this issue when I discuss environmental alarms. In that case science is really needed by politics and the elite politicians in power.

Next, the relationship between politics and economics should be mentioned. It is very simple and very complex at the same time, and I cannot pay too much attention to it here. Economic exploitation is the core of modern life when both welfare and security issues are taken into consideration. I want to emphasize both security and welfare, because these set the constraints within which politics (in the narrow sense) must work. Therefore, I would like to think that the two-sided influence between politics and economics is dominated by the latter. For instance, if Finnish agriculture is a national security issue, politics can hardly touch it. In the time of crisis, Finland needs its own crops, and that is that. If the security elite say so, then politics is powerless. Coal as an energy source is a security issue in, say, India, and that is why coal will also be used in the future. If we think of economic exploitation only from the point of view of national affluence and welfare, we cannot understand this relationship correctly. We need to be security realists here and understand that security is not a political question in the narrow sense. The recent WikiLeaks scandal shows extremely well in which ways foreign policy and security issues are outside parliamentary politics.

To summarize this discussion, let me draw the following sketch. The corner > indicates the main direction of influence in what follows.

> Traditional-Magical view > Politics
> Politics > Sciences (e.g., Environmental Science)
> Economics > Politics

The picture is not too flattering to politics and political power. It is true, of course, that the influence is not unidirectional, and thus, a politician is able to say that she has some real power and influence in environmental matters. Yet, it seems that this power is secondary to the informal power of voters and business. It is debatable whether this is good or bad, whether politicians and their elite deserve more power, and weather they could use more power for the advancement of good, whatever that might be. The political élite must serve the traditional-magical view. Science cannot advise politics as much as it would be desirable. Economical issues, especially in the name of national security, are so overpowering that politics cannot do too much to regulate and control it. Security concerns are secrets anyway.

4. Consensus to Antagonism

We now move on toward the deep waters of ecological conscience and its sensibilities. The upper triangle is a consensus triangle, the field of expected peace and cooperation. The lower triangle is the realm of conflict, the breakdown of cooperation, and antagonisms, where free floating anxiety reigns supreme. It is interesting that this clash of two realms, or worlds of thought and ideology, is so clear and evident. The essence of the debate here is not deliberation and peace but their opposites, action, and anxiety. At the same time both triangles are located in the space of politics in the widest sense of the term (see Mouffe 2006).

What I want to argue here is this: politics in the narrow sense is impotent and incapable of controlling the forces which damage and destroy our natural environments. If something can be done, it must be done in a much larger context in which some extra-political and antagonistic elements are utilized. In this sense, we discuss here radical politics, meaning as I said, extra-political and openly antagonistic ideas and methods. I distinguish between three such radical methods: eco-terrorism, direct action, and civil disobedience. This is a well-known group, but it seems to do the analytical work for us here. On the bottom of the lower triangle is the word "alarm." As we shall see, it has its own key role in this framework of thought.

First, let us look into eco-terrorism. The Finnish ecologist and thinker Pentti Linkola, who has a cult following in Finland, says that overpopulation is the key problem today. He has recommended killing people until the sustainable limit number can be reached. Such an idea belongs to the field of terrorism. Linkola actually publicly congratulated Bin Laden after 9/11 for killing so many people so quickly. I suppose Linkola also thought that those people in the Twin Towers were especially useless and also dangerous human beings. Be this as it may, Linkola did not return to this topic again. I am sure the American Embassy gave him a call or called the Finnish prime minister to ensure this. Linkola also hates cats that normally roam free in Finland and kill lots of birds every year. Their owners could not care less—another feature of the traditional-magical view of natural life and creatures. People love their cats when radical Linkola would kill them all. Linkola is of course right.

Eco-terrorism means any extra-political action or program which is designed to hurt people and violate their vital interests regardless of their rights in the name of saving the planet, nature, environment, a given species, or a natural individual (excluding humans). All such action is illegal. We may also find ecologically motivated nihilism and anarchism which seem to be more popular every year. The nihilist element is especially interesting and would warrant a separate study. These people are and want to be truly beyond the rule of law.

Only a fine line distinguishes this from direct action, or *action directe* in French. If eco-rebels and naturalist revolutionaries sneak into a mink farm in the dead of the night and release all the minks, what are they doing? This is not quite terrorism as no human victims are claimed and the harm is minor (except, paradoxically, to the minks), so it must be direct action. We can call these people activists who are engaged in direct action in order to realize their ecological and environmental goals. Some have put glue in the door locks of SUVs. Some like to throw paint on ladies' fur coats. This is direct action. But, if you do not attack the mink coat but you do attack its carrier so that you hurt her, you are not an activist but a terrorist. Bodily harm is the main feature that distinguishes a terrorist from an activist.

The third type is civil disobedience which is simply a form of ecology-oriented serious nonconformism. Its features are well known: an act belongs to the category of civil disobedience if and only if it is illegal (or otherwise somehow truly unacceptable), it is not done in search of personal gain and profit, it is a demonstration, and it is done publicly. If you chain yourself to a tree in order to save it from the axe, you perform an act of civil disobedience. The crucial point here is that you do it publicly, and you are ready to carry the responsibility of your action, for instance, the legal penalty which will follow. The mink farm visitors run away and go hiding. Other people do what they do publicly and surrender to the police.

I do not say this three-fold classification is especially important, mainly because the three types are simply the various forms of the very same idea and ideology. Some do it in a more sophisticated manner; some just break shop windows in demonstrations and fight the police. Their differences are not really very important. But their common features are remarkably important indeed. The political debate and its related actions cannot be understood without reference to them. These features are: anxiety, antagonistic feelings and thought, antidemocracy, radical action, illegality, violence, self-sacrifice, and utopian goals in the name of the planet Earth. In this way the lower triangle represents everything which the top triangle does not. Yet, somehow something good should follow from this clash of triangles. All this may sound quite amazing. I have already shown, however, that not much good can be expected from the upper, consensus-oriented political upper triangle alone, except in the dreams of political elites. So, if we expect a better future, it must come from the larger set of forces.

A key concept here is alarm, as described by Mary Douglas and Aaron Wildawsky. I find this idea quite illuminating. I present my own version of their powerful original view (see Douglas and Wildawsky 1983).

An alarm is a perception which causes deep-seated anxiety in the perceiver, such that he is motivated to start working on it in order to reduce his anxiety. The person is alarmed and hence also motivated. Alarms can be intended or not intended. The tsunami of 2004 was an unintended natural alarm which motivated the building of tsunami warning system on the ocean and dictated changes in the buildings by the sea. The Bhopal chemical factory disaster in India in December 1984 was an unintended technological alarm which necessitated changes in insurance systems and industrial security measures. Wikipedia says: "A leak of methyl isocyanate gas and other chemicals from the plant resulted in the exposure of hundreds of thousands of people. Estimates vary on the death toll. The official immediate death toll was 2,259 and the government of Madhya Pradesh has confirmed a total of 3,787 deaths related to the gas release." (Accessed 03-01-11).

Both events were alarming and charged with anxiety. In Chennai, India, a ceremony took place on the sixth anniversary of the great tsunami of 2004 in which local women poured hundreds of liters of milk into the sea to appease it and to remember the victims of the wave. All over the coast line around Chennai you can see little informal and unofficial memorials to the victims. All this feels good and does its work to reduce the anxiety still associated with the flood.

Then there are intentional alarms which range from communications of personal worries to grand scale designer alarms. Cats eat songbirds complains my elderly neighbor. Greenpeace harasses Japanese whaling ships out on the ocean in stormy weather, and we see it all on TV at home. These events are worlds apart, but they still mean the same. How terrible, I think, something must be done. I start looking around and try to find an outlet for my anger and anxiety. After an alarm sounds and it is heard, the ball starts rolling. It may be a juggernaut, but it can, as well, be something small and modest. Today we have a big alarm going against global warning. Some thirty years ago, the idea of an environmental catastrophe was associated with a nuclear holocaust and nuclear winter. We do not care anymore. And who cares about what was done when hydropower was built after the war in Northern Finland or the Tasmanian Western Highlands. If I want to see an ecocatastrophe, I go to Kemijoki in northern Finland. It used to be a grand salmon river. Now it is a big ugly ditch which produces cheap electricity, but who cares anymore?

Alarms are partial, partisan, and capricious things which tend to come and go according to some strange logic depending on an even stranger ecofashions. All this is somehow related to what Ulrich Beck has called a risk society (Beck 1992). We are superbly conscious of risks these days, and our natural environment is just full of them. The related anxiety must be managed and controlled somehow. What else could we do? Our love and admiration of nature is changing into the panic and fear of its mismanagement and destruction.

Douglas's and Wildawsky's idea is that the state tries to manage the alarm-induced fear and trembling. The success of this task is important to the state and its political elite mainly because the lower triangle must be controlled. If it is not, politics, in the narrow sense, does not work. The situation threatens to get out of hand which is a politically impossible situation. From the point of view of the lower triangle, the situation is ambiguous. It wants to disturb politics in order to initiate a real change, but who wants to go too far? Too much disturbance means chaos, and this is bad indeed. Only econihilists may wish this to happen and some more extreme anarchists too. But the mainstream responsible rebels cannot think so. Wildawsky says that the political elite use science to put oil on the waves. What they say is this: we are presently funding several key research projects which will in due course produce results which allow us to control this alarming situation. You citizens just wait. The situation is not really that bad, but it has been exaggerated. So, we take it seriously. First, we try some makeshift measures, and then our science solves it for good. Cancer risk research is a good example. We also study the problems of alternative energy sources. In the meanwhile, we recommend that you burn wood and turf (our countryside voters like the idea anyway). It is smoky but in many ways a good choice.

When the bottom triangle alarms and causes all that risk-related anxiety, who are called to manage it? The state and its elite politicians get the honor. This is somehow embarrassing. First, we say politics do not work and then, after the alarm has sounded, we put our trust in it. It is easy to see how uncomfortable and even inconsistent the situation is. Why would the politics suddenly start working for a good cause? And can we trust the alarms to be relevant, to the point, systematic, and to cover enough ground? What I mean is to ask whether the lower triangle warns us about all the relevant environmental and ecological dangers all the time, and does not stop alarming too easily, requires valid solutions, and monitors their continued efficiency. This is hardly possible, and you see why if you think of the nature of the lower triangle and its actors from the TV hungry Greenpeace to police fighting and window breaking econihilists. It is not a system and organized process—it is simply an idea of alarms and their implementation. Someone should hear the alarm and someone else should take systematic action. This is the work for politics, but it does not require much insight to realize that the state and its political elite cannot do it. A benevolent and well-informed ecodictator would do it, but we do not have one and, perhaps, we do not even want to have one. However, my message is this: we necessarily need the lower triangle, even if this is not really good news.

5. The Indian Way Is Our Way

Mr. Dunu Roy, the Director of the NGO, Hazards Centre in Delhi, India, writes in his column "Polluted India Needs an Erin Brockovich" to *Sunday Times of India* (Chennai, January 2, 2011) as follows:

> Thus, the [Central Pollution Control Board] applied [comprehensive environmental pollution index] calculations to about 88 industrial clusters and then declared 43 of them to be "critically polluted." For example, Ankleshwar and Vapi in Gujarat scored a high of 88.5 and 88.09, Chandrapur in Maharashtra stood at 83.88, Ludhiana in Punjab at 81.66, the Najafgarh drain in Delhi scoring a lower 79.54, and Kanpur in Uttar Pradesh only 78.09. The Maharashtra and Gujarat areas are essentially high industrial concentrations, Kanpur is polluted primarily by tanneries, the Najafgarh drain carries a cocktail of domestic, industrial, and agricultural effluents, and Punjab is sandwiched in between with indiscriminate use of pesticides and fertilizers.

What is done officially and politically to control the situation? Roy continues:

> Why have areas been declared as critically polluted through mathematical calculations, merely in order to collect more data in order to re-do the mathematics? . . . Which is why the action plan are basically an instrument for collecting the health data of an exposed (but unsuspecting) population and relating it to sampled pollutant data, in order that a more viable relationship can be established between cause and effect.

Roy's point is the familiar one, namely, the situation is not corrected as yet when more data must be collected. All this sounds too familiar to the reader of Douglas and Wildawsky. The situation is hopefully under cognitive control, but only under cognitive, not practical control. Anyway, as it seems, the Indian authorities worry about the situation. But how much weight can be put on these good intentions? Not much as it seems. The political elite and its relevant authorities seem to tolerate the situation for their own reasons.

What does Roy himself recommend? He refers to a Hollywood movie which tells a semi-fictional story of a beautiful working class woman who notices that there are too many cases of cancer in the town and successfully blames the local industries. Sensationally she wins. Fiction is fiction and a basis of populist dreams. To Roy, movies are the American reality, not violent rebellion. His modest point seems to be, however, this: a loud alarm is needed which leads to concrete action which cleans a bit of the Indian environment. I do not think that he wants to mention any conservationist issues.

Some ten years ago I took a taxi with my friend and philosophy colleague from Helsinki Mr. Juha Savolainen in Mumbai from our hotel to the airport. It was dark and the taxi drove slowly through the street full of cars, mopeds, shops, and cows. Everything was grey with dust and smelly with wood smoke, shit, and garbage. The place was overcrowded, dirty, messy, and certainly very impressive. We looked at it all and said to each other: this is not the past, this is our future, and this is how we will all live in the end. That was a very convincing thought and in a strange sense also consoling, not anxious at all. You get the same impression when you first live in Tokyo and then visit New York City. Tokyo is all glass and chrome, big, bright, modern, and impressive in every sense. It is one gleaming machine of a city. Then, there is New York. Manhattan is small, cramped, and dirty. Buildings are old and grey with sidewalks covered from plaster falling off the walls. It is an old and tired city just like London and ready to go the Mumbai route. Here is the question: should we care? And here we can apply the same intuitions which back our answers to ecological and environmental issues.

The question is, should we fight against the environmental degradation or should we quietly accept the idea of descending to the level of semi-rural India? So we care? In other words, what are our limits of caring? It is not the question of how resilient to change is your natural environment but how resilient we are. The Indian people do not have toilets in the countryside, but at the first dawn women go to the beach, bushes, or riverside to a secluded place to relieve themselves. Then the men follow. The women do it again the next morning, not before. Men urinate and defecate, more or less, publicly whenever needed. It is very natural and also culturally very restricted. In Finland, every house and hut must soon have their own waste water cleaning plant at the cost of 5000–10,000 Euros. In India, cows are everywhere, so people can enjoy wildlife. Beaches are good to swim during the dry season. The wet season is more dubious when rains flush the cities clean of all that accumulated shit into the sea. At the same time India has a nuclear weapons stockpile and an active program to put man on the moon in a couple of years' time. They even have their war in the north and an active terrorist threat. They are a high-tech nation and democracy which has its full and complete institutional infrastructure.

The question of whether we fight against chaos and degradation or let go may seem to be an impossible and even an unmentionable problem. It cannot even be asked seriously. But the problem is there anyway, and it is a real ideological and philosophical aporia (see Rescher 2009). Often, people take an answer to it to be intuitively given and even necessary and go directly to technical problems. How to save the last thylacines, flying squirrels, whales, and old trees and forests in Lapland and Tasmania? We want clean sea sides and swimming water, and we are afraid of air pollution. We want it all. We also want a high standard of living, conspicuous consumption, high-tech medical care, and cheap flights for everyone to Bangkok. We want animals we can hunt and fish to catch. We want to see seals in the Lake Saimaa in Eastern Finland. We want to pretend that all is well and nothing will change in nature anymore. We have seen enough change already. At least we want some clean pockets of natural life and an environment where life is as it has always been, undisturbed by the humans and their accursed technology. At least we should create some natural museums which we call a wilderness and original nature. We now have beavers in Finland after they were hunted to extinction one hundred years ago. These beavers were imported from Canada. They are not our beavers anymore, but they are so similar that we can pretend otherwise. Beavers live in Finland. The Tasmanian thylacines do not live anymore, and if they did live they would live on some isolated island where they never roamed before, in their own little museum and zoo-park. They would sort of pretend that they are there, just like our beavers do.

The question is an existentialist-philosophical one: if we fight a losing battle in the rich West, and our democratic politics cannot save us, why fight at all? Perhaps we care too much and tolerate too little, or we do it all in a wrong order? There are too many people on the planet already, there are too many conflicting interests, and too many battles have been lost to make it all more than the work of Sisyphus. Yet, as I fully realize, such an answer is nothing but an impossible outrage. We must fight, and we must get India involved. And they should not falsify their environmental statistics. They must be honest and fight the impending catastrophe with integrity and full commitment like we do. But do we? I have argued in this paper that the situation is not far from political chaos. Does that matter? No, it does not, most emphatically. (After one has said that much, perhaps one should add that at least the elite can save their own good relationship to the original nature.)

We do have (do we?) two competing major ideologies, human-centered and nature-centered. The near Eastern religions, like Christianity, are strongly human centered. Some indigenous religions, totemistic belief systems included, may be nature centered in the traditional-magical way. The economical view of nature is human centered even if nature plays a major role in it. Then we have the emerging scientific nature-centered view led by biology, ecology, and what can be called the environmental sciences. When they study fish, they work in their own natural field, but when they try to fly to the moon, the scientists' work is truly human centered. As we can see, even the idea of nature-centered thought is divided into different factions and camps. The human-centered view can be religious or nonreligious, which makes a difference: teaching is different, elites are different, and rewards and punishments are different. The nature-centered view has its own factions. Nevertheless, it is hard to see that these two major views could agree on all those major ecological questions and issues. The divide here is deep and clear cut. Perhaps they can agree on one thing though. This is the answer to the question, should we fight the environmental doom or not. Both sides may well say yes, because they can add to it their favorite caveat: yes, nature should be saved for the good of us human beings, or yes, nature should be saved for the good of the natural environment itself. Philosophically, the question is about instrumental and intrinsic values. The natural environment may be valuable in itself or as a means to human good. The agreement is largely illusory of course, but at least both parties agree that the fighting strategy is the correct one. To surrender to the destructive tendencies and to tolerate them is out of the question.

But is it really? To me this is the deepest possible question in the present context. If we cannot win, if all our victories are mere window dressing, if we cannot agree what methods to use or what the goals are, if the rich and poor countries go in different directions, if the dominant elites play their own hidden power games and have their secret agendas, if science, whose methods not one ordinary person can understand, assumes an imperialist rule, if traditional-magical views refuse to die, if the population of the Earth still grows and grows, why fight? A controlled descent to the level of India is still an alternative. Everyone should visit India at least once to force their eyes open. Or perhaps the traveler still hopes that these people would clean up the mess, collect their garbage, kill the cows and dogs, and buy four-stroke motors with exhaust gas cleaning apparatus, and stop honking the horns.

We are heading in a bad direction, I agree, and our elites have decided to fight back. We and I, as members of the faceless mass of humanity, have agreed to follow to the bitter end, and we have pledged our support to the political process which leads us there, peacefully, in the name of consensus. But we also have our eco-terrorists and nihilists who attack ladies wearing mink coats and slash the tires of SUVs. We need them because consensus is not enough. The political process does not take its own promises seriously enough, and they dismiss too many alarms. But if you ask, affirmatively, the question of whether we should fight or let go, you should also agree that the way to go is not consensual but essentially contested and deeply antagonist. You must be ready to fight, use violence, and in the end be, perhaps, ready to die defending your best values. Do we really want this? One can hardly answer affirmatively. We need politics, science, benevolent direct action, and environmental activism. But how is such a meta-consensus to be created?

My picture of two opposing triangles (above) is covered by the idea of politics in the general sense of the term. So politics should be in the key role in all that, but when it should create a consensus out of so many conflicting and in the end antagonistic elements, we have an interesting future ahead of us. What will happen next? Who can say? Can we save the natural environment? The question, as such, does not make much sense. Therefore, this is the most interesting and exciting future development of the idea of saving the natural environment. Can we expect that this key notion will get its fixed meaning in the future? Or should we expect that the meaning disappears altogether. This is a semantic battle.

I do not want to be a pessimist or defeatist. Let us do what can be done. The environmental issues are also concerned with life and death. Let us all try to do our best just like the elites of the rich countries do. We can show good examples to the developing countries in their efforts to reach the welfare level of ours without endangering the natural environment or their security. We may enjoy the fight.

Let us get our priorities right first. Should we think like Doctor Albert Schweitzer who wondered whether he could inject his African patients with penicillin which kills bacteria? Bacteria are as valuable living things as anything else. Should we worry about beavers and thylacines? Or should we think like they think with Dunu Roy that human survival is the first or even the only consideration? That is a moot political challenge for many of us.

References

Airaksinen, T., 2000, Isolation and Radicalization in Democracy, in *New Ethics—New Society, Acta Philosophica Fennica* 65: 9–26.

Beck, U., 1992, *Risk Society: Towards a New Modernity*, Sage, London.

Douglas, M. & Wildawsky, A., 1983, *Risk and Culture: An Essay on the Selection of Technological and Environmental Issues*, University of California Press, Berkeley, CA.

Gastil, J. & Levine, P. (eds.), 2005, *The Deliberative Democracy Handbook: Strategies for Effective Civic Engagement in the Twenty-First Century*, Wiley, New York.

Mouffe, Ch., 2006, *The Return of the Political*, Verso, London.

Owen, D., 2003, *Thylacine: The Tragic Story of the Tasmanian Tiger*, Allen and Unwin, Sydney.

Rescher, N., 2009, *Aporetics*, University of Pittsburgh Press, Pittsburgh, PA.

Ramo, J.C., 2009, *The Age of the Unthinkable*, Little, Brown and Company, New York.

A Designing Human Society:
A Chance or a Utopia?

Wojciech W. Gasparski
Kozminski University,
Warsaw,
Poland

A "Designing Human Society" Revisited

Over a quarter of a century ago, I presented a paper "A Designing Human Society: A Chance or a Utopia?" at the Design Policy Conference organized by the Design Research Society, London, 1982. Later the contribution was published in my collection (Gasparski 1984). The Global Forum "Managing as Designing in the Area of Massive Innovation" organized by Case Western Reserve University, June 2–5, 2009, was a good opportunity to revisit the idea expressed in my paper following the proverb that *novelty is an old stuff forgotten long enough.*

The Global Forum for Business as an Agent of World Benefit was established by the United Nations Global Compact, Academy of Management, and Case Western Reserve University. In relation to the track of "Management-As-Designing" the Call for Papers & Workshops of the 2009 Forum reads the following question: "What can management learn from the field of design and how might the design attitude help us turn social and global issues into bona fide business opportunities?"

In response to the question, I decided to punctuate the main issues raised in my paper and offer it for the virtual forum with the following summary: "[. . .] it seems that raising the idea of "designing society" could be a chance to overcome threats and to slow their rate of increase. [. . .] Acceptance of the proposed policy requires making rather difficult decisions on a global scale, decisions concerning three main problems:

- First, the fallacious axiom of unlimited resources available to man must be rejected with all its consequences.
- Second, the survival of mankind should be regarded as a supreme goal for all acting members of the species *Homo sapiens*, living now and in the future.
- Third, solving (in the epistemological sense) practical problems has to be regarded as the only method for making decisions concerning the practical behavior of man.

Design conceived as conceptual preparation of action (change) should become a way of solving practical problems; the society accepting this way and acting according to it is suggested to be called the designing society. The evidence of the importance of design, design approach, and design methodology is presented in Collen and Gasparski (1995), Gasparski (1987), Gasparski and Airaksinen (2007), and Schön (1992)."

The organizers of the Global Forum appreciated my contribution with the following letter:

Dear Wojciech,
    We want to express our sincere appreciation for your contribution to the Global Forum for Business as an Agent of World Benefit: Manage by Designing in an "Era of Massive Innovation," which was held June 2 through June 5, 2009, in Cleveland, Ohio.
    Thank you for the time, thought, and preparation that you put into creating a virtual presentation and paper for the Global Forum. Your work—"A 'Designing Human Society' Revisited"—made an important contribution to the dialogue that was taking place at the on-site event and on the Virtual Forum.
    Many thanks for your vision and presence and for the energy and excitement you brought to the Global Forum. On behalf of the Global Forum team and our partners, please know that it was a special privilege for all of us to connect, to collaborate, and to learn with you.
    The Global Forum brought together more than 500 leaders in the fields of design, management and sustainable value creation to explore humanity's ability to create positive change in the world through the power and promise of design. The ideas that were shared through keynotes, panel discussions, paper sessions, workshops, and presentations—combined with the creativity and engagement of all forum participants—generated initiatives that will change the field of management. The Virtual Forum (www.bawbglobalforum.ning.com) is now allowing for the participation of hundreds more from all over the world and is the platform where the conversations and initiatives of the Global Forum will continue to grow.

It was a pleasure to work with you and we look forward to welcoming you at the next Global Forum for Business as an Agent of World Benefit.

Sincerely,

David L. Cooperrider
Facilitator of the Global Forum for BAWB
Fairmount Minerals Professor of Social Entrepreneurship
Faculty Director of the Fowler Center for Sustainable Value
Weatherhead School of Management
Case Western Reserve University

Recently *The Journal of Corporate Citizenship* published a special issue on Managing by Design (2010) as "one direct offspring" of the Second Global Forum, as it was pointed out in the Editorial to the issue (Cooperrider and Fry 2010, p. 3). The issue is devoted to the design-inspired corporate citizenship.

* * * * *

1. Introduction

There comes a time in the history of a discipline, a moment in the life of a scientist, when from the perspective of the results achieved in research, in view of accepted and rejected hypotheses, it is desired to take a look at the surrounding world. The will to offer the world something more than a cool explanation appears. A desire emerges to serve society with ideas. The concern is then not with knowledge created by the discipline, but with trying to transform this knowledge and perhaps something more—intuition? beliefs? hopes? faith?—into wisdom.

I am not sure whether design science has yet reached the point in its development when most of its contributors are beginning to devote themselves to serving society. It seems that it has not. Personally—perhaps since I am of praxiological provenience—I feel the need to take up a subject that I regard as extremely important to society. It is the prospect of creating a society that is capable of reasonably solving problems arising from the practical situations of the people who are creating the society. This paper—which in the light of what had been said above is very personal—is intended as an outline of the idea of a designing human society.

It seems to me that implementing the idea of a designing society could be a chance, and may be the last chance (though such warnings have been misused so many times), to overcome threats and to slow their rate of increase. Perhaps I am overestimating the value of this idea—it is a sin of inventors to stick to their ideas. It is no more than another unreasonable utopia? Maybe it is, but even so, the extent of dangers threatening mankind is now so great that to find ways to minimize them is worth taking a look even as far as into the world of fantasy. And if the utopia would have an inspiring power only in part, then confined to realizable dimensions of the real world it could play a useful role indicating directions in which we ought to proceed. With this belief in mind, I dare to present publically the idea of a designing human society.

A conference devoted to design policy[1] is a dream of a forum for presenting the idea of a designing society, since it is an appeal for such a policy in regard to design that would be perceived as a policy of solving practical problems.

Acceptance of the proposed policy requires making rather difficult decisions on a global scale, decisions concerning three main problems. First, the fallacious axiom of unlimited resources available to man must be rejected with all its consequences. Second, the survival of mankind should be regarded as a supreme goal for all acting members of the species Homo sapiens, living now and in the future. Third, solving (in the epistemological sense) practical problems has to be regarded as the only method for making decisions concerning the practical behavior of man. Design conceived as conceptual preparation of actions (Gasparski 1979) should become a way of solving practical problems; the society accepting this way and acting according to it is what I will call designing society.

In the following the three subjects mentioned above are discussed in sequence.

2. The Fallacious Assumption

For forty thousand years (and some claim for sixty thousand), human behavior has been based, and it remains to be based, on the assumption that resources available to man are unlimited. This assumption underlies all human activities exerted hitherto. It is a manifestation of homocentrism, derived probably from the same belief upon which the ancient geocentrism was founded. Here is the proud Man, the proud inhabitant of the Earth who regards his planet as the center of the cosmos and himself as the center of the universe. Meanwhile, several centuries ago as a result of the contribution of the Polish astronomer Copernicus, it appeared that the Earth is only a planet in the solar system, and is neither the central nor is it the most important. This truth has been coming at minds slowly and at hearts even more slowly, and not without resistance. As evidence, the rehabilitation of Galileo by the church may serve; this did not come about until quite recently. If the acknowledgment of the fallacy of the second homocentric belief should come after a period of similar duration, then, I am afraid, it would never have acquired general acceptance. Mankind would have ceased to exist much earlier.

In ages when human knowledge was restricted both in volume and in degree of accessibility, the assumption mentioned above could remain unquestioned. There seemed to be such an abundance of resources that they appeared infinite. If there were shortages of same resources, they were replaced by other newly discovered ones. This led to the belief that the shortages were only local and temporary, which after a period of shorter or longer duration, turned out to be true. It seemed to confirm the belief, which, of course, was erroneous.

It might be thought that, in a time when both the quantity of facts and their common accessibility (if not knowledge) had shaken the assumption of unlimited resources, holding such a belief would be embarrassing. Where on the earth! Although the more enlightened members at our society regard our conduct as a manifestation of ordinary ignorance or extraordinary premeditation, we still cling to that belief, exactly as our ancestors clung to Ptolomaeus' geocentricity.

Despite numerous reports, prepared by many experts, and among them the famous Club of Rome Report, we still are proceeding as if the assumption of unlimited resources has never been in doubt. Are we distrusting the experts or are we manifesting our selfishness? But even if we give no credence to the experts' warnings, facts (and it is said that gentlemen do not quarrel about facts) such as the food crisis and the energy crisis should carry conviction. And we admit, certainly, that crises have occurred in the past, do happen now, and will in the future, but the art of life consist in arranging things so that the crises affect "them" not "us." "Them" means those who are living now but in other houses, on other streets, at other geographical latitudes, and, preferably, on other continents. However, "them" might also mean future generations, even those who may be living on the same streets or in the same houses. From the biological point of view, we know that in this case "them" means our descendants but so distant in time that there are no emotional links between "them" and "us," exactly as there are no such links between them far-away in space and "us."

Now, I dare to argue that regardless of the reasons causing us to cling with maniacal obstinacy (I am sorry if anyone feels offended) to the old assumption; the basic truth is that the whole of human culture rests on this assumption. Mankind has been creating the culture for tens of thousands of years. It cannot be regarded as a world external to us, since we ourselves belong to it and we are creating our own environment (Esser 1976). The culture is the entirety of our products, as well as we ourselves who are the main products of the artificialized world we have created. It consists of our knowledge, our science, the technology based on our science, our art, and our beliefs. Abandoning the assumption of unlimited resources means neither replacing one paradigm with another nor changing one epoch with another. All epochs have been based, implicitly or explicitly, on this assumption. All epochs have deduced from it assertions about the limitlessness of human potentialities playing up the homocentric minds.

To agree that the assumption is wrong and to reject it means taking leave of the culture created heretofore and regarding the history of mankind up to the present as a closed chapter. That is the reason it is so difficult. To reconcile with such ideas means to begin a new and diametrically different period in the history of mankind. In order to do so, we must free ourselves from the ties of the homocentric worldview. Although it may be painful, we must muster all our courage, just as those who decide on a painful operation for the sake of life.

To all appearances, what caused the art of life to consist in dividing people into "them" and "us" is not selfishness. They, who are remote both in space and in time, will succeed—this was a belief of our ancestors and it remains to be (with few exceptions) our belief. After all, enjoying the availability of unlimited resources, as promised by the axiom on which our belief and the belief of our ancestors has been based, they, the remote in space and in time, will succeed. If it happened that someone, say, John Smith, failed, then his brother, his neighbor, his son would succeed. Such was the way of thinking of John Smith's ancestors, and such is the core of his own beliefs. This way of thinking was prevalent in his family as he was growing up, and it was strengthened in school and by the social environment in which he lives. Ideologies have provided articulations of this way of thinking. The lives of John Smith, of his grandparents and great-grandparents has supplied arguments which—in his judgment have confirmed this belief. When he lacks arguments, he begins reasoning. He is so strong in his belief that he fails to distinguish between one thing and another. It is true that John Smith has not always succeeded in appropriating new supplies of resources, and sacrifices have been required. But after all, in his name, Columbuses discovered new continents and new lands, and acquired new sources of supply. The cost of discoveries and sacrifices turned out to be small against the benefits derived by successive generations. Who now is worried about Indians slaughtered by the invaders? And so, generation after generation, the conviction that the axiom is true has been successively strengthened, and it has been transformed in our social consciousness into a rule.

Yet, all propositions concerned with empirical reality, especially if the propositions are assumptions, can be regarded in the best case only as hypothetical utterances. Thus they are no more than suppositions. And—let me repeat an elementary assertion—even if a hypothesis has been confirmed in n cases, no matter how great n is, the n+1st case contradicting the hypothesis will falsify it once and for all. But what would we do if such n+1st case should follow after millennia of confirmation? In such a case, epistemology will not rise to speak, so, we ourselves ought to do it.

3. Revel or Survive?

"Revel or survive?" is a key question directed to every one of us—to the species of Homo sapiens as a whole. Without exaggeration it can be said that the future of mankind depends on the answer to this question. Everyone must answer and it ought to be done in the very near future since time is here a decisive factor. Lack of an answer is an answer too: it is a disguised decision against survival. Taking a position implicitly against survival (since there will be, probably, only a few explicit answers of this kind) would create a most serious threat to the existence of mankind. It is more dangerous than any technological means of mass extinction, since the use of such means requires decisions which depend on the decision-makers, their beliefs and views concerning the future of our species. If such decisions should have to be made by individuals declaring themselves against survival, woe betide mankind.

The future of mankind, however, might also be endangered when declaring ourselves in favor of survival if we remain adherent to dividing mankind into "us" and "them." Survival would then be conceived as survival of "us" at the expense of "them," a posture held often before in history. Such a possibility was indicated by Grzegorczyk (1979) and represents a totally fallacious view. There is no possibility for selective survival now as history does not repeat itself. Confining the struggle for survival to one group would cause counteractions in other groups.

Considering the power of contemporary means of struggle, this could lead only to one end—to an annihilation of all groups. And it does not depend on whether the group intending to survive at the expense of the other groups does it by monopolizing the access to resources or by deciding on extermination of the other groups.

In order to avoid extermination, collective action is required. This condition is necessary although not sufficient. Since a collective declaration against extinction is not yet a declaration in favor of survival of the species, it could limit us to one or two generations only. Collective declaration against extinction has two alternatives: future survival of the species, or present reveling of the living. However, attaining a non-ambiguous, authentic answer to this question is still more difficult. As in the case presented above, there will be few explicit answers in favor of reveling. Regardless of declarations, what can actually be expected is behavior that continues the present way of life, i.e. behavior which is objectively directed against survival. It could be exemplified by the reaction to the energy crisis. Is there a single house in which people have refrained from turning on a light bulb because of the energy crisis? Despite awareness of the world energy crisis, consumption of energy has been constantly increasing.

Therefore, it may happen that survival will be endangered by the gap between words and actions, by declarations in favor of survival without a change in behavior. As in the case of struggle, such behavior given the present circumstances, could provide an illusion of future success. Continuation of the present behavior, considering the growth of the world's population, would bring imminent disaster.[2]

If we consider seriously and with responsibility the problem of survival, not as a problem of survival of "us" at the expense of "them," of "our" generation at the expense of future generations, but as a problem concerning the survival of the species, then we should collectively initiate the work of creating a new culture. In deciding to form a new culture, and taking into account the scarcity of resources, we should organize contemporary life in such a way that whatever is done should not threaten any future generation in any future time. The success of such an undertaking will depend on joint action by all *for* the good of all.

4. Designing for Survival

If we decide on rejecting the axiom of unlimited resources and accepting survival, then the way of practical acting becomes most important. It is meant as a way of shaping reality which makes sure that the species will survive or, at least, as a way consistent with this supreme goal. Simultaneously, it must be a way ensuring that the intermediate states would provide sufficient satisfaction. Therefore, just as Francis Bacon who centuries ago thought it necessary to give the *Organum* a new shape and created the famous *Novum Organum*, so we have to create a new *Discourse on Method*, a sui generis *Novum Cartesianum*.

Here it may be asked whether the present way of acting, if adapted to attaining survival of the species, will ensure success. The answer is short—alas not. But the explanation of why not is longer.

It has been found that as far back as our (historical) memory can reach there has been a dichotomy dividing aspects of our activities into rational and emotional ones. The dichotomy is not a conceptual one derived from Aristotle but a factual one. For the sake of convenience, the sides of this dichotomy will here be called the "brain side" and the "heart side" respectively. On the brain side we have created science, on the heart side, art, each the highly specialized externalization of our rationalities or of our emotions respectively. Both sciences and art support cognition and are serving each in its own way, as the articulation of our perception of the world and of ourselves as part of it. Both science and art are concerned with intersubjective communication of their results and the deepening of individual perceptions. For this purpose, suitable "toolboxes" have been developed. In their extremely sophisticated form these "toolboxes," and science and art which are using them, appear as pure abstractions. It is believed, predominantly, that such a form testifies to the maturity of either. Within both science and art, applied science and applied art have been created at the pole opposite abstraction. Their most materialized representations are called technology and industrial design respectively.

Governed by macroparadigms of science on the one hand, and by macroparadigms of art on the other, methodologically similar spectra of methods and techniques have been developed. They are concerned with the rational and the emotional aspects of cognitive activities respectively. Among these methods are those that serve experienced critics as a basis for relating the results of activities which claim to belong to either, to science or to art. A familiarity with these methods is a basis for assessing the competence of the creators and for educating candidates. In the course of the development of either realm, i.e., science and art, views and beliefs have been changing and, within either macroparadigm, paradigms have been formed specific to particular divisions of science and art respectively. However, science as a whole and art as a whole are governed by rules specific to them.

However, neither the brain nor the heart are the only organs, and they do not work independently. Similarly, the two realms, science and art, do not encompass all activities. What remains is the practice of biological existence and of individual and social life. This third developing realm, was and remains to be an area of conquest for invaders from the other two worlds. The invasions result in artificializing the third world according to the rules of science or the rules of art. In this world, in the world of practice, we have oases of scientific correctness, and oases of artistic beauty. Encyclopedias, albums, and numerous accessional publications contain a lot of worked out exemplifications that—*pars pro toto*—should serve as demonstrations of the other two worlds' potentialities.

Aside from these oases, the Third World serves the two other worlds as a trash pile. Since scientific or artistic failures belong neither to science nor to art, the Third World is regarded as the only place beyond the other two worlds which is suitable for dumping that trash.

Finally, that third world also contains remnants of the nonartificialized nature. The Third World is the world of our lives, and also of private lives of those among us who spend their work hours in the other two worlds. It appears that for the Third World, the world of practice, the methods used in the other two worlds are inadequate. The third world requires methods specific to it, special "toolboxes," and a particular praxiological macroparadigm.

The Third World, i.e., the world of practice, is not a world which belongs to the scientific, artistic, and technological disciplines derived from the first two realms. The Third World is the world of practical situations of people, a world of facts and of values according to which the facts are assessed. The number of practical situations are enormous, and they influence each other to form a complex conglomeration. In simple, or apparently simple cases, and in cases of emergency, we act according to our ability. We prefer to act rather than do nothing because it is more important or more urgent or we are self-confident perhaps. In other cases, i.e., in cases of adequate time or great risk—in short, in cases of greater complexity—we prefer to prepare our actions. Among numerous kinds of such preparation of actions, I wish to distinguish one which consists of: developing patterns of actions, evaluating the patterns by considering various values which serve as a basis for appraisal, and selecting the pattern of highest relevance. Such a procedure, being in its essence a conceptual preparation of actions, is design.

However, what matters here is not simply an extension of all divisions of the kind of design known from past experience. The activities carried on by the majority of designers are derivatives of applied science or applied art. Such design, called traditional design, emphasizes the mastery of the workshop, but the scientific or artistic workshop. Traditional design can be regarded as a direct consequence of Cartesian methods inculcated in all of us by school and university education.

However, for design of the type we are discussing here, sometimes called modern design,[3] in which we see a way toward solving problems of survival, synthesis is required. The Third World—the world of practice of present and future generations of life—needs synthesis in order to deal in a harmonious way with practical situations. If survival is intended, we must cope with such situations in a manner which prevents disturbing the equilibrium of the conglomeration smoothly from one state of equilibrium to another. Let us repeat once more that what matters is the equilibrium of a conglomeration of practical situations (which if disturbed must be restored) rather than the equilibrium of particular, isolated situations.

Traditional design is concerned with particular situations which are fractional parts isolated from the conglomeration to form "design objects" given to the designer in advance for developing. The "design objects" are objects-desires specified by real customers, or objects-attractions for inciting designers in potential buyers. Traditional design is solution-oriented and regards a solution as better if it is more innovative. This approach follows from neglecting realizability, conceived as a holistic concept, and has its origins in the assumption, here put into doubt, of the limitlessness of resources.

Modern design, on the contrary, would be concerned with the "object of design" regarded as a pair of a given practical situation of a concrete subject (the core) and the context, i.e., the remaining world (the complement). This kind of design is situation-oriented and is meant to cope with the pair (core-complement) of practical situations. In design conceived in this way what belongs to the core part in one particular case is a fraction of the complement in other cases, and vice versa. And this is the reason why a synthesis is necessary, a synthesis which forms a basis for the postulated "unity of divided design" and for introducing the multi-dimensional relevance criterion (Gasparski 1979).

The reason for regarding design as a way of solving practical problems is the growing importance of meta-actions[4] under conditions characterized by the complexity of the conglomeration of practical situations. If it is desired to cope with practical situations genuinely, basing ourselves on the best knowledge and acting according to the best will (within limits determined by the requirement of maximization of conditions for survival and minimization of individual dissatisfaction), then it must be preceded by design solving the problems arising from these situations. The term "practical problem" is understood here as a description of a practical situation, as its mapping in a language which serves to formulate designs coping with these situations.

Design as a way of solving practical problems creates possibilities for overcoming our human inclination toward unreasonable or simply irrational[5] behavior.[6] This way necessitates an externalization of the problem-solving process which, in effect is becoming transparent. Design as such a way enforces explicit presentation of all pros and cons of particular candidate solutions thus providing evidence to support the selected solution. Design (planning, etc.) carried on in such a way ensures that actions thus conceptually prepared will be more relevant than actions not preceded by such preparation. We are stipulating the creation—centering on design understood in this way—of a paradigm and of "toolboxes" for the Third World—the world of practice. Design studies which have been developing for some time should help to attain this goal. They have been conducted hitherto in a way which has caused uncertainty of their status. They have been serving engineering disciplines and traditional design related to these disciplines and have been regarded as their "poor relatives." Undertaking the task of creating a paradigm for the world of practice would ensure proper status to design studies. It will provide design with designological knowledge, "toolboxes" (methods and techniques) for acting in conditions of complexity and for creating syntheses. In such a way, prerequisites could be created for transforming a society, which is acting in the name of individual desires and according to related irrationalities into a society designing reasonably and solving its problems in a way which ensures the survival of the human species.

I have discussed here only the prerequisites, since that is all that can be done by those who are aware of the dangers. The remainder depends on whether the other members of human society understand the seriousness of the present situation or neglect the dangers with premeditation. They, the remaining members of society, acting consciously or unconsciously, in fact, take the responsibility for the fate of the human species.

Notes

1. Contribution to the Design Policy Conference, London, 1982, organized by the Design Research Society, UK; published also in the collection: W. Gasparski, 1984, Understanding Design: The Praxiological-Systemic Perspective, Intersystems Publication, Seaside CA, pp. 194–209.

2. "Poverty is often accompanied by degradation to the immediate living environment. Moreover, persistence of mass poverty engrail harmful long-term consequences for the environment in general, and for the natural resource base in particular. The problem of achieving sustainable satisfaction of basic needs therefore has been becoming progressively more intractable. This is evidenced, for example, by desertification resulting from excessive use of firewood and fuel, and soil erosion resulting from intensive land use as rapidly increasing population try more and more desperately to live on it. Paradoxically, however, in terms of availability of essential natural resources, technology, and knowledge, the world has the capacity to achieve sustainable satisfaction of basic human needs for mankind as a whole"—which is not the same as unlimitedness of available resources—WG. "And while there are more impediments in the path of realizing this objective, the most important are perhaps lack of political commitment and absence of appropriate institutional mechanisms for cooperation and planning, for rapid assessment of potentialities as well as the risks and dangers" (Tolba 1978; Mr. Tolba was the Executive Director of the United Nations Environment Program).

3. Giving the design put forward here the name "modern" would not be objectionable provided that we remember that "novelty is an old stuff forgotten long enough," since Vitruvius appealed two millennia ago for understanding design in a way close to presented here.

4. "Perhaps we should distinguish actions and meta-actions in tie field of praxiology/decision theory, as we distinguish language and meta-language in the field of logic. Meta-actions would then be actions which would process other actions. If we were to agree to this proposition, then decision nuking (and also design, planning, etc. incorporating decision making in its scope) would be counted as neta-actions." (Gasparski 1981a).

5. "[. . .] the average man's attitude towards clear thinking is by no means merely passive; it is actively though unconsciously against clear-thinking. And the reason for this (. . .) is that he dislikes most of its immediate results. It is the active and unconscious resistance which renders abortive most appeals for sound sense and good judgment. It is not much good telling people to think rationally if, in their heart of hearts, they would rather not. It is even less good if they are entirely unaware of the possibility that irrational urges may exist. (. . .) during the greater parts of our lives, we, as human beings, tend to prefer unreason to reason and that, the more important the question, the greater is the tendency. (. . .) there is no reason whatsoever for feeling either worried by or ashamed of this tendency, provided we are aware of its dangers and of its peculiar temptations (Crawshay-Williwns 1947).

6. "In our work on volitional problems in addiction we have found that people often made a decision to quite their addictive behavior, but they rapidly find themselves in difficulties. Difficulties arise due to strong emotions which in turn are related to various wishes or desires. Under the influence of emotional stress, people reason in a twisted manner and many easily come up with low-quality reasoning and decisions that do not reflect their own best knowledge and they fail in their intention." (Sjöberg 1979).

References

Collen, A. & Gasparski, W.W., 1995, *Design and Systems: General Application of Methodology*, Transaction, New Brunswick, London.

Cooperrider, D. & Fry, R., 2010, Editorial: Design-inspired Corporate Citizenship, *The Journal of Corporate Citizenship*, Issue 37 Managing by Design, Spring, 3–5.

Crawshay-Williwns, R., 1947, *The Comfort of Unreason: The Study of Motives Behind Irrational Thought.* Kegan Paul, Tench, Trubner & Co., Ltd., London.

Esser, A.H., 1976, Design for Man–Environment Relations, in: A. Rapoport (ed.), *The Mutual Interaction of People and Their Built Environment.* Mouton, The Hague.

Gasparski, W.W., 1979, Praxiological—Systemic Approach to Design Studies, *Design Studies* 1 (2): 101–06.

———, 1981a, Decision Making and Action, *Praxiology Yearbook* 2: 123–42.

———, 1981b, Humanistic View on Design, in: R. Jacques and J. Powell (eds.), *Design: Accidence Retched Practice,* IPC.

———, 1984, *Understanding Design: The Praxiological-Systemic Perspective,* Intersystems Publications, Seaside, CA.

———, 1987, On Praxiology of Preparatory Actions, *International Journal of General Systems* 13: 345–53.

Gasparski, W.W. & Airaksinen, T. (eds.), 2007, *Praxiology and the Philosophy of Technology,* Transaction, New Brunswick, London.

Grzegorczyk, A., 1979, Filozofia czasu proby, (Philosophy for the Times of Trial, in Polish), *Editions du Dialogue,* Societe d'Editions Internationales, Paris.

Sjöberg, L, 1979, Contribution to the Working Group on Decision Making and Action, *Praxiology Yearbook* 2: 123–42.

Schön, D.A., 1992, The Crisis of Professional Knowledge and the Pursuit of an Epistemology of Practice, in: J.L. Auspitz, W.W. Gasparski et al. (eds.), *Praxiologies and the Philosophy of Economics,* Transaction, New Brunswick, London, pp. 163–86.

Tolba, M., 1978, Foreword, in: J. McHale & M.C. McHale (eds.), *Basie Human Needs: A Framework for Action,* Transaction Books, New Brunswick, NJ.

On the Role of Values in the World of Technology

Ladislav Tondl
Institute of Philosophy
Academy of Science
Prague
Czech Republic

1. Traditional Views of the World of Technology

Under the term "the world of technology" we traditionally understand those sets of human constructs, artifacts or everything that is artificial, that involved human creativity, skills or ability to do something, to change or suitably adjust something to meet specific purposes, to recreate something or, on the contrary, to prevent something from being made, thus protecting man. The Greek word "techné," originally denoting an ability to do, create, or provide something, was used to designate new objects, states, or situations man is capable of providing and putting together through his activities, of creating, thanks to his skills and knowledge. Another Greek word "logos" is added in some languages to accentuate the share and significance of knowledge application in such human works. A salient feature of those new man-created entities is that they form a new reality, a new state or situation fashioned by their human authors. They may differ from entities and events resulting from processes untouched by man, hence those created by nature. Technical entities and processes are, therefore, "artificial." They constitute a reality created by knowledge and skills or, as we most frequently put it, they are "artifacts." Another major trait is that man creates those works of his intentionally, purposefully, pinning on them specific expectations or, to put it differently, linking them with what is intended, wanted and anticipated, and, thus, associated with man's important property, called "intentionality." Therefore, human creativity and the activities related with it and with its substantial features figure among the specific qualities marking members of the human race, accompanying its development and fates throughout all the stages of its history.

While considering the areas or types of activities connected with production in the realm of artifacts and its latest forms, i.e., the world of technology, we can hardly ignore two main classes of such actions: the groups of artistic activities and, hence, the sphere of the arts, and the groups of handicraft skills associated with the production of useful and currently needed or desirable artifacts, including the necessary means, tools, and equipment. Both groups were noted for vital involvement of knowledge and of the carriers of such knowledge as well as the dissemination, acquisition, and naturally also development of this knowledge. Their significant trait lay in the connection of two types of knowledge, namely the "knowledge that" and the "knowledge and skills how," i.e., on the one hand, knowledge of materials, qualities, details and functions of what should be made, and, on the other hand, the knowledge of suitable procedures, methods, sequence and organization of activities involving the origin and creation of an artifact. Both in the sphere of artistic pursuits and in the fields of most handicrafts it was deemed important for a young apprentice or novice in those trades to acquire desirable knowledge and skills as well as required and recognized focus of his work by training underskilled experts and specialists in the given sphere of creative activity, not only at home but also in well-known centers abroad. As a result, specific groupings, workplaces, workshops or otherwise characterized centers of recognized creativity had been established since the Middle Ages, which proved to be traditional stepping grounds for schools of arts and handicrafts. That was also why Czech creative artists in the nineteenth century longed to have a chance of working, at least for some time, in Paris or elsewhere in France. While looking back at the time of my own youth, when readymade clothes were mostly a rarity, I remember that my first suit to be worn in higher grades of my grammar school was made by a tailor who was known as a "Viennese tailor" because during his apprenticeship he acquired his knowledge and skills in the capital city of the then monarchy. This only serves to demonstrate that already in the past a prominent role in the focus of creative activities was played by specific "models" of recognized, required, and appreciated better alternatives of desirable results and goals. A seminal role of such models is that, during the development of the realm of artifacts and thus the world of technology, we tend to seek not only new and more perfect solutions to our problems, but that we also imitate, copy the already made, successful and well-received or appreciated solutions, that the function of models is reasserted, being then promptly disseminated in keeping with the forms of information transfer used in a given period. In fact, this principle of applying the most advanced models and knowledge of creative activity in the sphere of arts and crafts grew to be an impetus for the establishment of one of the first highly qualified centers of technical education, i.e., the "National Conservatoire of Arts and Crafts" (Conservatoire national des arts et métiers) in Paris, set up by a decree of the Convent, the supreme body of the revolutionary French Republic on October 10, 1794 (or 19 Vendémiaire an III) at the suggestion of a member of this authority, abbot Gregoire. This new center was designed to create, provide, and display sets of machines, models, tools, projects, descriptions, and books from all walks of arts and crafts (today we would say from all the branches of technology), originals of new instruments and machinery, and newly invented or improved machines, to provide a way of explaining their design, application, and distribution for the benefit of the Republic.

In actual fact, this method of integrating developments in arts and crafts—together with accentuating the significance of specific knowledge, its generation, dissemination, and qualified mastering—highlights the relations and contexts of those spheres that create sets of such entities and their wholes, shaping the actual world of technology, doing so always within a specific development stage, within specific historic and social contexts. But this does not involve only sets of created works, their integral wholes and structures, instruments and machinery as well as their models, but also arrays of knowledge, methods or procedures associated with those entities and with their follow-up types of activities in which the appropriate knowledge is applied. Using only a very sketchy approach, we can distinguish in those spheres three main areas whose components are described by the mutually integrating attribute "technical":

- The field of technical thinking which also encompasses the sphere of decision-making and assessment, communication and expression or depiction, cognitive procedures and processes of verification and authentication;

- The field of technical activities also covering activities of intellectual nature, primarily in the sense of designing, fashioning verbal or other models of designed works and their functions, actions of material nature, finding and creating parts or components of planned technical artifacts or processes, activities ensuring their interconnection, concatenation, and thus creation of results;
- The area of technical artifacts, i.e., man-created units providing for the generation of planned functions, technical procedures, which—in connection with follow-up changes—lead to intended or designed goals.

When reviewing the interrelations existing in the technical world, its development patterns and sources, stimulation or initiative for its genesis, application and utilization of new components of that world, we have to realize that we spend most of our lives—from the cradle to the grave—in this world, growing up in it, learning and educating ourselves, working and resting in it, experiencing our joys and sorrows, and forms of our human self-fulfillment. We make use of elements of the world of technology, i.e., different tools, devices and human products, constructs or works, for the attainment of our defined goals, desirable changes, to implement specific plans and requirements, to meet—or facilitate the process of meeting—specific needs etc. Such situations, when we want to achieve an objective, effect a required or intended change or—on the contrary—prevent something that we take for a harmful or otherwise negative phenomenon, may be generally characterized as "problem situations." In keeping with the views expounded by K. R. Popper, we may, therefore, claim that life—or at least sum total of its major and decisive sections—offers a solution to problems or situations described as problem situations. It is natural that this particular characteristic of goal-directed activities in which man utilizes his knowledge, experience, and skills, but also the means and hence artifacts created or adopted for the self-same purposes, may be expressed by other conceptual patterns. One of such patterns is human effort to reduce the rate of uncertainty or indeterminateness within the immediate—and frequently—wider environment, thus reducing the level of entropy, as these natural endeavors and ambitions were described by N. Wiener. Another kind of description of goal-directed actions, characterized in this fashion, is the fact that the subject of such action is motivated by one's intention or—as sometimes termed—by one's intentionality, attaching to this activity an element of expectation, and hence an aspiration for a transition from the actual status to a desirable state, which the subject perceives as better, more profitable, less risky, etc. This also means that participating in the decision-making process on the startup of such an activity are—in addition to knowledge—also specific values, value-related attitudes or efforts to ensure that the prepared, considered, or anticipated result should display a higher level, a higher quality. Decision-making on the creation of new, planned and required entities, states or processes as elements of a preferred, newly built or future world, which we can describe by the attribute "teleological," i.e., desirable, anticipated, or connected with a target orientation, must always be based on known or available sources or capacities, on known or verifiable and practicable procedures and methods.

2. Elements of the Technical World as Means for Problem Solving

We all know states and situations we are dissatisfied with, which we would like to change or eschew, whenever possible and permissible. In such cases, we usually consider a given problem or problem situation, endeavors and intentions aimed at finding a solution to the problem situation in hand. The actual array of significant means, ways, and proceedings designed to solve problem situations includes the process of finding, devising, and fashioning the wherewithal, devices, and procedures that enable solution of a problem situation or—to put it in the terminology recommended by N. Wiener—to create facilities, works, or an arrangement of objects and processes capable of safeguarding such objectives, i.e., reducing the level of indeterminateness of objects and processes around us. A technical construct or technical process is capable of creating, albeit always solely in a limited and temporary fashion, what N. Wiener called "islands with the opposite direction of the development of entropic level."

The terms "problem" and the adjective derived therefrom—"problematic" thus express a complex of characteristic entities, their states or functions, which are the result of not only attained knowledge, but also an outcome of evaluation. Such a complex of characteristics includes primarily the following facts:

- We tend to perceive entities, their states or situations as problematic if they cause dissatisfaction, a critical attitude or demand for a better, more perfect or suitable form of analogous entity, state, or situation.
- Problem or a problem situation always represent issues confronting specific subjects. Hence they are always problems of somebody who has other views, assumes different value attitudes than those who do not regard—or have not hitherto regarded—the given entity or states as problematic.

- Problem recognition is a product of alternative reasoning, of a realization that a given state or a particular situation may be different, that besides the given situation perceived—previously and partly also presently—as common, there may also exist possible situations that are better, more perfect, more suitable.
- Identification, confirmation, and recognition of a given situation as problematic also constitutes the reason for or justification of the demand for a change, innovation of the hitherto used means or procedures. This may also turn out to be an impetus for seeking a new cognitive activity, for searching for new goals or a new content of some actions.
- Recognition of a specific state, situation, or hitherto used means and conditions as better, more suitable or profitable than those we take or will start to take as problematic is often associated with specific prognostic dimensions, especially with expectations of more suitable means, procedures, and conditions, and primarily with their better, more perfect and suitable results.

The subject of solving problems and problem situations usually results from an integration of two substantial human activities, namely cognitive activities, their intents, programs and target orientations on the one hand, and a specific assessment generally involving a comparison of the actual and the possible, the hitherto used and the future, the anticipated or the projected on the other. After all, the history of the human race is marked by the fact that—in addition to his actual world—man has always created images or ideas of those states or situations that can be called "possible worlds." Of great importance for directing human goals, intentions, and interrelated programs have been those "possible worlds" that were more perfect, suitable, acceptable, and not only as new elements, situations, and means gradually inserted into the actual world, but also as global images or ideas of a desirable, preferable and thus "teleological world." Images and visions of teleological worlds are invariably images or ideas created by specific subjects or groups or communities of those subjects. That is also why various teleological worlds existed not only in different historic and development stages; it is within a single stage that we come to identify several different teleological worlds existing concurrently, and thus also what is perceived by different subjects as desirable, more perfect or favorable. One of the major causes of conflict among people, and especially among their groups and large communities, are very often differences between their value attitudes, and hence differences between their own teleological worlds. This applies, for instance, to situations where some states are taken and accepted by some people or groups as problematic, while being regarded by others as "normal" or "standard."

As a result, some problem situations may easily degenerate into crisis or conflict situations. This is amply illustrated by a number of well-known cases from history as well as the present era, when an originally small and especially insignificant difference in value attitudes easily caused a conflict and a serious crisis and, therefore, when a problem situation simply flared up into a crisis situation or a conflict in general.

3. Technical Artifacts as More Perfect Alternatives to the Means Used

Progress in human activities is justifiably associated with procedures and interconnected changes that are generally described as transitory from imitation of what has been hitherto used to an innovation, involving innovations of target orientations as well as innovations of the applicable means. These procedures, too, are always connected with the knowledge of other alternative goals and means, with a comparison and evaluation of those alternatives. Already in the distant past, the primeval man knew that he could not break a hard object with his fist, that he had to use a stone. Later he found out that striking an object with a stone is more efficient if the stone is fixed onto a wooden handle, and turned into a hammer. The overall efficiency of a strike could be still enhanced when a stone hammer was replaced by the metal base of an axe whose handle could be anchored still more firmly, and an axe already had a cutting edge. This elementary example alone demonstrates the important preconditions of technical changes that include the following procedures:

- Thinking in alternatives
- Using different types of knowledge when reviewing and evaluating alternatives
- Selecting the best or most suitable practicable alternatives
- Confirming the chosen alternatives in practical terms

Thinking in alternatives is not limited solely to alternatives themselves or to alternatives understood in isolation. A typical as well as highly significant feature of various and divergent alternatives of technical artifacts is an array of their characteristics that may be described as forming their space of feasibility, i.e., sets of conditions for their creation, acquisition, and practical application, but also a sum total of the results or impacts of such applications. When assessing different alternative solutions of a problem situation—besides evaluating their space of feasibility—of no less importance is reviewing their possible risks or rather their adverse impacts, complete with the probability or—to put it otherwise—anticipation of such negative impacts.

Thinking in alternatives may proceed successfully, if and when accompanied by several major preconditions that may be briefly spelt out as follows:

- Conviction that a better and more perfect alternative solution of the identified problem situation is, indeed, feasible
- Decision to find, seek out, or create a better and more perfect alternative
- Courage to verify, confirm, and apply the found or created alternative after registering its positive results

These and other analogous prerequisites are bound up with what comprises the field of competence of the subject of thinking and decision-making on the topic of a given problem situation, on the genesis of stimulating initiatives in selecting goals and means for solving that particular situation. These and other demands placed on the sphere of application of technical facilities and procedures in different walks of human activities and the problems and calls for a change originating therein point to the significance of integrating different types of knowledge and, invariably, also knowledge and values, including ethical values and especially those involving the principles and requirements of responsibility. These also cover responsibility for potential and future risks, namely in parallel to the origin of new spheres of other changes, new demands and also new and originally absolutely unthought-of and previously unknown problem areas. This may be demonstrated by changes and contexts brought into existence by some major technical innovations, such as the mass introduction and application of motor vehicles in transport, and the large-scale and wide-ranging applications of information technologies. It is only natural that designers of the first automobiles, which resembled more coaches than anything else, even though the vehicles were driven by a thermal engine, did not and even could not suspect and anticipate what immense civilizational changes would be introduced by the mass development of automobile transport. As part of these changes, it was vital to build vast and costly transport networks, equipped with a system of petrol stations geared to meet the energy needs of cars, a network of other means necessary for providing other services; there has been an increase not only in accessibility of remote places and the population's mobility in general, there has been an upsurge in energy needs and the needs for a number of other services. This has been accompanied by a growing risk of road accidents and other dangers; as a result, many countries now register more road and traffic deaths than deaths caused by some feared diseases.

No less wide-ranging are arrays of other technical, social, and cultural changes brought about by the upswing in information technologies, which are crucial for most areas of human activities, including administrative, managerial, health-care, and many other areas. Risks of undesirable manipulations with human fates, their one-sided influence, and other dangers also tend to arise in the above spheres of application.

Working with alternatives involves all the characteristic aspects of the technical world. In technical thinking, learning and search for new knowledge and procedures, this particular task requires greater attention and care to be devoted to innovation trends and orientations, and, consequently, to paths that do not rule out unsuccessful attempts and mistakes. It is also in these particular aspects that thinking and related decision-making in the technical disciplines lay greater claims on creativity, differing from mere imitations, from repeating well-tested patterns or procedures. We have already singled out the relationship between technical training and technical cultivation, including the higher stages of technical education, on the one hand and the field of handicrafts and craftsmanship on the other. At the same time, one can hardly overlook the substantial differences between an artisan's way of thinking and technical reasoning and, in actual fact, specific engineering thinking, which should always involve variant reasoning, comparing possible options or alternative procedures of problem-solving, assessing their quality, their other perspectives, impacts, and risks in time.

4. Structure of Technical Artifacts and Values

We tend to take technical works and technical artifacts for constructs of a goal-directed activity engaging acquired, verified, and confirmed knowledge and facilitating solution of specific problems, implementation, and provision of specific goals, fulfillment of certain intentions or expectations. Of equal importance is also the fact that technical artifacts, whether specific entities, new objects, or new processes, make up a new whole comprising components of partial elements or constituents that enable the generation of new, necessary, or desirable properties or functions that separated elements or partial components have not yet been able to secure. As a result, these constitute structures that may be specified by pointing to several major aspects including the following in particular:

- Their characteristic function, target orientation or their pragmatic function relating to questions of the type: "what for," "for what purpose," "for whom," "what or who is to benefit" etc.

- Type or character of connection, concatenation of the individual elements or parts, preconditions for an adequate concatenation and efficient concatenability and thus links, relations or connections analogous to what we call syntax
- Rules for permissible and functional concatenation, complete with rules on how, what, with, and under which conditions is such a concatenation of elements feasible, hence "the knowledge how."

When considering, at a closer range, the above-mentioned or rather other major traits of concatenation which, in its entirety, leads to the creation of a human goal-directed work, to generating what we call "artificial," man-made, we find out that these particular aspects apply to any man's constructs, not only technical but also cultural and artistic works, to artifacts man creates with specific intentions, expectations of a desirable benefit, entertainment or other kinds of gratification in mind. These remarks pose questions pertaining to differences and connections of the elements of the technical world, and the field of artifacts in the arts and culture.

All the given aspects of human works, artifacts of technical nature as well as those we regard as works of culture and art (while these general characteristics of artifacts definitely are not disjunctive, they penetrate one another or they can participate in the overall concept of the resultant work to a varying degree) are closely connected with a value attitude, with selection or choice from different options, and with possibilities of implementation or application. It is not only a proponent or initiator of a new technical solution, designer or person implementing such a solution but also an artist, commissioner, and author of a work of art who invariably keeps in mind the target orientation of the future artifact, a set of viewpoints, criteria, and acknowledged models. Nothing can be changed in this by the well-known fact that such value attitudes may be commissioned externally and are—or at least should be—respected, or are inserted into the structures of anticipated, designed, or realized artifacts by subjects of the appropriate decision-making and creative activities. Seen in these contexts, one cannot ignore the prominent role played by recognized criteria and related models. Furthermore, the sphere of this recognition may be differently distributed and enforced, may be limited only to qualified groups of experts, to power or ideologically motivated groups, may be distributed through the media, the educational system and also, unfortunately, by monopoly power or ideology. Quite undoubtedly, the significant role played by the existing sets and systems of criteria as well as criteria and models, sometimes recognized and enforced only by monopoly power, deserves special attention. This role is then associated with the genesis and development of different phases or the so-called epoch styles, their development patterns and sequence, and, furthermore, it is often connected with stimulation effects, and sometimes also with influences giving rise to specific restrictions or even obstacles to new initiatives or inventions.

It is also definitely not recommended to underestimate the major aspect of a designed, projected, or already prepared artifact, and thus also what is its substantiation, justification, and also explication of its previously accepted selection. This also involves the task of winning over wider public support, or rather specific advertisement or promotion of the chosen procedures, goals, and orientations. When, after World War II, the ruling monopoly power in this country sought to gain support for the introduction of its dirigiste political and especially economic planning system, it launched advertising campaigns in which initially two-year and later five-year plans were promoted as measures "serving the people" or as "steps to welfare." (These "steps to welfare," with accents on enormous raw material and energy requirements only increased not only technological and economic delay and differences in living standards, but also exacerbated the existing load on the environment.) However, these remarks on the pragmatic function and namely on the possibility of abusing proper substantiation and justification of a designed or prepared artifact in no way challenge the rights of each and every citizen to be informed "why," "for whose benefit," and "in whose interest" are the planned or already prepared measures aimed at creating such technical and artistic artifacts made, and why they had to be realized in "public interest" and, consequently, why they had to be paid by the funds provided by the taxpayer.

The issues of concatenation and concatenability of different elements, materials, means of connection and forms of permissible linkage are not only a well-known subject of linguistic communication, meaningfulness of different possible verbal collocations, or a problem of contemporary logic, linguistics, and those areas where certain analogies to syntax are expected to appear, but also a topic of harmony or—as we often describe—compatibility of different entities, materials, processes, or events. The range of prerequisites, conditions as well as obstacles to concatenation, merging or other forms of ensuring compatibility, and also acceptable interplay of different entities, events, or processes is wide-ranging and diverse, encompassing, as it does, various substances, energy or information processes, as exemplified, for instance, by different material, chemical as well as biological procedures, as is well-known and confirmed, including the cases of verified and ordered restrictions in the field of building materials, pharmaceuticals, transplantations or various "implants," forms of the "artificial," etc. There exist notorious dangers posed by the use of some plastics and man-made materials used for the production of child toys. These last examples show in particular that the decisive criteria of contacts, connections, and other threats are associated with man, his health, age, with the conditions, surroundings and environment of his activities, and life in general. But this does not and should not concern solely health threats perceived in the physical sense. No less serious and often, in the first instances, imperceptible and thus frequently underestimated are threats posed to man's value-related and especially moral profile, namely during uncontrolled applications of information technologies and the mass media. The mass media in particular are in a position significantly to affect and also shape value attitudes, selection, and preferences applied therein in decision-making and when choosing from possible and especially offered alternatives; in fact, aggressive and obtrusive advertising surrounds today's man virtually at every step. Together with those influences and stimulating instructions that modify human steps and chosen directions and goals during their journey through the actual world, the mass media also fashion images of possible, often only illusory or fictitious worlds, while obfuscating other states or situations or at least distracting people's attention. However, in the annals of the development of human culture and civilization, there have always been people, social groups, or different ideological trends that tried to abuse such opportunities for shaping the views and attitudes of people, created models for such attitudes, albeit in the positive sense. But, in addition to the advantages and benefits of what we usually term the "information society," the danger of abuses and misapplications of information technologies also generates a vast area of "information risks" (as pointed out by Jean Jacques Salomon).

5. Can Technical and Artistic Artifacts be Distinguished Unequivocally?

A superficial look at the world of technology and its components and the sphere of artistic creativity may confirm great differences among tools, machinery, and automata on the one hand, and works of literary and fine arts, literature, music and other works of human creativity on the other. When considering the structure of artifacts regarded as technical ones, and works and constructs noted primarily for their artistic, aesthetic, and other analogous values, we find a lot of correspondence or at least analogy, as has already been emphasized in this study. It primarily holds that in all those spheres of human creativity, specific knowledge, including the type of knowledge termed the "knowledge how," comes into play. This kind of knowledge must be acquired, mastered, learnt, traditionally in specific knowledge centers, originally under the tutelage of carriers of such knowledge, in specific workshops, later schools and other facilities of the educational system. It is evident that mastering knowledge or generating knowledge itself involves some specific prerequisites, gift, talent, etc. Practical utilization of knowledge is also associated with specific intents, objectives, and previously defined tasks, wishes or needs, while their actual source may be external; but it may be the outcome of one's own initiatives. A created work and its impacts are usually connected with a body of expectations, with certain values that need not always be met or fully satisfied. The factors affecting the creation of artifacts of different nature and associated with various functions often include motifs of emotional nature, life experience or factors rather less rational. This also means that technical as well as artistic artifacts may have their own "reverse face," may be connected with possible risks or adverse effects.

An author of a work of art, too, makes use of actions, procedures, or methods that have the nature of concatenation, interconnection, creation of links among partial elements, parts, sequences of events and processes that make up new structures, and thus also bear the nature of emergence of new properties and functions. During this process, such an author has to respect or at least take into consideration certain rules that may be explicitly formulated or at least accepted, that may be matter-of-course or generally accepted and assumed. Genesis of a work of art also has its specific goals, missions, intentions, and impacts, bringing its own gratification, which may prove to be only satisfaction "for some" or even solely "for the author himself." Even works of art may—always to a varying degree and in varying contexts—pose risks. They also have different forms of reception, recognition, appreciation that usually is not and cannot be an appreciation by all and sundry, but mostly only by some.

The characteristics given above indicate that no sharp dividing line may be found between technical and artistic artifacts. On the contrary, there are many common features and identical or analogous dimensions, while inclusion of an artifact into a group defined and delineated in a specific fashion depends primarily on pragmatic aspects, notably on the forms and purposes of practical utilization, on value attitudes of the actual users. (This author is in a position to illustrate this by his personal memory: During a visit to Sicily in the 1960s, he saw in a small village on the southern edge of the island a capital of a Corinthian column that served the locals as a base for a large vessel containing soaked laundry). A typical feature of many technical as well as artistic artifacts is that these works have not only their own technical but also artistic dimensions, that they can be perceived as beautiful, appealing, or admirable, but that they still are technical works, notably works created thanks to great technical skills and knowledge. A case in point is an area that synthesizes and, in actual fact, is obliged to integrate both technical and aesthetic viewpoints, while also respecting the criteria associated with what we describe as the human dimensions, human friendliness, and attractiveness—the field of architecture.

Of considerable significance for the reception, recognition, and appreciation and for the motivation of applications and usage of technical as well as artistic artifacts in a given sphere of activity are the acknowledged and applied criteria of choice and decision-making, and hence also the values embodied in those criteria. This generally involves a plurality of different criteria and, consequently, sets or systems of criteria. A considerable risk in those contexts may be posed by overestimating some criteria, usually by subjects of decision-making and evaluation who exaggerate the actual importance of their own value attitudes or justify this particular significance by their own attitudes to monopoly power or to monopoly ideology (as we remember such attitudes from this country's totalitarian past and their still applied throwbacks). While emphasizing the positive role of the plurality of different criteria and values, this definitely does not mean any equality of used or usable criteria. We have and know many examples from the recent and more distant past when only some particular criteria were unilaterally accentuated and overestimated, mostly to advance somebody's own interests or benefits enforced by the powerful or the wealthy. That is why there is a vital need for introducing adequate controls of the system of criteria, specifications, and determination of their rate of relevance vis-à-vis the goals and purposes of a given decision-making or evaluating role, of the completeness of such a set in solving the task in hand, of securing an adequate level of selected experts and qualified participants in the decision-making process. It, therefore, comes as no surprise that neglecting such requirements, not respecting adequate criteria and levels of decision-making criteria often proves to be a breeding ground for such negative phenomena and losses as well as thefts of public resources, which are traditionally described by terms such as "corruption," "embezzlement" or, as we have come to know in this country of late, by the term "asset-stripping." This especially calls for the application of technical works and specific technical solutions in projects and programs involving large-scale investment operations subsidized from public funds and—in an analogous sense—engagement of artistic artifacts in similar events, for instance in case of honors awarded to officials of monopoly power.

6. New Areas of the Technical World and Values

A widespread perception of the sphere of the technical world focuses attention on those technical artifacts that expand and multiply man's capacities and skills, the human potential, power, and means of feasibility in production, while providing for materials and energy, in transportation and travel over great distances, and similar projects. In such areas, the dominating position is assumed by mechanics and in it forces, not only human ones, but also the power of draught animals, the power of water and wind, later power provided by thermal machines. Seen in this light, it is no accident that the very substance of technical artifacts was seen in forming some kind of a "plinth" for man (M. Heidegger, Gestell). This is, however, a very one-sided view of the sphere of technical artifacts, which—at present—definitely do not constitute only human constructs based on the knowledge of mechanics. A typical trait of today's technical world and its related branches is their interpenetration and overlapping into many other areas and thematic fields, into the sphere of information and communication processes, into processes typical for the animate nature, into the spheres of intellectual and cultural creativity, into the field of thinking and reasoning, into the vast distances, but also—as seen from the human perspective—into the minute dimensions of the micro world. In these contexts, such interpenetration of technology into other, formerly absolutely inaccessible spheres is sometimes termed as "converging technology." As a rule, the names of those newly developing technologies feature various specifying prefixes such as, for instance, info-, bio-, neuro-, nano-, etc.

The theme of converging technologies, a subject actually introduced by the pioneers of the "artificial elements of the world," "artificial worlds," and especially "artificial intelligence," has thus opened up new relations, dependencies and new forms of knowledge integration. This subject has also managed to give rise to new and vast spaces for the necessary application of values, criteria of different nature and diverse value attitudes. True to say, the contemporary society has been gradually getting used to the expansion of those components of the present-day world bearing the attribute "artificial" (their importance had been justifiably predicted already by H. Simon), whose representatives are "artificial kidney," "pacemaker," "artificial insemination," and other technical interventions, namely transplants of organs from other live organisms, but the diversity of value attitudes for some problem situations has survived to this day. However, it principally holds that the sphere of differences and sometimes contradictions between the two worlds, namely the "actual world" (Ist-Stand) and the "desirable or required world" (Soll-Stand), has considerably broadened. The importance and significance of this field have been strengthened primarily thanks to the results attained by biotechnology, genetics, and genetic information, genetically modified species, possibilities of cloning live creatures, complete with the prospects and possible interventions in those areas, which have been traditionally associated with world-view and especially with theological principles. This has reinforced the thinking that in those spheres it is possible—when proceeding in an acceptable fashion—to move solely within the framework of limits whose specification involves the use of criteria determined by values, limits of permissible or at least tolerable feasibility. Consequently, participating in the delineation of those limits are diverse values, especially those associated with health care considerations, with the task of maintaining sustainable developments and the environment, with a broadly based spectrum of human values and rights, and last but not least with ethical values. (Indeed, the roles and nature as well as significance of such limits and related restrictions were accentuated by an international conference entitled "Restriction of Freedom in Education and Science," held in 1991 by the Royal Academy of Canada. At a recommendation of Professor O. Wichterle, the author of this study attended that particular conference, presenting his paper on the assessment of the impacts of technology and on nonrespecting these subjects in the communist countries.)

Some areas of new technologies sometimes have to grapple with problems involving specific limits that cannot be transcended due to different reasons, justified not only by knowledge but also through accepted and acknowledged values. Various types of such boundaries may be distinguished, and the following forms of limits may be specified:

- Limits of human possibilities and feasibility
- Limits given by potential risks, dangers or serious threats
- Limits associated with the irreversibility of some procedures
- Limits of justified ethical viewpoints or values

Human possibilities are given by the capacities of the human senses, for example, to perceive or register, to see and hear normally, etc. It is natural that contemporary measuring and other registering devices are in a position to broaden in numerous directions the actual space of what is empirically attainable, even though such an extension is always finite. Similarly, it is now possible to put further away the limits of various risks and physical and mental limitations by using the present-day technical means, as corroborated by the procedures and protective aids used in space research. Some types of boundaries, primarily the limits delineated by the available means of what is actually feasible, may be justified by a complex of values of diverse nature and provenance. This applies, for instance, to the limits associated with the irreversibility of some processes. A traditional example illustrating such contexts, i.e., the liquidation of woodlands in Dalmatia, in Cyprus, or on some Greek islands due to the urgent need of wood for ship-building and thus an irreversible intervention into our environment, may be repeated on many occasions even at present, although usually in other areas. Still, it may bring much more drastic impacts.

A serious value-related issue is the thematic field connected with the application of new and previously unknown technologies, which is described as "exaggeration," as transcending or breaking the limits of what was formerly or hitherto traditionally practicable, which is characterized by the English term "enhancement." This involves, for example, the process of overstepping human possibilities to perceive, see, hear, register, and consequently to decide, choose adequate goals and means. Coming close to this topic is the possibility of representing action in possible worlds, in what are called virtual worlds, in applications of contemporary technologies, including the field of information technologies. As a matter of record, man has always been moving in different "possible worlds," and this particular subject has always been man's important specific trait, as confirmed by his past and current artifacts, particularly in the field of both verbal expression and in various spheres of culture. The present-day world of technology has greatly expanded and enriched those areas. Man's another major specific feature is that he has always associated the images, events, and acts in the "possible worlds" with the themes of values, the issues of good and evil, and the subject of ethics.

That is why it is quite understandable and justifiable that contemporary discussions on the direction of the current technology, primarily debates on converging technologies, on the theme of "enhancement" and risks existing in the sphere of "possible worlds" also include reflections on the necessary role of ethics, ethical values, consciousness, and especially of individual and social responsibility, including responsibility for the future generations of the human race.

References

Tondl, L., 2007, Problem Areas of the Philosophy of Technology, in: W. Gasparski & T. Airaksinen (eds.), *Praxiology and the Philosophy of Technology*, pp. 25–44.
Tondl L., 2009, *Člověk ve světě technologie (in Czech) (Man in the World of Technology)*, Bor Publishers, Plzeň.

On Green Economics: The Limits of Our Instrumental Valuations of Nature

Gabriel Malenfant
Faculty of History and Philosophy
School of Humanities
University of Iceland

1. Introduction

Green economics is a field of research and policy-making most popular in universities, governmental agencies, and businesses. It promises to integrate a variety of environmental value types that are then analyzed, compared, and promoted thanks to a methodology that pertains to economics. This combination of value diversity and quantitative methodology is rightly thought to be one of the greatest strength evinced by green economics. In the past years, its popularity has even began to overshadow environmental ethics proper as the entry door to reflection about environmental issues within environmental sciences and ethics programs: because green economics is relying heavily on cost-benefit analyses and other quantitatively-based devices, its methodology has acquired an aura of neutrality with regard to environmental values. The field has become so popular, in fact, that by criticizing it, one sometimes exposes oneself to charges of eccentricity, rent seeking, or romanticism.

Nevertheless, I will argue that nonanthropocentric environmental philosophers have been right in criticizing the preference-based anthropocentrism that lies at the heart of green economics. I will show that the two main valuation[1] methods offered by green economics require from us that we implicitly concur with a certain conception of human interactions and subjectivity, and that such a conception fails to deal with environmental values other than those which fall under the "instrumental" category even when it attempts to do so. But before I get to this, I will contend that a strictly preference-based approach to value assignation eludes certain types of values that should *prima facie* be included in deliberation processes about nonanthropogenic environments. I will also argue that we need a better account of values, human interactions, and human subjectivity before any proper weighing of environmental values can take place—even if it remains true that green economics can provide policy-makers with useful pragmatic tools to implement appropriate policies in specific contexts.

"Figure 1" synthesizes the first part of this chapter. In it, I will briefly present the basic principles of the two central valuation methods that attempt to value nature strictly from an economic viewpoint, since these clearly came to form in the past decades as the privileged manner in which to apply a morally anthropocentric value theory (cf., Anderson and Leal 2001, Costanza et al. 1997, Daly and Farley 2003, Hussen 2000, Millennium Assessment 2004). They are (1) the market-based valuation methods and (2) the contingent valuation methods. These are the two families of methods used by economists to assign values to nature, both of which are rooted in the assessment of human individual preferences. This exposition, albeit not exhaustive, will then allow me to present why such methods have both (i) internal problems and (ii) external limitations at the practical *and* theoretical level. Following Maris and Revéret (2009), I will be focusing first on the internal problems of the economic valuation methods, thereby exposing inconsistencies that will reflect important exogenous limitations to economically grounded value theories. By this I mean that some of the problems that arise from *within* the scope of economic valuation methods are related to the impossibility of these same methods to acknowledge values that are external to their scope. All in all, what I hope will become clearer from this presentation is that the taking into account of noninstrumental values of nature is tantamount to an evaluation that does not reduce nonanthropogenic nature to a pool of resources for the satisfaction of human preferences.

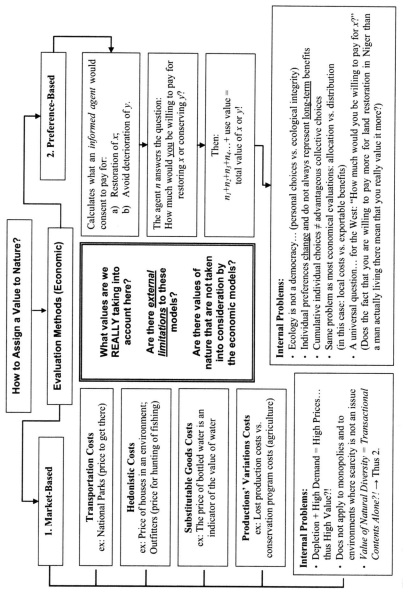

How to Assign a Value to Nature?

1. Market-Based

Transportation Costs
ex: National Parks (price to get there)

Hedonistic Costs
ex: Price of houses in an environment;
Outfitters (price for hunting of fishing)

Substitutable Goods Costs
ex: The price of bottled water is an
indicator of the value of water

Productions' Variations Costs
ex: Lost production costs vs.
conservation program costs (agriculture)

Internal Problems:
- Depletion + High Demand = High Prices...
  thus High Value?!
- Does not apply to monopolies and to
  environments where scarcity is not an issue
- *Value of Natural Diversity = Transactional
  Contents Alone?! → Thus 2.*

Evaluation Methods (Economic)

**What values are we
REALLY taking into
account here?**

**Are there *external
limitations* to these
models?**

**Are there values of
nature that are not taken
into consideration by
the economic models?**

2. Preference-Based

Calculates what an *informed agent* would
consent to pay for:
a) Restoration of *x*;
b) Avoid deterioration of *y*.

The agent *n* answers the question:
How much would <u>you</u> be willing to pay for
restoring *x* or conserving *y*?

Then:

$n_1+n_2+n_3+n_4...+$ use value =
total value of *x* or *y*!

Internal Problems:
- Ecology is not a democracy... (personal choices vs. ecological integrity)
- Individual preferences <u>change</u> and do not always represent <u>long-term</u> benefits
- Cumulative individual choices ≠ advantageous collective choices
- Same problem as most economical evaluations: allocation vs. distribution
  (in this case: local costs vs. exportable benefits)
- A universal question... for the West: "How much would you be willing to pay for *x*?"
  (Does the fact that you are willing to pay more for land restoration in Niger than
  a man actually living there mean that you really value it more?)

Figure 1

2. Market-based Valuation Methods

2.1. Preliminary considerations

A host of economically rooted valuation methods or rationales have been developed by environmentally concerned economists whose work attempts to give us an approximate account of how much nature is "worth," since, for them, valuations in monetary terms are seen as if not the only relevant valuative and evaluative tools, at least, as the only ones that can be applied, with a maximum of objectivity, both at a local and global scale. As I mentioned already, there exist market-based and contingent valuation methods, both of which are used by economists to assign value to nature. Yet, in both of these types of methods, what is valued is not nature itself but human preferences for services provided *by nature*—such valuative grounds should thus be described as morally anthropocentric.

Market-based valuation methods are used by economists who believe that "consumers' preferences are best expressed by a market economy" (Hussen 2000, p. 14), whereas the contingent valuation method is mainly used by economists, ecologists, or other kinds of environmental or social scientists who believe that values are, in some cases, best revealed by a direct expression of consumers' preferences. We will come back later to this second type of valuation method as we will first turn to the market-based valuation methods. It should however be noted that both of them aim at assessing the total worth of the services provided by nature; some methods target only ecosystem services that are *already* part of the market economy (i.e., the direct and indirect use value; e.g., minerals, wood, recreational activities tied to tourism, etc.) while other methods also include the *potential* monetary value of ecosystem services more generally (i.e., the option value; e.g., species of plants that could be used for pharmacological purposes, future recreational use of an environment, etc.). The integration of a *potential value* of natural resources and services is one of the reasons why scholars in this field nowadays speak of "ecosystem services" (Costanza et al. p. 1997). This concept is broader than the former (and more common) "natural resources" concept, because all benefits humans are said to obtain from nature are included therein, i.e., (i) provisioning (e.g., food, water, wood, etc.); (ii) regulating (e.g., regulation of climate, diseases, pollination, etc.); (iii) cultural (e.g., religious purposes, recreation, aesthetic appreciation, knowledge systems, etc.); and (iv) supporting services (processes necessary for the other three types of services to take place, such as nutrient cycling, soil formation, oxygen production, etc.) (cf., Millennium Assessment 2004). Of course, the "ecosystem services" concept is used to calculate the value of a particular service provided by a given ecosystem *in economic terms*.

On a global scale, Costanza et al. succeeded in calculating that the planetary ecosystem, the biosphere, provides us annually with approximately 33 trillion US dollars in services in average (between 16 and 54 trillion US dollars; Costanza et al. 1997, p. 253), a study that fast became one of the most cited works in the academic world. The study was indeed useful in showing that "because ecosystem services are largely outside the market and uncertain, they are too often ignored or undervalued, leading to the error of constructing projects whose social costs far outweigh their benefits" (Costanza et al. 1997, p. 259). One of the main goals of this study was to tentatively "internalize externalities," or integrate into the market what had thus far been left out of it to ensure that all (or at least most)[2] ecosystem services are assigned an economic value. This way, no benefits or costs that humans inherit from nature would be left without a human, economic attribution of value:

> Externalities are situations in which the production or consumption of one economic actor affects another who did not pay for the good produced or consumed, and externalities are viewed as either negative or positive. For example, environmental economists often cite pollution as an example of the former and preservation of biological diversity as an example of the latter. When these economists use the phrase 'environmental externalities', they are referring to environmental goods and services that are 'external' to market systems in the sense that they are presumed to exist outside of the allegedly lawful or law-like dynamics of these systems. (Nadeau 2008)

According to supporters of this approach, once the value of an externality (an ecosystem service) is internalized (assigned a value within the market), it can thereafter be expressed in a quantifiable currency used for the relative neutrality of its standard:

> To make this assumption is to be committed to *value commensurability*—the claim that there exists a common [neutral] measure of value through which different options or states of affair can be ordered . . . [In the end,] it promises the possibility of reducing social choice to a matter of a calculus. (O'Neill et al., 2008, p. 71)

And this attempt at "internalizing externalities" is shared to various extents (cf. infra, footnote 1) by all supporters of the "environmental economics" trend, as well as by some ecological economists:[3]

Environmental economics, a subset of neoclassical economics, recognizes that welfare also depends to a large extent on ecosystem services and suffers from pollution, but is still devoted to efficiency. As markets rarely exist in either ecosystem services or pollution, environmental economists use a variety of techniques to assign market values to them, so that they, too, may be incorporated into the market model. (Daly and Farley 2003, p. 5)

From this basic standpoint—that is to say, that using a neoclassical economics background in a new manner and within a different framework can help us assign a "real" (read "quantifiable") value to nature through the integration of ecosystem services into the market—many applicable methods have been developed to assign an economic value to ecosystem services, the most common of which have been outlined by Maris and Revéret (2009). Here are four that they lay down, with examples illustrating how these are said to succeed in assigning an economic value to nature.

- First, *transportation (or travel) costs*[4] can be used to evaluate how much a population actually pays to benefit from (recreational) services provided by an environment. For instance, the total amount of tourists' expenditures and the cost for locals to drive into the Icelandic highlands would give us an indication of the value of these environments.
- Second, *hedonic costs* can be used to calculate how much a sellable good is worth with regards to the qualities of the environment that surrounds it. For example, fishing in Laxá in Aðaldalur costs more than fishing at Reynisvatn, partly because of the pristine aesthetic qualities of the environment. The same would be true of a house built close to the coastline, or surrounded by old trees or parks, as compared to a similar house located in the industrial neighborhood of a city.
- Third, *substitutable goods costs* can be used to calculate the price of a resource that is not yet on the market, the most common example for this being bottled water: the price of water bottles could be an indicator for the value of the resource that these actually contain.
- Finally, *productions' variations costs* can be used to calculate, mainly in agriculture, the marginal discrepancies between a drop in crop production and implementation of a land conservation program with the help of a cost–benefit analysis.[5] The latter would thus justify the conservation of an area strictly by way of an economic argument if the benefits of the conservation program were to outweigh its cost in terms of lost crop production (e.g., drop in income), avoided costs (e.g., a need for irrigation or new machinery) and/or replacement costs (e.g., when land conservation costs less than the building of a water purification plant).

2.2. Internal problems of market-based evaluation methods

As some environmental economists and most ecological economists recognize, various internal issues arise when applying market-based evaluation methods, issues that have not been settled in recent years. By calling these problems "internal," I here mean that they come up because of shortcomings pertaining to the very method that is discussed. Some of these problems have to do with economic practicalities, which I will not go into as they are best addressed by economists themselves. (Recall that my ultimate goal in exploring "green" economic thought is to unearth both the value theory they champion as well as the conceptions of human subjectivity and interactions they rely upon.) But be that as it may, one can regroup more fundamental problems to these market-based evaluation methods under three categories:

2.2.1. Oligarchies, nonexclusivity of resources, and moral neutrality

The first is pervasive throughout all market or market-like systems: when and where there are economic monopolies or oligarchies, market-based valuation methods do a very poor job at representing the actual value of any of the goods or services they assess. Land lots, for instance, are in many areas owned by few parties[6] which can be problematic for the assessment of hedonic costs, since there is not a sufficient mass of competitors applying economic pressure to bring the cost of land down, or to push it up.[7] This fact could seem to provide support for an increase in privatization of land lots, and as a result, environmental economists championing market-based valuation methods often claim that "price distortions arising from externalities simply require minor fine-tuning of the market" (Hussen 2000, p. 149), i.e., better property rights and increased privatization. Yet this truly sounds like wishful thinking after decades of failed attempts at developing the "appropriate institutional adjustments" (Hussen 2000, p. 135).

For example, of the twenty three European countries that filled the UNECE/FAO questionnaire on forest land ownership, more than half "reported that the fragmentation of private holdings represents a hindrance to sustainable forest management" (Hirsch et al. 2007, p. 25). On the other hand, proper environmental land management does not seem to become easier when privatization of land ownership is *not* fragmented: large-scale land deals have been more frequent in Africa, in the past years, because of an increase in the value of biofuels and agricultural land (Cotula et al. 2009, pp. 37–38). As a result, foreign investors are increasingly buying large amounts of land in African countries, which at times results in resource depletion or in "local people . . . being arbitrarily dispossessed of their land" (Cotula et al. 2009, p. 10). To argue, like some environmental economists and free-market environmentalists[8] do, that such oligarchic situations (and what they entail) are a mere function of "the willingness of developers to outbid environmentalists" (Anderson and Leal 2001, p. 24) is to be ideologically blindfolded by a conception of the free market that does not exist, and that never truly existed in the ideal way portrayed by many neoclassical theorists.[9]

Despite such fallbacks, however, market-based valuation methods are still widely popular among environmental scientists, and the main reason for their popularity is that they are believed to be "value-free"—some kind of unbiased, "clean-slate" valuation tools. Accordingly, against those who say that one of the problems of market-based valuation methods is that they are replacing moral or ethical values with economic values, free-market environmentalists answer that "turning moral values into political issues and arguing that it is a matter of treading more lightly on the Earth . . . becomes another form of rent seeking, wherein people with one set of moral values get what they want at the expense of others" (Anderson and Leal 2001, p. 24). Clearly, they forget how their own notion of human freedom—basically understood through free-market individualism alone—is just as morally connoted a value as the environmentalists' notion of responsibility toward the Earth they so disapprove of. They omit to say that the market freedom, which they champion qua freedom *sans phrase*, is immediately turned by environmental economists into a political issue as well, as they are advocating for the expansion of private property rights over that of governmental duties toward public land. Promoting the withdrawal of public and governmental institutions from the land market, for instance, in favor of better defined private property rights for land ownership and ecosystem services is just as political a position as promoting the opposite view, a fact which free-market environmentalists and environmental economists refuse to recognize. By believing that market-based valuation methods are politically impartial and free of any ideological bias—which they obviously are not[10]— American environmental economists and free-market environmentalists also overlook issues related to the fact that corporations are considered legal moral persons (in the US, at least[11]), which provides them with the same rights (as regards property, among other things) as living persons even if these corporate entities have no recreational, aesthetic, spiritual, morally connoted, embodied, or emotional relationships at stake with the land and ecosystems they acquire. This means three things: first, that hedonic costs have few or no direct impact on corporations acquiring land for industrial purposes (unless the industry in question is a touristic one); second, that nonuse values can hardly be taken into account by corporations (we will come back to nonuse values in the section on the contingent valuation method); and third, that such corporate entities have a very clear advantage over individuals to appropriate land in terms of economic means, information, and incentives to do so. That is the case because individuals—having a variety of interests and relationships at stake—usually do not acquire land for the sole purpose of creating more wealth, which in turn means it is impossible for them to "put their money where their mouth is," as it were, when bidding against corporate entities that receive financial returns on their initial investments while having no affectively engaged relationships with the land they bid on in order to gain such financial benefits.

For all these reasons, that a true free market properly representing the value of nonanthropogenic environments does or even could exist is far from plausible: an equitable distribution of property rights is unlikely at best and utopian at worst. As economists Haab and McConnell claim: "markets cannot efficiently allocate public goods or resources with pervasive externalities, or for which property rights are not clearly defined" (Haab and McConnell 2002, p. 1). This is precisely why free-market environmentalists argue for better defined property rights while omitting to acknowledge, on the one hand, the part hitherto played by such property rights in the alteration of nonanthropogenic environments and, on the other hand, the possibility of valuing a natural entity or an environment on grounds other than its being owned, or than its yielding of actual or potential economic gains.

According to Haab and McConnell's (2002) definition of public goods and resources, many ecosystem services are furthermore not exclusive to an individual or an entity, in the case of national parks or other nonanthropogenic environments for example, a situation which makes hedonic costs nearly impossible to assess properly. Some nonanthropogenic environments are owned in commons or shared by communities even if they are managed by governmental agencies, which entails that their value can hardly be evaluated through market-based methods as there is no truly exclusive individual appropriation of ecosystem services by visitors. When one hikes in a public land, one does not buy or own it;

one merely enjoys it without hindering anybody else from doing so. Consequently, there is no relevant economic competition between visitors for the exclusivity of going into a land owned in commons either. As for the transportation costs approach, it is highly unconvincing that the value of an environment should depend on the travel expenditures of people. For example: one person travels by bicycle to visit a nonanthropogenic environment, another travels by car. The cyclist pays less to get there than the driver: does that mean that the cyclist values the given environment less than the driver? The opposite argument could, in fact, easily be made if one starts from other premises than economic ones.

Hence, even if it were the case that nonanthropogenic environments could be put into a state of market-like competition for visitors (which is unlikely because of issues regarding the possibility of having equitable distribution of property rights), it remains unclear how a market-based assessment of this kind (either in terms of transportation or hedonic costs) would give us an account of how valuable nonanthropogenic environments actually are.

2.2.2. The value of depletion

One of the major issues of market-based methods for assigning values to nonanthropogenic environments is that the values they assess rely in effect on the very scarcity of their benefits:

> There is . . . no doubt that once the scale of the economy has grown to the point that formerly free goods become scarce, it is better that these goods should have a positive price reflecting their scarcity than to continue to be priced at zero (Daly and Farley 2003, p. 53).

The scarcity of a given species of fish, for instance, increases the price of the resource (or of the "provisioning service," in other words), which suggests that the less fish there is, the more expensive the resource becomes and thus the more valuable it gets within a given economic zone. Economically, this argument is reasonable; environmentally, it rather seems irrational:

> One can remark the irony of evaluating biodiversity on market grounds, since the excessive commercialization of natural resources is an important factor for biodiversity erosion. In almost all cases . . .., one finds this paradox: benefits from commercial fisheries provide us with an indicator of the value of marine biodiversity although the highest threat for this biodiversity is the overfishing for commercial purposes (Maris and Revéret 2009, p. 56; my translation).

Even if biodiversity is not exactly the issue at hand here, the same could be said of most nonanthropogenic environments where scarcity of resources plays a role in their economic valuation: why should we rely on a valuation method that has scarcity as one of its premises to assign a value to natural entities or environments, given that this valuation method relies on the very mindset that allowed for the examined natural entities or environments to become scarce in the first place? No rationale is provided for this by economists; for them, the market simply is the default position for value assignation. Moreover, one can legitimately ask: from a prudential standpoint, where does the incentive lie for a person, a business, or a community owning a great quantity of land—land which, say, provides a variety of provisional services—to ensure that the owned land will be protected from massive alterations? There seems to be no such economic incentive inasmuch as there is no *full* depletion of the exploited resource(s) *and* that other landowners exploit their resource(s) in the same way: resources must remain scarce for their value to remain high; if the value drops, one will sell more of any given resources for the same price. To believe that the market can weigh in and solve this internal problem amounts to denying the existence of collective action problems such as "prisoner's dilemmas" or "tragedies of the commons," in which cooperation and self-interest should meet through a Pareto-*suboptimal* solution, *but do not* because of a lack of information, or because of the presence of perverse incentives. This is not to say that, in practice, central governmental regulations are a panacea,[12] but rather that the free market alone, if conceived in neoclassical terms at least, can hardly help us to value nature properly because it only assigns value to the *scarcity* of its ecosystem services. From a cost–benefit analysis point of view, conservation can sometimes be worthwhile only when an ecosystem service is on the verge of being completely depleted. As a result, market-based valuation methods such as "productions' variations costs" assess the value of the *depletion* of natural environments (at least until they reach their exploitation threshold) rather than their actual value. Provisional goods, as conceived in economic terms, are substitutable by other goods because of this lack of qualitative values assigned to ecosystem services by market-based valuation methods. This means that a substitutable value (since one here speaks of a "price") is assigned to nonsubstitutable ecosystem services or to irreversible damage made to ecosystems, which are also nonsubstitutable because they have, strictly speaking, no qualitative equivalent.

2.2.3. The value of nature via a transactional model

Hence, one could legitimately venture that the main reason why such inconsistencies *do* occur with market-based valuation methods is that they can only take into account the value of nature insofar as a *transaction* takes place. Thus, it is neither the *natural entity* that is valued, nor *natural diversity* (bio- or otherwise), nor even the *complex relationship* one has with the land: rather, the value here pertains to the transactional potential of natural entities against a monetary standard fixed by markets that are rarely truly "free" (if ever). The upshot of this is twofold: (1) market-based valuation methods can only take nature into account once it is reduced to its instrumental value—or, in other words, once nature is used for consumption (which includes recreational use) or transformation, which entails that (2) they can only value nature qua "provisional services."

Yet, despite this important flaw overarching the others, there are interesting arguments for such methods—arguments rooted mainly in the pragmatic approach of policy-makers and of certain economists as regards environmental regulations. For instance, ecological economists (here in opposition to environmental economists or free-market environmentalists) are undoubtedly right in saying that:

> What must be questioned is the prevailing belief that markets reveal all our desires; that they are ideal systems not only for allocating all resources efficiently, but also for distributing resources justly among people; and that markets automatically limit the overall macroeconomy to a physical scale that is sustainable within the biosphere. (Daly and Farley, 2003, p. 6)

And they are just as right to advocate for transdisciplinarity between economics, environmental ethics, and ecology. Indeed, for ecological economists—who, unlike their "environmental" colleagues, wish to do away with the neoclassical paradigm while using the market as a tool to achieve some of their goals—the attractive aspect of market-based valuation methods has to do with their expression of "value" qua "economic worth" (or "price"). And this is attractive for them because their economic integration of pollution and ecosystem services seems to provide policy-makers and business managers with a direct, calculable link between the value of nature as such and the quantifiable, economic value of services, goods, and waste that it offers to human societies for their sustenance and management. Therefore, such market-based methods are also conceived, by ecological economists, as offering a solid evaluative ground suitable for the implementation of MBIs (Market-Based Instruments), i.e., green policies such as eco-taxes (likely to yield revenues for public institutions either in "user charges" or "emission charges"), tradable permits (taking the form of tradable quotas, viz. CO_2 emissions) and/or deposit refunds (applied on sellable products which are reusable or recyclable in totality or in part, such as plastic bags or beer bottles). The convergence between market-based valuation methods and such political applicability appears to be true in certain cases and to a certain extent,[13] and it has allowed for real successes that should not be overlooked. But in spite of certain MBIs' advocates' self-proclaimed pragmatism, theoretical and practical objections can easily be found, since MBIs have often become a safe-conduct for a "more of the same" attitude in economic policy rather than true reform or improvement:

> Active political support for MBIs is (. . .) weak, not least among two constituencies—right-wing politicians and businesses—who might appear to have most affinity to the market rhetoric of the economists who enthusiastically advocate MBIs. Support for MBIs from the neo-liberal right is rather half-hearted and even disingenuous; their support for MBIs is driven primarily by a dislike of regulations rather than enthusiasm for improving environmental protection. The pro-market rhetoric of the UK Conservative government in the 1990s was, in practice, a recipe for inaction: its deregulatory zeal led to many 'unnecessary' regulations being removed, but the only eco-taxes it introduced were a discriminatory tax on leaded petrol and a landfill tax. (Carter 2007, p. 340)

In spite of the advocated efficiency of the practical, policy-oriented outcomes of market-based valuation methods, they thus rarely lead to MBIs that could be implemented globally or even nationally. It is also unlikely that the internalization of ecosystem services will, alone, change much of the way we act in terms of consumption since market-based valuation methods leave the door wide open for corporate discourses on "ecological modernization" which—although they can hardly be condemned unilaterally—nevertheless "ignore the issues of equity and social justice raised by the broader sustainable development discourse" (Carter 2007, p. 230). To be sure, their rhetoric focuses deliberately on the implementation of "best practices" (especially in Northern Europe and North America) instead of questioning the "overall level of consumption" (Carter 2007, p. 231). One should also recall that environmental econo-mists hold the basic assumption that "scarcity of resources (including natural resources) is continually augmented by technological advances" (Hussen 2000, p. 14) which supports their preoccupation for efficient allocation of resources and Pareto-optimal solutions to economic and social challenges rather than distribution of resources and cooperation. And even if ecological economists do not share this view of economics and have disproved it on many occasions, they remain vulnerable to the "ecological modernization"/"greenwashing" argument precisely because of their across-the-board, pragmatic use of the market as a crucial support for valuing nature.

But more importantly for us, the local importance of the values of nonanthropogenic environments is, in market-based valuation methods, brought to a minimum: unsurprisingly, macroeconomic tools are for the most part unable to assign value to the specific qualitatively acknowledgeable values of a given nonanthropogenic landscape (cf., Maris and Revéret 2009, p. 57). The monetary standard being the neutral wall against which *all* values are pinned down, nature loses most of its qualitative features. Nonmarketable natural qualities (i.e., the support of nonuse values) thus remain without "real" value, especially because one cannot understand, on the basis of their integration in a market, the preferences of individuals for eating wild berries while hiking in the Icelandic highlands, for the sound of glaciers cracking in the spring, or for experiencing the beauty of an ocean shore. And even if it were possible, the remaining question is to know if it would be desirable to see all of our preferences valued on the basis of their transactional nature alone: were it granted that our economy is based on a preference-based system of value assignation, *would the actual inclusion of all our desires and preferences into a transactional model of valuation be something we desire, or have a preference for?*

In sum, qualitative aspects of natural environments, such as the cultural meaningfulness of nonanthropogenic environments, are very hard to assess with these methods, since the value of a given culturally important landscape cannot be grasped by substitution with another landscape—their values are not commensurable. The value of a cultural landscape, for instance, also depends on much more than the total expenditures of its visitors, whether these are included in a cost–benefit analysis or not. Thus it becomes practically impossible for market-based valuation methods—even when they are associated with corresponding MBIs—to properly provide us with an account of the heritage value of nature, and the same is true of natural diversity (bio- or otherwise): market-based methods invariably reduce the heritage value of nonanthropogenic environments to a transactional value, and natural diversity to a flow of ecosystem services, all of which are then converted into a single universal monetary standard. Such a reduction leaves no place for nonuse values of natural environments (except, at times, for the option value of potentially marketable ecosystem services), which is one of the reasons why certain economists turned their focus toward the contingent valuation method; i.e., the second prominent tool rooted in economics used to evaluate natural environments.

3. The Contingent Valuation Methods

3.1. Preliminary considerations

The contingent valuation methods were specifically developed to incorporate nonuse values of natural environments into environmental assessments as it became clear that market-based methods were limited in scope and unable to account for important aspects of environmental valuations of populations. Instead of relying on the actual market to provide economists with information regarding the preferences of consumers, the contingent valuation methods propose to survey populations *directly* about their willingness to pay for the satisfaction of their preferences regarding nature. These methods are said to take a deeper look into what human beings value *without the a priori market-based exclusion of nonuse values*. Among these nonuse values, the "option value" (sometimes called "conservation value") was already mentioned: it concerns the preference of individuals for the *potential* use of certain ecosystem services, which supports a common argument made by conservationists. But two other types of values, which can be subsumed under the category of nonuse values, are of concern to economists using this preference-based method of evaluation: the "bequest value" and "existence value" (sometimes called "preservation value," when both are put together). The first refers to the preference of individuals who assign a value to the preservation of certain environments for future generations, while the second refers to the preference of individuals who assign a value to the existence of a given environment, whether they have an actual relationship with it or not. Therefore, theoretically at least, the contingent valuation methods are indeed more comprehensive than market-based evaluation methods: a monetary value is attributed to nonuse values *as well as* direct and indirect use values. For economists using the contingent valuation methods, the total value of an environment refers to the sum of use values and nonuse values altogether expressed through a preference-based survey, i.e. a survey in which participants assign an economic value to their preferences. According to these economists, avoiding the internal shortcomings of the imperfect market by way of a hypothetical market is tantamount to offering a proper economic translation of the overall value humans assign to nature.

Roughly speaking, the valuation technique goes as follows: economists survey a population comprehensively (i.e., through individual surveys), asking *how much a given agent would be willing to pay*[14] either to avoid the deterioration of an environment (for conservation or preservation purposes) or to restore an environment that has already suffered damage, and this, because . . .

> [. . .] techniques designed to estimate non-use values cannot use real market information, which means that willingness to pay for non-use values must be estimated by means of a hypothetical market condition. (Hussen, 2000, p. 311)

By answering the *how much* question on the basis of fictitious market conditions, the agent provides economists with information as to how he or she values the given environment; this information obviously is "a function of prices, income, and household tastes and conditioning variables such as household size, environmental attitudes, etc." (Turner 1999, p. 25). By generalizing their results through complex statistical methods, economists can subsequently build an approximate model of a population's preferences as regards a given environment. The three nonuse values that were mentioned can sometimes, in practice, be difficult to isolate from one another. But, for example, a survey inquiring into how much a given agent would be willing to pay for a nonanthropogenic environment to remain unspoiled for next generations would mirror the bequest value of the given landscape. The same would be true of the option value if the survey inquired into the agent's willingness to pay for the opportunity of benefitting from recreational visits to the nonanthropogenic area in the future, or of the existence value if the survey inquired into the agent's willingness to pay to know that the given nonanthropogenic environment exists without its being altered by some form of land use. As can be seen, the conservation value and preservation value do intersect (conservation for future use or preservation for future generations are preference justifications that do not automatically exclude one another), and the isolation of the type of value that is addressed in performing the survey can be, as a result, hard to perform. Still, contingent valuations recognize the importance of nonuse values altogether, which is already a clear improvement over the market-based valuation methods.

One could be tempted to immediately criticize this approach on the basis of the speculative character of the preference-based method: the survey questions are indeed hypothetical. Yet, many proponents have made studies which show that "contingent valuation has proved to be no less reliable than behavioral methods in a variety of tests" (Haab and McConnell 2002, p. 3), and that "contingent valuation and behavioral methods gave similar results across a variety of environmental improvements" (Haab and McConnell 2002, p. 4). The method, applied for example in Colorado (Walsh et al. 1983, pp. 14–29), showed that 37% of the total value of the wilderness areas in the State had to do with nonuse values, according to the population. Thus, even if there are downsides to contingent valuations—which will be stated explicitly in the next section of this chapter—the study was at least useful in showing that nonuse values of wild areas are acknowledged not only by environmentalists or activists, but on the contrary, by a large proportion of the population. Such a study is instrumental in proving that relying on use values *alone* cannot produce a significant picture of how people genuinely assign values to nature, and that, even if "researchers have found that CV (contingent valuation) results [which integrate nonuse values] were subject to a great deal of variability" (Kolstad 2000, p. 366).

3.2. Internal problems of the contingent valuation methods

In spite of many praiseworthy theoretical and practical successes, the contingent valuation methods still suffer from important problems not so much because of inconsistencies within the field of economics (after all, its markets are ideal and hypothetical), but rather because one's relationships with nature and others are hardly reducible to subjective preferences alone:

3.2.1. Ecology is not a democracy

When confronted with a "willingness to pay" question for the restoration of a formerly nonanthropogenic area, for instance, agents will respond in various manners, which is not surprising. However, what *is* surprising is that "people may place the same value on cleaning up one lake as on cleaning up ten lakes" (Kolstad 2000, p. 364), an anomaly called "imbedding" which arises because of the "partial knowledge of agents with regard to ecological processes as well as to the real implications of the protection of a species or habitat" (Maris and Revéret 2009, p. 58; my translation):

[O]ne of the lessons of ecology is that all matters in a natural ecosystem are mutually interrelated. Therefore, strictly from an ecological viewpoint, the value of a particular entity in the natural environment (an animal species, a valley, a river, humans, etc.) should be assessed on the basis of its overall contribution to the sustainability (health) of the ecosystem as a whole . . . .. Important ecological connections may be missed when valuing components of a system separately. (Hussen 2000, pp. 309, 312)

There is thus a qualitative difference between acting on the basis of shared preferences as regards nature and acting on the basis of an ecological rationale. What a population wants in terms of conservation or preservation and what should be done from the point of view of an environmental scholar can enter in conflict because of a lack of information, because of aesthetic preferences for one ecosystem's area over another, or because of a conflict between the importance attributed to use values or nonuse values. Thus, it is not because individual preferences are expressed by a multitude to the point of forming a majority or even a consensus, as in a democracy, that their cumulative choices are consistent with what should be done from an ecological perspective. In other words, what is willed by a given community—even one for which environmental issues matter—is not automatically tantamount to the best option as it would be defined in ecological terms.

3.2.2. Individual and social decision-making

This problem, related to the previous one, was already mentioned for market-based valuation methods, but, sadly, it also occurs in the contingent valuation methods: whether the market is hypothetical and ideal, or real and imperfect, collective action problems are often present, important, and unresolvable without relevant *social and regulatory institutions* or *proper incentives* conducive to cooperation:

The sum of individual preferences, as they can be expressed on hypothetical markets [*marchés simulés*], do not necessarily reflect collective preferences . . . .. The sum of prices that particular individuals would be willing to pay for conservation may be much inferior to that which they would consent collectively if they had the certainty that everyone would equally participate to the collective effort (Maris and Revéret 2009, p. 58; my translation).

The same is true of individual preferences as regards time. Both market-based and contingent valuation methods "appear to provide a rationale for displacing environmental damage into the future, since the value placed upon damage felt in the future will be smaller than the same value of current consumption" (O'Neill et al. 2008, p. 57). Collective decision-making includes questions touching on a given community's future, whereas individual preferences are unlikely to provide an appropriate picture of such long-term concerns.

3.2.3. Preferences and choices: local costs vs. exportable benefits

The agents' willingness to pay may depend on other variables than their actual preferences, i.e., they may value an environment while refusing to pay. In other words, the fact that environmental issues are part of a wider political debate on personal, governmental, and corporate responsibility can affect the response of certain individuals as regards their willingness to pay for the restoration of an environment. For example, if a nonanthropogenic area has already been altered by a multinational mining business which left the area to invest its accumulated profits elsewhere, it would be unreasonable to expect a population to be willing to pay for the restoration of the land, even hypothetically. Yet this unwillingness cannot itself be interpreted as carelessness for the given environment. It thus seems that value assignation is much more complex than consumer preferences—notably, because of moral ideals of social and environmental justice:

> A satisfactory method for eliciting preferences must be able, for some readily understandable scenario, to isolate the effects of preferences on choices. But it seems that in order to explain individual behaviour in relation to public goods— whether private contributions to public goods, or voting behaviour—we have to take account of other factors than preferences. In particular, we have to take account of the expressive value of actions, and of the moral norms to which individuals subscribe . . . As yet, no theory of choice seems sufficiently well-developed to do this reliably. (Sugden, 1999, p. 149)

3.2.4. A universal question?

Economic valuations of nature, broadly conceived, are sometimes said to rely on a Western tradition of assigning a monetary value to whatever should be recognized as valuable by a given society. This kind of claims often serves as a ground for criticizing the "economic obsession" of the West, and that is of course a discourse that has more supporters on the left side of the political spectrum. Regardless of such political sympathies however, this critique undeniably gains in relevance as one learns about the actual shortcomings of the contingent valuation method in poorer countries, such as the Philippines,

> where the analysis of households' environmental attitudes and perceptions shed some light on respondents' low willingness to pay for improved sanitation . . .While the study of attitudes and priorities sheds light on Calamba residents' low willingness to pay for piped sewage, it is important not to lose sight of the fact that households' income is also a key determinant . . . [since] incomes are simply not high enough to make full-cost recovery possible. Moreover, other conditions, such as the household level of education, will also have to improve before Calamba is ready for sewage (Lauria et al. 1999, p. 572).

As this example shows, because of a host of social factors such as education, economic context, lifestyle, day-to-day priorities, gender roles, religious background, and employment, different nations (and even different groups within a single nation) cannot be expected to react in the same way when asked about their willingness to pay for environmental protection and ecosystem services. Yet, some people's unwillingness to pay does not necessarily mean they value nature less. It can rather mean that they value money differently because of social or personal factors.

* * * * *

While presenting green economic valuation methods as well as their significant shortcomings, I have so far argued that the expressed preferences of human beings for nonanthropogenic environments and ecosystem services are incapable of properly reflecting their actual value, and that, regardless of the methodology used to gather or analyze those preferences. From what I have said, however, it still remains unclear what types of values are actually missing from those preference-based model we have seen. In the next section, we will see that those are values of the "moral" kind.

I call these values "moral" because they do not primarily focus on self-interested preference-satisfaction, as they rather focus on the value-worthiness of specific types of relationships that are, in turn, valued in and for themselves—in other words, my assignation of a value of these relationships does not depend on my having a personal preference for them. Rather these relationships will be shown to rely on my recognition that others value things too, and that their value assignation constitutes not only a sufficient ground for my assigning a value to something, but the actual basis of my valuing things morally at all. This is what the assignation of a "moral" value will mean in the context of this essay: to assign a moral value to x means assigning a value to x *for the sake of the other*.

Yet, I will show that this type of value assignation has no place in the valuation methods of green economics, even though it should be considered central for the evaluations we make of the total value of nonanthropogenic environments. This argument will crystallize the fact that environmental issues are first and foremost moral issues.

4. External Limitations to Economically Based Valuation Methods

4.1. What is preferred and what is good

We now need to go over the kinds of values that are identified in Figure 2. It shows the limitations that are external to the market-based valuation methods and contingent valuation methods, i.e., it presents an overview of the types of values one can find in the environmental ethics literature, some of which, I already argued, are ignored by the economic valuation methods.

In Figure 2, it could seem surprising that nonuse values are placed under the "instrumental values" category—a contradiction in terms, it could appear. But if instrumental values are understood as referring to the value assigned to x (a natural environment) by an agent n as means to do or achieve z for n, one has to recognize that nonuse values are accordingly defined by the willingness to pay of the agent n to achieve a goal or satisfy an individual preference that remains external to the valued natural environment. In other words, even in the case of the nonuse values as they are represented in contingent valuation methods, the value of the environment remains a means to the satisfaction of a person's preference, thereby falling under an instrumental account of values. This is the reason why the "existence value" of natural environments appears twice in the diagram, since in a nonanthropocentric account of the existence value, the existence of a landscape is conceived as having a value independently of anyone having a preference for it (thus falling under the "intrinsic value" category).

The heritage and bequest values could also be confused easily, as they both refer to the trans- or intergenerational value of nature. But again, the bequest value of a natural environment depends on the preference of individuals, whereas the heritage value is that which is assigned to natural environments without anybody having expressed an actual individual preference for it. The latter is however *not* a kind of intrinsic value either—and this is where it becomes important: even if agent n does not care much (i.e., has no individual preference) for natural environment x, n could still consider the *experience* of x to be valuable in and of

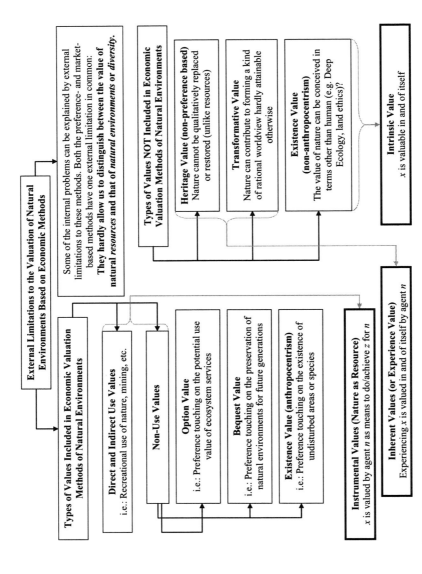

Figure 2

itself for intergenerational reasons—in other words, n can recognize the value-*worthiness* of x in spite of his own indifference toward x not because x has intrinsic value, but because x is *valuable*, or worthy of being valued *by others*. There is a subtle but important distinction to be noted and emphasized between the questions "do you desire that we preserve x for future generations?" (or "how much would you be willing to pay to ensure that we do?") and "should future generations have the possibility of experiencing and value x?" The first question focuses on individual preferences and desires, whereas the second focuses on the things that will provide possibilities and quality of life to others:[15]

> [S]ome preferences or values are impersonal even if they are for the agent, in the sense that they are desires for some objective state of affaire to occur—not for a particular agent's experiencing, enjoying, or causing it, but just for it to occur (cf. Darwall 1983, pp. 132–37). [Stephen] Darwall takes such impersonal preferences or values to be especially important for our moral lives. He calls this "a conception of value that is not relativized to ourselves as individuals" (Darwall 1983, p. 139). Such values are not natural, grounded in desire, nor are they objective in some ontological sense (Morgan 2009, p. 446).

Let us take an example outside of environmental ethics: I for one do not care much for patriotic military memorials built in homage to war veterans, an absence of preference which could be interpreted as insensitive or even offensive to some. Yet I readily admit the value-worthiness of war memorial and believe they should be preserved for heritage reasons even if I have no particular inclination to like or prefer them over a tree or park bench. They are however not intrinsically valuable either, since war memorials get their value from being seen, experienced, worshipped, or remembered. They are thus what I call "inherently" or "experientially" valuable,"[16] i.e., their value depends on their being worthy of value attribution according to an examination of their experiential and historical features inasmuch as these are tied to the other's possibilities and quality of life. It should however be clear that such values are identifiable in spite of the possible indifference of a given population's expression of preference. For example, even if no one has a preference for x, x could still be acknowledged as valuable not on the basis of it being intrinsically valuable, but rather on the basis of it being the support for experiences describable as valuable in and of themselves.

By contrast, economic valuation methods recognize as "value-worthy" preferences that are held by an agent n whether these preferences take into account their impact on others or not. Inherently valuable experiences, however, are not value-worthy simply on the basis of their being "preferred" by an agent n, but rather of their being reliant upon n's deference for others' experiences and lives (whether present, past, or future). Such experiential values express the epitome of values understood in light of what can be called "the good"—they are, as such, moral values.

Now, instrumental and experiential values do not necessarily stand in opposition to each other, obviously, but they certainly do not coincide either, which is why they are so difficult to identify even in our own value-laden judgments. The second kind of experiential values, the transformative value, provides us with a good example of this difficulty. Transformative values have chiefly been discussed by Bryan G. Norton and many of his followers over the last twenty years: a transformative value is that which can be assigned to x if and only if x triggers a modification of agent n's individual preferences. As such, many things can be identified as having a transformative value—war memorials, again, could perhaps transform the way n looks at the world and hence contribute to the formation of a different rational worldview for n. And again, the transformative value should not be conceived of as a subtype of intrinsic values, since the modification of n's preferences does not necessarily entail that one will hold a better, more accurate worldview according to all evaluative standards—i.e., neither the object provoking such a modification in n's preferences, nor n's worldviews will need to be recognized as having an intrinsic value for a transformative value to be assigned. Yet the evolution of n's preferences, values, and belief systems will. The evolution of one's preferences is commonly and understandably considered as a valuable experience in and of itself, which is why it can be considered a type of inherent or experiential value. One of Norton's main achievements has been to show that experiencing nonanthropogenic nature matters for humans' modifications of preferences. As such, assigning a transformative value to a nonanthropogenic environment is "wanting for some objective state of affair to occur—not for a particular agent's experiencing, enjoying, or causing it, but just for it to occur" (Morgan 2009, p. 446).

* * * * *

Going back to the valuation methods discussed earlier, what are we valuing when we apply the anthropocentric valuation techniques promoted by green economics? As it was already put forth, the answer is—both in the case of the market-based methods (valuation through real market situations) and in that of the contingent valuation method (valuation through hypothetical market-like surveys): individual human desires and preferences as regards nature expressed in the present. Unfortunately, for economists and philosophers holding the view that these are able to provide us with an comprehensive account of values that are relevant to an assessment of nonanthropogenic environments, individually expressed desires and preferences represent a variety of wants and fancies, some of which can stand in opposition to moral or ethical values. Individual preferences and desires (as they are supplying prudential reasons for action) can at times coincide with moral and ethical judgments, but because of the strictly formal nature of what an individual desire or preference is, one can in no conceivable way rely only on desires or preferences to elaborate an environmental ethics:

> When we promote the future good of young children, we do not merely aim at desire satisfaction in general, but we try to instill certain desires rather than others on the grounds that some things are worth developing a desire for, and others are not. I conclude from [this] that wanting something does not by itself confer desirability on what we want or getting it. (Kraut 2007, p. 318)

If this is true for ethics in general, one can infer that it is true for environmental ethics in particular. Richard Kraut continues:

> what makes a desire good to satisfy is its being a desire for something that has features that make it worth wanting . . . The desire theory [which seems to underlie the economic valuation methods, as we have seen] says that we confer goodness on objects by wanting them; by contrast, my idea is that the objects we desire must prove themselves worthy of being wanted by having certain characteristics. If they lack features that make them worth wanting, then the fact that we want them does not make up for that deficiency. (Kraut 2007, p. 319)

Such an argument is devastating for the valuation methods of green economics precisely because these methods do gather preferences and desires of individuals and then falsely and implicitly presuppose that these can all equally serve as reasonable premises for providing us with the actual value of a given natural entities or environments whether the valued preferences and desires are worth having or not. To make it worse, they also presuppose that no other valuation methods than those which are grounded in economics can give a relevant narrative concerning the values of nature. Such monist accounts of what is to be considered as a ground for establishing value (i.e., in their case, what a person prefers or wants) cannot but fail to grasp what should be considered "value-worthy," because there is no such thing as "value-worthy" for economic thought: either things are valued (preferred, desired), or they are not, which means they are never "valuable" unless an agent values them *in actu*. This argument, I believe, is significant for showing the importance of inherent or experiential values in environmental ethics, i.e., heritage and transformative values (and possibly, other kinds of aesthetic values). Nevertheless, to criticize green economics in this way does not imply that what is "value-worthy" should be established unilaterally by environmentalists, since

> if there is no supremely desirable object or life, in comparison with which all other objects or lives must be evaluated, then [value-worthiness] must be established on a case-by-case basis by showing why each proposed candidate fails to provide a plausible standard[, which also means that] we cannot bypass the task of evaluating our desires by asking whether their objects possess the qualities that make them worth wanting (Kraut 2007, p. 323).

Yet it is exactly what economic valuation methods are in effect bypassing. Therefore, I venture that this is the central, fundamental external issue explaining the four internal problems of the contingent valuation method as well as the failure of both the contingent and market-based methods' attempt at offering a substitute for moral and/or ethical values: both approaches are taking for granted that the wants and preferences of people can provide a unique and standardized ground for all valuation types, whereas moral values stand—at least in part—on other grounds; grounds such as social and moral norms (cf., Sugden 1999, p. 149), but also peoples' relationships with their past and future (heritage value), with their belief systems (existence value), and with the very possibility of forming new and different worldviews (transformative value). As regards the latter case, one should note that

> there is no self-contradiction in the idea that one might reason to the conclusion that there are activities that are better than reasoning, or that one's life goes best if reason plays a secondary or minor role. So the fact that reasoning is distinctive of human beings does not determine the proper place of reasoning in a human life. (Kraut 2007, p. 322)

Thus, the point here is not that one rational worldview should be valued in exclusivity. However, if there is no way of establishing what is worthy of being valued because of a lack of rational examination, or if what is worthy of being valued relies solely on the satisfaction of *in actu* human preferences and desires—as is the case in economic valuation methods—the very possibility of forming rational worldviews different than that which is already purported by anthropocentrism is completely denied:

Insofar as preferences felt by humans are not subject to any review within the value system of strong anthropocentrism, there is no way in which can be criticised the attitude of those for whom nature is no more than a store of raw materials to be extracted and used in manufacturing products to satisfy human preferences. (Afeissa 2008, p. 74)

This explains in part the difficulty of applying MBIs derived from market-based methods by ecological economists: because these instruments use the fundamental premises held by free-market and environmental economists—i.e., because they start from the same ground of unexamined human preferences to develop their green economic incentives—they can only follow the value paradigm of economic liberalism according to which what is preferred only has a "real" value insofar as it can be part of an economic transaction, either real or hypothetical. In the absence of an "objective list" of what preferences are worth having—a list with the help of which it would be possible to examine and compare preferences—economists and politicians are brought back to Costanza's statement that since "ecosystem services are largely outside the market and uncertain, they are too often ignored or undervalued, leading to the error of constructing projects whose social costs far outweigh their benefits" (Costanza et al. 1997, p. 259). Thus they recognize the problem. But instead of putting into question the way in which value assignation proceeds in economics, economists immediately infer, from the (very real) problem that Costanza identifies, that the only reasonable option is to internalize externalities into the economic system—in other words, to squeeze value types which are other-centered into self-centered valuation systems. Sadly, this "happy end" had already been decided from the start: for the economist, either something is included in a market (either real or hypothetical) and acquires a transactional value, or remains ignored or undervalued.

Notes

1. I will hereafter use the term "valuation" to refer to value assignation itself, and "evaluation" to refer to the weighing of values against one another.
2. This corresponds to the view, dubbed "ecological imperialism" by Daly and Farley (2003, pp. 50–55), which seeks to integrate all externalities into the economic systems. This is a largely popular trend, notably among environmentally concerned advocates of economic neoliberalism. Its counterpart is the "ecological reductionist" trend, which suggests instead that the economic system can be reduced to the many laws of nature. Daly and Farley criticize them both, as they both seek to impose a monist view either upon nature and/or the man-made economic system. The authors instead suggest reinterpreting John Stuart Mill's idea of the "steady-state subsystem," which is more complex than the other two propositions, but just as reliant on an instrumental view of nature. This "steady-state" or "stationary state"

idea aims at finding the sustainable limit of allocation of resources, the sustainable number of human beings that can live on the planet as well as their sustainable birth and death rates, so that the economic and demographic subsystems could be sustainable as well for the biosphere: "input equals to output equals to throughput" (Daly and Farley 2003, p. 55) is the motto for such a conception. Even though there is not enough space to get into its details, many problems can easily be foreseen if this scheme were to be implemented, notably as regards individual freedoms, or social and governmental control over birth rates. Peter Hay moreover points out that "whatever the ultimate validity of the zero growth case (some argue), if the practical consequence is to jeopardise ecological achievements that are attainable [by way of the development of greener technologies, for instance], it would make more sense to significantly reduce the current emphasis on zero-growthism" (Hay 2002, p. 252).

3.   "Ecological economists" are to be distinguished from "environmental economists" as the first attempt at finding the threshold of resource allocation at which an economy is no longer sustainable, insisting on resource distribution rather than Pareto efficient allocation. Their main goal is to "enlarge the framework of the neoclassical economic paradigm to include scientifically valid measures of the environmental costs of economic activities" (Nadeau 2008). Environmental economists, however, inquire more directly into the valuation of nature's worth in terms of ecosystem services, since their work is mainly directed at internalizing ecosystem services and pollution into the market-based economy (cf. Daly and Farley 2003, pp. 4–5), because "environmental economics seeks to redress this deficiency within the framework of assumptions essential to neo-classical economics" (Hay 2002, p. 221).

4.   The household production function approach includes the transportation costs among other expenditures that a household is willing to undertake to improve the quality of its environment. The mention of transportation costs is used here because it is the most relevant evaluation technique for landscapes and nonanthropogenic environments. In any events, the shortcomings of the household production function approach are very similar to that of the transportation costs (cf. Hussen 2000, p. 298).

5.   For example, O'Neill, Holland and Light (2008, p. 20) present the Pareto-optimal cost-benefit analysis test of Kaldor-Hicks in such terms: "a situation A is an improvement over B if the gains are greater than the losses, so that the gainers could compensate the losers and still be better off." It is "a method by which anyone, given a set of data about the outcomes of alternative actions, can work out mechanically which outcome is best" (O'Neill et al. 2008, p. 71).

6.   According to Siry et al., "86% of the forests in the world are publicly owned, [while] private forests provide proportionally more commodities" (Siry et al. 2009, p. 4). This proportion however drops to 50.1% in Europe (Hirsch et al. 2007, p. 23). In Western Europe, the proportion of private land ownership tends to be higher (as in the United Kingdom, Austria, Norway, Finland, France, and Iceland), but there is a great variability of ownership types among countries.

7.   One of the five basic assumptions of a proper market economy is that "for each item subjected to market transaction, the number of buyers and sellers is large. Thus, no one buyer or seller can single-handedly influence the terms of trade." This is not the actual situation for land ownership in most countries (Hussen 2000, p. 21).

8.   "Free-market environmentalism" is a branch of environmental economics suggesting an expansion of "well-specified property rights for natural and environmental resources": "in general, free-market environmentalism emphasizes the positive incentives associated with prices, profits, and entrepreneurship, as opposed to political environmentalism, which emphasizes negative incentives associated with regulation and taxes" (Anderson and Leal 2001, p. 4).

9. "The free-market was—and remains—an Anglo-Saxon singularity. It was constructed in a context not found in any other full-blown form for only about a generation [from the 1840 to the 1870s]. It could never have been created at all if ownership and economic life had not long been thoroughly individualistic in nineteenth-century England. It was an experiment in social engineering undertaken in exceptionally propitious circumstances . . . In the strictly economic terms of rising productivity and national wealth, the mid-Victorian period was one of boom. But it was a boom whose social costs were politically insupportable. As the democratic franchise was extended, so was state intervention in the economy. From the 1870s to the First World War, a spate of reforms was implemented, limiting market freedoms for the sake of social cohesion (and sometimes economic efficiency . . . It is the disappearance of the nineteenth-century free market, not its emergence, that occurred as a result of a slow historical evolution . . . The laissez-faire policies which produced the Great Transformation in nineteenth-century England were based on the theory that free markets are natural and political restraints on the market are artificial. The truth is that free markets are creatures of state power, and persist only so long as the state is able to prevent human needs for security and the control of economic risk from finding political expression" (Gray 1998, pp. 13–14, 17).

10. On the political partiality of the economic liberalism: "The free market has used the power of the state to achieve its ends but has weakened the institutions of the state in vital respects. In every case free market policies lost political legitimacy while at the same time altering the economy and society in ways that democratic choice cannot reverse" (Gray 1998, p. 24). On the ideological partiality of the free market creed: "Whilst claiming to liberate individuality, [the market] promotes cultural homogenisation. Whilst claiming to be the mechanism that will deliver sustainability, it destroys natural capital by transforming it into high-entropy, system-overloading wastes. Even its promised freedoms, defined as they are in the narrow terms of product choice on the supermarket shelf, are largely illusory" (Hay 2002, p. 247).

11. The Fourteenth Amendment of the United States Constitution was adopted in 1868, after the Civil War, to overrule the Dred Scott v. Sandford decision of 1857 which prevented slaves and their descendants from having constitutional rights. It did so by extending the notions of citizenship and person. However, through a bizarre series of events, two legal cases—Santa Clara County v. Southern Pacific Railroad Co. (1886) and Pembina Consolidated Silver Mining & Milling Co. v. Pennsylvania (1888)—confirmed that corporations would also thereafter be considered as "persons." One of the points made and discussed at length in the brief of counsel for defendants in error was that "corporations are persons within the meaning of the Fourteenth Amendment to the Constitution of the United States." Before argument, Mr. Chief Justice [Morrison R.] Waite said: "The Court does not wish to hear argument on the question whether the provision in the Fourteenth Amendment to the Constitution which forbids a state to deny to any person within its jurisdiction the equal protection of the laws applies to these corporations. We are all of opinion that it does" (Santa Clara County v. Southern Pacific Railroad Co. 118 U.S. 394 [1886]). According to Charles Wallace Collins, problems with corporations were not as rampant at the time. But already in 1912, as a result of the court's decisions, "what[ever] may be urged by people as a measure of social reform, to them takes the appearance of an attack on vested rights. These great organizations, having in their service well-trained lawyers, have been quick to seize upon every opportunity to check the activity of the State when their own interests are affected. Having great financial resources, they enter the field of politics to prevent the enactment of any statute that may operate to their immediate disadvantage. If they fail to stem

the tide of public opinion, and laws are made which will reduce their profits, they immediately set to work to prevent the enforcement of such laws" (Collins 1912, p. 130).

12. For example, 2009 Nobel Prize winner Elinor Olstrom claims: "I am opposed to the persistent reliance upon models like the 'Prisoner's dilemma' or the 'tragedy of the commons' after years of empirical research in both the lab and the field that has called their universal applicability into question . . .. Because common-pool resources, and their users, are viewed as relatively similar to one another, and because of the simplicity of the models, officials (assumed to be acting in the public interest) are thought to be capable of devising uniform and effective rules for an entire region . . .. However, empirical research does not support the idea that a central agency could solve all resource problems for a large region with simple, top-down directives . . .. Field studies have also found multiple cases where resource users have failed to self organize. Thus, the core empirical and theoretical question is why self-organization is successfully undertaken in some cases and not in others" (Aligica et al. 2003).

13. Neil Carter mentions that "Dutch water pollution charges have reduced organic emissions into waterways at low cost and encouraged firms to introduce cleaner technologies," and that "Swedish sulfur dioxide and nitrogen oxide taxes have produced significant emission reductions." Yet, success is quite variable, since similar MBIs introduced "in France and Germany have had mixed results" (Carter 2007, p. 337).

14. One of the debate arising between economists that use these methods regards the difference between the use of WTP (willingness to pay]) and WTA (willingness to accept), where the second concept refers to the willingness to accept a monetary compensation for an ecosystem service or a good. According to Kolstad, "theory suggests that there should be little difference between these two measures, yet there is considerable evidence that they are not the same" (Kolstad 2000, p. 366). For our purpose, we will only address the "willingness to pay" concept, which is the most common among ecological economists.

15. I here adapt an argument from Thomas Nagel who emphasizes that it is not necessary for one to act in order to be able to recognize that there is a sufficient reason to act. In the same way, it is not necessary for one to have a preference for something in order to recognize that this same thing is value-worthy: "The first-person acknowledgment of a sufficient reason for doing [or valuing] something is the acknowledgement of a justification for doing [or valuing] it, and is sufficient to explain one's doing [or valuing] it . . .. There is no need to hold that 'X acknowledges a reason to A' entails 'X does [or values, or "has a preference for"] A, or wants to do [or "have a preference for"] A,' or that the latter statement is part of the meaning of the former. Nor is it necessary to maintain that the first-person acknowledgement of a reason will produce a motivation unless other, contrary influences interfere . . .. Such an acknowledgement is by itself capable of providing a motivation in the appropriate direction" (Nagel 1970, pp. 110–11).

16. In a fascinating book on the encounter of Emmanuel Levinas with several analytic philosophers, Michael L. Morgan shows how Stephen Darwall's notion of "intersubjective values" could prove useful to move from Levinas's ethics to an understanding of ethics as the practical field within which justice is enacted. Here I dub this type of values "inherent" or "experiential" because it is the experience of a nonanthropogenic environment which provides the support for such values to occur. But be that as it may, I take Darwall's account of intersubjective values to mirror what I am purporting within the framework of this project as experiential or inherent values, and I concur with his analysis that these are crucial for our moral lives, as I am about to show.

References

Afeissa, H.-S., 2008, The Transformative Value of Ecological Pragmatism: An Introduction to the Work of Bryan G. Norton, in S.A.P.I.E.N.S., G. Mainguy, (ed.), *Institut Veolia Environnement* 1 (1): 73–79.

Aligica, P.D., Ostrom, V. & Ostrom, E., 2003, Rethinking Governance Systems and Challenging Disciplinary Boundaries—Interview with Elinor Ostrom, in *Rethinking Institutional Analysis and Development: The Bloomington School* (Mercatus Center, George Mason University), online: http://www.mercatus.org/PublicationDetails. aspx?id=15952.

Anderson, T.L. & Leal, D.R., 2001, *Free-Market Environmentalism* (revised ed.), Palgrave, New York.

Carter, N., 2007, *The Politics of the Environment: Ideas, Activism, Policy* (2nd ed.), Cambridge University Press, Cambridge.

Collins, Ch.W., 1912, *The Fourteenth Amendment and the State: A Study of the Operation of the Restraint Clauses of Section One of the Fourteenth Amendment to the Constitution of the United States*, Little, Brown and Company, Boston.

Costanza, R. et al., 1997, The Value of the World's Ecosystem Services and Natural Capital, *Nature* 387, 15 May 1997, 253–60.

Cotula, L. et al., 2009, *Land Grab or Development Opportunity? Agricultural Investment and International Land Deals in Africa*, FAO/IIED/IFAD, London and Rome, online: ftp://ftp.fao.org/docrep/fao/011/ak241e/ak241e.pdf.

Daly, H.E. & Farley, J., 2003, *Ecological Economics: Principles and Applications*, D.C. Island Press, Washington, DC.

Gray, J., 1998, *False Dawn: The Delusion of Global Capitalism*, Granta Books, London.

Haab, T.C. & McConnell, K.E., 2002, *Valuing Environmental and Natural Resources: The Econometrics of Non-Market Valuation*, Edward Elgar Publishing Limited, Cheltenham.

Hay, P., 2002, *A Companion to Environmental Thought*, Edinburgh University Press, Edinburgh.

Hirsch, F. et al., 2007, Private Forest Ownership in Europe, Unasylva 228, FAO/UNECE, Vol. 58, 23–25, online: ftp://ftp.fao.org/docrep/FAO/010/a1346e/a1346e06.pdf.

Hussen, A.M., 2000, *Principles of Environmental Economics: Economics, Ecology and Public Policy*, Routledge, London.

Kolstad, Ch.D., 2000, *Environmental Economics*, Oxford University Press, Oxford.

Kraut, R., 2007, Desire and the Human Good, in Russ Shafer-Landau (ed.), *Ethical Theory: An Anthology*, Wiley-Blackwell, Oxford, pp. 315–23.

Lauria, D. et al., 1999, Households Demand for Improved Sanitation Services: A Case Study of Calamba, The Philippines, in, Ian J. Bateman & Kenneth G. Willis (eds.), *Valuing Environmental Preferences: Theory and Practice of the Contingent Valuation Method in the US, EU and Developing Countries*, Oxford University Press, Oxford.

Maris, V. & Revéret, J.-P., 2009, Les limites de l'évaluation économique de la biodiversité, in *Les ateliers de l'éthique*, 4:1, CRÉUM, Montreal, pp. 52–64.

Millennium Assessment, Glossary, 2004, 17, online: http://www.millenniumassessment. org/documents/document.776.aspx.pdf.

Morgan, M. L., 2007, *Discovering Levinas*, Cambridge, Cambridge University Press.

Nadeau, R., 2008, Environmental and Ecological Economics, in Cutler J. Cleveland (ed.), *Encyclopedia of Earth*, Environmental Information Coalition, National Council for Science and the Environment, Washington, DC, online: http://www.eoearth.org/article/Environmental_and_ecological_economics.

Sugden, R., 1999, Public Good and Contingent Valuation, in Ian J. Bateman & Kenneth G. Willis (eds.), *Valuing Environmental Preferences: Theory and Practice of the Contingent Valuation Method in the US, EU and Developing Countries*, Oxford University Press, Oxford, pp. 152–82.

Siry, J.P. et al., 2009, *Global Forest Ownership: Implications for Forest Production, Management, and Protection*, Conference presented at the XIII World Forestry Congress, 18–23 October 2009, Buenos Aires, Argentina, online: http://www.cfm2009.org/es/ programapost/resumenes/uploads/global_forest_ownership_FD.pdf.

Turner, K., 1999, The Place of Economic Values in Environmental Valuations, in Ian J. Bateman & Kenneth G. Willis (eds.), *Valuing Environmental Preferences: Theory and Practice of the Contingent Valuation Method in the US, EU and Developing Countries*, Oxford University Press, Oxford, pp. 17–41.

Walsh, R.G., Miller, N.P. & Gilliam, L.O., 1983, Valuing Option, Existence, and Bequest Demands for Wilderness, in *Land Economics* 60 (1): 14–29.

Tackling Environmental Degradation and Poverty: A New Agenda for Entrepreneurs in Transition Economies

Boleslaw Rok
Kozminski University
Warsaw
Poland

1. Introduction

The proposition that businesses can play proactive role in solving development and environment challenges is a highly promising one. Encouraging firms to take seriously their social and environmental obligations to society is a new agenda for policy makers, business leaders, and academics (Newell and Frynas 2007). To eradicate poverty, ensure environmental sustainability and develop a global partnership for development, it is necessary to harness the power of business. Can this role be performed through business-as-usual practices or does it need to be driven, guided, and regulated by broader state-led developmental priorities? Business is a powerful force that can provide billions of people with better lives in a better environment. Several initiatives of this kind from transition economies will be presented in the last part of this text.

Poverty has many social and political dimensions in addition to income poverty, including material deprivation, discriminating social relations, lack of security, ineffective institutions and lack of information, education, and health. At the World Summit on Social Development in Copenhagen (UN 1995), extreme poverty was defined as depending on access to a range of services, a condition characterized by severe deprivation of basic human needs, including food, safe drinking water, sanitation facilities, health, shelter, education and information. Poverty means that income and resources are so inadequate as to preclude those people from having a standard of living considered acceptable in the society in which they live. They are often excluded and marginalized from participating in economic, social, and cultural activities that are the norm for other people.

Using monetary income to identify poverty has indeed a long tradition among academics, governments, and nongovernmental organizations. This traditional approach defines a person as poor if his or her income is below a poverty line. The poverty line may be subjective, objective, or hybrid and it is established at a nationally determined level based on a consumption basket or as a percentage of the overall income distribution. But there is a growing recognition that income level does not capture the social complexity of conditions that comprise poverty or qualify the level of well-being of an individual or a community.

Amartya Sen (1999) offers a broader conceptualization by defining poverty as a deprivation of human capabilities to exercise fundamental rights to survival, security, and freedom. These deprived capabilities include lack of access to employment, healthcare, basic resources, and the inability to remain secure from different conflicts. This conceptualization provides a multidimensional view of poverty as a phenomenon determined not only by financial measures, but environmental, social, and political forces as well. Social indicators are an important instrument enabling assessment of the level of a country's development as well as of the impact of its policies on human welfare. Environmental indicators as a nonmonetary measurement of living standard are equally important today as a part of multidimensional approach to poverty and well-being.

Of particular concern is the fact that poverty is often associated with unalterable characteristics such as environmental catastrophes that are beyond the control of those affected (Barbier 2010). The assetless poor are highly vulnerable to natural disaster shocks such as droughts, hurricanes, tsunamis, floods, and other extreme events. The problem of growing numbers of the poor without access to assets and their concentration in less favored areas remains a major development challenge. The dynamics of the poverty–environment trap can be even worse for the household if the environmental degradation problems are widespread in the region and affect many households.

The linkages between poverty and environment are characterized as "downward spiral" or "vicious circle." According to Brundtland Report, the impoverishment of poor people environment further impoverishes them, making their survival even more difficult and uncertain (Brundtland Commission 1987). The environmental degradation further reduces the income of the poor and forces them to overuse natural resources. This poverty–environment "vicious circle" implies that poverty is simultaneously a main reason and a result of the environmental degradation. But there are several stereotypes among economists, as it was pointed out by Dasgupta (2003). One of this says that economic growth is good for the environment because countries first need to put poverty behind them in order to care, or that trade improves the environment, because it raises incomes, and the richer people are, the more willing they are to devote resources to cleaning up their living space.

Sustainable development depends on addressing the contribution of the environment to human well-being and pro-poor economic growth into decision-making, a process known as poverty–environment mainstreaming (Mainstreaming 2009). It is a multi-stakeholder effort of integrating poverty–environment linkages into policymaking and implementation processes at national and international levels. In recent years, attention has focused on the key goal of reducing poverty and the pivotal contribution that better environmental management can make to improved livelihoods and income opportunities of the poor and other marginalized groups.

The relationship between poverty and natural resource degradation needs to be revised (Barbier 2010). Although poverty–environment traps are still prevalent, they encompass more complex relationships involving links between asset poverty, lack of income opportunities, or access to key markets for land, labor, and credit, and the availability and quality of natural resources. Barbier's study provides a new perspective on the poverty–resource degradation issue, by showing that the poor are less likely to be responsible for as much of the environmental degradation as previously believed, and suggesting novel policies targeted specifically at reducing labor, market, and asset constraints, which contribute to environmental poverty traps. There is a clear case to be made for promoting an integrated, more universal, more inclusive, and more holistic approach to deprivation (DESA 2009).

The poverty reduction and environmental protection are surely complementary goals. At the 2000 UN Millennium Summit, heads of state and governments from around the world signed the Millennium Declaration. The eight goals known as Millennium Development Goals were viewed as a set of eight interconnected aspects of human suffering and achievement which have formed the basis for guiding poverty reduction and for holding different partners accountable to citizens and motivate development policy decisions and actions. The environmental sustainability cannot be achieved without addressing poverty, and vice versa, the sustainable poverty reduction requires the environmental sustainability. These goals by promoting poverty reduction, education, maternal health, gender equality, combating child mortality, AIDS and other diseases, and protecting the environment set an ambitious target of halving the number of the world's poor by 2015.

Few years later, the Report of the UN Commission on the Private Sector and Development (Commission 2004), emphasized the essential role that entrepreneurs play in growing, dynamic, sustainable, and competitive economies that create sustainable livelihoods, put people to work and raise standards of living. The report also called for new and more creative models of engagement from different partners to accomplish these goals. A number of recommendations for public–private partnerships and private sector activity were proposed to make "business work for the poor" (SADC 2008). Today many governments, civil society organizations, and communities are looking towards private sector efficiency and creativity to help improve the standard of living of the world's poor. It is the case one can observe in different transition countries, including Eastern Europe and Commonwealth of Independent States.

Poverty and environmental degradation will not be overcome without a commitment on the part of all market players to create an economic playing field based on the principles of fairness and justice. To target poverty and environmental degradation more effectively while increasing revenues, business has several roles to play: by generating growth, by including poor people into their value chains, by contributing knowledge and capabilities, by developing innovative approaches, by replicating those approaches across borders, and by advocating for policies that will alleviate poverty and improve environment (UNDP 2010). But the effectiveness of business in fostering development depends on the necessary changes in management mindset and the quality of political, social, and economic institutions.

2. The Poverty Challenge in Transition Economies

Most of the countries in Eastern Europe (EE) and Commonwealth of Independent States (CIS) began their transition with extensive hidden unemployment and at least one-tenth of its population below the then subsistence level—as defined within the national context based on a "social minimum" consumption basket. The central issue during the transition era has been the movement of labor from the inefficient state sector to the emerging private sector. The socialist heritage and economic transition in most of the countries from the region have made the experience of post-socialist poverty unusual in some respects. Before the transition, people had secure jobs and anticipated pensions following retirement. The transition toward free market ended their guaranteed employment and retirement security.

The collapse of traditional state-owned industry and agriculture has led to a rapid fall in wages at the lower end of the distribution and an increase in short-term and long-term unemployment. Many people lost their jobs as state-owned enterprises reduced their workforce or closed entirely due to increasing competition. In rural areas, many state-owned agricultural cooperatives collapsed, leaving farm workers unemployed. Very few countries from the region have been successful in creating jobs to fully replace those that have been destroyed. At the same time, this was an opportunity for some people who under communist rule were only allowed to run very small "craft" or agribusinesses but in the new market realities had the opportunity to expand their operations and utilize their creative potential (Pradeep 2008).

The vast unemployment and the low level of main indicators for the material quality of life, sometimes also war-related circumstances in several countries, forced many citizens to seek economic opportunities for themselves and start their own businesses out of necessity. Although the economic recovery brought a noticeable improvement in the overall quality of life, several countries from this region are facing still a complex set of environmental challenges such as hazardous waste sites in residential areas, low energy efficiency, urban air pollution, and deteriorating water and sewage systems.

The recent global slowdown in economic activity can lead to rising unemployment levels across countries in this region. Different reports are showing that the crisis threatens the well-being of close to 40 million people who are still poor. It also threatens the welfare of an additional 120 million people who are living just above the relative poverty line and at risk of easily falling into poverty (The World Bank 2010). The poverty impact of the regional recession will be enormous. The results of simulations suggest that by 2010, there will be 11 million more people in poverty and over 23 million more people just above the international poverty line, relative to pre-crisis projections for growth and poverty. So, it is necessary to deal with an important question now: how to reduce poverty level even in the absence of high economic growth? And, who is primarily responsible for reducing or preventing poverty in the region?

Recently the European Commission published a new strategy "Europe 2020" putting forward for the coming future three mutually reinforcing priorities: smart, sustainable, and inclusive growth. For EC "inclusive growth" means empowering people through high levels of employment, investing in skills, fighting poverty, and modernizing labor markets, training and social protection systems so as to help people anticipate and manage change, and build a cohesive society. The Commission decided to work, together with the Member States, more intensively on establishing different instruments to foster commitment by public and private players to reduce social exclusion, to promote shared collective and individual responsibility in combating poverty, social exclusion and environmental degradation to design and implement programs to promote social innovation for the most vulnerable.

3. Global Challenges in a Changing Context

What has happened in the recent years that even one of the most developed parts of the world started to give highest priority to inclusiveness? We can elaborate on three new factors at least. The first factor is interconnectedness, so visible during recent discussions on the financial crisis. In fact we are facing several interrelated crises: economic recession, energy insecurity, food crisis, demographic challenges and the overarching climate crisis. We started to understand that solving any of these challenges requires addressing all. Development agenda relates not only to the economic growth but rather to the combination of economic development and social and environmental indicators of progress. So, there is a need to adopt a new approach focused on systemic change. We probably know better now how to proceed with global challenges in a changing context in a more holistic way, or at least there is a growing body of knowledge on those issues, but much more has to be done in order to reach a "new development consensus" in line with the sustainable development.

The second factor is related to the growing recognition that poverty reduction is a complex and vital issue not only for the developing world, with some of the poorest countries, but affects population in every country in the world, including the most developed countries and countries in transition. It is not about a country or a market, it is rather a demographic category. Technically, bottom of the pyramid (BoP) is a socioeconomic designation for the four billion people who live on less than USD 1,500 (according to the purchasing power parity exchange rate) per capita income. Every country has its own base of the pyramid sector, including the United States and Europe. Eastern Europe and Commonwealth of Independent States are the newest frontier where the poverty challenge is very serious and complementary to the environmental degradation.

The last factor is connected to the recognition that business plays an increasingly important role in development, using for example the benefits posed by knowledge and technology. The idea that businesses must embrace wider roles and responsibilities and respond in a proactive way to development challenges afflicting communities all over the world became a new source for innovation. Micro-entrepreneurs, local manufacturing companies, and multinational enterprises, all of them are investing in new ideas and new facilities that strengthen the foundation of economic growth and prosperity in the environmental-friendly way. But the poor must be participants in the design of a more inclusive process of economic development.

Some pioneering business-led approaches to poverty alleviation were known for years already, and we have come a long way from learning about innovation in enterprise development from Anglo American in South Africa, to exploring ways to finance and support entrepreneurs with Tribanco in Brazil, to looking at innovative BoP models like Jaipur Rugs in India (Jenkins and Ishikawa 2009). But only recently, it became widely recognized in both the corporate and development circles that firms of all types could be the central actors in this quest. They were significant achievements in the modern "philosophy of doing business" in the last ten years leading to a widely accepted proposition that businesses can play proactive role in solving development challenges by being an integral part of the solution to sustainable livelihoods of low-income communities all over the world.

The first achievement is connected to the growth of the corporate social responsibility (CSR) movement in business in its modern form as the innovative, sustainable management approach. The initial articulation of the groundbreaking idea of a base (or bottom)-of-the-pyramid (BoP) perspective on business strategy and poverty alleviation is the second achievement. And the third one is the development of the social entrepreneurship, sometimes named as the fourth sector activity.

3.1. Corporate responsibility as a solution

The business role in society was traditionally connected to the philanthropic attitudes, not to the strategic approach. Companies, in the least developed countries in particular, are expected to give back a portion of their profits to society, to help the disadvantaged, marginalized groups, and support community. It is a voluntary contribution to society, motivated mostly by ethical reasons. Philanthropy is an important, but not the only one, part of business–society equation in transition countries. CSR, connected to the more advanced strategies, is becoming gradually a powerful tool contributing towards sustainable development and societal regeneration in most countries in this region.

Looking at CSR from a development perspective, Michael Hopkins (2007) categorizes corporate involvement in development work into three types: charitable donation for purposes of philanthropy, development projects that serve to enhance the company's reputation, and development projects which directly have a positive impact on the company bottom line. Social development is widely perceived by commercial companies to be an overwhelming task, especially that in many cases the communities themselves call in business to do what the state cannot cope with on its own. Some assumptions under which business should become more involved in poverty alleviation and protection of the environment are discussed. One can conclude that poverty and environment are now on the agenda for business, and it is a hot topic as never before.

Responsible and sustainable business at the base of the pyramid is now starting to be a widely recognized model in business community. But CSR cannot continue to be perceived as a largely defensive tactic that is designed to protect companies against potential damage to their reputation, or we can say that new business models are beyond "CSR as usual." The modern corporate responsibility trend is based on achieving sustainability in the overall business activity (Blowfield 2010). CSR is the responsibility of an organization for the impacts of its decisions and activities on society and the environment through transparent and ethical behavior that contributes to sustainable development, including health and welfare of society, takes into account the expectations of stakeholders, is in compliance with applicable law and consistent with international norms of behavior and is integrated throughout the organization and practiced in its relationships.

Conceptually, this type of CSR engagement needs to be distinguished from defensive or reactive approach, where CSR is essentially treated as a supplementary function to a non-CSR-oriented core. CSR as a concept acknowledges now the fact that company behavior is subject to basic business operating principles like profitability and competitive performance. The emerging model is much more focused on operating the core business in an innovative, socially and environmentally responsible way, complemented by investment in communities for solid business case reasons. But at the same time, CSR recognizes that company behavior is key to the promotion of societal goals, including to the achievement of national or international strategies on sustainable development as an important part of market-based solutions.

3.2. BoP entrepreneurship as a solution

Today, there is little dispute that poverty is one of the most pressing global problems, calling for innovative solutions. The biggest challenge for the commercial sector lies in alleviating poverty in a socially, economically, and environmentally sustainable manner, without losing sight of poor people as individuals (Kandachar and Halme 2008). So, when Prahalad and Hart (2002) introduced the base-of-the-pyramid concept at the turn of this century, it was an idea whose time had come.

The perspective presented by Prahalad and Hart is based on the view that serving markets at the BoP is an economically viable business strategy generating reasonable economic and societal returns to the commercial organization and the local community at the same time. It is a win-win process, either by selling goods to, or sourcing products from, those at the base of the pyramid in a way that helps to improve the standard of living of the poor. The BoP market theory is based on the idea that commercial companies can simultaneously be profitable and help reduce global poverty by serving a market they have largely ignored until recently—over 4 billion people in the world. The base-of-the-pyramid strategy involves the private sector in helping reduce poverty by serving these people in ways responsive to their needs.

Although the idea of reaching a base of the pyramid through corporate initiatives was met with considerable acceptance and support within business and academic circles, it also raised several discussions. Some critics (Jaiswal 2008) claimed that one must not talk only about fortune at the base of the pyramid but also fortune for the base of the pyramid. It means that instead of selling to the poor, businesses could create opportunities first of all for the local population. Others (Kirnani 2007) concluded that that there is very little evidence that selling to the poor is a profitable venture which benefits large companies as well as the poor. But the list of the corporations looking for innovative strategies, transforming their business models required to reach the poor, was starting to grow rapidly, even if there is no consensus on mutual value creation. There are different collections of case studies already, reports from different markets looking for the best strategies and main constraints (Karamchandani et al. 2009, UNDP 2008, WEF 2009).

Some of the BoP strategies, based mostly on the demand side, but not exclusively, are still successful and could be seen as a first step, according to Simanis and Hart (2008). They pointed out already important differences between "first generation" BoP strategies (BoP 1.0)—which regard the poor as producers or consumers, with innovation only restricted to the structural aspect, and "second generation" BoP strategies (BoP 2.0), which include the poor as partners. The BoP 1.0 strategies are addressing a new market without clear understanding of the real needs or aspirations of those living there. The BoP 2.0 approach requires a personal relationship of trust, understanding, and respect through which new possibilities for locally embedded businesses can emerge. The second generation strategies are mostly operating on the supply side through engaging other partners and combining resources and capabilities.

According to Simanis and Hart, second generation BoP strategy requires an embedded process of coinvention and business cocreation that brings firms into close, personal business partnership with BoP communities. This helps promote embedded innovation, in which the new value propositions are jointly developed by a company and the community, creatively combining the capabilities of both parties. Therefore, the company and the BoP cocreate a new market, based on business intimacy in the sense that each party will find the other one irreplaceable and absolutely necessary.

3.3. Social enterprise development as a solution

The new phenomenon of the twenty-first century is the social enterprise development. For example, Bornstein (2004) has prepared a diverse collection of innovative cases from Ashoka members in several countries. They represent social service programs that can be replicated on a large scale, and some of them are self-sustaining initiatives that would not require ongoing influxes of funding aid in order to continue operations over the long-term. Social enterprises, or social ventures, are often described as businesses that operate with a social purpose to provide a service to disadvantaged individuals or the community (Darby and Jenkins 2006). The social enterprise movement is growing and gathering supporters across the globe as an innovative approach to business activity offering low-income or disadvantaged populations a path to sustainable development (Nielsen and Samia 2008).

Social entrepreneurship was greatly empowered by the work of Muhammad Yunus (2010). In his view, "unfettered markets in their current form are not meant to solve social problems and instead may actually exacerbate poverty, disease, pollution, corruption, crime, and inequality." Social business, as defined by Yunus, is a venture whose sole mission is to create a positive impact on society through its good or service, and is thoroughly sustainable, or covers its costs. All profits are reinvested into the company in order to expand and create a greater positive impact. As with any market-based approach, social businesses increase their efficiency and quality through competition, but on the basis of social and environmental impact rather than profit.

Most social enterprises are built on business models that combine a revenue-generating objective with a social value-generating structure, in order to launch products, services that function in the low-income markets. A growing number of entrepreneurs are setting up social businesses not to achieve limited personal gain but to pursue specific social goals. These entrepreneurs and their businesses are motivated by primarily "make a difference" (MAD) goals, often aiming to transform the system whose dysfunction help create or aggravate major socioeconomic, environmental, or political problems. Social enterprise is seen to represent a route both to solving some of the main social and environmental problems that the world faces and to new ways of creating jobs and social and environmental sustainability in a post-financial crisis world. These new organizations are operating in accordance with the best management principles, aiming for full cost recovery, but are concentrated on creating products or services that provide first of all social benefits for people.

Recently, social enterprises attracted strong interest in the discussions on poverty reduction and protection of the environment, in part due to the remarkable success of microfinance and the other local-based solutions. The most successful solutions pass two tests: they are self-funding, and they operate at sufficient scale to make a difference to larger poor communities. Social entrepreneurship can be an alternative or supplement to the traditional approaches of different assistance programs, donors, philanthropic foundations, purely commercial initiatives, or typical nongovernmental organizations.

There are numerous examples of the emerging convergence of for-profit money-making and nonprofit mission, sometimes labeled as "not-only-for-profit" or "for-benefits", "fourth sector organization." The term "fourth sector" derives from the fact that participants are creating hybrid organizations distinct from those operating in the government, business, and nonprofit sectors. They are driven by both social purpose and financial promise that fall somewhere between traditional companies and charities. The hybrid models leverage the capabilities of other actors in the market where they operate and find innovative ways to reduce transaction costs despite imperfect market conditions and drive innovation.

4. The Practice of Inclusive Business in Transition Economies

Through combining possibilities and resources of these three streams in business solutions for the poverty reduction—corporate responsible and sustainable models, BoP-entrepreneurs established in the cocreation process, and social entrepreneurship—there is a possibility to concentrate on awareness raising, providing access, affordability, and availability. Nevertheless, different kinds of support from governments, development experts, and social partners for innovative business models and value chains that demonstrate commercial and development impact having at the same time the potential of reaching sustainability and scale are crucial. But pursuing the BoP solutions forces us to rethink our conventional wisdom about business itself, its role in the society, and the motivation which lies behind the entrepreneurship.

The inclusive business approach was developed by the Netherlands Development Cooperation and the World Business Council for Sustainable Development (WBCSD 2009) as an initiative that seeks to contribute towards poverty reduction by including the base of the pyramid as consumers, suppliers, distributors or employees within the value chain of a company in a win-win relationship. Inclusive business has reached a stage where it is critical to look not only at what the models are, but also at how those models have started, evolved, reached commercial viability, and scaled over time (Jenkins and Ishikawa 2010).

Looking into different case studies from transition countries, it is easy to recognize a wide range of opportunities in the region of EE and CIS.[1] The solutions are as diverse as the national environments in which inclusive businesses are operating, legal status of an enterprise, its scale or sector, entrepreneur's personality, and their choice of partners. The social innovation that happens out of these activities, solving problems stemming from poverty and environmental degradation in the region, is almost certain to have implications for both private and public sectors in transition countries, but what is most important for this analysis, it has implications for future decision making process at different phases of the business cycle and establishment of the more effective and ethical business models.

This effectiveness is perceived not only in financial terms but also as a tool for social and economic empowerment of the low-income population. The ethical dimension of sustainable development is based on the idea of inter-generational and intra-generational accountability, along with its ecological corollary and the priority to be given to the poorest (Pesqueux 2009). Inclusive business models seen in a partnership perspective represent a form of radical innovation for long-term sustainability that may enforce real social responsibilities into corporate practice and bring to life new ideas, creating value for business and the low-income population at the same time.

The most successful organizations invest a great deal of time and energy to set up and develop its structure and strategy. So, it is crucial to identify the stages of business development through which the presented below enterprises from the region have evolved and to describe some critical points in every stage. The process of enterprise development is not fully predictable and linear; opportunities and constraints can shift businesses back and forth between stages. Nevertheless, there are at least four identifiable stages in this process to consider: concept development, model design, implementation, and achieving scale.

4.1. Concept development stage

At the concept development stage, the emphasis is on the purpose of the enterprise venture. In the social enterprise literature, there is a concept of blended value (Emerson 2003), saying that value is generated from the combined interplay between the component parts of economic, social, and environmental performance. In the literature on corporate responsibility, there is a concept of a shared value (Porter and Kramer 2006), which relates to policies and practices that enhance the competitiveness of a company while simultaneously advancing economic and social conditions in the communities in which it operates. Recently presented in details mutual value model (London et al. 2010) is based on the same idea that BoP venture has to generate economic value and social value in the same process. According to Ted London, venture development grounded in mutual value creation offers the best prospect for generating economically-viable enterprises that also enhance the quality of life in BoP communities. Inclusive business model presents a balanced picture, stressing the need to put in place mutually beneficial economic and social returns. It means that the way to a successful inclusive business is to create value for all stakeholders, in particular customers, suppliers, and employees, but also local communities.

The main question for analyzing the concept development stage of enterprises is about the ultimate driving force. Is it the pull from bottom-up demand or the push from the top-down development programs? These mutual value creation propositions are based on the connection of supply and demand, and escape traditional business logic representing a further step forward in business development. It started with the identification of opportunities and a kind of initial feasibility study. In some cases, mutual value creation is embedded at the level of concept development; other cases have creation of mutual value as an important outcome.

In the case of Begeli from Georgia, we can observe a process of creation a kind of commercial arm of the nongovernmental organization. The Biological Farming Association Elkana is a nongovernmental organization serving more than four hundred organic farmers from different regions of Georgia. Begeli as a newly created company is working directly with Elkana's members, who are producing organic food like cereals, honey, tea, juice, fruits, vegetables, and wine mostly for the local market. The company serves as a marketing and distribution tool for local farmers, using several sales channels, such as supermarkets, telephone ordering, and a recently launched online shop. The inclusion of farmers is the raison d'être of Begeli.

In Croatia, Zeljko Mavrovic, ex-boxing champion and a well-known public figure in ex-Yugoslavia, decided to produce best quality organic food in an environmentally responsible way. Starting his business, Mavrovic perceived a huge risk—he was afraid that entering the Croatian market as a first mover with an eco-related story could be misunderstood by the public. However, his social capital as a celebrity was a critical point. Mavrovic developed his inclusive business model as a system that tries to accommodate the basic economic, social, and environmental needs of the local population while preserving the natural resources.

There are opportunities for established businesses as well. Vitmark is a well-known company in the Ukrainian market and a recognized brand for juices, nectars, and still drinks. But juices and nectars were considered an unaffordable luxury product by many low-income customers in Ukraine. Additionally to its different products, Vitmark decided to offer a discount product for poorer segment of population in Ukraine, thanks to its own model of cost-efficient local sourcing and product design. With economical packaging, reducing overall marketing costs and using natural domestic fruits and vegetables, Vitmark was able to create low-priced quality product that addresses the demand of this particular market segment, at the same time including local farmers and providing access and long-term income opportunities to about 2,500 small-scale and 25 large suppliers from four regions. Consequently, Ukrainian consumers hailed the high quality and lower-priced eco-juice, since such a product for lower income customers had not been available in the country before.

In these three companies, the inclusive business model was an innovative attitude to fill gaps in the market, to offer new products or services adapted to the needs of low-income population, to ensure environmental sustainability in the region of operations by improving consumers' awareness and to create employment. The main driver in the concept development, or business idea planning, is connected to motivations of entrepreneurs, company managers, or partners. In some cases, the motivation is coming not from inside the business but from external partners, and the companies in the reactive way are starting their involvement. They need an external encouragement as a critical point for the concept development.

4.2. Model design stage

Often the decision made at the concept development stage is provisional, dependent on the organization's ability to design a solid business model, to manage the whole process of capacity building and to acquire financing. The most successful organizations invest a great deal of time to ensure that vital elements of the business model design are as resolved as possible before moving forward into implementation. The challenge is to innovate business models and apply them to produce desired environmental and social results cost-effectively and efficiently. For inclusive business model, the best solution to overcome different constraints at this stage can lie in collaboration with other stakeholders in the market, including communities, international and local organizations, and government.

Partnerships work best when they provide clear value to each party, and motivations are clearly and explicitly communicated from the outset. Partnership might be most effective where it focuses on supporting learning and change aimed at embedding new vision for business in all relevant processes. Capacity building as a critical point mostly refers to establishment of a partnership model that helps with investments in staff development, facilities, information systems, and technology improvements, allowing an organization to more effectively execute its mission and to create mutual value. In some cases, capacity was built by company investment, or by coinvestment, helping to combine resources and to reach financial sustainability in the later stages of company development.

Sometimes a proactive involvement to receive governmental support is needed. Marap, an Austrian company operating in several markets, founded DP Silk Road Organic Foods as a subsidiary in Uzbekistan. It collects, buys, processes, dries, packages, and exports approximately 2,000 tons of organically certified fruits and nuts from Uzbekistan to Austria each year. Marap and the Austrian Development Agency (ADA) in the partnership initiated the reforestation of related crops and the integration of organic cultivation techniques in Uzbekistan. During the Soviet era, many of Uzbekistan's natural forests and hillside orchards in areas surrounding human settlements have experienced significant degradation, or have disappeared entirely. The crucial input was provided by the State Forestry Administration in Uzbekistan, working with Marap, the UNDP, and the ADA in allowing DP as an intermediary to lease from the administration and on to the farmers, and changing the lease-holding agreements to ensure long-term commitment from farmers, thereby promoting sustainable land management practices.

In the business, reality of the inclusive models a partnership attitude is much more complex. It is not enough to have an initial financial support or a set of business-friendly legislation. The first two phases, concept development and model design, are important for having a good plan and starting up. The biggest challenge is to implement inclusive business model and to produce desired economic and social results for longer term. From the business perspective, it is the ability to compete while investing in inclusion and environment. The nature of the low-income market brings a necessity of innovative thinking about product packaging, service terms, delivery mechanisms, adapting products and processes, combining resources and the use of technology to reach consumers.

4.3. Implementation stage

Different kind of enablers can play a critical role at the stage of implementation. Strategic partnership can improve business environment for a particular venture and bring investment, advisory services, and better access to the market. Begeli in Georgia is strongly supported on a permanent basis by Elkana Association, for example in co-financing the certification, which makes it less costly for the farmers. An organic food certification allows them to have access to new local, regional and foreign markets. Farezi, one of Elkana member associations, provides the farmers machinery with 50% discount. This motivates farmers to actively engage in more advanced agricultural activities. Organizations like the UNDP along with the Global Environmental Facility and Eurasia Foundation have assisted and co-funded Elkana's biodiversity conservation programs, created networking opportunities with other local and foreign associations, and provided specialists for farmers' trainings and consulting in order to raise farmers' awareness on organic farming.

For some companies the most critical point in the process of implementation is to build the whole infrastructure to support business activity. In majority of transition countries the local nongovernmental sector is rather weak and the civil society activities are dominated by the type of donors and their goals. So, the best and innovative solution for Zeljko Mavrovic from Croatia in order to support the idea of organic farming in a country almost without civil society organizations was to create his own NGO. Eco centre Mavrovic, a nonprofit organization is responsible for public education and knowledge transfer of organic food production and usage for the different target groups. It can improve environmental consciousness among employees, farmers, business partners, and customers. One of the recent projects is based on social farming concept integrating people recovering from different addictions, psychiatric, mental, or physical diseases or handicaps, poor and long-term unemployed. Zeljko Mavrovic started a dialogue in the country to advance the practice of chemical-free, sustainable farming, becoming the new president of the Croatian farmer's union with 16,000 members. This activity was supported by eco-farm Mavrovic, a commercial entity responsible for growing, manufacturing and processing organic food. This strategy of combining resources from different types of organizations created by an entrepreneur was successful and now—after few years of development—it is the biggest organic food producer in the Western Balkans region.

There are major infrastructure and social-context problems in many transition countries, and companies, as part of their supply chain development, need to build their own operating infrastructure. In some cases it is about doing business differently through helping suppliers gain access to finance or building distribution channels where there is no infrastructure in place. The process of building a successful venture operating at the bottom-of-the-pyramid needs in many cases the fundamental redesign of the whole supply chain. It is not enough to build just separate, independent company and its manufacturing capacity. This means that for BoP-entrepreneurs it is important to build supplier capacity, the distribution systems, and customer demand on top of their manufacturing or production processes that would normally be considered their primary function.

4.4. Achieving scale

The ultimate role of the inclusive business models is to create long-term value for all. Some of these companies are profit-oriented; others are social enterprises trying to reach at least financial sustainability. But the top challenge for all of them is to achieve scale and generate self-financed growth. There is a growing recognition in the BoP field today that continuous growth of the inclusive business ventures and poverty alleviation can be synergistic. The strategic partnership model, implemented at every stage of business development, could raise the competitive advantage of the enterprise and generate benefits or competitiveness of all the players in an entire value chain.

A good example of a future-oriented, profitable, socially and environmentally beneficial model one can find in Ukraine. The business model and marketing innovation implemented by Vitmark have responded to the demand for quality, ecology, and affordable prices for low- and middle-income families. "Our Juice" brand share started from 1% in 2002 in the Ukrainian market of juices, nectars, and still drinks and grew to 16% in 2008. It is assumed that the share of the lower priced juice segment will increase, as price is becoming a crucial factor for many Ukrainians during the turbulent time and consumers are turning to less expensive alternatives. Through a well thought out marketing innovation, the low-income customers gained access to a cheap and healthy quality juice, with organic fruits and vegetables that provide essential vitamins and microelements.

Inclusive business models can provide an integrating opportunity for businesses, communities, governments, and civil society actors to construct a virtuous cycle of asset growth and sustainable outcomes. These sustainable outcomes include profits and reliable returns on investment, local economic development, enhanced quality of life for low-income communities, and environmental improvements. Organic farming promoted by Begeli in Georgia has significantly improved the quality and output of land, which increases the health benefits of consumers. One can observe an improvement of the socioeconomic conditions of the rural population of Georgia and the environmental protection through fostering the development of sustainable organic farming and increasing the self-reliance of the rural population. Begeli succeeded in actively promoting the organic products as more farmers turned to organic farming and more people now prefer organic food.

In the case of Uzbekistan, there are future prospects to expand the export of quality fruits and nuts, and the Marap's business model can bring sustainable jobs to impoverished rural communities and positively impact the environment through reforestation. Planting a fruit and nut tree orchard and encouraging the long-term commitment of local communities to cultivate and sustainably manage these plantations will increase Marap's turnover, improve the quality of its produce, and its capacity to more effectively meet demand for its organic dried fruit and nuts in the global market. Company estimates that both permanent and seasonal employment will double.

5. Future Prospects

The most important issue is to convince a growing number of businesses operating in transition economies, business partners, governments and nongovernmental organizations, that there is a tremendous opportunity to profitably and sustainably include the low-income and socially vulnerable in their value chains as consumers, employees, and entrepreneurs. There is a need for better understanding of how business can at the same time create financial value and improve people's lives, environmental conditions, to move beyond "business as usual" to innovative partnership with the value for all.

There is a need for better measurement tools which can help entrepreneurs in improving their solutions. No company is—or is ever likely to be—perfect. In general, the outlook is positive for the future of presented models as a mostly self-sustaining organization with multiple economic, social, and environmental results with lasting impact on the community at large. Companies can, however, put in place processes to determine social performance and provide for remediation, innovation, and learning that help to improve its impact. Appropriate measures can improve performance, because, as the accounting axiom goes, what gets measured and rewarded is what gets done. Inclusive business impact should be measured as the extent to which employed model contributes best to economic, social, and environmental welfare of the local population.

Poverty and environmental degradation are among the biggest challenges faced in the world today. The relationship between poverty and the environment is complex and highly influenced by the social and economic factors of a country or region. It is possible that in the second decade of this century, sustainable development may be advanced more by responsible and inclusive entrepreneurship than state directives and legislation. Business plays an increasingly important role in sustainable development. M. Blowfield addresses the issue of whether business can be expected to go beyond its conventional economic roles to become a more active agent of inclusive development, and how companies might be held to account for their development outcomes. He suggests that development ends can best be served when there is genuine collaboration whereby various actors pursue shared or complementary poverty end environmental objectives. This new kind of collaboration needs to move beyond the current reality of partnerships and involve different ways of connecting business with local needs and capabilities, voluntary initiatives and mandatory regulation (Blowfield 2010).

From a normative ethical perspective, poverty alleviation is an integral part of a true sustainable development. It becomes evident that new ways of sustainable consumption and production must be found to achieve sustainability's short-term, intragenerational goal of meeting the needs of the present and its long-term, intergenerational goal of an enduring utilization of resources (Hahn 2009). In fact, we need the new conceptual and institutional framework to align environmental protection and human development. The protection of the environment is central to sustainable human development and the eradication of poverty. There are already remarkable shifts and positive steps toward truly sustainable development from different actors involved but further action is needed (Halverson and McNeil 2008).

In recent years, business leaders, economists, and policymakers in different institutions have changed their appreciation of the role of business in society. With global societal challenges such as poverty, climate change, financial turbulences, and demographic ageing, the need for companies to adjust internal processes and partner with external stakeholders to find workable solutions at the local as well as regional level has increased. Businesses acting as businesses, not as charitable givers, are arguably the most powerful force for addressing many pressing issues facing our society. New strategies can address a wide range of economic, social, and environmental issues on the global and local level.

Note

1. Cases presented here were prepared under "The Growing Inclusive Markets Initiative for EE and CIS" project led by UNDP Bratislava Regional Centre, 2009–2010. The author is a principal consultant to this project. There is an emerging community of practitioners and researchers exploring inclusive business models. For more information: www.growinginclusivemarkets.org.The author wishes to thank local case writers from Croatia, Georgia, Ukraine, and Uzbekistan.

References

Barbier, E.B., 2010, Poverty, Development, and Environment, *Environment and Development Economics*, 15 (6): 635–60.

Blowfield, M.E., 2010, Business, Corporate Responsibility and Poverty Reduction, in P. Utting & J.C. Marques (eds.), *Corporate Social Responsibility and Regulatory Governance. Towards Inclusive Development?*, Palgrave Macmillan, Houndmills, Basingstoke, Hampshire, pp. 124–50.

Bornstein, D., 2004, *How to Change the World: Social Entrepreneurs and the Power of New Ideas*, Oxford University Press, New York.

Brundtland Commission, 1987, *Our Common Future. World Commission on Environment and Development*, Oxford University Press, New York.

Commission on the Private Sector and Development, 2004, *Unleashing Entrepreneurship: Making Business Work for the Poor*, UNDP, New York.

Darby, L. & Jenkins, H., 2006, Applying Sustainability Indicators to the Social Venture Business Model, *International Journal of Social Economics* 33 (5/6): 411–31.

Dasgupta, P., 2003, Population, Poverty, and the Natural Environment, in K.-G. Mäler & J.R. Vincent (eds.), *Handbook of Environmental Economics*, Vol. 1: Environmental Degradation and Institutional Responses, North Holland, Amsterdam, pp. 191–247.

Emerson, J., 2003, The Blended Value Proposition: Integrating Social and Financial Returns, *California Management Review* 45 (4): 35–51.

Department of Economic and Social Affairs, 2009, *Rethinking Poverty. Report on the World Social Situation 2010*, United Nations, New York.

Hahn, R., 2009, The Ethical Rational of Business for the Poor—Integrating the Concepts Bottom of the Pyramid, Sustainable Development, and Corporate Citizenship, *Journal of Business Ethics* 84: 313–24.

Halverson, E. & McNeil, C.I., 2008, Advancing a New Paradigm: Institutional and Policy Breakthroughs Toward Poverty Reduction and Sound Environmental Management, in P. Galizzi (ed.), *The Role of the Environment in Poverty Alleviation*, Fordham University Press, New York, pp. 3–29.

Hopkins, M., 2007, *Corporate Social Responsibility and International Development: Is Business the Solution?*, Earthscan, UK.

Jaiswal, A.K., 2008, The Fortune at the Bottom or the Middle of the Pyramid?, *Innovations: Technology, Governance, Globalization* 3 (1): 85–100.

Jenkins, B. & Ishikawa, E., 2009, *Business Linkages: Enabling Access to Markets at the Base of the Pyramid*, International Finance Corporation, International Business Leaders Forum, and the CSR Initiative at the Harvard Kennedy School.

————, 2010, *Scaling Up Inclusive Business: Advancing the Knowledge and Action Agenda*, International Finance Corporation and the CSR Initiative at the Harvard Kennedy School.

Kandachar, P. & Halme, M., 2008, Farewell to Pyramids: How Can Business and Technology Help to Eradicate poverty?, in P. Kandachar & M. Halme (eds.), *Sustainability Challenges and Solutions at the Base of the Pyramid: Business, Technology and the Poor*, Greenleaf Publishing, pp. 1–27.

Kirnani, A., 2007, The Mirage at the Bottom of the Pyramid, *California Management Review* 49 (4): 90–111.

London, T., Anupindi, R. & Sheth, S., 2010, Creating Mutual Value: Lessons Learned From Ventures Serving Base of the Pyramid Producers, *Journal of Business Research* 63 (6): 582–94.

Mainstreaming Poverty-Environment Linkages into Development Planning: A Handbook for Practitioners, 2009, UNDP-UNEP.

Karamchandani, A., Kubzansky, M. & Frandano, P., 2009, Emerging Markets, Emerging Models. Market-Based Solutions to the Challenges of Global Poverty, *Monitor Group*.

Newell, P. & Frynas, J. G., 2007, Beyond CSR? Business, Poverty and Social Justice: An Introduction, *Third World Quarterly*, 28 (4): 669–81.

Nielsen, C., & Samia, P. M., 2008, Understanding Key Factors in Social Enterprise Development of BOP, *Journal of Consumer Marketing*, 25 (7): 446–54.

Pesqueux, Y., 2009, Sustainable Development: A Vague and Ambiguous "Theory", *Society and Business Review*, 4 (3): 231–45.

Porter, M.E. & Kramer, M.R., 2006, Strategy and Society: The Link Between Competitive Advantage and Corporate Social Responsibility, *Harvard Business Review*, December, pp. 78–92.

Pradeep, M., 2008, *Innovation, Inclusion and Integration: from Transition to Convergence in Eastern Europe and the Former Soviet Union*, The International Bank for Reconstruction and Development/The World Bank.

Prahalad, C.K. & Hart, S.L., 2002, *The Fortune at the Bottom of the Pyramid, Strategy + Business*, issue 26, 1st quarter.

Sen, A., 1999, *Development as Freedom*, Anchor Books, New York.

Simanis, H. & Hart, S., 2008, *The Base of the Pyramid Protocol: Toward Next Generation BoP Strategy*, Cornell University Press, Ithaca, NY.

SADC—Swiss Agency for Development and Cooperation, 2008, *The Making Markets Work for the Poor (M4P) Approach*, Federal Department of Foreign Affairs, Bern.

The World Bank, 2010, *The Crisis Hits Home. Stress-Testing Households in Europe and Central Asia*, The International Bank for Reconstruction and Development.

The World Economic Forum, 2009, *The Next Billions: Unleashing Business Potential in Untapped Markets*, Davos.

United Nations Development Programme, 2008, *Creating Value for All: Strategies for Doing Business with the Poor*, New York.

————, 2010, *The MDGs: Everyone's Business. How Inclusive Business Models Contribute to Development and Who Supports Them*, New York.

United Nations, 1995, *World Summit on Social Development*, Copenhagen.

World Business Council for Sustainable Development, 2009, *From Challenge to Opportunity: The role of Business in Tomorrow's Society*, Geneva.

Yunus, M., 2010, *Building Social Business: The New Kind of Capitalism that Serves Humanity's Most Pressing Needs*, Public Affairs, Perseus Books Group.

Part 3
Changing Human Beings

The Role of Moral Status in Practice[1]

Külli Keerus
Department of Philosophy
Institute of Philosophy and Semiotics
University of Tartu,
Estonia

1. Introduction

One of the basic things that morality requires of us is to do good to others. At the outset, two issues should be specified: who are these others, and which actions are good. Think about the many kinds of things that surround us. Some of these should be taken into account in moral considerations and some seemingly should not. In philosophical language, some entities have moral status or moral standing and some do not. The standard examples of the opposite ends of such a spectrum are human beings and stones. Consider normal adult human beings. There are great many acts that one is not allowed to commit against them. Human beings are not to be experimented upon in laboratories, nor are they to be killed for food. Besides such restrictions, we also have positive duties toward human beings, such as helping them in cases of emergency. But now think about an ordinary small stone on the road. Does any moral issue touch upon it? Do we have obligations toward a stone? Hardly any come to mind.

Unlike these paradigmatic cases from opposite ends of the spectrum, there is no agreement with respect to the moral status of other entities, although the issues have been debated for centuries. Should a human embryo be protected to the same degree as an adult person? Should we

253

have moral concern for animals? Do trees have any moral standing? Should remote local ecosystems be protected, ecosystems which few people ever perceive and from which there is no direct benefit to any human being? These questions pertain to delineating the set of entities which have moral status. Very briefly, to have moral status means that the entity has to be taken directly into account in moral considerations by moral agents. If an entity is thought to have moral status, there are obligations toward it, which set limits to permissible actions. This means that the entity itself may be wronged and that this wrongfulness should be avoided. In the philosophical literature, there are many parallel terms to designate having moral status: an entity may be said to be an object of moral concern, belong to a moral community, have moral standing, or be morally considerable. But how could we decide which entities have such status? What are the criteria according to which moral status is ascribed?

As a field of practical ethics, one would expect environmental ethics to concentrate on the moral assessment of the *actions* regarding environment(s). However, since its emergence in the 1970s, the primary aim of environmental ethics has been first to define which *entities* can be the proper objects of moral concern, and only then to discuss what kind of actions will therefore be moral or immoral. In bioethics, the same question has taken the form of defining what is a "person."

The proposed moral status is then inserted—almost as a matter of fact—into the ensuing debate about which actions are permitted or prohibited. But what is or should be the particular impact of the "fact" of an entity's moral status on what we do, has received much less attention. Granted (it is sometimes admitted), rightness or wrongness of actions does not depend exclusively on the moral status of the affected entity: there are other considerations as well.[2] In practice, the most perplexing moral puzzles almost never arise merely concerning the moral status of just one entity, but from the collision of many of them. Concentrating on the moral status of just one entity in purified thought experiments may give us valuable knowledge. However, the way of articulating these issues has also caused a great deal of confusion. The role of the moral status of an entity in practical considerations should not be overestimated.

In this article, I introduce the most common criteria for ascribing moral status to several types of entities. I begin with the arguments for the claim that any and all human beings—and human beings only—can be the proper objects of direct moral concern, and discuss problems that arise from this claim. Thereafter, I shall examine criteria that are used to expand the scope of moral community to other entities besides human beings, and make some crucial and helpful conceptual distinctions. However, none of these accounts of the criteria of moral status is completely satisfactory, since in some cases they lead to strongly counter-intuitive results. In order to subsume into the conception of moral status certain strong intuitions which one cannot give up, some authors have used not only intrinsic, but also extrinsic or relational criteria. However, these concepts, to be explained below, do not seem to fit properly with the concept of moral status defined as a basis for *direct* moral obligations.

In the argumentation that follows, I will rely throughout on the method known as reflective equilibrium: moral theories or principles grow out of our considered judgments that are in turn based on our deepest moral convictions. Intuitive convictions are likewise controlled against the already existing general moral theories or against other areas of human knowledge. If a theory does not accord to our deepest convictions and other relevant accounts that we have a strong reason to believe, it may well be wrong. However, our intuitions may, of course, also be wrong and should be changed. One has to decide which ones to preserve and which ones should be corrected, and work back and forth to arrive at a correction. If some intuitions are given up, their origin must still be explained. The readers of this paper may have different initial intuitions across a range of issues. However, the basic aim of this work is not so much to reach a convincing general theory of moral status, but to give a very short overview of the possibilities and their attendant difficulties.

2. Moral Status as Ascribed to Human Beings Only

Throughout history, human beings have generally been held to be the first and surest candidates for moral status. There are two questions, though. First, are there any entities besides human beings which have moral status as well? In other words, is being human a necessary condition for possessing moral status? Secondly, do all people belong to this favored community, or are there such who do not? Or, to put it differently—to have moral status, is it sufficient to be a human?

The idea that no other entities besides human beings belong to moral community has been so common in Western moral philosophy that the possibility of direct obligations toward other entities—animals first and foremost—is barely ever mentioned. According to Aristotle's teaching, nature does not make anything without an aim: plants exist for animals and animals for humans. The idea that animals are for humans to use can also be found in the Bible: God gave humans the "dominion over the fish of the sea and over the birds of the air and over every living thing that moves upon the earth" (Genesis I, 29). This view, referred to as the Dominion Theory, is emphasized once again in the story of Noah (Genesis IX, 1–3).[3]

There is also another interpretation of the Bible, more favorable for animals: the Good Stewardship account, according to which humans are regarded as guardians of God's property. Animals and land are not completely under humans' discretion, but they must be well cared for. John Passmore has indicated that in contrast to the Dominion Theory, which has been more influenced by Aristotle's teaching, later adopted by Thomas Aquinas, the Stewardship account has its roots in the Hebrew tradition where God cares about animals and plants for their own sake. According to Passmore, the two traditions have a common basis in the idea that nature itself is not sacred. This core idea has influenced Western attitudes over the subsequent centuries. This has given some authors reason to accuse the Christian worldview of destroying nature with the help of technology created by humans (Passmore 1974, pp. 9–13).

Peter Singer notes that freedom to use animals for human purposes does not necessarily mean that the animals are seen as completely valueless. The right to take somebody's life does not mean that this life is valueless. To illustrate the point, Singer draws the example of killing an enemy soldier during wartime. Although it may be justified to kill an enemy, it does not mean that the life of this soldier is considered as lacking all value (Singer 1986, p. 350). However, while killing another valued human being under extreme circumstances may be an exception to the rule, the very point of the critics of the Western tradition is that, as a rule, animals are killed whenever it suits humans, not as a drastic exception as in war. Thus, it seems that providing extenuating interpretations is not enough: animals are still only seen as a property, however valuable, and they are seen as being under human discretion, be this despotic or favorable.

Secular theories of moral status are usually built upon some property of the entities. Mental characteristics or cognitive abilities are commonly taken as the ground of the special treatment of these entities. It is morally improper to ascribe moral status purely according to biological genus. Take the contemporary controversy of abortion: while the embryo is genetically a human organism, it is not clear whether or not it is already a person with proper moral status. To select out humans and to ascribe to them a privileged moral status may be just a prejudice.[4] Now, what are the properties that lift an entity up to the realm of justified moral protection? To divert us from disturbing prejudices, in her influential article of abortion, published in 1973, Mary Anne Warren asks us to imagine a space traveler who encounters some unfamiliar beings on a remote planet. On what basis should he decide how to behave toward them? Warren proposes five criteria on the basis of which the moral status of an entity should be assessed: consciousness, reasoning, self-motivated activity, capacity to communicate, and the presence of self-concepts or self-awareness.[5] Leaving open the question of whether an entity should satisfy all these criteria, she thinks that the first two alone, and probably also the third, are necessary and sufficient (Warren 1997, pp. 302–03).

There is a vast literature about animal minds and their psychology used to prove or to disprove their moral status. I will leave this issue aside, at least for the time being. It is philosophically more fundamental to ask, *why* mental characteristics and abilities are held to be so important in the determination of moral value. In other words, are the intuitions of the supposed space traveler justified?

The root of this conception of the importance of certain mental characteristics could be found in the supposition that morality must involve some principle of reciprocity. Thomas Hobbes, one of the founding fathers of ethical contractarianism, argues that without morality, people, while free but equal in capacities, would compete with each other for the possibility of attaining their own ends. In this condition, "every man has a right to every thing." This would be the condition of war, where there can be no security. To attain peace, people should lay down the right to all things (Hobbes 1996, pp. 82–87). But for an individual actor, this is reasonable only if others do the same. Therefore, covenants will be made. Promising is the basic sign of willingness to lay down the right to something. Additionally, according to Hobbes, a coercive power should be established to grant that everybody plays fair and adheres to the covenants made (Hobbes 1996, pp. 87–91). To this account Hobbes adds a short note that it is not possible to make covenants with beasts:

"To make covenants with brute beasts, is impossible; because not understanding our speech, they understand not, nor accept of any translation of right; nor can translate any right to another: and without mutual acceptation, there is no covenant" (Hobbes 1996, p. 92).

On this basis of communicability, animals, not to speak of other natural entities, are deemed not to belong to the moral community with us; consequently, we do not have any obligations toward them.

However, there are serious problems with these lines of thought regarding reciprocity. Morality does not seem to be reducible to mutual bargaining only. Many people believe that to be moral, good should be done also toward those who cannot reciprocate. This issue can be broken down into the distinction between moral agents and moral patients. *Moral agents* are those to whom moral demands apply, in the sense that they are expected to follow moral rules or be virtuous. They are morally accountable. *Moral patients*, on the other hand, are recipients of moral consideration: they count, but they themselves need not be accountable. To give an example, a wolf cannot be held morally accountable for killing a lamb while a human being normally can—whether or not the act is right or wrong. Thus, only a human being is said to be a moral agent. At the same time, a human being is also a moral patient, of whom other people should take account. There are, however, groups of human beings, such as mentally incompetent people, who are not held accountable. We may not be so sure about the moral status of embryos, but to allow killing of mentally disabled people is considered a horrifying idea. Although these people are usually not considered to be full moral agents, they are still moral patients and should be taken care of. Animals, too, are often said to possess the moral status as moral patients, even if they cannot be moral agents.

If anyone wishes to argue that moral considerability is conferred only because of certain intellectual capacities that enable their possessors to reason or to behave morally, it behooves them to explain the intuitions that one should not torture animals or experiment on people who do not have the mental capacities of moral reasoning. One way to spare oneself these difficulties while retaining the thesis that the capacity of reasoning is requisite for moral status is to claim that what seems to be a duty toward an animal or a child is actually simply a duty toward another person. Here we should introduce the next relevant pair of concepts: direct and indirect duties. *Direct duties* are duties *toward* an entity, while *indirect duties* are duties *regarding* something or somebody. For example, I may have a duty to keep an eye on my neighbor's house while she is away. It would be wrong to sell the house in the meanwhile. This is a duty toward the neighbor only regarding the house, not a duty toward the house. Hence, regarding the house, it is an indirect duty. However, if I am asked to keep an eye on my sister's five-year-old son, then my duty not to sell him to baby brokers is a duty not only toward my sister, but toward the child as well.[6] Hence, it is direct duty. Similar distinctions concerning animals are more disputable. If I slaughter my neighbor's pig for lunch during her absence, is this a wrong committed against the pig itself or just against the neighbor, whose property I destroyed? Moral status is often defined via the connection to the idea of *direct* obligations *toward* the entities to which it is ascribed. It is possible to argue that the pig does not actually have moral status, since the obligation not to kill it is an obligation toward its owner, not toward the pig itself.

If property relations alone could explain obligations regarding animals, it would be allowed for a farmer to beat his herd. Once again, this does not accord with our intuitions. Another way to argue for indirect duties regarding animals is articulated, for example, by Kant in whose *Lectures on Ethics* we find the famous declaration:

"[I]f a man has his dog shot, because it can no longer earn a living for him, he is by no means in breach of any duty to the dog, since the latter is incapable of judgment, but he thereby damages the kindly and humane qualities in himself, which he ought to exercise in virtue of his duties to mankind. Lest he extinguish such qualities, he must already practice a similar kindliness toward animals; for a person who already displays such cruelty to animals is also no less hardened toward men" (Kant 2001, p. 212; see also Kant 1999, pp. 563–64).

Thus, it is sometimes argued that we may indeed have obligations concerning nonrational animals, but only indirectly. It is, however, not so easy to adopt the same argument when talking of nonrational human beings, such as babies. Many people feel strongly that human babies still deserve *direct* moral consideration for their own sake. If this is so, rationality (or any other criteria connected to higher cognition) cannot be the sole criterion for ascribing moral status and perhaps these are not criteria for ascribing moral status at all.

3. Extending Moral Community: Which Entities Have a Good of Their Own?

In the previous section, I introduced the traditional way of thinking, which accords full moral status to human beings only. I also demonstrated why this is problematic. Firstly, being genetically human is not a morally neutral criterion for ascribing moral status and thus begs the question. Secondly, if one tries to ground moral status on specifically human capacities like rationality, since this alone enables moral agency, it could be replied that the question of moral status is about moral patients, not about moral agents. Tying moral status with certain specifically human capacities is also problematic in yet a third sense, since not every human being possesses each of these capacities. To leave such human beings without moral protection would be against strong intuitions of most people. Further, if these human beings have moral status, then nonhuman entities with relevantly similar capacities should have it as well. The last implication is called the argument from marginal cases, and although it concurs with another strong intuition—that human beings should be preferred to other entities—a serious attempt should nevertheless be made to extend the boundaries of moral community.

Depending on the version, the extension varies from covering only some higher mammals, like chimpanzees, to involving all living creatures, like plants and bacteria. Sometimes also complex wholes (like species and ecosystems), or even nonliving entities (rivers, mountains, or sacred places) are ascribed a value comparable to that of conceiving them as having moral status.

The general line of thought behind these accounts could be described as follows. As stated in the very beginning, morality pertains to doing good to others. The way to proceed in search for the criteria for moral status is to ask, which entities could have their own proper good? In the first place, this requires the specification of the term "good." In the general claim of morality, "good" may be replaced with the "ends," "aims," "interests," "preferences," "well-being," or "needs." For instance, in her initial definition of the concept of moral status Mary Anne Warren states:

"If an entity has moral status, then we may not treat it in just any way we please; we are morally obliged to give weight in our deliberations to its needs, interests, or well-being" (Warren 2000, p. 3).

Yet these specified terms cannot be understood unequivocally. Before they help us in ascribing moral status to any entity, they first need closer interpretation. Only then can we proceed to analyze which entities may be deemed to hold such "good" in this or other specified sense.

In his *Practical Ethics* Peter Singer claims the basic characteristic of ethics to be that ethical conduct must be acceptable from the universal point of view. He interprets ethical conduct as extending beyond one's own personal *interests*, i.e., to "give the same weight to the interests of others as one gives to one's own interests" (Singer 1993, p. 11). Singer does not restrict the scope of "others" any further: the interests of all beings, who can have interests at all, are taken into account. What remains to be interpreted is what is meant by "interests," and accordingly, which entities could meaningfully be said to have any interests? Here Singer relies on the utilitarian tradition and argues that living beings are interested above all in avoiding pain and experiencing pleasure: "If a being is not capable of suffering, or experiencing enjoyment or happiness, there is nothing to be taken into account" (Singer 1993, pp. 57–58). Thus the basic criterion for moral status turns out to be sentience.

Singer nevertheless amends his account by stating that sentience is to be taken merely as a "shorthand for the capacity to suffer or experience enjoyment or happiness," (Singer 1993, p. 58) thus allowing further interpretations. Restricting the definition to the capacity to feel pain would raise the issue of moral acceptance of painless killing. Many, maybe most people, would approve of using animals for food or other human purposes,[7] provided that the suffering of these animals is minimized. However, nobody accepts the painless killing of humans, be they either rational or nonrational. What, then, is the difference between humans and animals? In addition to the capacity to feel pleasure and pain, self-conscious and rational human beings, who are also aware of themselves as distinct entities with a past and a future, are capable of having *desires* about their future, among them the *preference* to continue living. According to preference-utilitarianism, such desires, or preferences, should also not be thwarted (Singer 1993, pp. 90, 94). Singer thinks it at least plausible that the strength of preference for one's life depends on the developmental level of the organism's consciousness, self-awareness, rationality, and breadth of possible experiences (Singer 1993, p. 107). Thus, according to Singer, "beings who cannot see themselves as entities with a future cannot have any preferences about their own future existence" (Singer 1993, p. 95). However, Singer treats the issue of drawing this line with extreme caution. Surely he does not want to imply that the lives of underdeveloped children or the senile are as cheap as those of the pigs or dogs have been. Nor does he argue that one should apply the doctrine of "sanctity of life" to pigs or dogs. Instead, Singer calls for an intermediate position:

"What we must do is bring nonhuman animals within our sphere of moral concern and cease to treat their lives as expendable for whatever trivial purposes we may have. At the same time, once we realize that the fact that a being is a member of our own species is not in itself enough to make it always wrong to kill that being, we may come to reconsider our policy of preserving human lives at all costs, even when there is no prospect of a meaningful life or of existence without terrible pain" (Singer 2002, p. 20).

On the whole, Singer stresses the importance of interests as preferences, the most important of which is to be free of pain and to have pleasurable experiences. May we then generalize and state simply that moral status is possessed by those beings which can be interested in or prefer something?

This approach may justifiably be placed in doubt. If a child wants to eat candies all day long, is this a preference that a caring mother should satisfy? Two types of interests can be distinguished: "preference-interests" and "welfare-interests."[8] A child may prefer eating more candies, but while it has also adverse effects on his health, it is doubtful if this diet augments his welfare. This difference in the use of the concept "interest" is often expressed as a distinction between somebody's being *interested in* something and something's being *in the interests of* somebody.[9]

It might be useful to refrain from the ambiguous term "interest" and to talk rather of *preferences* and *needs,* which cohere to this difference. Some people may subjectively prefer smoking, but as long as it is unhealthy, it is not what they need to do, objectively. Adult humans may be left free to decide for themselves whether or not to put their health at risk—provided that they are adequately informed. By contrast, in the case of children, what may be morally required of the mother is that she not allow her child to eat what he prefers, but only what contributes to his health and welfare.

When interpreting what morality demands us to do unto others, some philosophers attach more importance to considerations of needs than to considerations of preferences. For them, moral community is defined by the entities who have needs and who get benefits from their satisfaction. Kenneth E. Goodpaster has argued against philosophers who take sentience as a necessary criterion for moral consideration and who claim that without sentience there is nothing to take into account: "it is so clear that there is something to take into account, something that is not merely "potential sentience" and which surely does qualify beings as beneficiaries and capable of harm—namely, life" (Goodpaster 1978, p. 316).

The approach that centers on life as a criterion for moral worth, is developed at greater length by Paul W. Taylor, who agrees that without consciousness, plants, for instance, do not have interests in the sense of caring about something. Nevertheless, all living organisms are teleological (i.e., goal-oriented) centers of life that strive for maintaining the organism's existence. As such, they have a good of their own: the benefit or harm to them may thus be understood from the viewpoint of their survival, health, and well-being (Taylor 1989, pp. 60–68, 121–24). According to Taylor, having a good of its own makes it possible for a living thing to be the object of human duties. However, as Taylor admits, this does not logically imply that this good should be promoted by humans (Taylor 1989, pp. 71–72). Rather, the duties follow from a certain attitude of respect—which, as Taylor claims, is the only coherent attitude to adopt along with a system of beliefs—the biocentric outlook on nature (Taylor 1989, pp. 79–80). This consists of the following four beliefs: first, all human beings are equally members of the Earth's Community of Life with any other living things; second, all species, including humans are part of an interdependent system; third, all organisms are teleological centers of life, pursuing their own good in their own way; and fourth, humans are not superior to other living things (Taylor 1989, pp. 99–100).

In brief, to be coherent with these beliefs, which are conjoined to factual knowledge, one should also adopt respect for nature as an ethical standpoint. According to Taylor, this forces us to undertake direct moral duties toward all living beings and to promote their goods even if they themselves are not able to care about them.

However, if life is made the criterion for ascribing moral status and if, accordingly, morality demands us to take into account all needs of every living being, we soon get into trouble. If animals have moral status and we should not kill them nor raise them for food, we should become vegetarians. But should we care about plants since they are living organisms, too? Does this involve a prohibition against cutting them for consumption? What about destroying parasites? Do we really have to grant what constitutes a good life for bacteria?

Both Taylor and Goodpaster actually saw these problems and tried to solve them. One possibility is to understand moral status not as an absolute but as a measurable value: as an issue of more or less. Some entities may have stronger moral status than others. This is the strategy chosen by Goodpaster, who distinguishes moral considerability from moral significance. Moral considerability is to be understood as a threshold of being taken into account or valued for one's own sake. How much an entity counts in comparison to other entities in conflict situations, is an issue of that being's moral significance. While being alive is a criterion for ascribing general considerability to an entity, a different criterion such as sentience may function as a criterion of moral significance (Goodpaster 1978).

Taylor takes another route for solving these conflicts. He does not use any sliding scale account of moral status, whereby this status can be higher or lower. For him, moral status is the same for all living beings, including humans. However, if the claims that follow from moral status should come into conflict, the priority and procedural rules will solve them. It is not possible to enter into a detailed account of these rules and principles here. To give a general idea, let me outline the principles that are meant to solve conflicts between humans and nonhumans. First, the principle of self-defense permits to protect oneself against any other entities, even by destroying them. Secondly, the principle of proportionality requires that greater weight should be given to basic than nonbasic interests, regardless of whose interests they are. Third, the principle of minimum wrong admits that if moral agents decide to pursue a value regardless of the wrong that will be done to other living beings, this wrong should at least be minimized. The fourth—the principle of distributive justice—regulates the conflict between basic interests of different parties by demanding that moral agents provide them an equal share of a benefit which satisfies these interests.

Last comes the principle of restitutive justice, which supplements the principles of minimum wrong and distributive justice by requiring the restitution of any harm that is done while these two other principles are followed (Taylor 1989, pp. 263–307). In these ways, life-centered or biocentric theories can avoid the main accusation with regard to value conflicts and possible absurd conclusions, such as prohibitions on brushing one's teeth. Nevertheless, there are yet other important aspects to consider in ascribing moral status.

4. Moral Status as Derived from Nonintrinsic Properties

As I have tried to show in the previous sections, problems arise both from limiting moral status according to the special capacities of human beings (e.g., Why would it be wrong to torture animals? What about the marginal cases of humans, such as embryos, newborns or mentally retarded?); and also from extending the moral community to include entities with more general properties of being able to have interests or needs (e.g., How do we survive then ourselves: can we even breathe without harming any living being?). One possible solution is to create a hierarchy of moral statuses where each level is submitted to a hierarchy of criteria. For example, one may set a higher value on rationality and a lower value on sentience. According to this scheme, rational human beings have stronger moral status than any nonrational but sentient being. This account is not speciesist as long as those human beings that do not satisfy the rationality criterion are on the same level as animals are according to the sentience criterion. Therefore these human beings do not completely lack moral status. Nor must one think that they can be slaughtered like animals, if one holds that slaughtering sentient animals is wrong. Another type of hierarchy—based on priority rules of the principles—was presented in the above discussion about Paul W. Taylor's ethics.

Besides such hierarchies, some authors have directed their attention to certain relational properties as a basis of moral status. In contrast to intrinsic properties (like life or sentience), relational properties of an entity depend for their existence on other entities. Being a mother and being unique are good examples of nonintrinsic properties. Somebody can be a mother only if there exists or has existed another entity—that is, her offspring. And an entity is unique, if there do not exist other relevantly similar entities.

The following is a simple example of how one may argue in favor of relational properties. Think about the problem of famine. Are we obligated to aid starving people in faraway regions? If so, how much should one give? Usually, one is allowed or even obligated to care for one's own children first and also to provide them more than mere subsistence, even if donating to organizations would help to prevent deaths of many others somewhere in the other side of the world. If the intuition that these obligations toward kin are stronger (some may even think that there are no positive moral obligations toward people in faraway places at all), this gives a reason to claim that moral status can be based on relational properties.

The example is familiar, but placing it into the framework of the criteria for moral status is more recent. One author who suggests using relational properties as a criterion for ascribing moral status is Mary Anne Warren. She develops this idea from the basis of two earlier theories. One of these is J.B. Callicott's biosocial moral theory, which stresses the importance of human bond with nature; an entity (be it organism, species or even nonliving one like waters or soils) is entitled to moral status in reference to the role it plays in the ecosystem. The other theory, Nel Noddings' ethics of care, emphasizes the moral importance of the emotional relationship between a carer and a cared-for. Moral obligations arise from affectionate relationships which give natural motivation to meet the needs of particular others. According to the interpretation, moral status is ascribed to those that are cared-for (Warren 2000, pp. 19, 21, 137–42).

Although Warren argues in favor of including such relational properties amongst the determinants of moral status, she is critical toward using them as the sole criterion. She herself supports a multicriterial account where several intrinsic and extrinsic criteria are bound together into a set of principles that allow us to judge the moral status of any kind of entity (Warren 2000, pp. 148–84). Rather than digging deeper into these interesting multicriterial or pluralist[10] accounts of moral status, my concern here is with a more specific issue: is it proper to involve relational properties into the account of moral status at all? Firstly, *if* moral status was meant to involve *direct* obligations *toward* certain entities, is this definition truly retained in the arguments for including relational properties? Secondly, do relational properties play a part in determining moral *considerability* or merely moral *significance*, i.e., the relative strength of the moral status of the entities when compared to each other? I will now turn to these issues and consider them each separately.

To illustrate the first problem, we can look at one of the Warren's principles, the ecological principle, which is based on relational criteria. Here, the living or nonliving entities are argued to have moral status because of their relation to the ecosystem. But can it really be claimed that these entities themselves are valued so that we have direct obligations toward themselves or because of themselves? It seems to me that here one is rather dealing with the obligations *regarding* these entities. If the moral status may cease after the relationship ceases, isn't this a sign that the entity was not valued for itself? The moral status actually belongs to the ecosystem, or even to human beings for whom the ecosystem provides a suitable environment.

Warren herself seems to disaffirm that the ecological principle is ground for true moral status. She tries to find a way out by claiming that the ecological principle "permits us to recognize moral obligations toward water, air, plant and animal species," but does not *require* it. Tentatively, Warren admits that because nonliving parts of nature cannot be harmed, "it is implausible to insist that our obligations regarding them must be understood as obligations toward them." However, Warren claims it to be reasonable for people to hold that these nonliving parts of nature "have a more than instrumental value" and that "we might be wise sometimes to accord moral status" to these entities "if we wish humanity to survive and flourish into the distant future" (Warren 2000, pp. 167–68). Thus, Warren's arguments for ascribing moral status on the basis of the relational worth of certain nonliving entities to the ecosystem boils down to a noble lie with the aim of the survival of the human species.

It nevertheless seems convincing that relational properties still have some role in determining our obligations toward certain entities. This brings us to the second problem: what exactly is the role that relational or extrinsic properties play in theories of moral status? Of those three among Warren's principles which are based on relational properties, two (the Ecological and the Interspecific Principle)[11] are articulated with the help of the condition that the entity specified with a relational criteria "has stronger moral status than could be based upon their intrinsic properties alone." Thus, moral status is already there, and the relational aspect merely fleshes it out. At least in Warren's account, relational properties are used as *criteria not* for moral *considerability*, but rather for moral *significance,* i.e., they determine the relative strength of the moral status of the entities compared to each other.

It is not just Warren who seems to offer up a criterion of relative moral strength as a criterion for the moral status itself. In a recent article Bernard Baertschi and Alexandre Mauron propose to "modify the traditional concept of moral status and to consider it as referring not only to intrinsic properties, but to extrinsic or relational ones" (Baertschi and Mauron 2010, p. 96). However, they must also actually mean "moral significance," not "moral considerability" in Goodpaster's sense. They explicitly concentrate themselves on "moral weight or importance" (Baertschi and Mauron 2010, p. 98) and note that relational properties may both enhance and diminish the moral status of an entity. For example, being placed in a uterus enhances the moral status of an embryo; not being implanted or destined to be experimented on diminishes it (Baertschi and Mauron 2010, pp. 101–02). What is most perplexing here is that the properties which Baertschi and Mauron present as relational properties depend on certain actions the permissibility of which may itself depend on the moral status of an embryo. May we really experiment on someone because this someone is *destined* to be experimented upon?

Due to these problems, I hesitate to ascribe importance to the relational or extrinsic properties in determining the moral status of an entity—understood as "moral considerability," not just "moral significance" in Goodpasterian sense, and as grounding direct obligations toward these entities. If relational properties play some role in determining our moral obligations, they do it in the form of indirect obligations or, rather, they merely specify the strength of moral status, which, needs to be ascribed independently in the first place.

5. Alternative Developments and Conclusions

What should we conclude from these discussions? First, it may well be that the usage of the notion "moral status" should not be restricted merely to that which is bound to direct obligations. However, if its usage is multifarious, other terms must be found to convey the different meanings.

Frances M. Kamm, for example, brings out three main senses according to which entities could count morally. Firstly, an entity could count *in its own right*. In such case, the entity is valued because of itself, as an end, not just as an instrument for attaining some other end. An entity may have value as an end both because of its intrinsic or extrinsic properties. Examples of this may be a work of art or a tree. Secondly, an entity may count *for its own sake*, and in this case, the entity itself can get something out of the moral protection. For this, a capacity for sentience or consciousness is needed. It is for this purpose that Kamm decides specifically to reserve the term "moral status." Thirdly, to some entities we *owe* certain duties. Only at this point does Kamm resort to the notion of "directed duty," to distinguish this from just having a duty to do something without owing it to a specific entity. The entity, to which a duty is owed, has a corresponding right or claim (Kamm 2008, pp. 227–30).

What is especially interesting in Kamm's account is the explanation how these three moral accountabilities cannot be clearly ranked in a conflict case where we need to decide which one to honor. An entity with each of these types of counting may occur as more significant than an entity with another in a given situation. According to Kamm, for example, if the situation ever arises where we have to choose between preserving the Grand Canyon and saving a bird, we may have more reason to favor the first, even if the Grand Canyon "only" counts for its own right, but cannot have a "sake." In Kamm's formulation, "This illustrates how something can count morally because it can get something out of life, and so have moral status, without it giving us more reason to act in its favor than other things whose going on in existence, in their own right, is more significant. Sometimes, the remarkableness of something or its uniqueness calls for more protection than does something else's having moral status" (Kamm 2008, p. 230). Also, it seems that it is sometimes at least permissible to override someone's right.

Another conclusion may be that it is not even possible to draw lines between different entity classes according to some of their common properties, thus justifying the different treatment of these separate classes. James Rachels (2004) analyses two questions simultaneously: toward what kinds of beings do we have any obligations, and what are these obligations? He notes that the existing theories about moral status bind the issues of how an entity may be treated with certain facts about these entities or their characteristics. But the specific characteristics may justify only some specific types of treatments and may not concern other types. For example, Betty can be given Prozac because she is depressive but not because she cannot sing (Rachels 2004, p. 167). Similarly, being sentient is a reason not to be beaten. In relation to this specific treatment it does not matter whether or not the entity is also autonomous or self-conscious: being sentient is sufficient. However, the ability to feel pain does not matter in the issue of having been admitted to the university; instead, what counts is intelligence. By way of such examples, Rachels reaches the conclusion that there is no such limited number of properties, according to which all entities of a certain category could have moral status,[12] and which, in turn, would determine all the possible permissible and prohibited actions regarding this entity. There is no such thing as moral status *simpliciter*: "There is no characteristic, or reasonably small set of characteristics, that sets some creatures apart from others as meriting respectful treatment. (. . .) Instead we have an array of characteristics and an array of treatments, with each characteristic relevant to justifying some types of treatment but not others" (Rachels 2004, p. 169).

To sum up, I have demonstrated that it is very difficult to choose a criterion or even a multiple set of criteria that accords fully with our strong intuitions regarding those types of entities toward which we have moral obligations and what we take these obligations to be. Whatever criterion we choose, some entities that we deeply care about will be left out, or we will include entities, the protection of which becomes too costly for us. Furthermore, the debate about moral status is full of conceptual ambiguities. Do we consider only direct duties here or indirect ones as well? Do we speak about different types of moral considerability, or just about the steady scale of significance? It must be very carefully noted which terms are used and what exactly is meant by them. Moreover, it may well prove unfruitful to concentrate on creating a theory of moral status in this way. As we have seen, a more productive approach might be to turn our attention directly toward reasons for action and to skip the "moral status" as one of these.

Notes

1.   The author cordially thanks her supervisors, professors Olli Loukola and Margit Sutrop. Many thanks belong also to Prof. Tiina Ann Kirss who corrected both my grammar and style. The work on this article was supported by European Union from the ESF project "Graduate School for Linguistics, Philosophy, and Semiotics" and by the Estonian Science Foundation grant (in the European Economic Area/

Norwegian financial mechanisms scheme) "New ethical frameworks for genetic and electronic health record databases" funded from 2008 to 2010.

2. For instance, Mary Anne Warren who has written a frequently cited book on moral status, mentions briefly that our obligations may also be based "upon situational factors, such as a promise we have made, a personal relationship in which we are involved, a civil or criminal law that has been justly enacted, or a wrongful past action of our own that requires restitution or compensation" (Warren 2000, p. 9).
3. More about arguments for unique status of human beings can be found in Singer (1986, pp. 342–53) and a thorough overview about the attitude to animals in Western tradition in Passmore (1974, pp. 3–40).
4. Peter Singer's comparison of this view, which he calls "speciesism," to that of racism is well known: to ascribe moral status according to purely genetic difference is as prejudicial as to ascribe it on the basis of skin color (Singer 2002, p. 6).
5. Warren notes that it is difficult to produce precise definitions of these traits; and indeed, in different reprints of the article they are given slightly differently.
6. The example is borrowed from Warren (2000, p. 10).
7. Singer himself, generally, is against it.
8. For example, Tom Regan uses these terms and explains them in his "The Case for Animal Rights" (1983, pp. 87–88).
9. Paul W. Taylor, for instance, explains it in his "Respect for Nature" (1989, pp. 63–64).
10. A pluralist account is proposed by Christopher Stone in "Earth and Other Ethics."
11. And it is possible to interpret the third one—the transitivity of respect principle—in a similar way.
12. Rachels himself uses the term "moral standing" throughout, but he defines it in the same way—with reference to direct duties (Rachels 2004, p. 164).

References

Baertschi, B. & Mauron, A., 2010, Moral Status Revisited: The Challenge of Reversed Potency, *Bioethics* 24 (2): 96–103 (doi: 10.1111/j.1467-8519.2008.00686.x).

Goodpaster, K.E., 1978, On Being Morally Considerable, *The Journal of Philosophy* 75 (6): 308–25. JSTOR: http://www.jstor.org.

Hobbes, T., 1996, *Leviathan*, in R. Tuck (ed.), Cambridge University Press, Cambridge.

Kamm, F.M., 2008, *Moral Status, Intricate Ethics: Rights, Responsibilities, and Permissible Harm*, Oxford University Press, Oxford, pp. 227–36.

Kant, I., 1999, Metaphysics of Morals, in *The Cambridge Edition of the Works of Immanuel Kant: Practical Philosophy*, M.J. Gregor (transl. and ed.), Cambridge University Press, Cambridge.

———, 2001, *Lectures on Ethics*, P. Heath and J.B. Schneewind (eds.), transl. by P. Heath, Cambridge University Press, Cambridge.

Passmore, J., 1974, *Man's Responsibility for Nature: Ecological Problems and Western Traditions*, Duckworth, London.

Rachels, J., 2004, *Drawing Lines, Animal Rights: Current Debates and New Directions*, Oxford University Press, Oxford, NY.

Regan, T., 1983, *The Case for Animal Rights*, University of California Press, Berkeley, Los Angeles.

Singer, P., 1993, *Practical Ethics* (2nd ed.), Cambridge University Press, Cambridge.

———, 1986, Animals and the Value of Life, in T. Regan (ed.), *Matters of Life and Death: New Introductory Essays in Moral Philosophy* (2nd ed.), McGraw-Hill, Inc., New York, NY, pp. 338–77.

————, 2002, *Animal Liberation*, Ecco, New York.
Taylor, P.W., 1989, *Respect for Nature. A Theory of Environmental Ethics*, second printing, with corrections, Princeton University Press, Princeton, NJ.
Warren, M.A., 1997, On the Moral and Legal Status of Abortion, L. Gruen & G.E. Panichas (eds.), *Sex, Morality and the Law*, Routledge, New York, pp. 296–307.
————, 2000, *Moral Status. Obligations to Persons and Other Living Things*, Clarendon Press, Oxford.

Romance, Reason, and Poetry in Ecological Philosophy

Erazim Kohák
Philosophy/Centre for Global Studies
Philosophy Institute
Czech Republic Academy of Science
Prague,
Czech Republic

The night comes softly, beyond the power-line and the blacktop, where the long-abandoned wagon road fades amid the new growth. It does not crowd the lingering day. There is a time of passage as the bright light of the summer day, cool green and intensely blue, slowly yields to the deep, virgin darkness. Quietly, the darkness grows in the forest, seeping into the clearing and penetrating the soul, all-healing, all-reconciling, renewing the world for a new day. Were there no darkness to restore the soul, humans would quickly burn out their finite store of dreams. Unresting, unreconciled, they would grow brittle and break easily, like an oak flag dried through the seasons. When electric glare takes away the all-reconciling night, the hours added to the day are but a dubious gain . . ..

In the global city of our civilisation we have banished the night and abolished the dusk. Here the merciless glare of electric lights extends the harshness of the day deep into a night restless with the hum of machinery and the eerie glow of neon . . .—. . . A human alone, surrounded by the gleaming surfaces of his artefacts, cannot bear the vast surplus of grief that darkness never has a chance to reconcile. (Kohák 1982, pp. 29, 33, altered)

1.

The passage just cited is rather typical of what we wrote and thought in the heady early years of what we then called *the ecological movement.*[1] In America, which offered me refuge all through the Cold War years, it was a time of ferment. Thousands of young people, for the most part veterans of the bitter struggles over the war in Vietnam, took to the woods to seek their roots in *nature's* peace. They—or we, since I was one of them—were the uprooted product of an urban civilization. That civilization, grown affluent and technological, no longer offered us a sense of either order or purpose. We had rejected its order of accumulating and controlling when we took our stand against "the war." When it ended, we found ourselves too deeply marked to blend in with the rising yuppie generation. We were a generation lost between the age of burnt-out ideologies and the new upwardly mobile age of unabashed greed.

We encountered *nature* and its peace in that frame of mind, as an ageless order with its own purpose, made neither for nor by humans. On our make-believe homesteads, *nature* surrounded us, grand, ageless, mysterious, with an order and a purpose of its own. We stood before it in awe, painfully ill-fitting with our urban assumptions, yet convinced that, if only we could shed the veneer technology, we could merge with the harmony of *nature's* great green peace, finding both order and purpose therein. The *ecological movement* that emerged from that conviction was often as naive as we were and as well-meaning, convinced that the conflict between humans and *nature* was basically a misunderstanding which would yield to noble vision and our earnest goodwill.

Our ecological movement was in that sense fundamentally—and often naively—philosophical. It was a quest both for personal meaning and for the meaning of the whole of our lives and world. Our orientation was teleological, not mechanical; our questions focused on what being human means in the order of nature. It was also fundamentally moral. We were concerned less with it than with what we *ought do* and *ought avoid doing.*

Yet, already eight years before the first Earth Day, Rachel Carson introduced a different orientation with her epoch making book, *Silent Spring.*[2] She wrote with the same dream-like sensitivity as Aldo Leopold[3] or Joseph Wood Krutch,[4] but her book was packed with hard information about the impact of commercially used chemicals on both plants and wildlife. The silence of which she wrote was the silence of a world without songbirds. DDT, considered harmless and indiscriminately used, was weakening their egg shells (Carson 1987, pp. 159–81). On the ponds of New Hampshire, we could see nests abandoned by loons whose eggs could not support their body weight in hatching. The *nature* which for us had been the great presence in whose comforting embrace we sought solace and renewal now came to seem an endangered species, needing out active help. The biologist and the forester replaced the philosopher and the poet as the iconic figures of what we increasingly called the environmental movement.

Today, that practical emphasis has prevailed almost exclusively. In face of detailed, painstakingly documented environmental studies like the United Nations' *Human Development Report* (United Nations 1998) of more recently the AR4, *Fourth Assessment Report of the Intergovernmental Panel on Climate Change* 2007 (IPCC 2007a,b)—result of an intense, global effort of the best scientific minds and laboratories—makes the ecological philosophy and poetry of the sixties seem vastly beside the point—and, actually, somewhat embarrassing. The threat is present and pressing, clearly presented, and calling for urgent action on both intergovernmental and interpersonal level. The clash of intractable human attitudes—specifically, the fundamental assumption that *growth* is the meaning of being human—and the equally intractable finite ability of the Earth to tolerate ever growing human numbers and human expectations—appears irresoluble and apocalyptic.

Thus far, for many good reasons, our environmental efforts have focused entirely on the scientific side of the equation. We have assessed the resources of the Earth with impressive accuracy and have made major strides in using them effectively. Yet even the most optimistic assessments of our ability to cope with environmental degradation, such as the report *Mitigation of Climate Change* (Metz 2007), cannot avoid the hard reality that *infinite growth is not compatible with finite Earth*. Even our best scientific effort cannot make earth infinite.

This, I shall suggest, is an excellent reason to dust off the long neglected philosophical pole of the equation and start posing critical questions about human assumption and attitudes which have driven our civilization into the blind alley of infinite *growth* on a finite Earth. That, admittedly, is no longer a hard-nosed empirical study, constructing theoretical generalizations upon sets of verified data. We are no longer posing the question of theoretical reason, *what is in fact the case*, but rather questions of practical and ultimately poetic reason—what *could be* the case and what *ought to be* the case. Are the ways we experience and assess our life and world genetically given or historically conditioned? If the latter, how can and ought we modify our ways of experiencing and assessing our lived reality—vulgarly stated, our "values"—to make our civilization compatible with our Earth?

2.

With that we have come a full turn of the spiral, returning from our extended detour in scientific environmental study to the question of values and so to philosophy, though in a rather specific sense of that much abused word.[5] We are not turning to philosophical ecology solely because scientific environmentalism has ended in the blind alley of infinite *growth* on a finite Earth, but far more basically because, *volens-nolens*, scientific theories as such are grounded in pre-scientific experiential attitudes and assumptions.

Half a century ago, that topic emerged in the form of the question of whether scientific theories are necessarily theory-laden. Tom Kuhn, in another epoch-making book, *Structure of Scientific Revolutions*, (Kuhn 1970) made the point that the science of any period age operates with what he called a *paradigm*—a set of postulates which seem so obvious as to appear as simply *the way it is*. Those the age does not question. Rather, it assumes them as that which orders lived experience as intelligible. This paradigm—a way of experiencing as much as of thinking—defines what will appear as a problem and what as a solution. Scientific revolutions are essentially paradigm shifts. They come about not with a change in theory but rather with a shift in assumption that appear self-evident.

Kuhn chooses his examples from the natural sciences, though for our purposes, the assumption that *growth* is both the basic ordering principle of life and a moral imperative of all action. To the age of progress, that seemed too self-evident to question. To many researchers, it still does. Even in a period of economic crisis signaling the system's breakdown, the problem continues to be defined as one of restoring *growth*. Yet it is precisely the assumption that growth is something both natural and desirable that leads us to the dilemma of infinite growth on a finite Earth and the double damning conclusion that our civilization—or perhaps our species must needs perish either of overextension or of stagnation. If we foster *growth*, we shall destroy the prerequisites of our living and choke on our abundance. If we give up *growth*, we shall lose our very *raison d'être* and perish of decadence. There is ample reason to undertake a philosophical inquiry into the pre-reflective attitudes and assumptions that structure our humanity.

Here we are evidently dealing with something more basic than a set of scientific postulates grown habitual, as in the case of Kuhn's paradigm.

Edmund Husserl's conception of *the natural world* (Husserl 1983), lived experience so fundamental as to appear simply *natural*, the way things are, might prove rather more useful.[6]

Husserl starts with the recognition that in all our knowing we are dealing not with some putatively "objective" reality, but with *reality as lived*, with *Sein als Bewußtsein*. Lived experience—*Erlebnis*, which Ricoeur translates helpfully as *le vécu* (Husserl 1950, pp. 140–41)—is not an outer layer of *appearance* masking an inaccessible core of reality we can only conjecture. Rather, lived experience *is* reality's way of being, the way reality presents itself. It is reality as knowable—for only as such can we know it. There is, however, nothing *mere* about it. Appearance is reality, *reality appearing*, making itself actual. The putative "objective reality" with which our sciences operate is an abstraction, a construct of theoretical reason abstracted from the primary given, *lived experience, le vécu*. The task of dealing with it, both theoretical and practical, is not an "objective" one, wholly independent of the observer. Neither, though, is it "subjective" in the sense of being merely mental. Rather, it is *phenomenological*, dealing with phenomena, that is, with *reality standing out into appearance* and so actual rather than merely abstract or theoretical.

This fine bit of obfuscation makes one basic point—that reality always comes to us ordered and rendered intelligible by prereflective experiencing encoded in attitudes and expectations. All our reflective judgments are always inevitably grounded in a more basic, prereflective— or prepredicative—lived experience. Thus they do not present us with some intractable reality-in-itself, but with reality intrinsically ordered by experience. The order which appears to us as die *Härte des Realen*—such as orientation of life to *growth*—is grounded in prereflective experiencing. Or, translating into *lingua vulgaris*, it is not the case that "people are like that," but only that *people act like that* in the context of experience.

Were the patterns of meaning—or more accurately, the ways we live our experience—genetically coded, it would amount to the same *hardness of the real*, whether without us or with us. However, if we live those patterns of experiencing as historically conditioned, then they may be deeply rooted, to be sure, yet be susceptible to change. Continuing with our example, perhaps our fatal fascination with unceasing *growth* is not our fate, only our current condition.

Husserl scholars still argue whether Husserl understood the essential structure of our being as absolute and static or as dynamic and so historically conditioned. His early work, especially his *Logical Investigation*, clearly suggests a static conception, and most scholars so read his entire project. So Kersten translates *Erlebnis* as mental process (Husserl 1983, p. 140f *et passim*). The self-consciously phenomenological studies of the *Ideen* period allow some latitude, so Ricoeur can translate *Erlebnis* as *le vécu*. Husserl's last great work, *Die Krisis der europäischen Wissenschaften* suggests a dynamic view of *Wesen* as historically conditioned, offering latitude for translating *Erlebnis* as structural patterns of being (Husserl 1970, pp. 21–101 esp. 70–73).

Our concern, however, is not with Husserl's *mens auctoris* but with the use we can make of Husserl's insight of reflective judgments as grounded in prereflective experience and of the tools he offers for the purposes of ecological philosophy. Purists may dismiss it as *Tammigold*—fool's gold—though in truth we are taking Husserl at his word and treating phenomenology not as the definitive philosophy, but rather as a prolegomenon to any future ecological philosophy (Kohák 2010).

There is, first of all, the basic recognition that reflection is grounded in prereflective experience. There is, then, a set of philosophical tools which Husserl offers. One of those is the distinction between contingent instantiation and ideal meaning patterns, present in such instantiations yet intrinsically prior to them. That is how we are reading Husserl's distinction *Tatsache und Wesen: Wesen* is an ideal possibility, a possible way of being which a contingent individual takes on. Factual instantiation gives the idea actuality, idea gives that instance meaning. Or, translating once more into *lingua vulgaris*, this is what happens when a stone at a camp site assumes the role of a hammer (Kohák 2007).

Husserl calls the second crucial tool somewhat misleadingly *bracketing*, opening a possibility of a confusion with Descartes' methodological denial. That, though, is not the point. Husserl is not concerned to prove the "existence" of something but rather to grasp its meaning—not to prove objectivity but to understand it. He bids us see each actual occasion as an ideal possibility, defined by a context prior to any actual instantiation, as the need for hammering precedes all actual hammers. For that reason he proposes to set aside all causal explanation, based on the actual occurrence of something, and look rather for its place in the context of a web of meanings, whether that something actually exists or not. Putting it differently still, we are concerned with the idea, the essential possibility of justice, normatively *reel* whether or not it ever occurs in our courts of law. Our task is to grasp the ideal of justice, even though on all actual occasions our verdicts may fall short of it. That does not render the idea irrelevant. Quite the contrary it enables us to understand its actual, imperfect occasions.

There is yet a third tool which Husserl, in a moment of enchantment with Kant, called *transcendental subjectivity*. Perhaps the first point to note is that *subjectivity* is not a subject. Rather, it is a way or ordering experience as intelligible by relating it to a subject. Objectivity describes an ordering of experienced reality as if it were not experienced, in terms of efficient causal relations. Subjectivity similarly refers to ordering experienced reality in subject-related categories of meaning, purpose, and value. The important point is that such an ordering need not be "subjective" in the common sense of the word. It can mean ordering (*as if* related) to a subject, any possible subject, *in principle*. The alternative to objectivity is not private "subjectivity" of this or that subject, but rather subjectivity in principle, an ordering in terms of value and meaning.

Such, I would submit, may be the most useful prolegomena to ecological philosophy. It needs be a descriptive study of the meaning structures of lived experience.[7] If there is any point in recalling ecology as once done by philosophers and poets, it is to trace the patterns of meaning of our ecological experience so we can assess critically and consciously what once we simply lived.

3.

And so to work. What are the meaning patterns structuring our experience of nature as reflected in the writings we traditionally labeled *ecological*? Or, to mix metaphors a bit, what paradigm enframes the authors' experience of their living environment?

Consider the text we quoted at the start of this paper. Forty years ago, the volume we cited (Kohák 1978) sold quite well and even today retains a small but faithful following. This suggests that it articulated faithfully something in lived experience shared by many readers. What was it? The most noticeable mark of the text is a heavy sense of nostalgia. The author evidently experienced nature in its purity as a paradise lost. He experienced—or, he might say, *saw—nature* with the antelapsarian eye of fond recollection as fundamentally harmonious, all embracing, all healing, all reconciling. It is *nature* as a primeval home of ancestral dreams. At its core, there is a Christian vision of a created world, though unscarred by the Fall. Discord enters that harmony with the works of humans. Those are intrinsically *artifices*, product of human art, not of natural spontaneity, and so not structured by the harmony of *nature's* peace. The author experiences electric light painfully as a violation of nature's cycle of night and day, of outgoing effort and reconciliation. He feels comforted by the golden glow of his petroleum lamp even though he is presumably aware, in theory at least, that such lamps represented a dramatic and actually quite recent technological innovation.

In the author's experience, it is not humans as such that represent the violation of nature's order. He evidently experiences his own humanity as natural and so himself as a part of nature's order. Presumably humans who lived in harmony with that natural order—who rose at dawn, lay down at dusk, raised or gathered their sustenance with their hands—perhaps as the peasant farmers in nineteenth century novels or the noble savages a century earlier—would be at peace with *nature* and themselves. The sole difference would be that while for all non-human beings that order is a natural order, inscribed in their very being and obeyed instinctively, for humans, even humans living most naturally, it would still be a *moral* order, one they ought to honor but are able to disregard.

Thought out in detail and practical implication, that vision appears naive, bearing a contradiction within it. Once humans become self-conscious and so free—or in nineteenth century idiom, *moral*—they cease being *natural*. It is not technology, but reflection, the ability to visualize contra-factual conditionals and act on those, that strip *the usual* of the aura of *the natural*. But ideas make facts meaningful; they are not derived from them. Not being able to think through an idea as fact does not invalidate it as an ideal, just as a helmsman's evident inability to reach the Pole Star does not invalidate it as a star by which to steer his ship.

In its outline, that ideal is simple enough. It is the vision of a world created and ordered by a benevolent God as a harmonious creation, which humans disrupt when they follow the desires of their hearts rather than God's law. After that point, history becomes *Heilsgeschichte*, the drama of their quest for restoration of the once and future harmony, presently and contingently disrupted.

That is a seductive paradigm for enframing the perennial human experience of the goodness of life disrupted by fortuitous evil. It is not the only possible, but it seems to fit so well—and it is so adaptable! Latterly, we have seen it embodied in the Marxist vision of a (natural) primitive communism disrupted by the introduction of (artificial) private ownership—though therein Marxism may be more indebted to Friedrich Engels than to Karl Marx. In contrast with the ongoing social meliorism of the Social Democrats, the Communists clung to the faith that if only the disruptive element (here private property) could be removed from the face of the earth, harmony would blossom, history would cease, and humans would live in a timeless peaceable state, at most competing peacefully in meeting production norms. Perhaps, that is why Marx refused to explain just how he visualized his once and future communism. It is not easy to visualize perfection in time (Kolakowski 1978, pp. 399–407, also 39–44).

The same paradigm underlies the essays of the *nature writers* in the first half of the twentieth century, direct precursors of romantic ecology. Here Henry David Thoreau's *Walden* (Thoreau 1956) is the prototype most often invoked. Thoreau's admirers usually overlook Thoreau's evidently thinking himself the proponent of a viable alternative rather than an uncommitted dreamer of dreams (Ibid., pp. 59–71). He did devote his first and longest chapter to the economics of living on the land, had practical advice to his Irish neighbor, and located his hut within an easy walk of town. Still, his readers in the 1960s justly recognized the paradigm as central. Life consistent with the order of nature is in principle harmonious. It is the drive for progress, symbolized for Henry David by the steam train and by his neighbor's love of his *tay*, that is the fortuitous disruptive factor through which evil enters into *nature's* harmony.[8]

That is the paradigm we can trace no less in the writings of John Muir (1916, 1980) to whom America owes its system of national parks. Muir wrote not only of nature, but of the *harmony* of nature, viciously violated by human rapacity as symbolized by the deforestation of New England for lumber and firewood. He strove to preserve patches of wilderness, of nature in its purity, as a reminder of the harmony whose devastation he witnessed, though without a hope that humans could mend their ways by their efforts. If there is a glimpse of hope in his writings, it is not that humans will mend their ways by their own efforts. In Muir's writings, hope has a religious tinge of the Creator healing his devastated creation.

Something similar can be said of the gentle, urbane nature writings of Joseph Wood Krutch (Krutch 1957), now largely and unjustly forgotten, and of the acclaimed nature essays of Aldo Leopold (Leopold 1990), a forester with a poet's soul and a philosopher's need to systematize. It was Leopold who provided the ecological movement with a clear vision of good and evil: *A thing is right, he writes, when it tends to preserve the integrity, stability and beauty of the biotic community. It is wrong when it tends otherwise* (Ibid., p. 262). Leopold earned significant criticism for this implicit recognition that "Man" is not the measure of all things and that even legitimate human needs might actually be destructive. It was still the *age of progress*, and America was not ready to give up the primacy of "Man" and the hope of the golden age which romantic ecology put in question.

Leopold saw beyond his time, or perhaps looked at it from above, *sub specie aeternitatis*. In his *Sand County Almanach* (Ibid., pp. 137–39), he gives the example of humans who thought it in their interest to exterminate wolves in a particular mountain range. Wolves kill deer whom humans find appealing. Yet uncontrolled overpopulation of deer grazed the mountain bare. Subsequent erosion left a barren stony rise where a lush forest teeming with life had been. Each of the actors in the story had their particular interest, yet there is a higher interest, the interest of the mountain which Leopold uses as the long range good of the biotic community as a whole. The mountain does not side with humans, wolves, or deer. To *think like the mountain* means to rise above the conflict of partial interests to the transcendent viewpoint of the whole. It means rising above time with its progress to the perspective of eternity. That is romantic ecology at its grandest, transcending the particular to the perspective of the whole.

Yet there is something infinitely poignant about the intense empathy with which Leopold writes about surviving patches of land left free of cultivation and about the resignation with which he accepts the inevitable *march of progress*. It takes immense courage to love what is finite, cherishing its value yet accepting the pain of its mortality. Most humans find the pain of finitude too great a burden. Some give up love and grow hard, indifferent to pain in what Heidegger, in a step into dark romanticism, called *Entschlossenheit* and his English translators *anticipatory resoluteness*.[9] Others sink into comforting nostalgia, transforming pain into poetry. Those, too, are paradigms for enframing lived experience. The Enlightenment and its heirs chose a different alternative: effective action guided by the hope that doom is not inevitable, that with will and effort we can change the outcome. Or, for the lovers of labels, we can say that Western modernity is an attempt to dispel the gloom of romanticism with the historical optimism of the Enlightenment.

Here, though, a brief detour is in order. In the concluding third of the twentieth century, a movement calling itself *deep ecology* sought to break through the gloom of paradise lost by changing the other horn of the ecological dilemma. If we cannot avoid doom by changing the finitude of the Earth, perhaps we can escape it by changing the infinite rapacity of humans. Arne Naess, the Norwegian philosopher trained originally in analytic philosophy, coined the designation as a synonym for philosophical ecology (Naess 1998). He interpreted ecology's task primarily as one of reconciling humans with to the nature they bear within and directly about them. So understood, ecology does not seek to change the world directly. Rather, it seeks to change the passions of the heart in the hope that once humans are no longer driven by lust for power and greed for possession, they will be able to approach nature no longer as an opponent to be conquered but as their home to be cherished. Naess in effect shifted the emphasis of ecology from the way humans relate to nature to the way they relate to all that is *natural* within them—spontaneous, free, forced by no artifice. It was a noble attempt. Though it seemed naive, it was the finest the romantic paradigm had to offer, the recognition that evil—here environmental degradation—needs be countered at the source, in the hearts and minds of humans. It inspired Naess' students, among them Bill Devall, George Session (Devall and Sessions 1985), and David Rothenberg. They presented Naes's thought and charisma to America and evoked a widespread positive response.

Unfortunately and rather unfairly, when *deep ecology* moved from Norway to California, it underwent something of a metamorphosis. The authors of a manual entitled *Thinking like a Mountain: Towards a Council of All Beings* (Seed et al. 1988), appealing to a rather special clientele, gave a wholly new meaning to Leopold's phrase, interpreting it as an emphatic identification with the lived experience of suffering creation. Mingling deep ecology with fashionable mysticism and a rather idiosyncratic depth psychology, they transformed *deep ecology* into an introspective psycho-hygiene. Their manual recommended adepts a discipline of incense and drumming culminating in donning *papier-mâché* masks of individual species and reliving the distress of a cow trapped in *agrobusiness* or of a loon unable to hatch her eggs because her eggshells have been weakened by DDT. Actually, when lived rather than described at a distance, it can be a powerful emotional experience. It can change a person's attitude toward the nonhuman world dramatically, though at the cost of critical reason—and so is ill-suited for projecting a strategy of dealing with environmental deterioration.

That, ultimately, may be at the root of the problem of all romantic ecology. It can provide inspiration and insight, helping humans break out of their homocentric blindness. For all its failings as professional philosophy, it has brought into question the central assumption of modern thought—that *"'Man' is the measure of all things."* Yet while neither the measure nor the center of all things, humans, for better or worse, have placed themselves at the center of responsibility for the drift of our civilization to environmental oblivion. As we become increasingly aware of the environmental crisis—and reports like that of the Intergovernmental Panel on Climate Change, *Climate Change 2007* (IPCC 2007a), leave little room for honest doubt—we need a strategy for action and a blueprint for effective action.

4.

The environmental movement which sought to respond to that need owes more to Rachel Carson's *Silent Spring* than to Aldo Leopold's *Sand County Almanach*. Its focus is far more practical: there is a specific problem, we need effective solutions. Yet even in environmental theory and philosophy at their most practical, we can discern a paradigm enframing the authors' experience and shaping both their perception of the problem and their vision of solutions.

The paradigm which emerges here is one bequeathed to us by the Enlightenment with its Stoic ancestors, though now in a Christian context. Here, too, the world is not random; it is ordered by the *reason* which the Stoics called the Divine Logos, albeit by our time rather secularized. The ordering of the cosmos is good; it is unruly passions through which evil enters. However, the Enlightenment set its stoic understanding of the place rational order and disruptive passion in a context that owes less to Marcus Aurelius than to Aurelius Augustinus, reflecting a distinctively Hebrew-Christian sense of history as the locus of significant change. There is rational order and irrational chaos, but there is also a growth from chaos to order, from bestiality to humanity.

Perhaps the best sketch is one offered by a largely forgotten father of modernity, Johann Gottlob Herder. Herder, heir of the Enlightenment, rejected the Christian conception of evil as fatal product of the fall (or "alienation") of an originally good creation (Herder 1784). The creation is good, ordered by God's reason, only it is still imperfect. There is a dynamic strain to Herder's conception: creation is *ab initio* incomplete, has yet to grow to completion. Being is becoming, *growth* is its inmost thrust. Whatever there is, begins as mere possibility, much as the grain of mustard seed only gradually grows into a plant so great that birds can nest therein. So humans at their birth—or humanity at the dawn of history—are neither perfect nor fallen, but simply unfinished, raw material of future humanity. That beginning, in humans and in humanity alike, is marked by wholly self-centered selfishness leading to a constant fight of all against all, much as Hobbes described it. That is *bestiality*, the condition which Herder ascribes to nonhuman animals, incidentally showing his lack of socio-biological knowledge. It is also the condition which both savages and newborns share. However, unlike other animals, Herder's humans are endowed with *reason*, the capacity for discerning the order of divine *reason* in nature, and with "noble sentiment," the ability to sympathize with the joy and suffering of others.

Humans in the course of life—and humanity in the course of history—are guided by critical *reason* and noble sentiment in developing, gradually, to the full stature of humanity. *Humanitas*, the potential of growing to the fullness of human potential, is the common element in all Enlightenment thinking from which both romanticism and (Enlightenment) rationalism derive. The split between them comes only when those Enlightenment thinkers whom we normally count as *romantics* despair of critical reason as the path to full humanity and opt for noble sentiment instead. Herder defies classification. For him, both *reason* and *sentiment* are ways to growth. It was up to his heirs to cope with the problem of coping with the conflict of rational humanism and sentimental nationalism.

For our purposes, though, the central point is Herder's conviction that evil is imperfection and that the task of humans and humanity alike is to outgrow it, maturing under the guidance of critical *reason* and noble *sentiment* from bestiality to the fullness of humanity. *Bestiality* is for Herder a condition rather like *laissez-faire* capitalism gone wild—blind conflict of all against all for everything, much as Hobbes visualized the *state of nature*. Humanity, the goal for which we strive, he envisioned as a condition of peaceable living in a community structured by mutual understanding (reason) and mutual goodwill (noble sentiment). The point, though, is that, unlike for the Romantic paradigm, this is not a once and future state, once had, then lost, some day to be regained. Rather, it is an ongoing task in which both individual humans and humanity as a whole strive for the fullness of their humanity. Being human is not a constant state. It is becoming.

As Herder imagined it in the final decades of the eighteenth century, that growth was not yet an evolution, much less *progress* in the nineteenth century sense. Rather, it was a moral growth, an ongoing nurturing of our humanity. However, thinkers like Jan Evangelista Purkyně and Charles Darwin soon transformed that moral growth into biological evolution, which in turn gave rise to the idea of social evolution as well. The age of steam and electricity in turn interpreted evolution as *progress*, now understood as ever greater releasing of energy for human use. While Marxism in its Communist form projected essentially a romantic vision of a once and future perfect society, capitalism here projected an essentially Enlightenment vision of perpetual growth as the fundamental law both natural and moral and as a cure for all ills.

To a culture which enframed its experience in the paradigm of progress, growth would understandably appear not only as a moral imperative but as the shining path to human fulfillment, once called *salvation*, more recently *happiness*, whose pursuit American revolutionaries held for a right as inalienable as life and liberty. In that paradigm, the environmental concerns of romantic ecologists like Muir or Krutch would understandably appear as a fortuitous obstacle on the path of progress and a threat to all the age held dear. The mass of humankind convinced that *progress* held the key to happiness might have been willing to indulge sentimental "nature lovers" and "tree-huggers" as long as their peculiar predilections did not interfere with *growth*. They certainly were not willing to alter their project of open-ended expansion of production and consumption for the sake of what they regarded as a personal aesthetic or emotional predilection, the "love of nature," said with a strong sense of irony. The apostles of *progress* thought themselves tough-minded, not tender-minded thinkers.

Interestingly enough, the dominant response of the heirs of the Enlightenment to environmental warnings and appeals conformed to the five stages which Elisabeth Kübler-Ross identified among patients seeking to come to terms with a terminal diagnosis (Kübler-Ross 1970). It was as if the recognition of fatal environmental degradation spelled the death of the dream they had been living ever since they accepted the message that *progress* will dry every tear and solve every problem within the foreseeable future, and not without reason. Implicit in such concern was the unspoken message that progress, the proposed cure, may be the cause of the environmental crisis. That would indeed be the end of the dream.

So indeed the first critical reaction for Rachel Carson's *Silent Spring* was *denial*, much as Kübler-Ross describes it. What Carson described was so utterly contrary to *the American dream* that it simply could not be true. American society at the time—and global society after the usual ten, twenty years—was willing to tolerate *nature lovers* as harmless and perhaps even allow them some decorative social value, but was not willing to entertain the possibility that its *pursuit of happiness might* endanger the very happiness they sought. In America, the 1960s were an age of the fad, and ecology appeared as one of them. The more romantic among us, with their sandals, Indian drums, and something rather resembling nature worship, encouraged the impression that ecology was but a fad that would in time go the way of the lindy and the jitterbug.

It was hard, however, to dismiss as fad authors like Rachel Carson who presented not only their love for nature and concern for its future but also a vast array of hard scientific data. The first report of the Club of Rome, *The Limits of Growth*, made it clear that even if ecological fashions were to go away, environmental problems would not. That recognition triggered what Kübler-Ross describes as the second stage of coming to terms with what is unacceptable yet cannot be denied, *anger*—or, in this case, veritable rage. Rachel Carson, the gentlest of souls, found herself attacked viciously as everything from a "bleedin' heart" through a cancer on national self-confidence to a Communist agent trying to undermine America's faith and morals. Ironically, as environmental concerns spread to what was then the Soviet bloc, Communists returned the compliment and attacked environmentalists as agents of capitalism seeking to block the people's triumphant march to Communism. Even today, Václav Klaus, currently president of the Czech Republic and a passionate defender of neoconservative causes, attacks the environmentalists as charlatans using bad science to endanger free enterprise, insisting that this is *a blue, not a green planet* (Klaus 2007). In all such attacks, there is little logic or reason, but a great deal of passionate denial of what, though undeniable, is simply unacceptable—much like a terminal diagnosis.

Kübler-Ross calls the third stage in coming to terms with the inevitable *bargaining*. Patients will bargain with their physician or perhaps with death. *If I cut down on smoking, won't you change my diagnosis? If I stop altogether?* At this stage, the "patients"—people of affluent culture—make a common cause with practical environmentalists in an urgent quest for innovative approaches and technologies which would reduce the cost of our affluence without endangering it. In part, many of the scorned gestures of romantic ecologists return to favor—burning wood instead of coal, travelling by railway or at least fuel-efficient motor cars, once derided as "econo-boxes," in place of their cherished gas guzzlers. A great hit of this stage was a book promising twice the affluence at half the energy cost, Ulrich von Weizsäcker's *Factor Four: Doubling Wealth—Halving Resource Use* (Weizsäcker 1997). Significantly enough, at the time it was actually published as *The New Report of the Club of Rome*. The Enlightenment wing of the environmental movement was joining in the bargaining. *If we produce more efficiently and consume more considerately, can we please keep our affluence?* To avoid prejudging the answer, no one at the time paid much attention to the role of geometrically rising populations in the equation.

Even so, the answer was negative. Even excluding the population factor, environmental research had gone past the many specific problems that could be amenable to a particular solution. The problem now stood out in its global, systematic simplicity. Our civilization, regardless of local variations, places an infinite demand on the Earth. The Earth's ability to sustain such demands is. QED.

That recognition heralds the fourth stage of Kübler-Ross's process—*depression*. The patient gives up. Not just gives up struggling. Just gives up. James Lovelock paraphrases Garret Hardin's summary of the message of doom of another generation, the three laws of thermodynamics, as "1. We cannot win. 2. We are sure to lose. 3. We cannot get out of the game" (Hardin 1985, Lovelock 1995, p. 116). Ecology in the spirit of the Enlightenment sought to counter the melancholy conclusions of Romantic ecology's *noble sentiments* with the vigorous action of *reason*. It ended in a recognition of the impotence of action in face of a reality which we find utterly unacceptable—the demise of our global civilization—but which the dynamics of that very civilization, summed up in the slogan of *growth*, make inevitable.

In Kübler-Ross's far-ranging observations, after depression exhaust itself, the final stage is *acceptance*. Yes, I shall die. Not sometime, in principle. I shall die in the foreseeable future—and there is nothing, nothing I can do about it. There is nothing for it except to resume living, only knowing what I knew all along, *I shall die*. Nothing has changed, except perhaps I shall not purchase any long playing records. So, eleven years later, James Lovelock bids his readers give up worrying, buy a farm in East Anglia, and enjoy a little corner of nature while it lasts (Lovelock 1988, pp. 237–40 *et passim*). A. O. Wilson, one of the world's most knowledgeable researchers in the field, concludes that we are witnessing the sixth great die-out which this time includes our own species. We are about to turn over the planet to a less destructive species, to insects, perhaps the ants in particular. They have colonized all five habitable continents and with their perfect social organization, not corroded by the acid of individuality, are well suited to inherit the earth. In the meantime, A. O. Wilson continues in his painstaking research in his formidable studies of formicology (Wilson 1992).

Hope may die last, but when it does, hopelessness is beside the point. All that remains is acceptance. We are doomed by the very logic of our efforts. Enlightenment environmentalism has *come by the highway home, and lo, it is ended*. But is that not what romantic ecologists have been telling us all along?

5.

"Out through the fields and the wood and over the walls I have wended. I have come by the highway home, and lo, it is ended." sings Robert Frost, the great poet of the New England of another age. We have paraphrased him at the end of the preceding section. Yet the poem goes on: *"Ah, when to the heart of man was it ever less than a treason / To go with the drift of things, To yield with a grace to reason, / and bow and accept the end of a love or a season?"* (Frost 1979, pp. 29–30).

If not romance or reason, perhaps poetry—or philosophy in a poetic mode—leads on to another question. Are our habitual ways of enframing experience, whether in a romantic of a rationalist mode, really *the way things are?* Their roots do run deep. Ever since Parmenides triumphed over Heraclites, we have sought *true reality* in the murky depth of what we thought eternal, unchanging, firm. Yet the evident reality of our lived experience is a process, not a state. It is a story we live and tell. We ourselves are living organisms in the organic context of all life. When we ponder our relation to our environment, we ought to think not of static entities like "Man" [sic] and "nature," but rather of *ways of being*—or as we have put it earlier, to the patterns that emerge in the process of living.

There is precedent not only in Heraclites and Hegel, but also in ideas of *Creative Evolution* (Bergson 1911) or *Process and Reality* (Whitehead 1960). Here nature appears not as "fact" but as process, the grand stream of all life with all that sustains it. There is no one state we could or ought to fixate for all eternity. There are, however, rules for acting out the story of life in the story of nature. Rather than speaking of the way nature *is*, we can speak more accurately of the way *nature does*. Such is the reality of our lived experience—*nature as the system of all life*, including our own.

The same is true of what we are wont to call *culture*, the world of human activities. That, too, is a dynamic (sub)system of integrated processes, dependent on the system of all life. The crucial point is that while the system of all life—*nature*—is relatively closed and independent, its counterpart, the world of human culture with all it entails, is radically dependent. In biological terms, the world of human acts is a parasitic subsystem, a gondola suspended from the balloon of all life. As a parasite, "culture" draws on "nature" not out of some cosmic ill will or technological inadequacy, but simply because that is a parasite's way of being. Consequently, the basic rule for a successful parasite—say, the *ethic of parasitism*—is to draw on its host with respect for its integrity. "Respect for nature" is not just a noble sentiment, but also a structural necessity of our being. To survive, we must use our host but also respect its *integrity, stability, and beauty* (Leopold 1990, p. 262).

The basic rule of parasitism, respect for the host, is thus both an ethical demand, a structural necessity—and the starting point for all environmental ethics. We are neither *nature's* wayward children nor its shepherds and masters, but rather its dependents, in a parasite's unequal partnership with its host. That need not be an adversarial relation, as the Czech environmental writer Josef Šmajs would have it (Šmajs 1995), as long as our demands upon our host do not endanger its survival.

Seen in so simple terms, environmental degradation appears to have a similarly simple solution, in principle at least. Humans (or "culture") need but live within the limits of *nature's* capacity for self-renewal. True—but it tempts environmental thinkers to formulate that fundamental insight as *their philosophy*, setting themselves up as prophets convinced that if all humans would accept their particular doctrine, the problem would solve itself. Thinkers as different as Arne Naess, John Seed or Ulrich von Weizsäcker tend to yield to that temptation.

After our experience with assorted saving creeds and ideologies it is hard to believe that converting humankind to a creed, however noble, would be likely to transform its way of being on Earth—and in this case, the transformation would need be dramatic indeed. Living within the Earth's limitations would require a drastic reduction in human populations as a major shift of material resources from the over-consuming parts of the world to the Third World—and from individual consumption to common welfare not of humans only, but of the entire biotic community.

Are we humans capable of so great a behavior modification? Not easily. Ecological and environmental pessimism grows from the assumption that the human pole of the environmental equation is as intractable as the environmental pole. Yet humans have repeatedly shown that they can accept limitation and loss for the sake of values they hold dear. Here British response to Churchill's call for "blood, sweat and tears" bears witness. So do the immense sacrifices of the Russian people in the Great Patriotic War. *In extremis*, other things prove more important than short-term individual advantage—though rational theoretical understanding, though a *conditio sine qua non* for coping with the threat, need be augmented not with romantic illusion but with poetic comprehension of the challenge.

To be sure, such transformation would require far more than living as usual, only learning to love nature and use it more efficiently. For starters, we should need to overcome the gap between the insanely rich and the insufferably poor, a major source of both environmental degradation and of social tension. We should need to abjure violence as a means of conflict resolution, even though wars mean profit for the oligarchs and adrenalin for the masses. Most of all, we should need to break free of the illusion that the meaning and fulfillment of being human is open-ended *growth*. We should need to consider the possibility that that fulfillment is not somewhere else but here, in the contentment of being at peace with oneself, one's neighbor, and the entire grand system of all life, if not outright God.

That may seem the greatest challenge. Yet no one ever joined an NGO for mercenary motives. Humans even now notoriously find fulfillment even on the simplest level of consumption. What they require is not ever-rising standard of consumption but a confidence that what they are doing is meaningful, that they are doing it well and that those who matter to them appreciate it. Both great prophets and base demagogues inspired their following by offering just that. Self-respect and the respect of others are the basic human needs—and, unlike tawdry substitutes as riches, fame, or power, they are ecologically sustainable.

The challenge of reversing our drift to environmental oblivion needs be confronted also rationally, to separate visionaries from demagogues. It needs be confronted with the keenest technology and science. Ultimately, though, it is not a matter of technology or theory, but of transforming the deeply ingrained value structure of our experiencing from strife to solidarity, from greed to justice, from hate to love. Yes, even were we to succeed in such a transformation, we should still need make full use of our theory and technology, our reason and sympathy. Should we fail in that transformation, we should definitely fail in theory and practice as well. The missing component, though, may be the poetic perspective which romantic ecology at its best provided. Perhaps it would take poets to save humankind from its technical rationalism and its rational technology.

6.

Hold, though—isn't that sheer fantasy, a goal beyond our reach? Most probably it is. It is a distant star by which to steer our ship while knowing we shall never reach it. Or perhaps it is but an idle dream. Dreamers have repeatedly called for such a transformation, in vain. Perhaps humankind simply cannot change and is doomed to perish. There is a great deal of evidence to suggest that that is so.

If so, it is that much more a reason not to postpone acting until after God or some engineer of human souls shall have transformed humanity. We need to strive for finite practical goals, relying on tools available to us, on technology, regulation, education, setting partial goals, and welcoming partial successes. A reduction in carbon dioxide will not bring salvation, only slightly better breathing. Protection of green spaces will not save the atmosphere, only make the Earth a little bit greener. Resolution of particular conflicts will not bring peace, just save some people from premature death and needless suffering. Alleviation of the most blatant instances of social injustice will not bring the Kingdom of God to earth, but it will make life a bit more bearable for the most downtrodden. All these are significant achievement, even if they are for a finite time and cannot preserve civilization for all time. After all, we, too, live in a finite time.

We have one advantage which writers like Karl Jaspers (Jaspers 1957) or Milan Machovec (Machovec 1998) recognize. This time we face not just the decline of one civilization, but its global annihilation. Perhaps that will shake us humans out of our affluent lethargy. Admittedly, it is not likely. Those among us who are confident that, come what may, the cosmos is in good hands, have an advantage. Yet whether we share their faith or not, if we wish to look ourselves in the mirror in the eye, we cannot abandon the urgent tasks of technological environmentalism. Neither can we stop dreaming great dreams. Dreams without technology may be powerless, but technology without dreams is blind—and can be deadly, as the mushroom cloud over Chernobyl reminds us.

So, act locally, as Greenpeace teach. Think globally, as they do. But, most of all, *do not stop dreaming great dreams*!

Notes

1. The distinction between the ecological and the environmental movement is artificial yet useful. Both refer to the concern about the impact of human activities on the whole of life and all that sustains it (usually nature). We shall follow the usage which uses the term ecological for that part of the movement whose primary concern is philosophical, with humans, their self-understanding and their understanding of nature. We shall use the term environmental for the part whose concern is primarily practical, with nature, including humans, and its needs. The ecological strand is as old as Virgil, the environmental strand as the first recognition of the finitude of natural resources, primarily coal, in the Industrial Revolution. Whereof more anon.

2. In the United States, Sen. Gaylord Nelson's (D–WI) proclamation of April 22 as Earth Day in 1970 tends to serve as the date of the birth of the ecological movement, while the publication of Rachel Carson's *Silent Spring* in 1962 (Carson 1987) serves a similar function for the environmental movement (Kohák 2000, pp. 3, 143).

3. Aldo Leopold (+1948) was an active forester who in his "Land Ethic" gave America its first environmental philosophy though his classic, *A Sand County Almanach*, consists mostly of sensitive reflections on nature (Leopold 1987, pp. 237–95 *et passim*).

4. Remembered today mostly by lovers of noble English nature prose, Joseph Wood Krutch (+1970), Krutch is the author of the memorable observation that when humans destroy something replaceable made by them, we call them vandals, when they destroy something irreplaceable made by God, we call them developers (Krutch 1957).

5. The following section, rather technical, is intended specifically for readers interested in the intricacies of interpreting Husserlian phenomenology. Readers content simply to make use of its result for an enquiry into ecology and environmentalism without delving into such Husserlian scholasticism can skim over it and take up the argument on p.000 below without loss of continuity.

6. The following interpretation of phenomenology, though indebted to Husserl, does not claim to represent a reading of Husserl but only one possibly fruitful application of his insights. See references cited, also my earlier work, *Idea and Experience* (Kohák 1978).

7. "Die Phänomenologie als deskriptive Wesenslehre der reinen Erlebnisse" (Husserl 1995, p. 156). I am purposely citing the original German because of the ambiguities in the translation of Erlebnis explained above.

8. I have dealt with the authors here mentioned at some length in *The Green Halo* (Kohák 2000) to which I would refer the enquiring reader. Here I shall restrict myself to brief sketches and references as reading suggestions.

9. This may be the most problematic moment in Heidegger's Being and Time. Heidegger recognizes death as an integral part of life. That is a fundamental recognition to which faith responds with the love of life which makes possible acceptance of all it entails. There is little love in Heidegger. He faces death rather as an enemy, in a stance of defiance (Heidegger 1929, pp. 25–300), leaving the reader wondering whether Heidegger's opting for death rather than life as the inmost human possibility might not have something to do with his political stance in 1933 and thereafter. That, however, wildly exceeds the limits of this enquiry and so we shall not pursue it here further.

References

Bergson, H., 1911, *Creative Evolution*, Mitchell, A., (trans.), Henry Holt and Company, New York.

Carson, R., 1987, *Silent Spring* (1st ed.), 1962, Houghton Mifflin Company, Boston.

Devall, B. & Sessions, G., 1985, *Deep Ecology: Living as if Nature Mattered*, Peregrine Smith Books, Salt Lake City, UT.

Frost, R., 1979, *The Poetry of Robert Frost*, E.C. Lathem, (ed.), Henry Holt and Company, New York.

Hardin, G., 1985, *Filter Against Folly: How to Survive Despite Economics, Ecologists and the Merely Eloquent*, Viking, New York.

Heidegger, M., 1929, *Sein und Zeit*, Halle a.d.S.: Max Niemeyer Verlag; English in Macquarrie, J. and Robinson, E., Being and Time, Harper & Brothers, New York, 1962.

Herder, J.G., 1784, *Ideen zur Philosophie der Geschichte der Menschheit*, czech translation, Patočka, J., trans, Vývoj lidskosti, Laichter, Praha, 1941.

Husserl, E., 1950, *Idées directrices pour une phénoménologie*, Ricoeur, P. trad., Gallimard, Paris.

————, 1970, *Die Krisis der europäischen Wissenschaften und die transzendentale Phänomenologie*, English in Carr, D., The Crisis of European Sciences and Transcendental Phenomenology, Northwestern University Press, Evanston, IL.

————, 1983, *Ideen zu einer reinen Phänomenologie und phänomenologischen Philosophie*, Erstes Buch (1st ed.), 1911, English in Kersten, F., tr., Ideas pertaining to a pure phenomenology and phenomenological philosophy, First Book, General introduction to a pure Phenomenology, The Hague, Martinus Nijhoff Publishers.

————, 1995, *Ideen zu einer reinen Phänomenologie und phänomenologischen Philosophie*, K. Schuhmann (ed.), Kluwer Academic Publishers, Dortrecht.

IPCC, 2007a, Salomon, R.D. et al., *Climate Change 2007: Fourth Assessment Report* of the Intergovernmental Panel on Climate Change, Cambridge University Press [cited as AR4], Cambridge, UK.

————, 2007b, Metz, B. et al. (eds.), *Mitigation of Climate Change*, Climate Change 2007 Report of the Third Working Group of the Intergovernmental Panel on Climate Change, Cambridge University Press, Cambridge, UK.

Jaspers, K., 1957, *Die Atombombe und die Zukunft des Menschen*, Piper, München.

Kohák, E., 1978, *Idea and Experience: The Project of Phenomenology in Ideas I*, University of Chicago Press, Chicago.

————, 1982, *The Embers and the Stars: A Philosophical Inquiry into the Moral Sense of Nature*, University of Chicago Press, Chicago, IL.

————, 2000, *The Green Halo: A Bird's-Eye View of Ecological Ethics*, Open Court Press, Chicago, IL.

————, 2007, Významy a vrtochy Wesen (The Vagaries of Wesen), *Reflexe* 16 (32): 65–74.

————, 2010, *Consequences of Phenomenology*, Presented at the conference Geburt der Phänomenologie, Österreichisches Kulturforum Prag, 11 January 2010, Publication pending in supplemental band of Filosofický Casopis, vol. 58, no. 5 (October 2010).

Klaus, V., 2007, *Blue Planet in Green Shackles: What is Endangered, Climate or Freedom?*, Competitive Enterprise Institute, Washington, DC.

Kolakowski, L., 1978, *Main Currents of Marxism: The Founders*, Falla, P.S., (trans.), Clarendon Press, Oxford.

Krutch, J.W., 1957, *The Best Nature Writing of Joseph Wood Krutch*, Pocket Books, New York.

Kübler-Ross, E., 1970, *On Death and Dying*, Macmillan, New York.

Kuhn, T., 1970, *The Structure of Scientific Revolutions* (2d ed.), University of Chicago Press, Chicago, IL.

Leopold, A., 1990, *A Sand County Almanach* (1st ed.), Ballantine Books, New York, 1946.

Lovelock, J., 1988, *The Ages of Gaia: A Biography of our Living Earth*, W.W. Norton & Company, New York.

————, 1995, *Gaia: A new Look at Life on Earth* (1st ed.), Oxford University Press, Oxford, 1979.

Machovec, M., 1998, *Filosofie tváří v tvář zániku* (Philosophy in Face of Annihilation), Nakladatelství "Zvláštní vydání", Brno (CZ).

Muir, J., 1916, *A Thousand Mile Walk to the Gulf*, Houghton Mifflin, Boston, MA.

————, 1980, *Wilderness Essays*, Peregrine Smith Books, Salt Lake City, UT.

Naess, A., 1998, *Ecology, Community and Life-Style*, D. Rothenberg (ed.), Cambridge University Press, New York.

Seed, J., Macy, J. & Fleming, P., 1988, *Thinking Like a Mountain: Towards a Council of All Beings*, New Society Publishers, Philadelphia, PA.

Šmajs, J., 1995, *Ohrožená kultura: Od evoluční ontology k ekologické politice*, Zvláštní vydání, Brno (CZ).

Thoreau, H.D., 1956, *Walden and Other Writings*, Mentor Books, New York, NY.

United Nations Human Development Report, 1998, *Special Issue: Consumption for Human Development*, Oxford University Press, New York, NY.

Weizsäcker, E.U., 1997, *Factor Four: Doubling Wealth—Halving Resource Use: The New Report of the Club of Rome*, Earthscan Publications, London.

Whitehead, A.N., 1960, *Process and Reality*, Harper Torchbook, New York, NY.

Wilson, E.O., 1992, *The Diversity of Life*, Penguin, New York, NY.

Sustainable Development as an Axiological and a Civilizational Challenge

Tadeusz Borys
Sustainable Development and Quality of Life
Department of Quality and Environment Management
Wrocław University of Economics
Poland

1. Introduction

The paper presents the consequences of evident axiological volatility experienced in many fields of social, economic, and political lives. In particular, the educational system is vulnerably exposed to that sui generis schizophrenia. Compared with the past century, when axiology was obviously marginalized, the twenty-first century will be a major axiological challenge based on a new development paradigm. The paradigm is characterized by balance, durability, and sustainability, thus determining essence and logic of the second road. General idea of the new development paradigm and its increasingly many concretizations demonstrate a strong stream of more mitigated anthropocentrism that is based on a holistic vision of humaneness.

A new development paradigm naturally serving as an alternative concept of development is applied worldwide as balanced development, durable development, and sustainable development or sometimes, yet less frequently, ecodevelopment. Unfortunately, the new development paradigm, notwithstanding its fundamental importance, is not only in

Poland relatively unknown, is perceived as controversial, and generally, it is not a special favorite of the current civilization.

In twenty-first century, a new development paradigm is first of all an axiological challenge—a challenge for the systems of values. The present-day civilization is characterized by evident axiological volatility experienced in many areas of social, economic, and political lives. In particular, the educational system is vulnerably exposed to that *sui generis* schizophrenia, as basic consequences of that volatility are particularly acute and intense due to the fundamental role of education in social life. This introductory reflection should be supplemented by a necessary dose of optimism contained in a statement that it is precisely the idea of *sustainable development* which slowly becomes a real basis of a major change in the quality of life—and becomes a key civilizational challenge for the twenty-first century with many favorable chances to be successful.

What is an axiological sense of *development*? What will the current century be like? What are the chances to create a new model of *quality of life* based on the *new development paradigm*? These are key questions and problems of our times (Borys 2010, pp. 5–6).

2. What is an Axiological Sense of Category of Development?

The category of development is especially exposed in economy and economic sciences (with regard to *economic development*), in social sciences (with reference to *social development*), and in technical sciences (in relation to *technical* and *technological development*). There are also areas in which development is, to a great extent, undistinguishable or seems a forgotten category. One can also agree with the idea, that this category often becomes the subject for peculiar sociotechnics in different ideologies or politics.

The condition for better progress in discussing new development paradigm is to reach an agreement regarding *the general concept of development itself*. This is the fundamental premise for the creation of a uniform terminological convention of derivative concepts, consisting mostly in adding to the term "development" either prefixes (e.g., *eco*development) or adjectives (e.g., *sustainable or durable* development).

While considering the subject of development, three closely connected terms have to be taken into account: the *development* itself, *regression*—as opposed to development (underdevelopment, holding back in development), and *stabilization* (lack of changes). In attempting to define the first two categories, the role of constitutive attribute is played by the term of *changes* or synonyms of change (e.g., *passing from to*, etc.). In this respect, one can distinguish: *developmental changes* and *regressive changes*.

Establishing whether development should be perceived as a positive or negative notion becomes the first important step in explaining the general concept of *development*. There are many arguments which support *positive* understanding of development,[1] and they support the acceptance of *positive aspect of changes as a constitutive attribute of the definition of development*.

Therefore, development is the stimulant (stimulator), i.e., an attribute which higher values mean higher level of an analyzed phenomenon (an increasing function of preference), which in our case means, that "the higher the level of the development the better" (e.g., the development of a human being or commune, etc.).

Concluding, it can be agreed that *development* means *the process of changes regarding an object assessed in a positive way from the point of view of a defined criterion (or set of criterions)* or in a more extensive form as *the process of object transformation from less desirable stages (less positive ones; considered as inferior, less developed, from less perfect forms) to more desirable stages (more positive ones; considered as better, more developed, to more perfect forms) from the point of view of a defined criterion (or a set of criteria)*. Therefore, it is assumed, that the later stage is better from the earlier one.

This general definition constitutes a favorable background for the construction of derivative, more explication type of definitions based on progressing substantiality of the criterion assessing to what extent such changes are positive, as well as to an obvious—based on analogy—definition of *regression*.

There definitely exist many criteria of assessing how positive the changes are, although few of them are explicitly revealed. Basically, one can distinguish two groups of criteria among them:

- Criteria of a detailed nature with a *hidden axiological aspect*. For example, while applying the *object complexity criterion*, complexity is understood as a positive value ("the more complex the better"); without disclosing its axiological aspect, this criterion becomes a disputable one, since the positive value may become, say, *simplicity*, while development may be perceived as the "process of changes toward simplicity," just like, for example, in the case of spiritual development. Another example of this type of criterion may be the *criterion of quality* (qualitative

development), using which quality is recognized as a positive value—the higher the quality the better;
- Global criteria with a *disclosed axiological aspect*. This is the *value system criterion* (in other words—an axiological criterion), which means the criterion of the principles based on, say, the category of good. An equally important and complementary criterion for the one of quality system is the *criterion of an objective*; the significance of this criterion is revealed in any kind of strategic planning.

It goes beyond any doubt, that in the process of human development, but also in social and economic development, an *axiological system* should take over the role of a criterion deciding about the positive value of changes, understood as a defined system of values (given set of principles describing this system).[2]

Apart from the discussion on the term *value* itself, it can be stated that the whole world of values can be divided into:

- *Material values* (also referred to as "cold" ones; all material objects, including money and values related to them, e.g., power);
- *Spiritual values* (also called "warm" values; e.g., goodness, truth, courage, friendship, love, empathy, conscience, honesty, justice, sensitiveness, respect, faith, wisdom, etc.).

It has to be pointed out that not only in the Polish world of science, apart from few academic circles, especially those of philosophers and psychologists, discussions concerning accomplishments of ones own research area with regard to "warm" values seem a bit inappropriate. These few, who try to take it up, encounter most often a lack of understanding or even surprise, despite an apparent paradox—peculiar fashion for crating subsequent "external," with regard to a human being, ethical codes (an ethics of teachers, medical doctors, of business, etc.) accompanied by a dramatic erosion of morality, inside which there are no codes, regulations, settlements, and standards—but just an "internal," practiced through feelings, emotions and activities, system of "warm" values (good/goodness, sympathy, love, etc.). The statement that science and knowledge should be neutral in an axiological sense (since otherwise they become an ideology) is to a great extent untrue, because both science and knowledge present genuine interest in axiology on a daily basis, however predominantly in axiology of "cold" values (*technocratic axiology*), while at the same time each true scientist undergoes "training" in avoiding public speaking about "warm" values.

Therefore, the first explication of the suggested above general definition of development will be the understanding of *development* as *the process of changes of an object (country, region, etc.) assessed positively from the point of view of a defined system of values (i.e., the set of principles which describe this system)* (see Borys 2005b, pp. 18–26).

Such development, having used the assessment criterion of how positive the *axiological system* is (just as in case of every other criterion), reveals its *relativism.* It is therefore an obvious issue, that the same process of changes which is assessed by a given person or a group of people as development may be evaluated as regression (*nondevelopment*) by another individual or a group. Therefore, while expressing positive assessments, related to changes, one should disclose (at best by its name—e.g., development from the point of view of an egocentric system of values or just an *egocentric development = hard anthropocentric development*) which system of values or level of a given system to refer to. It is worth illustrating it briefly. For example, *egocentric development*, i.e., the one based on an egocentric system of values is a positive category, from the point of view of an egocentric, while negative (regressive; damaging concept) from the point of view of soft/moderate anthropocentric individual. Moderate anthropocentric may use the term regression with reference not only to an egocentric concept of development, but also to regressive changes within the framework of the concept of an *anthropocentric development* (e.g., going backward in sustainable development means its getting closer the concept of egocentrism).

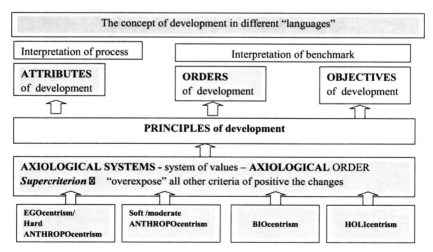

Figure 1a.   Complementary methods for expressing the concept of development

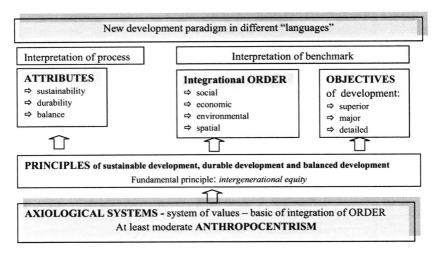

Figure 1b.   Complementary methods for expressing new development paradigm

Source: author's compilation

An opportunity for operational approach, including taking advantage of indicators, depends in a decisive way on the relative uniqueness of complementary description of a substantial developmental concept. The concept of the category may be expressed by means of different languages: as a set of attributes, principles, objectives, or in the language of orders. The synthesis of this description is presented in Figure 1a and for new development paradigm in Figure 1b. As it is illustrated, principles of development become the main carrier of information about the accepted axiological system.

3. What will the Twenty-first Century be Like?— Three Answers and Two Roads

This question is certainly fundamental. It emphasizes that the suggestion contained in the title of the article should be carefully examined considering all diversity of views, preferences, and priorities, especially while differentiating a political class and circles of creators.

The main source of the differentiation is definitely axiology, i.e., often nonexplicit and rarely disclosed system of values. A scheme shown in Figure 2 clearly suggests that the twenty-first century will primarily be an age of major axiological awakening. In the past century, the axiology was obviously marginalized, either nonexistent or embarrassing topic,

Figure 2.   Superiority of axiological challenge

Source: own elaboration

and in some disciplines (e.g., in economic and engineering sciences) treated as nonscience.

There emerges now the most important question: why do current civilization and its significant modules, i.e., culture and education, avoid, just like *the devils flee from the holy water*, an unambiguous disclosure of value systems, and instead, prefer their fuzziness and "sleep"?

It is worth emphasizing that without disclosing our systems of values, we are not able to clearly answer the question as to which social, economic, ecological, spatial, political, and institutional orders we want to accomplish. Without axiology we do not know and we cannot know what those orders mean as diverse systems of values generate diverse orders. Without clearly exposing axiological aspects, we fail to answer the question: what is the true reason of the current economic crisis.

It is worth reminding that the collapse of Enron began in 1997 when a clear and human-friendly management style created by Richard Kinder was transformed to its opposite by Jeff Skilling who believed that the best motivation to work are negative emotions—greed and fear that guarantee survival of the fittest. More and more evidence emerged that the current economic crisis actually results from an axiological crisis. A part of the evidence is quoted by Michael Shermer in his excellent book entitled *The Mind of the Market* (Shermer 2009, pp. 344–45).

When seeking an answer to the question what the twenty-first century will be, axiology offers two preliminary answers resulting from two different levels of ethical field that determine *who has the right to development and to quality of life* (cf. Figure 3). Two first anthropocentric levels acknowledge that only a human being has such a right. However, as we will show later, the answers of an egocentric and a moderate anthropocentric are significantly different. Other levels of wider ethical fields that grant nonhuman beings the right to development and to quality of life

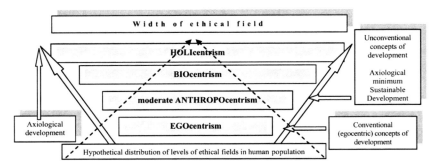

Figure 3. Systems of values according to the width of ethical field: Who has the right to development and to quality of life?

Source: own elaboration

are not easily acceptable within Western civilization. Consequently, let us focus on two first levels of that field.

Hence, how to make an axiological diagnosis of a human? In my opinion, a good way—even if not the only one—to recognize a presented system of values is to answer the following fundamental question: What is a human (person) by nature? Or: What is a human's nature? Typically, we obtain one of the *three answers* (cf. Figure 4):

1. The first answer holds that a human is bad by nature (greedy, egoistic, acquisitive, aggressive, etc.), hence, a human by nature is an egocentric with an excessive *ego* (cf. Figure 5). In terms of light, there is plenty of shadow in a human (quantum collapses) that results mainly in life goals; the primary goal becomes making money and material wealth based on a motto: "one can buy everybody and everything—depending on the price" which means that in an egocentric's opinion one can buy a human and human's feelings. Thus we obtain an "inhumane" human, whose humaneness is more or less deformed. Now, a quite rhetorical question emerges: *Can a human have a deformed humaneness by nature?* In spite of a seemingly obvious answer to this question, it is not adequately appreciated by lots of people in many fields of science (e.g., in economics).
2. The second answer is hybrid, i.e., a human is by nature a bit good and a bit bad, or "grey," a bit honest and a bit dishonest, a bit friendly and a bit unfriendly, etc. Thus, such a human is by implication a schizophrenic, and perversion is originally built into the human's essence. The inconsistency of this opinion seems obvious as it implies that humaneness is deformed "by nature"—could it be possible that the *constructor* was wrong?
3. The third answer implies that a human is by nature good (empathic, friendly, etc.), while due to some weaknesses, there are some departures

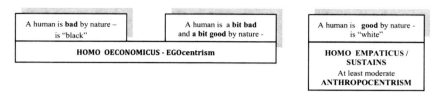

Figure 4.   Recognition of a human's systems of values: What is a human by nature?

Source: own elaboration

from the humaneness caused among others by educational errors in family, flaws in educational system, pressure by milieu, etc.

Answers one and two represent a *first road* leading to an *unbalanced quality of life*. Answer three is a *second road* leading to a *holistic/balanced quality of life*.

A First Road

A *first road* basically reflects the answers given by modern civilization that unfortunately refer to an African parable of two hungers: the great one and the little one. The little one wants whatever is necessary for life: goods and services, money to buy them. The great one is the hunger for understanding the meaning of life, the hunger for seeking after the sense of life and the feeling of essence of humaneness—the hunger for being simply a human being (sensitive, empathic, honest, friendly, . . .) toward the self and another human.

Our Western civilization used to presume comfortably and yet illusively that it is possible to satisfy the *great* hunger (for sense of life, awareness of one's humaneness) by satisfying the little one (when making money becomes a major goal and not just one of the means for life), and thus satisfying the little hunger replaces the *great* one—especially noticeable nowadays. It is worth noting that the first and second road mean different worlds of values, different worlds of energy, and different systems of axiological patterns and anti-patterns. All compromises create and widen schizophrenia, both on an individual and social scale.

The first road, therefore, is a conventional development based on old paradigms, and in axiological terms, based on egocentric stream that reveals:

- human's egoism and greed (*homo oeconomicus*);
- domination of one generation's perspective in thinking, e.g., as regards natural resources;

- commercialization of practically everything, including human relationships and assessing people exclusively based on their material success; and
- reluctance to business ethics and business social responsibility.

In a social field, it prefers the following:

- *Cold values*—material and financial, and linked values, e.g., striving for power, greed for power, etc.
- *A reversal of the polarity of warm values* that is leading to redefinitions, e.g., honesty becomes naivety; public service that was declared during election campaign soon becomes imperceptibly transformed into power (sharing a cake after the election victory);
- Suppression of feelings (spiritual sphere), i.e., conscience, empathy, sensitivity, dignity;
- Building a vision of tool societies, e.g., information society, network society, that hide axiology or *are void* of values;
- Legal and institutional over-regulation.

With respect to environment, it reveals the following opinions:

- Environmentalism is just a fashion, a must, or even a kind of terrorism;
- Environmental movements restrict economic growth.

The consequences of following the first egocentric (technocratic) road are manifest in all aspects of life. We have become increasingly aware of contradictory trends (tendencies and countertendencies) within certain systems of values. Possibly, such phenomenon was seen in all ages, but its recent intensification demonstrates that we are dealing now with *sui generis* civilization crash. Very often we want to build a *consumer society* (or more precisely, over-consumer society) and at the same time, a *self-restricting consumer society* (protecting resources).

As mentioned above, the challenges of the present century, expressed as expectations or desires, define the essence of the first and second road. Advocates of a technocratic conventional development warn that *the twenty-first century will*:

- be rational,
- be competitive,
- be knowledgeable, and
- see fast technological progress *or there will be no twenty-first century*.

The promoters of such a vision of a current century create diverse terms to name the twenty-first century society as a direct consequence of priorities that were mentioned before, e.g., information society, network society, knowledge society, etc. The vision of development in the current century is sought after in techniques and tools.

A Second Road

The supporters of alternative development based on moderate anthropocentrism and on fundamental balancing have a different vision of this century and warn that *the twenty-first century will*

- be *ecological* (Skolimowski 1999, p. 8),
- be an age of *quality* (the quality specialists emphasize the fundamental significance of quality, warn against poor quality, and against fascination of quantity),
- be based on *partnership* (this view stresses a particular weight of nonabusive interpersonal relationships and prefers cooperation to rivalry or competition),
- and finally—be founded on *wisdom or there will be no twenty-first century* (thus emphasizing that knowledge itself is not enough if it does not contribute to building more wisdom!).

All the above prognostic assertions form a specific charity auction and paraphrase Andre Malraux famous statement that the *twenty-first century* will be *spiritual or it shall not be at all.* They are also consistent with the essence of one major thought by Al Gore who was awarded the Nobel Peace Prize in 2007. He said that *either the twenty-first century will be an age of sustainable development or the world will stand on the brink* (Gore 1992, p. 273). It means that technocratism (egocentrism) of development under the *old paradigm* will threaten the very foundations of today's civilization.

A new paradigm of development defining the essence of the *second road* will always be criticized by egocentric individual, because it presumes a different axiological foundation. The doubts emerging in literature and during conferences are mainly about a dilemma: Is the idea of new paradigm of development (created by conceptions: *sustainable, durable and balanced development*), a utopia, illusion, or a nonscientific and fuzzy or a real, holistic conception of development (cf. e.g., Sztumski 2008)? A new paradigm of development without its axiological essence eliminates foundations from the discussion on the conception, thus transforming it into meaningless divagations. In doing so, one forgets that a new paradigm is both a general idea[3] and its ongoing concretization.

For example, sustainable development as a *general idea* or a concept of development is typically identified with a principle of intergenerational equity in access to many habitats: nature, culture, economic, etc. It was highlighted for the first time by the Brundtland Commission in a historical definition of sustainable development presented in "Our Common Future" in 1987. The report pronounced *hope conditioned upon the establishment of a new era of international cooperation based on the premise that every human being—those here and those who are to come—has the right to life, and to a decent life* (1987, p. 47). This last-century definition based on intentions was clearly reducing *sustainability* to a sustained access to a natural habitat. Over time though, the interpretation of *sustainability* was extended to more environments: human, cultural, etc. The stages of the development in the concept of sustainable development are marked by successive mega-conferences, called Earth Summits, that were organized in 1972 (Stockholm), 1992 (Rio de Janeiro), and 2002 (Johannesburg).

A subsequent concretization of a new paradigm of development caused that it has become mostly an operational category today. An increasingly better recognition of the paradigm is due to describing three key features that define its conceptual domain, i.e., sustainability, durability, and balance, and also to concretizing as regards:

- law (in Poland it is provided by the Constitution—article 5),
- diagnoses, plans (strategies),
- axiology,
- measurement (indicators),
- areas or sectors (sustainable development in transport, tourism, production, consumption, etc.).

To sum up, both a general idea of the new development paradigm and its increasingly many concretizations demonstrate a strong stream of more moderate anthropocentrism that is based on a *holistic vision of humaneness* (see Figure 5) and highlights:

- warm values—honesty, friendliness, empathy of a human (*homo empaticus*),
- domination of thinking about the quality of life of a present and future generations,
- selective commercialization,
- preferring business ethics (as being an organization's "conscience") and business social responsibility (as acting in favor of business ethics),

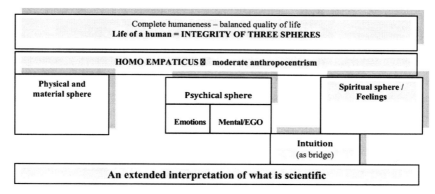

Figure 5.   Quality of life in a new development paradigm

Source: own elaboration

- environmental protection as a condition of a human's survival on planet Earth, and
- supporting balanced/holistic human development, i.e., a human's physical, psychical (emotional and mental), and spiritual (feelings) spheres; a holistic approach to human development is a fundamental discriminant of *education for sustainable development*.

That synthesizes the essence of the *second road* being currently the largest axiological and civilizational challenge that is unfortunately not enough established in individual and social awareness.

Notes

1. These arguments are presented, among others, in Borys (2005a, pp. 24–36).
2. Broad understanding of axiology as a science of values or in functional quantification—as a science of valuation is assumed here.
3. It is not just vagueness that is triggering the attacks on historical commentary of the essence of sustainable development, but also still a narrow understanding of a new paradigm that prevails not only in common speech, but also in scientific discourse. Such a narrow definition of sustainability generated a category of ecodevelopment to large extent.

References

Borys, T., 2005a, *Wskazniki zrównowazonego rozwoju* (Indicators of sustainable development), Ekonomia i Srodowisko, Białystok–Warszawa, pp. 24–36.

———, 2005b, *Indicators for Sustainable Development—Polish Experiences*, Ekonomia i Srodowisko, Białystok–Warszawa, pp. 18–26.

———, 2010, Sustainable Development as an Educational Challenge, *Argumenta Oeconomica*, 1 (24): 5–6, 5–21, Wrocław University of Economics.

Gore, A., 1992, *Earth in the Balance. Ecology and Human* Spirit, Houghton Mifflin Company, Boston, New York, p. 273.

Shermer, M., 2009, *Rynkowy umysł* (The mind of the market), Cis, Warszawa, pp. 344–45.

Skolimowski, H., 1999, *Wizje nowego millenium* (Visions of a new millennium), EJB, Kraków, p. 8.

Sztumski, W., 2008, Reflection about Sustainable Development (Is sustainable development fiction, utopia, illusion or swindle?), *Problems of Sustainable Development* 2: pp. 133–39.

Our Common Future, 1987, United Nations, New York, p. 47.

Educating for Sustainability

Caitlin Wilson
Environment and Natural Resources
Department of Life and Environmental Sciences
Faculty of Natural Sciences
University of Iceland,
Iceland

1. Introduction

Civilizations have risen and fallen since the dawn of humanity. In his book *Collapse*, a sweeping analysis of why some societies collapse while others succeed, Jared Diamond concludes that the interaction of the following factors have in the past determined the fate of any given society: deforestation and habitat destruction, soil problems, water management problems, overhunting, overfishing, effects of introduced species on native species, overpopulation, and increased per capita impact of people. Furthermore, he propounds that four additional factors will be significant in the present and future fate of society: human-caused climate change, buildup of toxins in the environment, energy shortages, and full human utilization of the earth's photosynthetic capacity (Diamond 2005). While this analysis, and the many others like it, leads one to conclude that we are doomed, I believe that in reflection lies our salvation. The fact that we do painfully muster self-awareness and take measures to improve our situation and prevent self-destruction distinguishes us from societies who blindly chopped down the last tree and fished the last fish (such as the Easter Islands). In this simple act of thoughtfulness do I find greatest reason for hope that we can sustain modern society. But it will require more: we must not only think, but also act on our intelligence.

As the latter half of the twentieth century progressed, the concept of sustainable development went from being radical to progressive to necessary to popular and widely accepted. It is almost commonplace today. The movement was motivated by the collective impact of population growth, environmental degradation, and socio-economic class disparity, both within and among the nations of the world. Sustainability is now generally accepted to be the mode of existence in which present generations thrive such that future generations may have the same opportunities to thrive; or, the harmonious balance among industrial activity, environmental conservation, and social justice. But it is more than the sum of its three parts—economy, environment, society—it shall comprehend in its grasp all of the cultures of the world and their respective ways of being. Sustainability is the means to an end, and the end is not so much a static target itself, but a dynamic equilibrium in which a global metacivilization thrives perpetually on a healthy planet. Thus sustainable development is not an easily contained concept, but relates to every school of thought and every human activity.

Institutionalized thoughtfulness, or education, is a powerful tool in the hands of society. Education does the work of "social reproduction: the social process by which each new generation is initiated into the language, rituals, roles, relationships, and routines which its members have to learn in order to become members of a society" (Carr and Kemmis 1986). Education plays the important role in society of maintaining practical continuity within and among generations. However, society is constantly changing, so education also serves a "transformative" function in which the educating generation attempts to improve the life of the generation receiving the education (Carr and Kemmis 1986). In this way, education is both conservative and progressive at once, so the questions of what to teach and how to teach it are necessarily controversial. Thus, to engage in educational research is to engage in political debate because it is to evaluate the educational agenda and the ideology it propagates.

In my research on education for sustainability, I took a close look at a group of students studying abroad from North America to Iceland on a summer program, which I facilitated, on renewable energy and sustainable development (SIT Study Abroad 2009). The students traveled around the country, stayed with host families, underwent intensive, interdisciplinary coursework, visited power plants and research and development as well as policy firms, and conducted independent study projects. My case study evaluated the program through in-depth interviews, qualitative analysis, and discussion of the emergent theory and its implications for practice. My goal was to characterize their learning experience such that my conclusions could be extrapolated to shed light on the wider fields of education, sustainable development, and education for sustainable development.

Responses from the students expressed three broad categories of influential experiences from the program in Iceland: cultural and personal expansion from studying abroad, the experience of Iceland's natural environment, and the experience of seeing renewable energy in practice. The following is a selection of some student responses.

"It made me realize more about myself than I was expecting to learn."

"I gained a much stronger sense of how interconnected the world is."

"It opened my eyes to how different the US is from foreign countries."

"I became a part of the [host] family in those three weeks. That will undoubtedly last a lifetime."

"Renewable energy in Iceland made much more sense with the perspective gained from the homestay."

"I was blown away by the beauty of the country and the vast differences in the landscape."

"[Icelandic culture values] respect for retaining the country's native landscape."

"It was awesome to see that the stuff we learned about in the classroom wasn't just theoretical, but was actually happening."

"I was impressed by the implementation of renewable energy types that are only discussed in mass in the United States rather than used in mass."

"There was just a sense that it is possible for countries and societies to function in a sustainable manner."

"The experiential learning process certainly made me feel like what I was learning was much more applicable and relevant."

"I also appreciated that we had so many different people teaching us throughout the program. It helped the course stay fresh and it was interesting to learn from people with so many different backgrounds. This reinforced the idea that there are so many ways for a society to become more sustainable since achieving it requires synthesis in economics, science, technology, and the social sciences."

Lately, I've personally been feeling more and more like the political powers of the world just aren't going to be able to sort out the issues regarding climate change and sustainable policies. However, my time in Iceland was a reminder that it is possible. Despite having to rely on imports for a lot of things, I was really impressed with how well Icelanders take advantage of their local resources when possible, and I think it's a model and a frame of mind that would do wonders for the rest of the world. Overall, my time in Iceland gave me a frame of reference for what I think a "sustainable society" should, or at least could, look like.

2. Discussion

Study abroad has steadily grown in popularity along with the emphasis on internationalization of universities (Chan and Dimmock 2008). Students have historically chosen to study abroad in order to learn a foreign language, experience another culture, as well as for the desire to travel (Talburt and Stewart 1999). Studies investigating how students benefit from study abroad have found that, according to the students, they include: learning a foreign language, gaining a critical perspective on the U.S., receiving insight into a foreign culture, and becoming more socially competent (Talburt and Stewart 1999). With more demanding lines of study constraining students' ability to leave their home universities for a year or even a semester of study abroad and universities reticent to lose their customers, short-term study-abroad programs, such as the seven-week Iceland program, have been on the rise. They have been given a critical eye for their ability to deliver a meaningful study-abroad experience (Talburt and Stewart 1999).

The results of my study challenge this criticism. Although students only spent three and a half weeks with their host families, they claim the same benefits that students of more traditional, long-term study-abroad programs do. The most significant gain students claimed from the homestay was that of cultural insight. The effects on the students were manifold: greater understanding of Icelandic culture and society as a whole, the self-reflection triggered by experience of another culture, and their personal relationships with their new Icelandic families, which in some cases may well be lifelong. It seems this contact to Icelandic culture is also beneficial for learning about renewable energy in Iceland. Through this cultural insight, students cited being able to understand how Iceland could develop sustainably. Furthermore, because this program is a shorter study-abroad program offered in the summer, it attracts engineering students who follow a very structured line of study and would not otherwise be able to study abroad. One such student, who was in fact skeptical and dismissive of "the cultural and political" aspects of sustainability as "hippie stuff," actually claimed that he got the most out of "all of the cultural expansion I experienced while in Iceland." For this student, the study-abroad experience, though short, was clearly transformative.

On the whole, there was a noted lack of a critical view of Icelandic nature from the students. Only one or two remarked that the landscape was fragile or had been degraded; many more praised Icelandic conservation efforts. This indicates a lack of deeper understanding of the environmental situation in Iceland, which has actually been heavily impacted since human settlement (Arnalds and Gretarsson 2000). Erosion is the greatest problem facing the nation currently, with satellite images showing the land literally blowing away into the sea. This false perception of Icelandic nature as a pristine wilderness is propagated by the tourist board. Their marketing has been all too successful, and actually undermines environmental efforts in Iceland. Though the students had access to some information about the geological formation of Iceland in class and the human history since settlement in museums, this knowledge is overridden by powerful images of Iceland as pure and untouched, which it surely looks like on the surface compared to their hometowns in the U.S.

Based on the lack of deeper experience in nature, I must conclude that the students either did not have enough or the appropriate access to nature. In his article "The Mechanics of Nature Appreciation," David Pepi calls on the spirit of Henry David Thoreau and Aldo Leopold when he suggests that "a critical approach to nature appreciation offers an alternative to much of present practice, because it teaches students how to apprehend, assess, and make reasonable claims about inherent values, in order to achieve the richest and most satisfying experiences possible" (1994). To this end he recommends "direct intercourse with nature" (Pepi 1994). In order to amplify students' learning experience in the natural environment, students should spend more time outdoors and engage in discussion on the social and natural history of the land as well as environmental ethics and aesthetics to deepen their understanding.

The students described the difference between what they learned inside the classroom and what they learned outside it. Below is a table compiling their responses.

Inside	Outside
Facts	Application
Theory	Real-life implementation
Basic background	Holistic understanding
Science	Culture
Technology	Physical limitations
Concepts	Interaction
Energy economics	Functions of society

For almost all the students, the experiential or field component of the program was transformative for learning. The more enthusiastic among them felt it was rewarding and essential for learning about sustainability while the less enthusiastic, though they stated they enjoyed seeing the subject firsthand, felt the program suffered from lack of structure and consistency. Several are quoted as saying some form of the sentiment "science is best learned in a classroom." I remember one point during the intensive lecture portion of the program (in which lecturers changed twice a week and covered topics ranging from resource economics to fuel cell technology) in which the students complained of the chaotic presentation of course material. When it was explained that it was supposed to be that way, that they should take each lecture as a piece of a puzzle and put it together themselves, their attitudes changed instantly. Suddenly, instead of receiving the lecture with consternation about how to understand it, they were open and active in their education. I realized in that moment that they had become agents of their own education.

A critical characteristic of experiential learning is learner control or involvement in learning. Illeris (2007) gives a survey of attempted definitions of experiential learning from the influential scholars John Dewey, David Kolb and Roger Fry, Susan Warner Weil and Ian McGill, and David Boud to conclude that each contributes to ideas that make up experiential learning. Dewey wrote of connecting past and future experiences through worthwhile learning experiences (Dewey in Illeris 2007); Kolb and Fry depicted it as concrete experience, observation and reflection, formation of abstract concepts, and testing in new situations (Kolb and Fry in Illeris 2007); Weil and McGill contributed their idea of learning villages based on primary experience in different settings (Weil and McGill in Illeris 2007); and Boud put forward the learner-centered approach and importance of freedom in learning (Boud in Illeris 2007). Illeris finds that none of these satisfactorily encompasses experiential learning and goes on to attempt his own. On learner involvement,

Illeris writes that each learner brings to the learning environment his or her own specific culture, place, time, and experience, which in the late modern globalized world "offers unlimited, and to a great extent also unstructured, possibilities for learning" (2007). He goes on: "Hence, the often formulated need for learning to learn, that is creating a personal structure or a value system to sort out what is worth learning from what is not" (Illeris 2007).

Illeris's description of the modern learner rings true with my experience with the students. They sensed the unstructured, multidisciplinary nature of the course material, and were unprepared from their more traditional university educational settings to interpret the information for themselves. But how does a facilitator teach students to learn? In the case of the Iceland summer program, a discussion on philosophy, ethics, and spirituality is missing in the debate. The students need the opportunity to understand their own personal structure or value system. This motivational or emotional facet of understanding is also part of experiential learning. Jean Piaget and David Ausubel authored in the fifties and sixties seminal theories concerning individual acquisition during a learner experience and the linking of past with present learning. This is often the domain of cognitive psychology, and psychologist Hans Furth expanded the theories of Piaget and Freud to show importance of emotions in learning (Furth in Illeris 2007). Illeris (2007) elaborates that this emotional side incorporates feelings, volition, motivation, and incentives. Thus I would argue that it is through personal codes of ethics that we understand our emotions and motivations in relation to experiential learning about sustainability.

3. Conclusion

Education for sustainable development, in my opinion, is best accomplished with multidisciplinarity, active student participation, immersion in nature, experiential learning elements such as field study, a critical approach, holistic presentation, firm grounding in reality, as well as consideration of ethical issues on the personal, subjective, and sociocultural levels. In the time outside the classroom, students recorded experiencing some benefits of some of these elements, such as greater and more practical understanding, more balanced and holistic perspective, and realization of the reality of renewable energy. These aspects of their education in Iceland appear to have at least informed their conceptions of sustainability.

Three researchers, Camino et al. (2009), as part of a larger Science Education Research Group, designed a course on sustainability based on their past experiences. They followed these guidelines: provide a variety of choices of educational offerings that enable all students to be stimulated; use a variety of strategies that range from silence to open exchanges, from individual reflection to group cooperation, and that link disciplinary knowledge to everyday life to contextualize scientific knowledge; employ a multiplicity of relational approaches to break down hierarchical relationships into equality, respect, and value for difference but nonviolence (Camino et al. 2009). Their primary objective was to move beyond "a simple exchange of information" to lay bare the differences in methodologies "as well as their implicit assumptions and paradigms" (Camino et al. 2009). Among the course participants were chemists, physicists, other scientists, a linguist, a psychologist, and performance artists. In engaging in this transdisciplinary dialogue, they reported having "a deeper insight into their own as well as others' disciplines, from both a methodological and an epistemological point of view" (Camino et al. 2009).

Moreover, students were given the opportunity of developing metacognitive competences (Bateson 1973, Varela et al. 1991) for dealing with problems by going beyond the empirical evidence, and above all, for accepting—at least in part—the sense of limitedness of human knowledge and the importance of creativity and intuition in the production of new knowledge (Camino et al. 2009).

Students of the course in Italy reported undergoing a "total change of mindset . . . their view of things had changed" (Camino et al. 2009). They had gained new conceptual tools and new interpretive schemes rather than simply transferring ideas (Camino et al. 2009). The researchers note that this did not come quickly and easily, but was learned over time. They then unveil their approaches that were most effective. On bringing to light different disciplinary angles: "From a student's point of view, becoming aware of what are the interpretive schemes guiding scholars in exploring the problems that are typical of their own discipline can be extremely useful for understanding the motives that guided, as well as for making the objectives of the inquiry explicit" (Camino et al. 2009).

The concept of boundary, a practical way to divide among things which is natural and useful, is analyzed in its use in academia. The example they use to help students understand their point is ecology: it is almost impossible to draw boundaries between ecosystems because they are so interconnected. One study even comes to the conclusion that "the discrepancies between scientists accurately reflect the diversity of the real world" (Corn 1993 cited in Camino et al. 2009). They propose relationships and flows instead of boundaries as a way to organize thought on not only ecosystems but also climate change and other sustainability issues. They move from the conceptual tool of boundary to energy flows and matter transformations to discuss the energy needs of humanity. Energy study is divided among the scientific disciplines of physics, chemistry, biology, and engineering, and each uses a different measurement and scale to quantify energy—volts, calories, joules, watts. The tutors lead a critical discussion on energy flows, production and consumption, and scales of energy, slowly increasing in complexity. They use a number of techniques including narratives, thought experiments, artistic representations, and sharing personal experiences. Concluding their study, Camino et al. present some study responses to the course which show how their perspectives and understandings changed rather drastically through the course (2009).

Cultural-historical activity theory provides a useful framework for understanding and evaluating the renewable energy program in Iceland. Roth et al. (2009) tout its useful application to modern science education. Since activity theory is not only about understanding but also about transforming practice, it can aid in shaping sustainable development education to the goals of transforming learner attitudes, values, and behavior. By acknowledging all aspects of the learner context, it can be used to improve science learning environments and create opportunities for expansive learning (Roth and Lee 2007). But, it is more than just being aware of the context; the interaction among the elements of the learning experience is critical for producing the outcome. Roth gives the example of a seventh grade class tackling community water quality issues (2007; Roth and Lee 2007). Rather than the teacher assigning tasks to the students, they are allowed to decide for themselves one aspect of the problem to approach, the tools they will use to investigate it, and present their projects themselves to the class and the community. Parents, local experts, and journalists were involved in the project, which was quite successful.

The most prominent characteristics of such an educational environment appear to be: larger community and societal involvement in the learning process (which subsequently also grounds the subject material in reality), variety of tools employed in attaining the object of learning, and student freedom of choice and control in the educational environment. The Iceland program achieves each of these to a certain degree but can also improve in all directions. It emerged from the discussion that the experiential learning aspect effectively rooted the course in reality and made students feel that what they learned in the classroom was significant outside of it. The students' access to community via the homestay was overwhelmingly positive and enhanced their educational experience. The variety of lecturers, settings, and learning styles provided for a more comprehensive understanding of renewable energy and sustainability. Students appreciated the freedom they were given to explore the country, though it must be noted that in spite of the fact that this forms an informal, rather peripheral aspect of the educational program, it was nevertheless meaningful for the students.

Through all of the students' responses to their experience on the program in Iceland, for many different reasons, there is the common thread of students cultivating a positive outlook. The main way in which Iceland influenced students' thoughts on and understanding of sustainability was that it made them feel a sustainable future was "possible" and "feasible." They wrote that a sustainable society is one that considers the future. Overall, the students reported gaining a positive outlook for the future. Futures studies is a field that clarifies goals and values, analyzes and interprets the recent past and present, explores projections of current trends, and carries out systematic studies of possible, probable, and preferable futures (Lloyd and Wallace 2004). David Lloyd and John Wallace make the case that future studies are a necessary and valuable dimension in science learning (2004). As became apparent to me from reading the overwhelming inclusion of the word "future" in student responses which did not specifically ask them about the future, it is a concept inextricable to sustainable development.

Students' ability to imagine the future depends largely on factors like confidence and comfort and relationship to the class and teacher (Lloyd in Lloyd and Wallace 2004). Students' images of the future subsequently act as a type of interpretative framework and therefore influence learning (Bloom in Lloyd and Wallace 2004). From the results of the interview, the most common effect on students, from a variety of experiences on the program, was quoted as an increase in confidence in some form or another—feeling hope, undergoing personal growth, believing that sustainability is possible, and having a more positive outlook on the world. This effect is not unintentional, but I do not think the program can take full credit for having such a good influence. Some of these benefits are the byproduct of study abroad, particularly the homestay, and some are directly related to Iceland and its renewable energy practices. But that does not diminish the rather dramatic overall effect of empowerment and growth in confidence. Because many of the students of the program take home from Iceland a positive, future-oriented experience—developed competence, practical knowledge, and optimism—their interpretative frameworks also developed and will in turn contribute positively to their future learning and their futures generally.

In a course in my graduate study in Spring 2009 entitled "Educational Action for Sustainable Development," Education and Philosophy Professor Ólafur Páll Jónsson (University of Iceland) and Philosophy Professor Nigel Dower (University of Aberdeen) discussed the ethical implications of sustainable development. The challenge, it appears, is to extend our ethical considerations to distant places and times—that is to say, across the globe and into the future. No education can be for sustainable development then without this ethical dimension. The students in my study appear to have rather unintentionally and unconsciously developed somewhat in this direction. The conglomerate effect of the study-abroad experience, the homestay, being in Iceland, and the formal and informal educational experiences about renewable energy all together promoted positive personal development, expanded and diversified worldview, created deep and memorable learning moments, and left students with a general sense of possibility and hope for the future. Their awareness was raised regarding their own culture and identity as well as a culture outside their own, the vastness of the world, and the importance of present action for the future. While this is indeed a positive evaluation of the Iceland program, there are several notable areas for improvement. Primarily, bringing a level of consciousness to the process of change would enhance their ability to learn in a meaningful way.

Student agency in their education is valued by proponents of cultural-historical activity theory, experiential learning, and education for sustainable development. Almlöv and Moberg (2008) find that student leadership within a course encouraged an authentic democratic process and a sense of individual responsibility. They go on to argue that these are important aspects of education for sustainable development because "students develop knowledge and insights as well as perceptions of their future lives, their visions and their ability to act responsibly" which is important for developing the "ability to evaluate global and inter-generational issues" (Almlöv and Moberg 2008). This is the kind of education I hope to foster with the Iceland program, one which develops the whole person, and that person knows for himself or herself what "the right relationship to nature" is (Bonnett 1999).

The remaining question then is how educators and facilitators can accomplish these improvements well. We must carefully contemplate how we can enable this kind of transformative education. This goes beyond changing what one does to changing how one does it. At an educator workshop on education for sustainable development that I attended last fall in Visby, Sweden, one seasoned educator told me the most important thing any teacher needs to know: "You cannot teach students anything at all. Knowledge can only grow." I took him to mean that transmissive education, the business of telling students what they should know, at best produces in the student the ability to recite pieces of information. But if we want to create transformative education whose students embody knowledge and are able to understand the world and its problems in their complexity and remain undaunted, then we must enable empowering educational experiences. During that workshop, I realized that most teachers need to stop talking so much and let learning happen. Educators needs to be very perceptive to try to see and understand the learning process each of their students is undergoing in order to tailor the situation to best stimulate them.

Alice and David Kolb (2005) argue that "learning is best conceived of as a process, not in terms of outcomes," and quoting John Dewey, "'the process and goal of education are one and the same thing'" (Dewey in Kolb and Kolb 2005). They propose the following principles to create learning spaces for the enhancement of experiential learning (Kolb and Kolb 2005):

1. Respect for learners and their experience
2. Begin learning with the learner's experience of the subject matter
3. Creating and holding a hospitable space for learning
4. Making space for conversational learning
5. Making space for development of expertise
6. Making spaces for acting and reflecting
7. Making space for feeling and thinking
8. Making space for inside-out learning
9. Making space for learners to take charge of their own learning

The first two principles deal with experiential learning in two senses: that the students experience the subject matter so learn by directly relating to it and that the past experience of the students is recognized and valued. The latter contributes to confidence building in students, who are treated as already having a body of knowledge which they can contribute to the class. Because students process new knowledge through their personal interpretative frameworks that in turn determine their values, attitudes, and behaviors, the best way to create an educational experience that influences both knowledge and the framework is by acknowledging the experience of each student. The second two principles address the learning environment. Kolb and Kolb hold that critical thought and discussion of issues and differences are only constructive in a positive, safe, hospitable environment. The ambience in the class must encourage fearless communication and expression of differences by welcoming and supporting each individual (Kolb and Kolb 2005). Furthermore, discussion should be more conversational and conducive to natural thought and speech, as opposed to the rules of the traditional lecture method of sitting and listening. "Making space for good conversation as part of the educational process provides the opportunity for reflection on and meaning making about experiences that improve the effectiveness of experiential learning" (Keeton, Sheckly, and Griggs, and Bunker in Kolb and Kolb 2005). Principles 5 through 8 talk about letting student interest guide their education. Emotion influences whether and what we learn, and can determine cultivation of life purpose out of education (Kolb and Kolb 2005, Dewey in Kolb and Kolb 2005). The final principle regarding student ownership of his or her education echoes the same sentiment that has sprouted up from many directions in this thesis. Kolb and Kolb (2005) emphasize that it enables students to learn in a meaningful way that ultimately influences their self-perception and life goals.

What we see from the above discussion is that (1) direct experience of the learning object, (2) connection to community and society, (3) critical, multidisciplinary approach to course material, (4) a supportive, expressive learning environment, and (5) student autonomy cultivate transformative educational experiences. It emerged from this research process that the Iceland program succeeded in creating these kinds of transformative educational experiences to some extent and with varying degrees of intention. It was most strong in fostering positive growth among the students, enabling meaningful cultural exchange, and creating experiential, interactive education about renewable energy and sustainability. In the future the program can benefit from a more purposeful approach to strengthen these program elements even more. I will also be cognizant with my attitude as facilitator of acknowledging and incorporating the students' experiences, bringing in critical perspectives to the subject material, fostering holistic understanding through multidisciplinarity, and, above all, promoting synthesis of the complex educational experience by raising student awareness and self-reflection about their experience in open discussion.

One unexpected and significant realization I had from doing this research is that study abroad could be a powerful tool for education for sustainable development. From my personal experience studying abroad as an undergraduate, one forms uniquely strong bonds with one's classmates. I saw this as well in the group of students on the Iceland program. They come from a wide variety of backgrounds and experiences but are motivated by a common interest, and then share the powerful experience of study abroad together. This is naturally conducive to creating a supportive learning environment in which their differences can be openly and conversationally discussed. Study abroad also naturally widens worldview, extends cultural understanding, and engages interest. To be an effective educator in this extraordinarily dynamic setting, I need to understand and acknowledge the various forces at play and facilitate their constructive interaction. My goal in the future with this program is to streamline all these levels of stimulation and development into a cohesive, meaningful, authentic educational experience of sustainability. My greatest hope as an educator is that this educational experience would build part of the students' own sustainable frame of mind.

References

Almlöv, M. & Moberg, E., 2008, Students in Possession of the Issues of Tomorrow: An Innovative Studentled Course Project, *Journal of Education for Sustainable Development* 2 (2): 173–79.

Arnalds, O. & Gretarsson, E., 2000, Soil Erosion in Iceland—Results, *Agricultural Research Institute of Iceland*, Retrieved in February 2010 from http://www.rala.is/desert/4-1.html.

Bonnett, M., 1999, Education for Sustainable Development: A Coherent Philosophy for Environmental Education?, *Cambridge Journal of Education* 29 (3): 313–24.

Camino, E., Barbiero, G. & Marchetti, D., 2009, Science Education for Sustainability: Teaching Learning Processes with Science Researchers and Trainee Teachers, in D. Gray, L. Colucci-Gray & E. Camino (eds.), *Science, Society and Sustainability: Education and Empowerment for an Uncertain World*, Routledge, New York, NY, pp. 119–53.

Carr, W. & Kemmis, S., 1986, *Becoming Critical: Education, Knowledge and Action Research*, Deakin University Press, Oxon, UK.

Chan, W. & Dimmock, C., 2008, The Internationalization of Universities: Globalist, Internationalist and Translocalist Models, *Journal of Research in International Education* 7 (2): 184–204.

Diamond, J., 2005, *Collapse: How Societies Choose to Fail or Succeed*, Penguin Group, New York, NY.

Illeris, K., 2007, What Do We Actually Mean By Experiential Learning?, *Human Resource Development Review* 6 (1): 84–95.

Kolb, A.Y. & Kolb, D.A., 2005, Learning Styles and Learning Spaces: Enhancing Experiential Learning in Higher Education, *Academy of Management Learning & Education* 4 (2): 193–212.

Lloyd, D. & Wallace, J., 2004, Imaging the Future of Science Education: The Case for Making Futures Studies Explicit in Student Learning, *Studies in Science Education* 40: 139–78.

Pepi, D., 1994, The Mechanics of Nature Appreciation, *Journal of Environmental Education* 25 (3): 5–14.

Roth, W.-M. & Lee, Y.-J., 2007, "Vygotsky's Neglected Legacy": Cultural-historical Activity Theory, *Review of Educational Research* 77 (2): 186–232.

Roth, W.-M., Lee, Y.-J. & Hsu, P.-L., 2009, A Tool for Changing the World: Possibilities of Cultural-historical Activity Theory to Reinvigorate Science Education, *Studies in Science Education* 45 (2): 131–67.

SIT Study Abroad, 2009, *Iceland: Renewable Energy, Technology, and Resource Economics*, Retrieved in June 2009 from http://www.sit.edu/studyabroad/sss_ice.cfm.

Talburt, S. & Stewart, M.A., 1999, What's the Subject of Study Abroad? Race, Gender, and "Living Culture", *The Modern Language Journal* 83 (2): 163–75.

The Creators of Global Warming

Tomas Kavaliauskas
Department of Social and Political Theory
Faculty of Political Science and Diplomacy
Vytautas Magnus University
Kaunas, Lithuania

With the rise of temperature, with the melting ice, and with the deepening awareness of the negative impact of industrialization on the Earth, the division between human beings and nature has once again fortified. Humans are treated as the destroyers as well as the pests of the planet, although we are also the innovators. Nature is perceived as a victim of *homo economicus*, and it now seeks revenge for the wrongdoing. True, scientists working on climate change today regard human beings as directly acting upon nature and directly influencing it. We are treated as geological actors, and in this sense, the distinction between humankind and the planet Earth is diminishing, while the planet and its rational dweller are brought closer: the epoch of our climate now is called anthropogenic, i.e., human climate epoch (Crutzen and Stoermer 2000). The journal of Geologists Association of America, *GSA Today*, argues that anthropogenic era is based upon the new consequences of human activity (Zalasiewicz and Williams 2008) and CO_2 emission caused by humans is higher today than it was during the most active period of volcanoes. In the remote future, if mankind still exists for someone to undertake anthropological excavations, only a lot of concrete will be found. And that will be found not just in metropolises, but also on the foothills where highways are built. The beginning of anthropogenic era coincides with the invention of the steam engine, industrialization.

It means that we end up treating ourselves as the exceptional life form that has extraordinary say in the planet's well-being, quality of functioning, cycles of seasons, and its evolutionary rhythm. But can this anthropogenic approach overcome this dualism between nature and humankind?

Asserting that the climate epoch is anthropogenic, involuntarily stresses the unique evolution of the climate. Involuntary, because the texts on the anthropogenic stage analyze human impact on nature, but do not conclude that this stage is evolutionary. However, if it is a new stage—dated to the Industrial Revolution—then it is evolutionary. Of course, we may call it devolutionary, if we are to believe that anthropogenic stage is morally wrong, hurts natural processes, leaves too much asphalt, and cuts too many trees. But for that we would also have to believe that natural processes without human intervention are morally right. Otherwise we cannot call it devolutionary. However, that thesis is subject to substantial critique as nature itself has destructive forces such as virus and natural disasters that kill and destroy. In the history of philosophy, this issue is best represented by Leibniz theodicy, justification of natural evil as not related to God, and Voltaire's reaction to the Lisbon earthquake in 1755. The earthquake that showed the scale of nature's evil led Voltaire to call philosophy false and vain:

> *Oh wretched* man, earth-fated to be cursed;
> Abyss of plagues, and miseries the worst!
> Horrors on horrors, griefs on griefs must show,
> That man's the victim of unceasing woe,
> And lamentations which inspire my strain,
> Prove that philosophy is false and vain.
> Approach in crowds, and meditate awhile
> Yon shattered walls, and view each ruined pile,
> Women and children heaped up mountain high,
> Limbs crushed which under ponderous marble lie;
> Wretches unnumbered in the pangs of death,
> Who mangled, torn, and panting for their breath,
> Buried beneath their sinking roofs expire,
> And end their wretched lives in torments dire.
> Say, when you hear their piteous, half-formed cries,
> Or from their ashes see the smoke arise,
> Say, will you then eternal laws maintain,
> Which God to cruelties like these constrain?
> Whilst you these facts replete with horror view,
> Will you maintain death to their crimes was due? (Voltaire 1901)

Following Voltaire's disbelief in justification of evil against humans, the anthropogenic era has not eliminated catastrophes—nature still acts independently and hits with all its destructive power whimsically. Thus, albeit that the anthropogenic era is evolutionary, it is not the era of progress in terms of harmony between humans and nature. The relationship between the two is tense. Being a part of nature, being the dwellers of the Earth, means that it is an inside experience, not outside. Therefore, the anthropogenic stage is also an evolutionary experience of climate transformation in relation to man's activity.

The inside perspective bring humans and nature closer together, and the philosophical gap between the two narrows down. But our perspective and interpretation is limited to our point of view. .From this limited perspective, we regard ourselves as geopolitical actors who are capable of influencing climate change. Thus, being the ones who are capable of such influence, we turn out to be the Other to nature, i.e., the Other who acts upon the planet. In this sense an element of estrangement remains. Green ideology attempts to eliminate this estrangement. When we see in a supermarket a T-shirt saying "This T-shirt is GREEN" (and the word "green" is colored in green), the message is that the T-shirt is for wearing with pride as it is not against the nature. The educational idea behind it is: if everyone acts ecologically, according to the green standards, the gap between the planet's nature and a human being will close. Supposedly, it is possible to be on the same side with the planet.

Science rhetoric of global warming promotes a kind of ingratiating with nature. At the same time we expect to temper the extremes of the climate change and silence our consciousness by being green, loving what is "natural" and caring for the signs of climate change. This way nature is caressed, calmed, and condoled. Humane care for the planet Earth is demonstrated as if humans were saying, "We, who think green, show solidarity with all the natural disasters as they are the sign of the planet's suffering, crying, and sighing."

We, Homo Sapiens, tend to show solidarity with the victims of storms or drought. But scientific data leading to interpretation that the major challenge seems to be carbon capture and its sequestration (Snieder and Young 2009) also indicates solidarity with the planet itself as a live organism that is poisoned by us. This way the Earth is personalized, the soul of the planet is animated. The storms, untamed hurricanes, emaciating heat waves, in the sun-scorched wheat, expresses the condition of the planet's soul—fury and rage. When the body of the Earth is cemented, when the rivers are damned, and the sky from dawn to sunset is polluted by emitted jet fuel, when the sea beds are covered with gas pipes, then such a disfigured body is wailing, the soul of the planet is in the condition of fury and rage.

Animated Earth submits to being treated merely as the means of natural resources. . The climate change has made us reconsider the view—perhaps the body of the planet and its parts in the continents are not just for materialistic economy? Perhaps we can think about the planet's unique character as well.

When nineteenth century Russian mystic Nikolai Fiodorov spoke of the Earth as a space shuttle in which humans travel through the cosmos, it seemed like a mystical language indeed. Today, in spite of a modest positioning of our Milky Way galaxy in the Universe (we are practically in the periphery of the Universe, centrewise insignificant, too distant), we recognize the planet's vital function—to fly us in the solar orbit. But we are incapable of moving the planet; we are not the first movers of the Earth, rather we are dependent on its life and speed in the orbit positioned amongst the other planets, stars, satellites, ruled by the laws of gravitation. True, if we used all nuclear weapons perhaps we could become the final movers disbalancing the planet.

Everyday spinning around the axis of the Earth provides us with the impression of the sunrise and the sunset. The planet Earth provides us with the seasons, four at the most. In this sense, whatever influence mankind can have upon the planet, s/he has that influence only because of the pre-given conditions to act so in daylight or at twilight. In this sense, the term of anthropogenic climate change—the term which underlines human power to transform or correct the planet's "habits"—is misguiding because it gives an impression of a Homo Sapiens' capability to create that anthropogenic epoch of the climate change. The effort is of our species, but the conditions under which that effort is made come from the nature of the planet. And that is not without the context of the Universe, cosmos. After all, it is only due to the unique positioning of the Earth within the Solar system that the Earth has life. The Earth has life on the basis of contingency. Otherwise, the planet would be lifeless and such would be circling the orbit as a huge chunk of a cosmic cave. That is the function of the other planets. The Earth has a privilege to carry civilizations.

In the eighteenth and in the nineteenth centuries, the separation of nature and man underwent transformation: instead of treating nature as superior, hierarchically higher, man pushed nature downward by replacing human persons into its position. A human being, perceived as a rational creature, which supposedly freed from religious superstitions thanks to advanced science, was able of conquer the Earth. Knowledge of the laws of nature led to the false belief that man no longer needs to be the victim of whimsical behavior of nature—diseases can be cured, coal can be mined out, Africans enslaved, chimneys erected, train tracks laid across the continents. Comte wrote his doctrine of positivism disregarding the value of metaphysical thinking and putting his scholarly faith into sociology. The Renaissance distinction between the history of nature and the history of mankind in the nineteenth century writings of Karl Marx went as far as his belief in Hegelian conclusion of history, only this time through the means of economy, the end of capitalism, and the end of classes thanks to the final revolution of proletariat in the name of economic communism. Thus, the history of mankind was supposed to end because of human effort and rational thought. Conclusively, a human being is the master of mankind's history. By eliminating the irrational aspect of history and by believing in progress, God no longer has anything to do with the salvation of mankind. In this sense, Marx's political economy is Hegel applied to practice, since for Hegel, history is rational and it progresses systematically as *Geist* travels through epochs till the culmination when the mind of the philosopher understands it.

Once the history of mankind was perceived as something to be controlled and rationally advanced, a human being became emancipated as it is s/he who changes history. This narcissistic self-masterhood was doubled by the belief in the ability to master the planet, its resources. The homo self-glorification found its basis in self-mastery in history and in the mastering of nature.

Lithuanian philosopher, Arvydas Šliogeris, contends in almost all his writings that we are facing total hominization, i.e., imposed culture and human activity upon nature. Nature is stripped of its essence—nature. In his book *Alpha and Omega* (Šliogeris 1999), this Lithuanian author says that alpha reality is loaded with created meanings of omega reality and for that reason Šliogeris seeks being by the river Šešuola, walks on the hills trying to listen to the words of being, to the breathing of nature. To him, even the most detailed description of nature does not say anything about being. A human with the words and their meanings takes away the true meaning of the nature. A human hominizes what was authentic and archaic in pre-hominization—untouched being.

Šliogeris feels that proliferation of language separates him from that to what he was attached to when fishing trout in Šešuola river; nevertheless, he feels an inexorable need to catch trout and the clouds hanging over the river specifically by words. He wants to utter a word in such a way that by some absurd miracle the word itself would turn into a cloud or a trout. Šliogeris himself desires to put omega reality on alpha reality. Apparently, human nature desires to describe and cultivate the surroundings. In the end, the humans lay asphalt and concrete on the hills that stretch by the rivers. Then gas stations are built for the cars to run . . ..

Šliogeris is a great critic of man being as self-glorifying master of nature. He intends to decrown that master. Moreover, he accuses human culture of covering being with the layers of culture and artificial meanings. Because of proliferating meanings it is hard to find the original meaning, to see things as they are. Not coincidentally Šliogeris, á la Nietzsche's madman, claims his joy in *Potato Metaphysics* (Šliogeris 2010), when he finds a potato in the countryside field. Potato here is a reference to untamed land with its alpha meaning of being.

What is important in this case of Šliogeris is his typical adherence to the distinction between nature and man, nature and culture. In essence, man here is once again the despot who abuses nature, land, rivers, hills. S/he is the engineer who constructs on top of being, natural land, and takes away the alpha meaning. In this romantic tradition of philosophy, civilization as such is the enemy of nature. American transcendentalist and romantic Henry David Thoreau even longed for a spiritual direction of America's development instead of industrialization. He even preferred going westward for a walk and loathed to turn around to walk back eastward as the west of the United States signified untamed and untouched nature.

My thesis is that the typical dichotomy between man and nature is vicious, misguiding. What if there is no distinction between the two? Namely, because a human being is an element of nature, the product of evolution under conditions provided for living. The life form of any organism, including human, is natural—the cells are nature with the DNA code system inherited from the natural process of development. Humans have nothing that would be unnatural, artificial. Every blood vessel and nerve is nature nurtured, passed from one generation to another by natural instinct of breeding. Finally, humans come from nature and die in nature.

But more importantly, for the purpose of this essay, everything that a human creates in this world or whatever s/he destroys, is done so because nature allows it by providing conditions. To build bridges or to burn libraries one can only do so in a day or night time, standing on the Earth and submitting to the law of gravity, certain pressure of atmosphere either in winter or in summer, in spring or in autumn. No one can perform anything morally valuable or despicable without the conditions of the planet Earth. Civilization is not counter to nature, but its product. Climate change and damaged ecosystem due to economic brutality is taking place because nature itself allows it—a human being cannot do anything that would not be allowed to do.

It reminds me of the conversation between Pilate—having political power—and Jesus as the Son of God. In the gospel of John, Pilate asks: "Knowest thee not that I have power to crucify thee, and have power to release thee." Jesus replied: "You have no authority over me at all, except what was given to you from above." (Jn 19:9, 11)

In other words, the entire human self-glorification stems out of self-separation from the nature by having a belief that humans can act independently from nature. What is forgotten is the question: who or what gave the power to create anthropogenic climate epoch?

Today we are overwhelmed by social responsibility propaganda, when ecological values are hierarchically superior, stimulating ecological self-awareness, because of the belief that humans must be responsible consumers of the planet's resources. Also the expectation is that humans can be responsible creators of global processes, innovative and green. In other words, if we are already living in anthropogenic epoch, then it should be managed responsibly in spite of the fact that no one planned the climate change responsibly. Industrial Revolution did not foresee predator like pumping out of the resources of the oceans with all possible drills. It turns out that Enlightenment at the age of Industrial Revolution had nothing to do with social responsibility.

If friendliness to the planet is promoted only because its nature has started to bite, then the source of responsibility is rather primitive, kindergarten level: children always test their limits; they are eager to see what happens if they do this and that. The acceptance of responsibility on a global corporate level is not voluntary, but obligatory. Mother Nature no longer permits its children to play with the resources irresponsibly. Still the political decisions are being late. Copenhagen climate change forum failed—no serious action has been taken. Perhaps, the climate change is not sufficiently rapid? Or perhaps it is sufficiently rapid and corporations are awaiting the global warming benefits? Canada, Russia, and Norway are in competition to get control over the melted North Pole. There are more and more articles on the benefits of global warming with a quite noticeable change in rhetoric as if increased flooding, storms, droughts, and heat temperature records did not exist with all the consequences.

Nevertheless, the global consensus is that the planet is in danger, that dramatic change is taking place in front of our eyes. Corporations have adopted green rhetoric and often policies; green innovations are popular and respected. However, at the same time we are also witnessing the abuse of ecological rhetoric.

In ancient Greek philosophy we find an understanding of the Earth as a live organism. For Heraclitus nature is comprised of laws—hot and cold, dark and light, dry and wet—and we live under the conditions of those laws. Knowledge of it is the task of the wise man. Twenty-first-century scientists discovered so much about global climate change that Heraclitus could only envy, but he probably would be disappointed at the thought that human wisdom depends so much on political institutions that environmental rhetoric can remain separated from action and will to act. The U.S. ignorance of Kyoto agreement to reduce CO_2 and the failure of Copenhagen climate change forum has demonstrated just that—green rhetoric and knowledge is not enough for action. CO_2 emissions are reduced gradually, air planes pollute just as before without regulations, China and the U.S. are untamed, Brazil continues cutting its rain forest, The Netherlands helplessly plan more powerful pumping of the water at its cost.

In the meanwhile—talking in terms of Nikolai Fiodorov—we continue flying in cosmos on our planet/shuttle. Flying in cosmos, a human being overlooks who or what gives the conditions for being the cause for global warming. So much is taken for granted—the existence of nature is regarded as a self-evident fact as if surrounding planets also were full of blue oceans and green forests. But the Earth as a live organism might be gradually starting to get rid of its rational species who, by caring about global economy, forgot global spirituality, higher meaning of Homo Sapiens species, higher purpose while living here-and-now on the generous planet—the real master of nature. The planet Earth as the real master of nature is also the ultimate master of homo civilizations as they depend on the behavior of the planet.

The Earth can function without humans perfectly well just as it did for a few billion years. We tend to forget that. It has been taken for granted that humans belong to this green planet, however, from the evolutionary perspective we are guests and potentially extinct species.

If humans would not cause global warming if they were not allowed to from above, given conditions to act so, then the real creator of the climate change is the planet itself merely using humans as a means for self-destruction, and the results of that destruction will hit civilizations much harder than the planet. Global warming is not just about melted ice and summer heat discomfort—it is about the spread of diseases and cataclysms that cause painful redemographication process that establishes new poverty stricken areas. The planet—as a chunk of mass in the orbit—can always continue its journey in the Milky Way on its own with its alpha meaning of being. Then the river Šešuola—with trout or without it—would be a tiny part of no longer "hominized nature", but also without a philosopher like Šliogeris to reflect upon it. But then, his dream for purification of nature from hominized omega meaning would come true. The dualism between nature and civilization would no longer be relevant.

Most likely global warming consequences won't be that severe; probably, humans won't become extinct as a species. There are too many of us. More likely, nature by the means of global warming will make major corrections in the number of its inhabitants as nature has been doing throughout its history through diseases and cataclysms. If that happens, it could be wise not to place human economic history above the history of nature and to rethink human mastery on this planet.

Postscript

It is important to note that climate change discourse has been changing as well. New well-argued articles that do not believe in Global Warming keep emerging. Scholars argue that CO_2 does not cause temperature rise, that ice melting is confused with ice breaking, new layers of ice keep forming. The following are a couple of representative quotations that are worthy of consideration:Last March, global warming fanatic Al Gore used a picture of two polar bears purportedly stranded on melting ice off the coast of Alaska as a visual aide to support his claim that man-made global warming is doing great harm to Mother Earth. The one he chose, but didn't offer to pay for right away, turned out to be a photo of a polar bear and her cub outdoing what healthy, happy polar bears do on a wave-eroded chunk of ice not all that far from shore in the Beaufort Sea north of Barstow, Alaska. Byrd, a marine biology grad student at the time, was gathering zooplankton for a multi-year study of the Arctic Ocean. Crosbie, who was also on the trip, pilfered the polar bear photo from a shared computer onboard the Canadian icebreaker where Ms. Byrd downloaded her snapshots; he saved it in his personal file. Several months later, Crosbie, who is known as an avid photographer, gave the photo to the Canadian Ice Service, which then allowed Environment Canada to use it as an illustration for an online magazine. Today that photo, with credit given to photographer Dan Crosbie and the Canadian Ice Service, can be found all over the Internet, generally with the caption "Two polar bears are stranded on a chunk of melting ice". The picture, wrongly credited to Dan Crosbie, an ice observer specialist for the Canadian Ice Service, was actually taken by Amanda Byrd while she was on a university-related research cruise in August of 2004, a time of year when the fringe of the Arctic ice cap normally melts." (Middleburry Networks 2009)

"We found 50 glaciers are advancing in New Zealand, others are growing in Alaska, Switzerland, the Himalayas, and even our old friend, Mt. St. Helens is sprouting a brand new crater glacier that is advancing at 3 feet per year. And down south last September, NASA satellites showed the Antarctic Ice Field to be the largest it has ever been in the 30 years it has been observed by satellite (based on an analysis of 347 million radar altimeter measurements made by the European Space Agency's ERS-1 and ERS-2 satellites). (Middleburry Networks 2009)

References

Crutzen, P.J. & Stoermer, E.F., 2000, The Anthropocene, *Global Change Newsletter* (41): 17–18, available at: http://www.mpch-mainz.mpg.de/~air/anthropocene/Text.html.
Middleburry Networks, 2009, Editorial: *The Great Global Warming Hoax*, available at: http://www.middlebury.net/op-ed/global-warming-01.html.
Snieder, R. & Young, T., 2009, Facing Major Challenges in Carbon Capture and Sequestration, *The Geological Society of America* 19 (11), 36–37
Šliogeris, A., 1999, *Alfa ir Omega*, Vilnius: Pradai.
———, 2010, *Bulves Metafizika (Potato Metaphysics)*, Vilnius: Apostrofa.
Voltaire, 1901, *The Lisbon Earthquake and Other Poems*, Paris.
Zalasiewicz, J. & Williams, M., 2008, Are We Now Living in the Anthropocene?, *GSA Today*, available at: http://www.geosociety.org/gsatoday/archive/18/2/pdf/i1052-5173-18-2-4.pdf.

Notes about the Authors

Timo Airaksinen (PhD, Turku University, Finland, 1975) is professor of moral and social philosophy, University of Helsinki, Finland. He is a life member of Clare Hall, Cambridge, and vice president of the Philosophical Society of Finland and the International Berkeley Society. He is managing editor of Hobbes Studies. He has written *The Philosophy of the Marquis de Sade* (Routledge, 1995), *The Philosophy of H. P. Lovecraft* (Lang, 1988), and *The Ethics of Coercion and Authority* (University of Pittsburgh Press, 1988). He has also written high school and university textbooks in philosophy and non-religious moral education. Professor Airaksinen is a member of the International Advisory Board of the Praxiology series within which he co-edited Practical Philosophy and Action Theory (Transaction, 1993) and Praxiology and the Philosophy of Technology (Transaction, 2008). He is a life honorary member of the Learned Society of Praxiology.

Tadeusz Borys is professor of economic sciences. He is head of quality and Environment Management Chair at Wrocław University of Economics, and a faculty in Jelenia Góra. He is UNDP consultant for sustainable development strategies and audits, member of the European Association of Environment and Natural Resources, the National Council for Sustainable Development, and the State Environmental Council of Poland. For many years, he has been involved in research, combining three scientific domains: statistics, quality of life, and theoretical basics of new paradigms. He is author of 250 articles and books such as *Qualimetrics* (1991), *Indicators of Sustainable Development* (2005), and *Education for Sustainable Development* (2010).

Wojciech Gasparski, professor of humanities, Dr. Sc., director and founder of the Business Ethics Centre (a joint unit of Kozminski

University and Polish Academy of Sciences, Institute of Philosophy and Sociology). He is the immediate past vice rector for research of the Kozminski University. He is professor emeritus of the Institute of Philosophy and Sociology, Polish Academy of Sciences (PAS) where he chaired the academic board and headed the department of praxiology as well as the research group for ethics in business and the economy. His publications on human action theory (praxiology), business ethics, methodology, science studies, and systems theory are numerous. He is a member of the Warsaw Learned Society; Learned Society of Praxiology (Founder and Honorary President); Polish Philosophical Society; International Society of Business, Economics, and Ethics; Academy of Management (USA); Society for Business Ethics; Science Studies Committee PAS (Honorary Member), Management Science Committee PAS. He was editor-in-chief of *Praxiology: The International Annual of Practical Philosophy and Methodology* (Transaction Publishers, USA). In 2006, he was nominated to the European Faculty Pioneer Award for Business in Society by Aspen Foundation (USA) and the European Academy of Business and Society. He was awarded The Tadeusz Kotarbinski Medal by the Polish Academy of Sciences for his achievements in management science (2008).

Tomas Kavaliauskas is Lithuanian social critic, essayist as well as a lecturer at Vytautas Magnus University. His academic interests are interwoven with his essay writing on European identity, the political and cultural character of European regions. He lectures political philosophy, business ethics, and Central Eastern European Transition courses. The author has been contributing his essay writing to Lithuanian monthly Kultūros barai (The Domains of Culture) for the last seven years and some of the writings have been published on www.eurozine.com. T. Kavaliauskas has published a collection of essays titled *Business, Christianity, and Consumerist Culture* (Vilnius, Versus Aureus, 2008) a monography *The Individual in Business Ethics: An American Cultural Perspective* (Palgrave, 2010). The author is a member of SPES—spirituality in economics and society—and a member of Lithuanian PEN club.

Külli Keerus has been a researcher and PhD student of philosophy in Tartu University. She graduated from Tartu University in 2000 with BA in philosophy, and in 2003 with MA in philosophy. Her research interests include environmental ethics and bioethics.

Erazim Kohák (PhD, Yale, 1958). Born in 1933 in Prague, Czechoslovakia, he was a political refugee in United States from 1949 to 1989, and is now living in Prague, Czech Republic. Bearer of Czech Republic Medal of Merit. Professor emeritus, Boston University (MA, USA) and Charles

University, Prague, he is currently Senior Research Fellow, Philosophy Institute of Academy of Science of Czech Republic. He is author of numerous books in Czech and English, including *The Embers and the Stars*, *Idea and Experience*, *Jan Patočka*, *The Green Halo*, *Člověk, dobro a zlo*, *Zelená svatozář*, *Svoboda svědomí soužití*, *Domov a dálava*, and the recent *Hearth and Horizon*, honored by the annual Excellence in Scholarship Award of the Czech Republic Ministry of Education.

Simo Kyllönen is a researcher and doctoral student at the University of Helsinki. His research interests are in the field of environmental political philosophy; particularly on the linkages between environmental concerns and democratic governance and citizenship. Currently he is working in the Helsinki University Centre for Environment (HENVI) project *The Anatomy of Environmental Responsibility*.

Marjukka Laakso is Master of Social Sciences. She has been a researcher and postgraduate student in the department of social and moral philosophy, University of Helsinki, Finland. Laakso's research topic has been environmental political philosophy in the context of liberal theory in the research projects of, for example, *Redefining Concepts and Practices of Environmental Law and Decision-Making*, and *Sustainability in Forest Use*.

Olli Loukola (Doctor of Social Sciences, University of Helsinki, 1999) is Docent of Practical Philosophy and senior lecturer in social and moral philosophy in Department of Political and Economic Studies, University of Helsinki. He has led a number of research projects of environmental philosophy, among them *The Anatomy of Environmental Responsibility*, *Redefining Concepts and Practices of Environmental Law and Decision-Making*, and *Sustainability in Forest Use*. He is the head of the Baltic Philosophy Network (BalPhiN, http://balphin.org/).

Gabriel Malenfant received his MA degree in philosophy from the Université de Montréal and is currently completing a PhD in philosophy at the University of Iceland, where he is a postdoctoral researcher, at the EDDA Center of Excellence. He has published papers in ethics, environmental philosophy, and phenomenology. He also translated works by Jean-Luc Nancy, Daniel Weinstock, and Georges Leroux.

Paul McLaughlin is Senior Lecturer in Practical Philosophy at the University of Tartu, Estonia. He is the author of *Anarchism and Authority: A Philosophical Introduction to Classical Anarchism* (2007) and *Mikhail Bakunin: The Philosophical Basis of His Anarchism* (2002).

Boleslaw Rok, PhD, is associate professor at Business Ethics Centre and academic director of Corporate Responsibility Executive Programme at Kozminski University, Warsaw, Poland. He specializes in innovative entrepreneurship, sustainability management, and public policy. He cooperates extensively with the Academy of Business in Society, UNDP, European Commission, The Director General for Enterprise, and different professional associations on business ethics, sustainability, and inclusive business models. He is consultant and lecturer to many commercial organizations. He is cofounder of the Responsible Business Forum (2000), a membership organization affiliated to CSR Europe, and also of European Business Ethics Network, Poland (1999). He is the author of the *Responsible Companies Ranking in Poland* (from 2007).

Christopher Stevens is a PhD candidate at the University of Maryland, College Park, and a 2010–11 Fulbright Fellow at the University of Oslo's Centre for Development and the Environment. He earned an MA from the City University of New York Graduate Center.

Ladislav Tondl, PhD, is full professor at the philosophical faculty at Charles University in Prague. Studied philosophy, sociology, and economy at Charles University in Prague. He was an associate professor and from 1968, has been a full professor. Director of the Institute for Theory and Methodology of Science at the Czechoslovak Academy 1968, 1969; president of Science Policy Commission UNESCO 1968–1970; honorary life member of the Association for the Philosophy of Science, USA; member of some learned societies abroad, of editorial boards of some international journals and book editions. Because of political reasons, he was dismissed from Charles University after 1950, and after the invasion in 1968 from the Academy, he worked many years in the Institute of Information Theory and Automation in Prague engaged in the problems of logical semantics, scientific procedures, and the relationship between modern information theory and decision theory. After the Soviet invasion, he was dismissed from the Academy and worked in the sphere of computer-aided design and computer-graphics in a design organization. After his full rehabilitation in 1989, he has been head of the Centre for Science Technology and Society Studies, Academy of Sciences, Czech Republic.

Caitlin Wilson is a PhD candidate in the School of Education at the University of Iceland. She holds a Master's degree in Environment and Natural Resource Management from the University of Iceland, and a BA in English literature from the College of William and Mary in Williamsburg, Virginia. She currently works as a higher education consultant and as academic director for the SIT study abroad program "Iceland: Renewable energy, technology, and resource economics."

CPSIA information can be obtained at www.ICGtesting.com
Printed in the USA
BVOW080245090212

282474BV00001B/7/P